Four Romances of England

King Horn, Havelok the Dane, Bevis of Hampton, Athelston

Middle English Texts

General Editor

Russell A. Peck
University of Rochester

Associate Editor

Alan Lupack
University of Rochester

Advisory Board

Rita Copeland
University of Minnesota

Thomas G. Hahn
University of Rochester

Lisa Kiser
Ohio State University

Thomas Seiler
Western Michigan University

R. A. Shoaf
University of Florida

Bonnie Wheeler
Southern Methodist University

The Middle English Texts Series is designed for classroom use. Its goal is to make available to teachers and students texts which occupy an important place in the literary and cultural canon but which have not been readily available in student editions. The series does not include those authors such as Chaucer, Langland, or Malory, whose English works are normally in print in good student editions. The focus is, instead, upon Middle English literature adjacent to those authors that teachers need in compiling the syllabuses they wish to teach. The editions maintain the linguistic integrity of the original work but within the parameters of modern reading conventions. The texts are printed in the modern alphabet and follow the practices of modern capitalization and punctuation. Manuscript abbreviations are silently expanded, and *u/v* and *j/i* spellings are regularized according to modern orthography. Hard words, difficult phrases, and unusual idioms are glossed on the page, either in the right margin or at the foot of the page. Textual notes appear at the end of the text, along with a glossary. The editions include short introductions on the history of the work, its merits and points of topical interest, and also include briefly annotated bibliographies.

Four Romances of England

King Horn, Havelok the Dane, Bevis of Hampton, Athelston

Edited by
Ronald B. Herzman, Graham Drake, Eve Salisbury

Published for TEAMS
(The Consortium for the Teaching of the Middle Ages)
in Association with the University of Rochester

by

Medieval Institute Publications

WESTERN MICHIGAN UNIVERSITY

Kalamazoo, Michigan — 1999

Library of Congress Cataloging-in-Publication Data

Four romances of England : King Horn, Havelock the Dane, Bevis of Hampton, Athelston / edited by Ronald B. Herzman, Graham Drake, Eve Salisbury.
p. cm. – (Middle English texts)
Includes bibliographical references.
ISBN 1-58044-017-7 (pbk. : alk. paper)
1. Romances, English. 2. Havelock the Dane (Legendary character)--Romances I. Herzman, Ronald B. II. Drake, Graham. III. Salisbury, Eve. IV. Series: Middle English texts (Kalamazoo, Mich.)
PR2064.F685 1999
821'. 109--dc21

98-46398
CIP

ISBN 1-58044-017-7
Copyright 1999 by the Board of the Medieval Institute
Printed in the United States of America
P 5 4

Cover design by Linda K. Judy

Contents

Acknowledgments

Preparing this edition of four romances from the thirteenth and fourteenth centuries has produced its own adventures — including journeys by sea, car, subway, and bus, the perils of snow, and the languid haze of summer. Through all these peregrinations both earthly and editorial, we have relied on the help of numerous colleagues, students, friends, and family members.

In the first place, we wish to thank the Consortium for the Teaching of the Middle Ages and all its supervisory members for their help and encouragement. Special thanks go to our friends at the Robbins Library, particularly Russell A. Peck for setting an editorial standard requiring the best we had to give; Alan Lupack, Curator for providing often obscure research materials and for his careful reading of the manuscript; Karen Saupe, who as assistant editor of METS in its early days proved herself invaluable as troubleshooter, whether giving technical advice about Word Perfect, double-checking references on baffling place names, or providing careful editorial scrutiny. So too do we wish to thank Dong Choon Lee, for his help checking texts against photocopies of the manuscripts, and Mara Amster and Jennifer Church, whose many talents have made the camera-ready process infinitely more efficient.

At Geneseo, we were deeply fortunate to have two of our finest undergraduates, Lisa Lucenti and Laura Sythes, read our glosses and notes to provide a student reader's perspective. Marie Henry and Gail English supported us in many ways from the English Department Office.

We also wish to thank some special people in our lives who intersected with the production of this volume. Sarah Higley provided an insightful reading of an early draft of the general introduction. Graham in particular thanks his sister and brother-in-law, Susan Drake Cumbie and Seán Cumbie, for their hospitality in Georgia and California while he worked on this manuscript, and his cousins, Donnie and Margaret Johnston of Cunningsburgh, Shetland Isles, who provided their American cousin with a quiet sitting room to work in and even iced tea (despite their personal distaste for it) during a working summer in Scotland. Equally gracious was the hospitality of Mrs. Veronica Herzman in Geneseo. Ron would also like to thank Veronica Herzman, though for different reasons: recently a favorite student and earlier his most important teacher. In addition to the usual gang, Ellen, Suzanne, and Edward Herzman, Wes Kennison, and Bill Cook, Ron also thanks two e-mail buddies — Anne Clark Bartlett (who kept telling him how much an edition of *Bevis* was needed), and Rick Emmerson. Eve wishes to thank daughter Meghan for her cheerful optimism and ongoing contributions to a rich and diversified domestic life.

Finally, we are grateful to the National Endowment for the Humanities, whose support, even in difficult times, has kept the Middle English Texts Series alive.

Four Romances of England

Introduction

The English word "romance" has accrued multiple meanings over the centuries: the joys of private love, heroic adventure on land and sea, the choice of the risky and exotic over the mundane. Romance is also a generic term that has been applied to such disparate works as ancient Hellenistic and Latin narratives, twentieth-century novels by authors such as Barbara Cartland, and even the mass-produced fantasies of Harlequin. *Roman*, from which the word "romance" derives, is still the word used for "novel" in several modern European languages. The poems in this volume are also known as romances, a particular type of vernacular narrative which saw popularity in late medieval western Europe.

Of the four romances of England presented here, *King Horn* (c. 1225) is probably the earliest (other than, arguably, Layamon's *Brut*, itself a translation of Wace's twelfth-century Anglo-Norman poem on Arthurian themes).[1] *Havelok the Dane* is dated at approximately 1290, with *Bevis of Hampton* following shortly thereafter (about ten years before Dante began to write his *Divine Comedy*). *Athelston*, the latest of the four, was probably composed between 1355 and 1399; thus it was completed shortly after Boccaccio's *Decameron* (1349–51) and around the time Chaucer was becoming the "father" of English poetry.

These were not the only English romances, of course. Romance was an extremely popular genre in medieval England; from the thirteenth through the fifteenth centuries dozens of English romances were produced, including, for example, *Guy of Warwick*, *Sir Perceval of Galles*, *Sir Isumbras*, *Octavian*, *Sir Eglamour of Artois*, *Sir Tryamour*, and *Ywain and Gawain*; numerous retellings of Trojan and Theban history, the deeds of Alexander the Great and Richard the Lionhearted as well as the exploits of Charlemagne and his followers exist in Middle English versions; the legends of King Arthur and his knights, originally in Latin, French, and Welsh narratives, experienced a flowering in England in such classics as the *Alliterative Morte Arthure* (c. 1350–1400) and *Sir Gawain and the Green Knight*. But the romances in this volume bring together some of the finest

[1] See Introduction to *King Horn* in this volume for an alternative dating of *King Horn* in the middle of the thirteenth century.

imaginative work in what became known as the Matter of England, the non-Arthurian romances dealing largely with English subjects and locales. They stand out as well by their reduced interest in the nuances of courtly behavior so characteristic of French romance, as they pay more attention to the socio-political issues contained within folktale motifs. Manuscript evidence suggests that romance reading in England was hardly confined to the nobility but became part of the increasingly prosperous and literate middle classes' attempts to style themselves after the upper classes.[2]

Romance and the Epic

It was in the Middle Ages that the word "romanz" was first used to describe vernacular narratives as opposed to Latin poetry. But the meaning of the word narrowed to tales of knightly adventure and love together, linking the masculine, battlefield world of the *chanson de geste* with the increasing upper-class interest in what we would now call "romantic love." The idea of a personal love-interest between a man and woman, devoid of dynastic or financial concerns, had already taken root in the oral poetry of Provençal *trouvères* and the court of Marie, Countess of Champagne, which produced courtly love debates and nuanced descriptions of love-relationships set down by her chaplain, Andreas, in his *De Amore*. This combination of battlefield and boudoir, so to speak, is perhaps the chief way that romance diverges from epic. In the epic genre, an individual character of extraordinary strength demonstrates his martial skills and wisdom as he leads a nation or a group of comrades in great crisis — Odysseus in the *Odyssey*, Aeneas in the *Aeneid*, Beowulf in his eponymous epic. While love interests are of some concern to the protagonist, they are incidental to larger dynastic and foundational concerns. For example, Odysseus' return to Penelope is subordinated to his re-establishing the hereditary monarchy on Ithaca. Aeneas' dalliance with Dido delays him from his ultimate goal: to win Italy for the Trojans and to found a line through marriage with King Latinus' daughter, Lavinia. Indeed, Beowulf seems to have little intimacy beyond his band of warriors. Dynasty and glory are the point; love is not.

Romance itself can be distinguished in a number of other ways from epic. In the first place, it invests more heavily than epic in the personal story of the main character, in his response to challenges which test his strength, courage, and knightly courtesy. One can

---

[2] W. R. J. Barron, *English Medieval Romance* (London: Longman, 1987), p. 54. See also Derek Pearsall, "The Development of Middle English Romance," *Mediaeval Studies* 27 (1965), 91–116; Susan Crane, *Insular Romance: Politics, Faith, and Culture in Anglo-Norman and Middle English Literature* (Berkeley: University of California Press, 1986); Harriet Hudson, "Middle English Popular Romances: The Manuscript Evidence," *Manuscripta* 28 (1984), 67–78.

even argue that this happens in Arthurian legend, in which the dominance of the Round Table is eclipsed by the lonely quests for the Holy Grail or by the torn loyalties and madness of Lancelot or Tristan. At times, one may see, with Gabriel Josopovici, that fairy tale and romance "function in a timeless present in which the hero is the centre of the universe," a paradigm in which the nation takes second place.[3] Another equally important component of the hero's development is the challenge of love, making women major players in the action, whereas in epic women more usually lure the hero with dilatory lusts, commune weirdly with dead spirits, or stay at home and weave. And this greater centrality of women reminds us of the social and political functions of romance, which to many critics display a class consciousness and a certain anxiety over the instability of feudal relationships.

Romances, especially in England, nevertheless combine social realism with superhuman or supernatural events. This lends a "mixed" quality to romance, the combination of the real and the ideal. As W. R. J. Barron argues, romance is less a genre than a mode of writing:

> The expressive conventions of the literary form reflect in their antithetical nature — adventure and instruction, fantasy and idealism, symbolism and realism — the mixed nature of the romantic mode, poised between the mythic and the mimetic. The tension between the various expressive means reflects the paradox within the mixed mode, which in turn reflects the dual nature of man as sensualist and idealist, escapist and moralist. . . . Throughout the Middle Ages [this mode] was all-pervasive, showing itself not only in almost every literary genre, including the professedly mimetic categories of chronicle, history, and biography, but in the other arts and even the forms and ceremonies of courtly life.[4]

The protean nature of romance, poised as it is between binary oppositions, or existing within a "mixed mode," as Barron describes, renders a potentiality for expression and possibility for transformation that few other "modes of writing" can claim.[5] Thus what appears in the beginning to offer dim prospects for the future for a disenfranchised hero may be transformed into success by the end. Perhaps this marks yet another distinction between epic and romance. While epics often conclude in tragedy — the deaths of Hector, Beowulf, and Arthur in the *Alliterative Morte Arthure*, even the "unfinished" twelfth book

---

[3] Gabriel Josopovici, *The Book of God: A Response to the Bible* (New Haven: Yale University Press, 1988), p. 199.

[4] Barron, pp. 5–6.

[5] For a comprehensive discussion of the hybrid nature and transformative potential of romance see Kevin and Marina Scordilis Brownlee, *Romance: Generic Transformation from Chrétien de Troyes to Cervantes* (Hanover: University Press of New England, 1985).

of the *Aeneid* which describes the death of Turnus but no actual wedding between Aeneas and Lavinia — romances are basically comic in structure. Life may be hard for Horn, Bevis, Havelok, or Athelston in the beginning, but by the end they receive rewards for their perseverance and valor: honor and glory for themselves, wedded bliss, and a restored kingdom to rule.

The Character of the Romance Hero

While romances have a similar paradigm of exile and return, the development of the hero's virtue through danger and hardship, there is no such singular scheme of romance composition. Sometimes, as in *King Horn* or *Athelston*, the structure is carefully symmetrical, while at other times it is more asymmetrical and episodic. The plot of *Bevis*, for instance, is far more complicated, switching from one location to another or adding new adventures that do not seem to build on earlier adventures as keenly as in these shorter, relatively simpler romances. Often, the plot of a romance moves from a position of high privilege to a loss of that privilege followed by subsequent recovery. Horn, for instance, becomes a child exile, serves two different foreign kings to prove himself, and eventually wins back his rightful kingdom from Saracen invaders. Bevis' mother sells him off to Armenian merchants; he later returns to oppose his stepfather and reclaim his patrimony.

This U-shaped motif (called the "monomyth" by such modern mythographers as Joseph Campbell)[6] is common to most epic and romance, and especially in romance it helps focus attention on the development of the central hero. Romance follows a pattern of separation and reunion or, as Northrop Frye views it, a journey of descent followed by ascent and a corresponding resolution of the hero's purpose and place in the world.[7] Because the very structure of such romances is the development of the hero towards maturity, achievement, and resumption of his rightful title, they often focus on questions of identity — as initial concealment followed by gradual revelation. Havelok conceals his identity as a fisherman; Bevis becomes, at various points in the narrative, a shepherd, messenger, and pilgrim; Athelston begins as a lowly messenger but gradually grows into his identity as king.

Inevitably, the hero will have to prove himself through his valor by some test, usually in warfare. Romance tends to zero in on individual combat more than the expansive and highly exaggerated battle scenes of epic. The chivalric code, not always explicitly spelled out in romance, is nevertheless implied in the bravery, justice, and glory of knightly

---

[6] See Joseph Campbell, *The Hero with a Thousand Faces* (New York: Pantheon, 1949).

[7] Northrop Frye, *The Secular Scripture: A Study of the Structure of Romance* (Cambridge: Harvard University Press, 1976).

combat — as, for instance, in the single combat between Yvor and Bevis on an island, and the bravery and triumph that the hero asserts throughout his life.

The Politics of Love and Class

A significant love-relationship, usually ending in marriage, is not only integral to romance as a genre but also to the hero's development. Typically, the hero will fall in love with a high-born woman, whom he marries only after significant obstacles impeding their union have been overcome. Both Horn and Bevis nearly lose their loved ones in marriage to an evil or unwanted man; a neat variation on the idea occurs in *Havelok*, as Goldeboru is forced to marry against her will a man she thinks is a vulgar peasant, only to discover by a sign from heaven that the peasant is Havelok, of royal lineage equal to her own. In *Bevis* Josian endures two forced marriages to unsavory men until she is finally wedded to her beloved. For Dame Edyff and Athelston's queen it is not marital union that is impeded, but reunion and reconciliation of family members brought about through their personal sufferings.

The reason these women figure so prominently, in fact, has mostly to do with heterosexual love and courtship. Yet the hero is not always the active pursuer and agent, nor is his female counterpart always the hapless damsel in distress. As if demonstrating the inherent power of transformation, gender roles can surprisingly reverse themselves in romance. Goldeboru, for example, often acts as an equal partner and companion to Havelok. Rymenhild — dismissed by some readers as a cardboard character known mostly for her overwhelming passions — takes the lead in wooing the gallant young Horn. Dame Edyff and Athelston's queen demonstrate an integrity and fortitude that set an example for the men around them, while Josian, one of the most active and well-developed of all medieval heroines, shows remarkable strength through a series of amazingly adverse situations. Medieval romance heroines, just as women in the real medieval world, are prohibited from participating in military combat, but they take an active role in personal relationships in these narratives. This may be in part because the relatively new concept of romantic love in companionate marriage was making its way into popular culture. Marriage was slowly moving away from being mostly an exchange of property (the woman and her dowry being the items of exchange) and towards a loving if not always socially equal partnership.[8]

---

[8] For general discussions of medieval marriage, see Georges Duby, *Medieval Marriage: Two Models from Twelfth-Century France*, trans. Elborg Forster (Baltimore: The Johns Hopkins University Press, 1978), and Frances and Joseph Gies, *Marriage and the Family in the Middle Ages* (New York: Harper and Row, 1987), especially pp. 141 ff. See also Christopher Brooke, *The*

The importance of women to romance reminds us that issues of gender in these tales are intertwined with matters of class and the vicissitudes of political power in medieval England. Some political issues had already become ancient history: the attacks by the Saracens in *Horn* are probably memories of the Viking invasions that had plagued England in the ninth to eleventh centuries. A world that joined a son of Southampton with the daughter of the King of Armenia in *Bevis of Hampton* may have had its historical roots in England's active role in the Crusades of the eleventh and twelfth centuries. In *Athelston*, trial by ordeal recalls an already discarded practice. Yet the power struggle between the king and clergy in this romance was a continual reality in England. From the Crusades to the Barons' Revolts and the civil uprisings of 1381 to armed conflict with France in the Hundred Years' War, the unglamorous realities of war were well known to the English.

Besides conflict between royalty and clergy, English romance reveals the changing status of the nobility. Throughout the later Middle Ages, the nobility faced innovative legal arrangements and centralized royal power on the one hand and the growing power of the mercantile classes on the other. The increasing practice of primogeniture created an uneasy position for the younger sons of noble families with no inheritance and little else to do except take holy orders or fight. Stephen Knight argues that the figure of the solitary knight, who must prove himself in arms by winning back his patrimony, reflects this uneasy position in contemporary English life.[9] In such "family romances" as *Amis and Amiloun*, *The Avowing of Arthur*, *King Horn*, and *Athelston*, Knight sees that "competitive assertiveness is the inner strain upon the fraternal bond [between knights]."[10] But even in the imaginative world of romance, the solitary chivalric hero is sometimes overpowered by a dialectic of multiple interests — as Knight observes, *Havelok* "shows 'lower-class' features in its village games and physical work, royal myth in its hero and his revelation, urban connections in its links to an origin legend for Grimsby. This text is much broader than the specifically knightly and feudal world, being both older than and marginal to the main romance pattern."[11]

A threat from below was imposing even more reality on English romance in the changing value of peasant labor in the fourteenth century and in an independent merchant class that would eventually replace feudal society with a dependence on money, capital, deeded property, and litigation. Indeed, congruent with a genre aware of the vicissitudes of contemporary daily life, there is an engaging realism in these romances. *Havelok*

Medieval Idea of Marriage (Oxford: Oxford University Press, 1989).

[9] Stephen Knight, "The Social Function of the Middle English Romance." In *Medieval Literature: Criticism, Ideology, & History*, ed. David Aers (New York: St. Martin's Press, Inc., 1986), p. 107.

[10] Knight, p. 113.

[11] Knight, pp. 109–10.

features lists of particular fish on sale in Lincoln, and the hero engages in peasant wrestling contests. Horn is a convincing sooty beggar when he decides to approach Rymenhild in disguise. *Athelston's* four main characters are initially messengers before they acquire higher social status. Bevis plays various roles from the lower classes before regaining his patrimony. Furthermore, local colors in the form of place names and graphic descriptions of a variety of battles and methods of execution point to the realities of social and political discontent emanating from the lower classes. Even so, Barron's reading of the Matter of England romances suggests a caveat against universalizing class analysis. In comparison to the models of French Romance, "The struggles in which [English romance heroes] are caught up spring not from the internal contradictions of courtly codes but the oppressive forces of a wicked world."[12]

Everyday life in this wicked world nonetheless comes with eerie surprises. In the simple home of the fisherman Grim, Havelok is identified as a special figure by a mysterious light and a cross-shaped birthmark. Much of the plot of *Athelston* hangs on a miraculous outcome of a trial by ordeal; Bevis is often saved *deus-ex-machina* style from certain death. Such intrusions of the supernatural mark the romance hero's life as rather extraordinary. The very real and immediate body of the hero becomes the slate upon which the truth of God's will is indelibly and infallibly written. It is this combination of supernaturalism and a kind of homey realism that gives the Middle English romances in this volume the distinctive "mixed" quality so often seen as definitive of the notion of romance.

[12] Barron, p. 85.

Select Bibliography

Barron, W. R. J. *English Medieval Romance.* London: Longman, 1987. [A general discussion of the genre, audience, and historical backgrounds.]

Brownlee, Kevin, and Marina Scordilis. *Romance: Generic Transformation from Chrétien de Troyes to Cervantes.* Hanover: University Press of New England, 1985.

Crane, Susan. *Insular Romance: Politics, Faith, and Culture in Anglo-Norman and Middle English Literature.* Berkeley: University of California Press, 1986. [Delineates distinguishing features of English romance as well as cultural and ideological issues.]

Fewster, Carol. *Traditionality and Genre in Middle English Romance.* Cambridge: D. S. Brewer, 1987. [Discusses theories and approaches, implied audiences, style, structure, and romance narrativity.]

Frye, Northrop. *The Secular Scripture: A Study of the Structure of Romance.* Cambridge: Harvard University Press, 1976.

Hudson, Harriet. "Middle English Popular Romances: The Manuscript Evidence." *Manuscripta* 28 (1984), 67–78. [Discusses the provenance of romance manuscripts and their probable audiences.]

Hume, Kathryn. "The Formal Nature of Middle English Romance." *Philological Quarterly* 53 (1974), 158–80. [Distinguishes three types of romance based upon the hero's ability to fulfill his destiny.]

Knight, Stephen. "The Social Function of the Middle English Romance." In *Medieval Literature: Criticism, Ideology, & History.* Ed. David Aers. New York: St. Martin's Press, 1986. Pp. 99–122.

Loomis, Laura A. [Hibbard]. "The Auchinleck Manuscript and a Possible London Bookshop of 1330–1340." *PMLA* 57 (1942), 595–627. [Study of internal evidence in order to locate the manuscript's production in a commercial scriptorium in London.]

———. *Mediæval Romance in England: A Study of the Sources and Analogues of the Non-Cyclic Metrical Romances.* 1924; rpt. New York: Burt Franklin, 1960. [A useful study of various versions of thirty-nine English romances.]

Mehl, Dieter. *The Middle English Romances of the Thirteenth and Fourteenth Centuries*. London: Routledge & Kegan Paul, 1968. Pp. 146–52. [Addresses historical contexts, audience, generic definitions, narrative techniques of several categories of romance.]

Pearsall, Derek. "The Development of Middle English Romance." *Mediaeval Studies* 27 (1965), 91–116. [Follows the growth and development of the genre from 1240 to 1400.]

———. "Middle English Romance and Its Audience." In *Historical & Editorial Studies in Medieval & Early Modern English for Johan Gerritsen*. Ed. MaryJo Arn and Hanneke Wirtjes, with Hans Jansen. Froningen: Wolters-Noordhoof, 1985. Pp. 37–47. [Discusses a range of possible audiences from urban to provincial.]

Ramsey, Lee C. *Chivalric Romances: Popular Literature in Medieval England*. Bloomington: Indiana University Press, 1983. [A general survey of the origins of medieval romance as well as the major types of English romance plots. Includes a chronological list of romances.]

Strohm, Paul. "Storie, Spelle, Geste, Romaunce, Tragedie: Generic Distinctions in the Middle English Troy Narratives." *Speculum* 46 (1971), 348–59. [A useful study of genre as perceived by medieval writers.]

———. "The Origin and Meaning of Middle Engish Romaunce." *Genre* 10 (1977), 1–28. [Discusses the use of the term from the twelfth through the fifteenth centuries and addresses such related terms as storie, geste, and lay.]

Wittig, Susan. *Stylistic and Narrative Structures in the Middle English Romances*. Austin: University of Texas Press, 1978. [A study of the problems of stylistic analysis and various structural units.]

King Horn

Introduction

Written in the last part of the thirteenth century, *King Horn* is probably the oldest surviving Middle English romance.[1] While *Horn's* meter may show some influence from the rhyming ballad meters of Anglo-Norman poetry, it is just as likely that the poem retains characteristics of Old English verse in a century when French-speaking Normans dominated English culture.[2] Like Old English verse, its meter depends on several heavy stresses per line, though rhymed couplets have overshadowed the alliteration common to earlier English poems. Even though an Anglo-Norman poem, *Horn et Rimenhild*, contains roughly the same plot, some scholars believe that the English poem derives from an earlier source.[3] Both *Horn* and *Havelok the Dane* belong to a group of poems known as the Matter of England, late medieval romances based in part on the oral folk culture that survived the Norman Conquest. This category also usually includes *Athelston* and *Bevis of Hampton*.

King Horn begins with the death of the hero's father at the hands of the Saracens who send Horn and his companions into exile. The young Horn finds himself with his twelve companions abandoned in Westernesse (identified with the Wirral peninsula near modern-day Liverpool). There the king's daughter, Rymenhild, declares her passion for Horn, and persuades her father to make him a knight. But Horn will not marry her until he has proved his worthiness, which he does by killing some invading Saracens. Jealous of his exploits, Horn's companion Fikenhild tells the king that Horn plans to kill him. Horn goes into exile again, this time in Ireland where he proves his military skill further by killing yet more invading Saracens. Though King Thurston offers his daughter Reynild in marriage as a reward, Horn remains loyal to Rymenhild. He returns in disguise when she is about to be forced into marriage with one King Mody, but then goes off to defeat the Saracens who

---

[1] The date for the poem has been traditionally acknowledged as about 1225, but recent scholarship has challenged that date, placing it later in the thirteenth century. For a review of the arguments see Rosemund Allen, "Date and Provenance of *King Horn*: Some Interim Reassessments," *Medieval English Studies Presented to George Kane*, ed. Edward Donald Kennedy, Ronald Waldron, and Joseph S. Wittig (Suffolk, England: St. Edmundsburg Press, 1988), 99–126.

[2] W. R. J. Barron, *English Medieval Romance* (London: Longman, 1987), p. 223.

[3] J. A. W. Bennett, *Middle English Literature*, edited and completed by Douglas Gray (Oxford: Clarendon Press, 1986), p. 135.

murdered his father. When he returns he discovers that the evil Fikenhild has just forced Rymenhild to marry him. Horn quickly kills the traitor comrade, and he and Rymenhild then marry. Reynild, Thurston's daughter, is given in marriage to Horn's faithful comrade, Athulf, and everyone lives happily ever after.

Unlike the loosely organized compositions of many French romances, *King Horn* uses repetition to create a rather tight, symmetrical structure. One may see this repetition on the simplest level, as in two-or-three word formulas, recaps of earlier parts of the story, and even large parallel portions of the plot. This structure of repetition and parallel helps underscore a major theme of the romance — the development of the hero towards maturity. Horn begins as a frightened noble child who develops a love life, achieves several military victories, becomes a sophisticated strategist with his use of disguises and coded statements to Rymenhild, and ultimately wins back his love and his kingdom, both of which have been taken away from him unjustly. Georgianna Ziegler identifies four distinct stages in this development: destruction (lines 1–152), learning (lines 153–756), initiation (757–1008) and reconstruction (1009–end).[4] The three battles show Horn's increased skill and confidence, as do repetition of hunting and love motifs and dream symbolism, which mark a "change from boy to man, from innocence to self-assertion, from hunted to hunter. . . ."[5]

Another theme of the romance is the stark contrast of good and evil. *Horn's* moral world divides distinctly between loyal friends and evil traitors — the never-failing Athulf vs. that "wurste moder sone" Fikenhild, who double-crosses Horn not once but twice. On a larger scale, Horn's Christian world is threatened by the Saracens — usually thought of as Muslims, yet also clearly representative of the Vikings; they are an abstract, thoroughly evil enemy that must be defeated.[6] And, of course, Horn does; he beats back the threatening hordes, and brutally mows down Fikenhild, hewing him to pieces. As W. R. J. Barron observes, English romance heroes such as Bevis, Guy of Warwick, Horn, and Havelok are not dealing with a courtly code but "the oppressive forces of a wicked world."[7]

Indeed, the fine sentiments of the courtly love code so popular in late twelfth-century continental poetry is missing from *Horn*. Rather than putting the heroine on a pedestal and praising her virtues, Horn is pursued by her; his physical beauty sparks a passion for him that drives Rymenhild wild (lines 256, 300, 956). Nor does the poem contain much reference to the related code of chivalry, though Horn does think it unfair for three of King Thurston's men to fight one Saracen.

---

[4] Georgianna Ziegler, "Structural Repetition in *King Horn*," *Neuphilologische Mitteilungen* 81 (1980), 403.

[5] Ziegler, p. 406.

[6] See Diane Speed, "The Saracens of *King Horn*," *Speculum* 65 (1990), 564–95.

[7] Barron, p. 85.

Many of *Horn*'s motifs — sea voyages, exile and return, revenge and marriage — do belong to romance tradition. The two near or broken-off weddings in the poem replay a timeless situation that not only appears in Chrétien de Troyes' *Erec et Enide* or Malory's *Le Morte Darthur*, but also in modern films such as *The Graduate* and *Monty Python and the Holy Grail*. Some scholars see folk tale motifs as even more prominent: the voyages and exiles, yes, but as well Horn's disguises, the symbols of rings and fish, the significance of dreams, even the simple but effective patterns of repetition themselves. All this is put together without the digressions and interlacing that typify continental romances of this period.

The streamlined, folksy directness of *King Horn* should not fool us, however. The story contains unexplained actions and situations that can only be explained because the poet is referring, sometimes incompletely, to folk tale sources. One "folk-tale non sequitur" Barron notes is that Horn gives no particular reason for hiding his true identity. And John Speirs sees misty connections to mythology in the symbol of Horn himself — to the Horn of Plenty and ultimately the Holy Grail.[8]

Horn is also an object lesson about loyalty and betrayal in a real-world political sense. For Lee C. Ramsay the poem "seems to say that internal dissension is the ultimate threat to a state."[9] Yet *King Horn* is not as much a "mirror for princes" as is *Havelok the Dane*; rather, it is more a chronicle of martial and romantic achievement, a chronicle concerned with political gains.

Finally, the manuscripts in which *King Horn* appears say something about how it may have been viewed by contemporary readers and listeners. Both *Horn* and *Havelok* appear, for example, in a Bodleian Library manuscript (Laud Misc. 108) whose contents also include popularized saints' lives, scientific information, and current events; perhaps, as Barron observes, these romances along with the Reader's Digest version of contemporary knowledge "would appeal to an audience of limited sophistication anxious for instruction and moral edification."[10] Cambridge Gg.4.27.2 (the manuscript on which our text is based) is an equally diverse anthology compiled in the late fifteenth or early sixteenth century. In it *Horn* appears with other romances, saints' lives, a collection of homilies, devotional works, didactic narratives, and several miscellaneous items. *Horn* also appears as the only romance in a third manuscript anthology — British Library MS Harley 2253 — this time, with Latin and French verse, religious material, and love poems.[11] These very different

---

[8] John Speirs, *Medieval English Poetry: The Non-Chaucerian Tradition* (London: Faber and Faber, 1971), p. 187.

[9] Lee C. Ramsey, *Chivalric Romance: Popular Literature in Medieval England* (Bloomington: Indiana University Press, 1983), p. 32.

[10] Barron, p. 54.

[11] Barron, p. 233.

locations for *Horn* suggest a complexity of attraction that modern readers need to know about.

Select Bibliography

Manuscripts

Cambridge University Library MS Gg.4.27.2.

British Library MS Harley 2253.

Bodleian Library MS Laud Misc. 108.

Critical Editions

Allen, Rosamund S., ed. *King Horn*. New York: Garland Medieval Texts, 1984.

Hall, Joseph, ed. *King Horn*. Oxford: Oxford University Press, 1901

French, Walter Hoyt, and Charles Brockway Hale, eds. *Middle English Metrical Romances*. New York: Prentice-Hall, 1930.

Gibbs, A. C., ed. *King Horn, Havelok, Floriz & Blauncheflur, Orfeo, Amis & Amiloun*. Evanston: Northwestern University Press, 1966.

McKnight, George H. ed. *King Horn, Floriz & Blauncheflur, The Assumption of Our Lady*. EETS o.s. 14. London: Oxford University Press, 1901; rpt. 1962.

Sands, Donald B., ed. *Middle English Verse Romances*. New York: Holt, Rinehart and Winston, 1966.

Related Studies

Allen, Rosamund "The Date and Provenance of *King Horn*: Some Interim Reassessments." In *Medieval English Studies Presented to George Kane*. Ed. Edward Donald Kennedy, Ronald Waldron, and Joseph S. Wittig. Suffolk, England: St. Edmundsburg

Press, 1988. Pp. 99–126. [Based on both internal and external evidence, argues a later date for all MSS than previously thought.]

———. "Some Textual Cruces in *King Horn*." *Medium Aevum* 53 (1984), 73–77. [Isolates six examples where cruces occur by comparing three MS versions.]

Dannebaum, Susan. "'Fairer Bi One Ribbe/Thane Eni Man That Libbe' (*King Horn* C315–16)." *Notes and Queries* 226 (1981), 116–17. [Posits a masculine ideal for physical beauty operating within the poem that derives from Adam and Christ.]

French, Walter H. *Essays on King Horn*. Ithaca: Cornell University Press, 1940. [Contains theories about meter, text, and personal names.]

Hearn, Matthew. "Twins of Infidelity: The Double Antagonists of *King Horn*." *Medieval Perspectives* 8 (1993), 78–86. ["*King Horn* deals with the turbulent historical forces of its time in a rather oblique fashion, repressing the real or 'historically accurate' traces of domestic social tensions and projecting them instead onto a set of fictional antagonists more ideologically digestible to its audience: infidel Saracens and the traitor Fikenhild" (p. 79).]

Hurt, James R. "The Texts of *King Horn*." *Journal of the Folklore Institute* 7 (1970), 47–59.

Hynes-Berry, Mary. "Cohesion in *King Horn* and *Sir Orfeo*." *Speculum* 50 (1975), 652–70. [Argues that all episodes fit into a "cohesively progressive pattern" in which every incident contributes to narrative development.]

Jamison, Carol. "A Description of the Medieval Romance Based upon *King Horn*." *Quondam-et-Futurus* 1:2 (Summer 1991), 44–58. [General discussion of generic evolution, poetic style, audience, and structural principles.]

McLaughlin, John. "The Return Song in Medieval Romance and Ballad: *King Horn* and *King Orfeo*." *Journal of American Folklore* 88 (1975), 304–07. [Links twentieth-century Serbo-Croatian heroic poetry, medieval French romances, and nineteenth-century Scottish ballads, by recognizing a "return song" pattern common to all.]

Nimchinsky, Howard. "Orfeo, Guillaume, and Horn." *Romance Philology* 22 (1968), 1–14. [Comparative cross-cultural study of similar passages.]

O'Brien, Timothy. "Word Play in the Allegory of *King Horn*." *Allegorica* 7 (1982), 110–22. [Magic rings, Horn's disguises, and the love triangle "comment upon the political and psychological meanings contained in the poem's word play" (p. 121).]

Purdon, Liam. "*King Horn* and the Medieval Trope of Christ the Lover-Knight." *Proceedings of the PMR Conference at Villanova* 10 (1985), 137–47. [Horn is not only physically beautiful but achieves a state of moral perfection. By incorporating features of the trope of Christ the Lover-Knight the poet establishes the logic of Horn's many trials and generates the poem's suspense.]

Quinn, William A. *Jongleur: A Modified Theory of Oral Improvisation and Its Effects on the Performance and Transmission of Middle English Romance*. Washington, D.C.: University Press of America, 1982. [Discusses the close relationship between oral performance and the making of written texts.]

Scott, Anne. "Plans, Predictions, and Promises: Traditional Story Techniques and the Configuration of Word and Deed in *King Horn*." In *Studies in Medieval English Romances: Some New Approaches*. Ed. D. S. Brewer. Cambridge: Brewer, 1988. Pp. 37–68. [Explores the "binding power of promises, intentions, and desires" and the poet's means of reaffirming and challenging "traditional narrative techniques" (p. 47).]

Speed, Diane. "The Saracens of *King Horn*." *Speculum* 65 (1990), 564–95. [The Saracens named in the poem are not "figures from real life," but rather a "literary phenomenon."]

Ziegler, Georgianna. "Structural Repetition in *King Horn*." *Neuphilologische Mitteilungen* 81 (1980), 403–08. [Divides the narrative into four parts and draws attention to "the skillful interweaving of matter with form" (p. 403).]

King Horn

	Alle beon he blithe	*be happy*
	That to my song lythe!	*[Who]; listen*
	A sang ich schal you singe	
	Of Murry the Kinge.	
5	King he was biweste	*in the west*
	So longe so hit laste.	*it (i.e., his life)*
	Godhild het his quen;	*was called*
	Faire ne mighte non ben.	*Fairer*
	He hadde a sone that het Horn;	
10	Fairer ne mighte non beo born,	*be*
	Ne no rein upon birine,	*rain fell upon*
	Ne sunne upon bischine.	*or sun shone*
	Fairer nis non thane he was:	
	He was bright so the glas;	*as*
15	He was whit so the flur;	*flower*
	Rose red was his colur.	
	He was fayr and eke bold,	*also*
	And of fiftene winter hold.	*old (see note)*
	In none kinge riche	*no other kingdom*
20	Nas non his iliche.	*anyone like him*
	Twelf feren he hadde	*companions*
	That he alle with him ladde,	*led*
	Alle riche mannes sones,	
	And alle hi were faire gomes,	*they; good fellows*
25	With him for to pleie,	
	And mest he luvede tweie;	*most*
	That on him het Hathulf child,	*one of them was called Athulf*
	And that other Fikenild.	
	Athulf was the beste,	
30	And Fikenylde the werste.	
	Hit was upon a someres day,	
	Also ich you telle may,	*As I*
	Murri, the gode King,	

	Rod on his pleing	*Rode for sport*
35	Bi the se side,	*seaside*
	Ase he was woned ride.	*used to*
	With him riden bote two —	
	Al to fewe ware tho!	*too; were they (see note)*
	He fond bi the stronde,	*shore*
40	Arived on his londe,	
	Schipes fiftene	*Ships*
	With Sarazins kene	*Saracens bold*
	He axede what hi soghte	*asked; they sought*
	Other to londe broghte.	*Or*
45	A payn hit ofherde,	*pagan heard it*
	And hym wel sone answarede:	
	"Thy lond folk we schulle slon,	*slay*
	And alle that Crist luveth upon	
	And the selve right anon.	
50	Ne shaltu todai henne gon."	*Nor shall you; hence*
	The king alighte of his stede,	*off*
	For tho he havede nede,	*then; had*
	And his gode knightes two;	
	Al to fewe he hadde tho.	*then*
55	Swerd hi gunne gripe	*they began*
	And togadere smite.	
	Hy smyten under schelde	
	That sume hit yfelde.	*So that; felt*
	The king hadde al to fewe	
60	Togenes so fele schrewe;	*Against so many villains*
	So wele mighten ythe	*easily; they*
	Bringe hem thre to dithe.	*death*
	The pains come to londe	*pagans came*
	And neme hit in here honde	*took it into their possession*
65	That folc hi gunne quelle,	*folk; kill*
	And churchen for to felle.	*churches to destroy*
	Ther ne moste libbe	*might not live*
	The fremde ne the sibbe.	*strangers; relatives*
	Bute hi here laye asoke,	*Unless they their religion forsook*
70	And to here toke.	*theirs took*
	Of alle wymmanne	
	Wurst was Godhild thanne.	*Most miserable*

	For Murri heo weop sore	*she wept*
	And for Horn yute more.	*yet (even)*
75	He wente ut of halle	*out*
	Fram hire maidenes alle	
	Under a roche of stone	
	Ther heo livede alone.	
	Ther heo servede Gode	
80	Aghenes the paynes forbode.	*Against the pagans' injunction*
	Ther he servede Criste	*she*
	That no payn hit ne wiste.	*So that no pagan knew it*
	Evre heo bad for Horn child	*Ever she prayed*
	That Jesu Crist him beo myld.	*might be gracious to him*
85	Horn was in paynes honde	*hands of the pagans*
	With his feren of the londe.	*companions*
	Muchel was his fairhede,	*Great; beauty*
	For Jhesu Crist him makede.	
	Payns him wolde slen,	*wanted to kill him*
90	Other al quic flen,	*Or flay him alive*
	Yef his fairnesse nere:	*If it were not for*
	The children alle aslaye were.	*slain*
	Thanne spak on admirad —	*one emir*
	Of wordes he was bald, —	*bold*
95	"Horn, thu art well kene,	*you; eager*
	And that is wel isene.	*seen*
	Thu art gret and strong,	
	Fair and evene long;	*quite tall*
	Thu schalt waxe more	*grow bigger*
100	Bi fulle seve yere.	*seven*
	Yef thu mote to live go	*If; were to go away alive*
	And thine feren also,	*companions*
	Yef hit so bi falle,	*befall (happen)*
	Ye scholde slen us alle:	*might; slay*
105	Tharvore thu most to stere,	*Therefore; must go; boat*
	Thu and thine ifere;	*companions*
	To schupe schulle ye funde,	*ship; hurry*
	And sinke to the grunde.	*bottom [of the sea]*
	The se you schal adrenche,	*drown in*
110	Ne schal hit us noght ofthinche.	*Nor shall [we] regret it*
	For if thu were alive,	

	With swerd other with knive,	*or*
	We scholden alle deie,	
	And thi fader deth abeie."	*pay for*
115	The children hi broghte to stronde,	*shore*
	Wringinde here honde,	
	Into schupes borde	
	At the furste worde.	*command*
	Ofte hadde Horn beo wo,	*been woeful*
120	Ac nevre wurs than him was tho.	*But; then*
	The se bigan to flowe,	*(see note)*
	And Horn child to rowe;	*rue (regret bitterly)*
	The se that schup so fasste drof	*drove*
	The children dradde therof.	*were afraid*
125	Hi wenden towisse	*They expected for certain*
	Of here lif to misse,	*their life to lose*
	Al the day and al the night	
	Til hit sprang dailight,	
	Til Horn sagh on the stronde	*saw; shore*
130	Men gon in the londe.	*going about*
	"Feren," quath he, "yonge,	*"Friends," said; young*
	Ich telle you tithinge:	*news*
	Ich here foyeles singe	*hear; birds*
	And that gras him springe.	
135	Blithe beo we on lyve;	*Let us be happy [to be] alive*
	Ure schup is on ryve."	*Our ship; shore*
	Of schup hi gunne funde,	*Off; they hasten*
	And setten fout to grunde.	*foot to ground*
	Bi the se side	
140	Hi leten that schup ride.	
	Thanne spak him child Horn,	
	In Suddene he was iborn:	*(see note)*
	"Schup bi the se flode,	
	Daies have thu gode.	
145	Bi the se brinke,	*sea's edge*
	No water the nadrinke.	*have you to drink*
	Yef thu cume to Suddene,	
	Gret thu wel of myne kenne,	*Greet; family*
	Gret thu wel my moder,	
150	Godhild, Quen the gode,	

	And seie the paene king,	*say to; pagan*
	Jesu Cristes withering,	*enemy*
	That ich am hol and fer	*sound; well*
	On this lond arived her;	*here*
155	And seie that hei schal fonde	*they; experience*
	The dent of myne honde."	*blow*
	The children yede to tune,	*went their way*
	Bi dales and bi dune.	*hills*
	Hy metten with Almair King,	*King Alymar*
160	Crist yeven him His blessing	*give*
	King of Westernesse	
	Crist yive him muchel blisse!	*much*
	He him spac to Horn child	*spoke*
	Wordes that were mild:	*soft*
165	"Whannes beo ye, faire gumes,	*Whence (from where); young ones*
	That her to londe beoth icume,	*have come*
	Alle throttene,	*thirteen*
	Of bodie swithe kene?	*very bold*
	Bi God that me makede,	
170	A swich fair verade	*very; group of companions*
	Ne saugh ich in none stunde,	*never*
	Bi westene londe:	*land of the west*
	Seie me wat ye seche."	*Tell; seek*
	Horn spak here speche,	
175	He spak for hem alle,	
	Vor so hit moste bivalle:	*For; befall*
	He was the faireste	
	And of wit the beste.	*intelligence*
	"We beoth of Suddenne,	*are from*
180	Icome of gode kenne,	*family*
	Of Cristene blode,	
	And kynges swthe gode.	*so very*
	Payns ther gunne arive	*did arrive*
	And duden hem of lyve.	*deprived; life*
185	Hi sloghen and todroghe	*tore apart*
	Cristene men inoghe.	*enough*
	So Crist me mote rede,	*So help me God*
	Us hi dude lede	
	Into a galeie,	*galley*

190	With the se to pleie,	*On; sport*
	Dai hit is igon and other,	*[One] day; another*
	Withute sail and rother:	*Without; rudder*
	Ure schip bigan to swymme	*Our; drift*
	To this londes brymme.	*edge*
195	Nu thu might us slen and binde	*Now; slay*
	Ore honde bihynde.	*Our; hands*
	Bute yef hit beo thi wille,	
	Helpe that we ne spille."	*die*
	Thanne spak the gode kyng	
200	Iwis he nas no nithing	*truly; villain*
	"Seie me, child, what is thi name?	*Tell*
	Ne schaltu have bute game."	*sport*
	The child him answerde,	
	Sone so he hit herde:	*As soon as*
205	"Horn ich am ihote,	*called*
	Icomen ut of the bote,	*Come out; boat*
	Fram the se side.	
	Kyng, wel mote thee tide."	*you prosper*
	Thanne hym spak the gode king,	
210	"Well bruc thu thin evening.	*bear; name*
	Horn, thu go wel schulle	
	Bi dales and bi hulle;	*hill*
	Horn, thu lude sune,	*loudly shall sound*
	Bi dales and bi dune;	
215	So schal thi name springe	
	Fram kynge to kynge,	
	And thi fairnesse	
	Abute Westernesse,	*[All] about*
	The strengthe of thine honde	
220	Into evrech londe.	*each and every*
	Horn, thu art so swete,	
	Ne may ich the forlete."	*not abandon you*
	Hom rod Aylmar the Kyng	*homewards*
	And Horn mid him, his fundling,	*with; foundling*
225	And alle his ifere,	*companions*
	That were him so dere.	
	The kyng com into halle	
	Among his knightes alle;	

	Forth he clupede Athelbrus,	*called*
230	That was stiward of his hus.	*steward*
	"Stiward, tak nu here	*now*
	My fundlyng for to lere	*teach*
	Of thine mestere,	*occupation*
	Of wude and of rivere,	*hunting; hawking*
235	And tech him to harpe	
	With his nayles scharpe,	*fingernails*
	Bivore me to kerve,	*Before; carve [meat]*
	And of the cupe serve.	
	Thu tech him of alle the liste	*skills*
240	That thu evre of wiste,	*knew about*
	And his feiren thou wise	*companions; teach*
	In to othere servise.	
	Horn thu undervonge	*take charge of*
	And tech him of harpe and songe."	
245	Ailbrus gan lere	*Athelbrus; teach*
	Horn and his yfere.	
	Horn in herte laghte	*in his heart; understood*
	Al that he him taghte.	
	In the curt and ute,	*court; out*
250	And elles al abute	*everywhere else*
	Luvede men Horn child,	
	And mest him luvede Rymenhild,	*Rymenhild loved him the most*
	The kynges owene doghter.	
	He was mest in thoghte;	*foremost in her thoughts*
255	Heo luvede so Horn child	*She*
	That negh heo gan wexe wild:	*she nearly went crazy*
	For heo ne mighte at borde	*dinner table*
	With him speke no worde,	
	Ne noght in the halle	
260	Among the knightes alle,	
	Ne nowhar in non othere stede.	*place*
	Of folk heo hadde drede:	
	Bi daie ne bi nighte	
	With him speke ne mighte.	*she could not speak*
265	Hire soreghe ne hire pine	*Her sorrow nor her pain*
	Ne mighte nevre fine.	*end*
	In heorte heo hadde wo,	

	And thus hire bithoghte tho:	*decided then*
	Heo sende hire sonde	*She; her message*
270	Athelbrus to honde,	*into Athelbrus' presence*
	That he come hire to,	
	And also scholde Horn do,	
	Al in to bure,	*private chamber*
	For heo gan to lure;	*appear downcast*
275	And the sonde seide	*message*
	That sik lai that maide,	*sick*
	And bad him come swithe	*immediately*
	For heo nas nothing blithe.	*was not a bit well*
	The stward was in herte wo,	*pained in his heart*
280	For he nuste what to do.	*did not know*
	Wat Rymenhild hure thoghte	
	Gret wunder him thughte,	*Seemed very strange to him*
	Abute Horn the yonge	
	To bure for to bringe.	*bower*
285	He thoghte upon his mode	*mind*
	Hit nas for none gode:	*It was for no good*
	He tok him another,	
	Athulf, Hornes brother.	
	"Athulf," he sede, "right anon	*immediately*
290	Thu schalt with me to bure gon	*bower*
	To speke with Rymenhild stille	*in private*
	And witen hure wille.	*know about her desire*
	In Hornes ilike	*Horn's likeness*
	Thu schalt hure biswike:	*deceive*
295	Sore ich me ofdrede	*fear greatly*
	Heo wolde Horn misrede."	*advise badly*
	Athelbrus gan Athulf lede,	
	And into bure with him yede:	*went*
	Anon upon Athulf child	
300	Rymenhild gan wexe wild:	*grew very passionate*
	Heo wende that Horn hit were	*thought*
	That heo havede there:	*had*
	Heo sette him on bedde;	
	With Athulf child he wedde;	*revealed passion*
305	On hire armes tweie	*In; two*
	Athulf heo gan leie.	*embrace*

"Horn," quath heo, "wel longe — *said*
Ich habbe thee luved stronge.
Thu schalt thi trewthe plighte — *swear fidelity*
310 On myn hond her righte, — *right here*
Me to spuse holde, — *to be a spouse*
And ich thee lord to wolde." — *to have as lord*
Athulf sede on hire ire — *in her ear*
So stille so hit were, — *As quietly as possible*
315 "Thi tale nu thu lynne, — *finish*
For Horn nis noght her inne.
Ne beo we noght iliche: — *alike*
Horn is fairer and riche,
Fairer bi one ribbe
320 Thane eni man that libbe: — *lives*
Thegh Horn were under molde — *Even if; earth*
Other elles wher he wolde — *Or wherever*
Other henne a thusend mile, — *from here*
Ich nolde him ne thee bigile." — *would not beguile him nor you*
325 Rymenhild hire biwente, — *changed*
And Athelbrus fule heo schente. — *foully; denounced*
"Hennes thu go, thu fule theof, — *From here; wicked thief*
Ne wurstu me nevre more leof; — *will you be; dear*
Went ut of my bur, — *Get out; bower*
330 With muchel mesaventur. — *much bad luck*
Schame mote thu fonge — *overtake you*
And on highe rode anhonge. — *gallows hang*
Ne spek ich noght with Horn:
Nis he noght so unorn; — *ugly*
335 Horn is fairer thane beo he: — *he (i.e., Athulf)*
With muchel schame mote thu deie." — *die*
Athelbrus in a stunde — *right away*
Fel anon to grunde. — *immediately*
"Lefdi min oghe, — *My own lady*
340 Lithe me a litel throghe! — *Listen to me for a moment*
Lust whi ich wonde — *Hear; hesitated*
Bringe thee Horn to honde.
For Horn is fair and riche,
Nis no whar his iliche. — *Nowhere; equal*
345 Aylmar, the gode Kyng,

	Dude him on mi lokyng.	*Placed; care*
	Yef Horn were her abute,	*If*
	Sore I me dute	*Greatly; fear*
	With him ye wolden pleie	*take pleasure*
350	Bitwex you selve tweie.	
	Thanne scholde withuten othe	*beyond doubt*
	The kyng maken us wrothe.	*angry*
	Rymenhild, foryef me thi tene,	*forgive; anger*
	Lefdi, my quene,	
355	And Horn ich schal thee fecche,	
	Wham so hit recche."	*Whoever may care*
	Rymenhild, yef he cuthe,	*as much as she could*
	Gan lynne with hire muthe.	*keep quiet*
	Heo makede hire wel blithe;	*She made herself*
360	Wel was hire that sithe.	*[It was] well with her; time*
	"Go nu," quath heo, "sone,	*she said; soon*
	And send him after none,	*noontime*
	On a squieres wise.	*dressed as a squire*
	Whane the kyng arise	
365	To wude for to pleie,	*woods; sport*
	Nis non that him biwreie.	*No one; will betray*
	He schal with me bileve	*stay*
	Til hit beo nir eve,	*close to evening*
	To haven of him mi wille;	*desire*
370	After ne recche ich what me telle." [1]	
	Aylbrus wende hire fro;	*turned away from her*
	Horn in halle fond he tho	*then*
	Bifore the kyng on benche,	
	Wyn for to schenche.	*Wine; pour*
375	"Horn," quath he, "so hende,	*gracious*
	To bure nu thu wende,	*bedchamber; go*
	After mete stille,	*meal quietly*
	With Rymenhild to dwelle;	
	Wordes swthe bolde,	*very*
380	In herte thu hem holde.	*them keep (i.e., be quiet)*
	Horn, beo me wel trewe;	

[1] *Afterwards I do not care what people say*

	Ne schal hit thee nevre rewe."	*you will not regret it*
	Horn in herte leide	*took to heart*
	Al that he him seide;	
385	He yeode in wel righte	*went*
	To Rymenhild the brighte.	*beautiful*
	On knes he him sette,	
	And sweteliche hure grette.	*sweetly greeted her*
	Of his feire sighte	*appearance*
390	Al the bur gan lighte.	*glow*
	He spac faire speche —	
	Ne dorte him noman teche.	*needed*
	"Wel thu sitte and softe,	
	Rymenhild the brighte,	
395	With thine maidenes sixe	
	That the sitteth nixte.	*sit next to you*
	Kinges stward ure	*our*
	Sende me in to bure;	*Sent*
	With thee speke ich scholde.	
400	Seie me what thu woldest:	*Tell*
	Seie, and ich schal here	
	What thi wille were."	
	Rymenhild up gan stonde	
	And tok him bi the honde:	
405	Heo sette him on pelle	*fur mantle*
	Of wyn to drinke his fulle:	
	Heo makede him faire chere	*She showed him*
	And tok him abute the swere.	*neck*
	Ofte heo him custe,	*kissed*
410	So wel so hire luste.	*as much as she liked*
	"Horn," heo sede, "withute strif,	*doubtless*
	Thu schalt have me to thi wif.	*for your wife*
	Horn, have of me rewthe,	*pity*
	And plist me thi trewthe.	*pledge; oath (fidelity)*
415	Horn tho him bithoghte	*thought to himself*
	What he speke mighte.	
	"Crist," quath he, "thee wisse,	*guide*
	And yive thee hevene blisse	
	Of thine husebonde,	
420	Wher he beo in londe.	*Wherever*

	Ich am ibore to lowe	*born; too low*
	Such wimman to knowe.	
	Ich am icome of thralle	*a serf*
	And fundling bifalle.	*have become a foundling*
425	Ne feolle hit the of cunde	*Nor would it be natural*
	To spuse beo me bunde.	*As a spouse; united*
	Hit nere no fair wedding	*would be*
	Bitwexe a thral and a king."	
	Tho gan Rymenhild mislyke	*Then; be displeased*
430	And sore gan to sike:	*sigh*
	Armes heo gan bughe;	*to bend (raise)*
	Adun heo feol iswoghe.	*Down; fell unconscious*
	Horn in herte was ful wo	*in much grief*
	And tok hire on his armes two.	
435	He gan hire for to kesse	*kiss*
	Wel ofte mid ywisse.	*with certainty*
	"Lemman," he sede, "dere,	*Beloved*
	Thin herte nu thu stere.	*control*
	Help me to knighte	*become a knight*
440	Bi al thine mighte,	
	To my lord the king	
	That he me yive dubbing:	*dub me*
	Thanne is mi thralhod	*serf-like status*
	I went in to knighthod	*turned*
445	And I schal wexe more,	*grow*
	And do, lemman, thi lore."	*instruction*
	Rymenhild, that swete thing,	
	Wakede of hire swoghning.	*swoon*
	"Horn," quath heo, "wel sone	
450	That schal beon idone.	
	Thu schalt beo dubbed knight	
	Are come seve night.	*Before a week is up*
	Have her this cuppe	*Take*
	And this ryng ther uppe	*along with it*
455	To Aylbrus the stuard,	
	And se he holde foreward.	*see to it; keep the agreement*
	Seie ich him biseche,	*Say I ask him*
	With loveliche speche,	
	That he adun falle	*fall down (humble himself)*

460	Bifore the king in halle,	
	And bidde the king arighte	*immediately*
	Dubbe thee to knighte.	
	With selver and with golde	*silver*
	Hit wurth him wel iyolde.	*He will be well-rewarded*
465	Crist him lene spede	*grant success*
	Thin erende to bede."	*Make known your business*
	Horn tok his leve,	
	For hit was negh eve.	*nearly evening*
	Athelbrus he soghte	
470	And yaf him that he broghte,	*gave him what*
	And tolde him ful yare	*quickly*
	Hu he hadde ifare,	*How; fared*
	And sede him his nede,	*what he wanted*
	And bihet him his mede.	*promised; reward*
475	Athelbrus also swithe	*as soon as possible*
	Wente to halle blive.	*quickly*
	"Kyng," he sede, "thu leste	*listen*
	A tale mid the beste.	*The best of all tales*
	Thu schalt bere crune	*crown*
480	Tomoreghe in this tune;	*Tomorrow; town*
	Tomoreghe is thi feste:	*feast*
	Ther bihoveth geste.	*It is fitting to have a good time*
	Hit nere noght for loren	*It is not a lost cause*
	For to knighti child Horn,	*young man*
485	Thine armes for to welde:	*bear*
	God knight he schal yelde."	*Good; turn out to be*
	The king sede sone,	
	"That is wel idone.	*good idea*
	Horn me wel iquemeth;	*pleases*
490	God knight him bisemeth.	*seems*
	He schal have mi dubbing	
	And after wurth mi derling.	*become; favorite*
	And alle his feren twelf	*companions*
	He schal knighten himself:	
495	Alle he schal hem knighte	*them all*
	Bifore me this nighte."	
	Til the light of day sprang	
	Ailmar him thughte lang.	*thought to himself*

The day bigan to springe;
500 Horn com bivore the kinge, — *before*
Mid his twelf yfere, — *With; companions*
Sume hi were luthere. — *Some of them; evil*
Horn he dubbede to knighte
With swerd and spures brighte. — *spurs*
505 He sette him on a stede whit: — *white horse*
Ther nas no knight hym ilik. — *was no; like him*
He smot him a litel wight — *light blow*
And bed him beon a god knight. — *ordered; good*
  Athulf fel aknes thar — *on his knees*
510 Bivore the King Aylmar.
"King," he sede, "so kene — *bold*
Grante me a bene: — *favor*
Nu is knight Sire Horn — *Now as*
That in Suddene was iboren;
515 Lord he is of londe
Over us that bi him stonde;
Thin armes he hath and scheld
To fighte with upon the feld:
Let him us alle knighte
520 For that is ure righte." — *our*
Aylmar sede sone ywis, — *responded quickly*
"Do nu that thi wille is." — *what*
Horn adun lighte — *got down*
And makede hem alle knightes.
525 Murie was the feste — *Merry*
Al of faire gestes: — *entertainments*
Ac Rymenhild nas noght ther, — *But*
And that hire thughte seve yer. — *she thought seven years*
After Horn heo sente, — *sent for*
530 And he to bure wente. — *chamber*
Nolde he noght go one; — *alone*
Athulf was his mone. — *companion*
Rymenhild on flore stod:
Hornes come hire thughte god: — *Horn's coming seemed good to her*
535 And sede, "Welcome, Sire Horn,
And Athulf knight the biforn. — *before you*
Knight, nu is thi time

For to sitte bi me.
Do nu that thu er of spake: *spoke about before*
540 To thy wif thu me take.
Ef thu art trewe of dedes, *i.e., a man of your word*
Do nu ase thu sedes. *said*
Nu thu hast wille thine,
Unbind me of my pine." *Release; pain*
545 "Rymenhild," quath he, "beo stille!
Ich wulle don al thi wille,
Also hit mot bitide. *When the time is right*
Mid spere I schal furst ride, *With spear*
And mi knighthod prove,
550 Ar ich thee ginne to woghe. *Before; begin; woo*
We beth knightes yonge, *are*
Of o dai al isprunge; *one; sprung up*
And of ure mestere *our mastery*
So is the manere: *manner*
555 With sume othere knighte
Wel for his lemman fighte *lover*
Or he eni wif take; *Before*
Forthi me stondeth the more rape. *For you; greater haste*
Today, so Crist me blesse,
560 Ich wulle do pruesse, *I will do knightly deeds*
For thi luve in the felde
Mid spere and mid schelde. *With*
If ich come to lyve, *return alive*
Ich schal thee take to wyve."
565 "Knight," quath heo, "trewe, *she said*
Ich wene ich mai thee leve: *believe; love*
Tak nu her this gold ring:
God him is the dubbing; *Good; adornment*
Ther is upon the ringe
570 Igrave "Rymenhild the yonge": *Engraved*
Ther nis non betere anonder sunne *under the sun*
That eni man of telle cunne. *can tell of*
For my luve thu hit were
And on thi finger thu him bere.
575 The stones beoth of suche grace *power*
That thu ne schalt in none place

	Of none duntes beon ofdrad,	*blows be afraid*
	Ne on bataille beon amad,	*battle; go crazy*
	Ef thu loke theran	*If; on it*
580	And thenke upon thi lemman.	
	And Sire Athulf, thi brother,	*[sworn] brother*
	He schal have another.	
	Horn, ich thee biseche	
	With loveliche speche,	
585	Crist yeve god erndinge	*success*
	Thee aghen to bringe."	
	The knight hire gan kesse,	*kiss*
	And heo him to blesse.	
	Leve at hire he nam,	*He took leave of her*
590	And in to halle cam:	
	The knightes yeden to table,	*went*
	And Horne yede to stable:	
	Thar he tok his gode fole,	*horse*
	Also blak so eny cole.	*As black as*
595	The fole schok the brunie	*horse; armor*
	That al the curt gan denie.	*court; resounded*
	The fole bigan to springe,	*buck*
	And Horn murie to singe.	*merrily*
	Horn rod in a while	
600	More than a myle.	
	He fond o schup stonde	*a ship anchored*
	With hethene honde.	*heathen hounds*
	He axede what hi soghte	*they*
	Other to londe broghte.	*Or*
605	An hund him gan bihelde	*One heathen*
	That spac wordes belde:	*bold*
	"This lond we wullegh winne	*wish to conquer*
	And sle that ther is inne."	*[the inhabitants]*
	Horn gan his swerd gripe	
610	And on his arme wype.	
	The Sarazins he smatte	*hit*
	That his blod hatte;	*blood [grew] hot*
	At evreche dunte	*each and every blow*
	The heved of wente;	*head; off*
615	Tho gunne the hundes gone	*rush*

Abute Horn a lone: — *Surround*
He lokede on the ringe,
And thoghte on Rimenilde;
He slogh ther on haste — *killed; quickly*
620 On hundred bi the laste, — *One*
Ne mighte noman telle — *count*
That folc that he gan quelle. — *subdue*
Of alle that were alive,
Ne mighte ther non thrive.
625 Horn tok the maisteres heved, — *leader's head*
That he hadde him bireved — *deprived of*
And sette hit on his swerde,
Anoven at than orde. — *On top on the point*
He verde hom into halle, — *went*
630 Among the knightes alle.
"Kyng," he sede, "wel thu sitte,
And alle thine knightes mitte. — *with you*
Today, after mi dubbing,
So I rod on my pleing — *As I rode for sport*
635 I fond o schup rowe — *row of ships*
Mid watere al byflowe — *With water surrounded*
Al with Sarazines kyn, — *kin*
And none londisse men — *native*
To dai for to pine — *torment*
640 Thee and alle thine.
Hi gonne me assaille: — *attack*
Mi swerd me nolde faille: — *would not*
I smot hem alle to grunde,
Other yaf hem dithes wunde. — *Or gave them deadly wounds*
645 That heved I thee bringe — *head*
Of the maister kinge. — *principal*
Nu is thi wile iyolde, — *trouble rewarded*
King, that thu me knighty woldest."
  A moreghe tho the day gan springe, — *In the morning when*
650 The king him rod an huntinge.
At hom lefte Fikenhild,
That was the wurste moder child. — *worst child of woman*
Horn ferde into bure — *went; chamber*
To sen aventure. — *seek*

655 He saw Rymenild sitte
Also heo were of witte. — *As if; out of her mind*
Heo sat on the sunne — *i.e., at a sunny window*
With tieres al birunne. — *tears; covered*
Horn sede, "Lef, thin ore! — *Beloved, grant me your favor*
660 Wi wepestu so sore?"
Heo sede, "Noght I ne wepe, — *I do not weep for nothing*
Bute ase I lay aslepe
To the se my net I caste, — *sea*
And hit nolde noght ilaste; — *stay intact*
665 A gret fiss at the furste — *fish; immediately*
Mi net he gan to berste. — *burst*
Ich wene that ich schal leose — *know; lose*
The fiss that ich wolde cheose."
"Crist," quath Horn, "and Seint Stevene
670 Turne thine swevene. — *Interpret; dream*
Ne schal I thee biswike, — *deceive*
Ne do that thee mislike. — *displease*
I schal me make thin owe — *own*
To holden and to knowe — *keep*
675 For everech othere wighte, — *Above any other creature*
And tharto mi treuthe I thee plighte." — *oath; pledge*
Muchel was the ruthe — *sadness*
That was at thare truthe, — *betrothal*
For Rymenhild weop ille, — *bitterly*
680 And Horn let the tires stille. — *tears stop*
"Lemman, quath he, "dere, — *my love*
Thu schalt more ihere. — *hear*
Thi sweven schal wende — *dream; turn [favorably]*
Other sum man schal us schende. — *Or someone will harm us*
685 The fiss that brak the lyne,
Ywis he doth us pine. — *Certainly; torment*
That schal don us tene, — *cause us pain*
And wurth wel sone isene." — *will be seen*
Aylmar rod bi Sture, — *the Mersey*
690 And Horn lai in bure. — *chamber*
Fykenhild hadde envye
And sede thes folye: — *spoke these lies*
"Aylmar, ich thee warne

	Horn thee wule berne:	*destroy you*
695	Ich herde whar he sede,	
	And his swerd forth leide,	
	To bringe thee of lyve,	*to kill you*
	And take Rymenhild to wyve.	
	He lith in bure	*lies; chamber*
700	Under coverture	*the bedcovers*
	By Rymenhild thi doghter,	
	And so he doth wel ofte.	
	And thider thu go al right,	
	Ther thu him finde might.	
705	Thu do him ut of londe,	*force him out*
	Other he doth thee schonde!"	*Before; harm*
	Aylmar aghen gan turne	
	Wel modi and wel murne.	*angry; sorrowful*
	He fond Horn in arme	*embrace*
710	On Rymenhilde barme.	*bosom*
	"Awey ut," he sede, "fule theof,	*out; foul thief*
	Ne wurstu me nevremore leof!	*Nor will you ever be dear to me*
	Wend ut of my bure	*Get out; bower*
	With muchel messaventure.	*bad luck*
715	Wel sone bute thu flitte,	*Unless you flee at once*
	With swerde ich thee anhitte.	*hit*
	Wend ut of my londe,	
	Other thu schalt have schonde."	*injury*
	Horn sadelede his stede	
720	And his armes he gan sprede.	*armor; laid out*
	His brunie he gan lace	*chain mail tunic*
	So he scholde in to place.	*As if he; battle*
	His swerd he gan fonge:	*grab*
	Nabod he noght to longe.	*He wasted no time*
725	He yede forth blive	*went; immediately*
	To Rymenhild his wyve.	*betrothed*
	He sede, "Lemman derling,	*dear love*
	Nu havestu thi swevening.	*dream*
	The fiss that thi net rente,	*tore*
730	Fram thee he me sente.	
	Rymenhild, have wel godne day:	*have a good day*
	No leng abiden I ne may.	*No longer; stay*

	In to uncuthe londe,	*unknown*
	Wel more for to fonde;	*find*
735	I schal wune there	*live*
	Fulle seve yere.	*seven*
	At seve yeres ende,	
	Yef I ne come ne sende,	*If I do not return or send a message*
	Tak thee husebonde;	
740	For me thu ne wonde.	*wait*
	In armes thu me fonge,	*take*
	And kes me wel longe."	*kiss*
	Heo custe him wel a stunde	*kissed; a while*
	And Rymenhild feol to grunde.	*swooned*
745	Horn tok his leve:	
	Ne mighte he no leng bileve;	*longer stay*
	He tok Athulf, his fere,	*companion*
	Al abute the swere,	*neck*
	And sede, "Knight so trewe,	
750	Kep wel mi luve newe.	*Take care of*
	Thu nevre me ne forsoke:	
	Rymenhild thu kep and loke.	*look after*
	His stede he gan bistride,	*mount*
	And forth he gan ride:	
755	To the havene he ferde,	*harbor; went*
	And a god schup he hurede,	*good; rented*
	That him scholde londe	
	In westene londe.	*western*
	Athulf weop with ighe	*eyes*
760	And al that him isighe.	*he saw all of that*
	The whyght him gan stonde,	*seabreeze sustained him*
	And drof til Hirelonde.	*drove; Ireland (see note)*
	To londe he him sette	*disembarked*
	And fot on stirop sette.	
765	He fond bi the weie	*found*
	Kynges sones tweie;	*two*
	That on him het Harild,	*one called himself Harold*
	And that other Berild.	
	Berild gan him preie	*ask*
770	That he scholde him seie	
	What his name were	

	And what he wolde there.	*wanted*
	"Cutberd," he sede, "ich hote,	*I am called*
	Icomen ut of the bote,	*Come out; boat*
775	Wel feor fram biweste	*From far away in the west*
	To seche mine beste."	*seek my fortune*
	Berild gan him nier ride	*nearer*
	And tok him by the bridel:	
	"Wel beo thu, knight, ifounde;	
780	With me thu lef a stunde.	*remain a while*
	Also mote I sterve,	*As surely as I must die*
	The king thu schalt serve.	
	Ne sagh I nevre my lyve	*in my life*
	So fair knight aryve."	
785	Cutberd heo ladde in to halle,	
	And hi a kne gan falle:	*they on their knees*
	He sette him a knewelyng	*made them kneel*
	And grette wel the gode king.	
	Thanne sede Berild sone:	
790	"Sire King, of him thu hast to done;	*do [business] with him*
	Bitak him thi lond to werie;	*Entrust; defend*
	Ne schal hit noman derie,	*harm*
	For he is the faireste man	
	That evre yut on thi londe cam."	*yet*
795	Thanne sede the king so dere,	
	"Welcome beo thu here.	
	Go nu, Berild, swithe,	*quickly*
	And make him ful blithe.	
	And whan thu farst to woghe,	*go wooing*
800	Tak him thine glove:	
	Iment thu havest to wyve,	*[Whatever] intention; marry*
	Awai he schal thee dryve;	
	For Cutberdes fairhede	*for the sake of; beauty*
	Ne schal thee nevre wel spede."	*prosper*
805	Hit was at Cristemasse,	
	Neither more ne lasse;	
	Ther cam in at none	
	A geaunt swthe sone,	*giant very quickly*
	Iarmed fram paynyme	*non-Christian lands*
810	And seide thes ryme:	*rhyme*

	"Site stille, Sire Kyng,	
	And herkne this tything:	*listen to; message*
	Her buth paens arived;	*There are pagans*
	Wel mo thane five	*[knights]*
815	Her beoth on the sonde,	*There are; sand*
	King, upon thy londe;	
	On of hem wile fighte	*One*
	Aghen thre knightes.	*Against*
	Yef other thre slen ure,	*If your three slay our [one]*
820	Al this lond beo youre;	
	Yef ure on overcometh your threo,	*our one; three*
	Al this lond schal ure beo.	*ours*
	Tomoreghe be the fightinge,	
	Whane the light of daye springe."	
825	Thanne sede the Kyng Thurston,	
	"Cutberd schal beo that on;	*one*
	Berild schal beo that other,	*second*
	The thridde Alrid his brother;	
	For hi beoth the strengeste	*they are*
830	And of armes the beste.	
	Bute what schal us to rede?	*What advice shall we take*
	Ich wene we beth alle dede."	*believe*
	Cutberd sat at borde	*table*
	And sede thes wordes:	
835	"Sire King, hit nis no righte	
	On with thre to fighte:	*One*
	Aghen one hunde,	*Against; heathen hound*
	Thre Cristen men to fonde.	*attack*
	Sire, I schal alone,	
840	Withute more ymone,	*companions*
	With mi swerd wel ethe	*easily*
	Bringe hem thre to dethe."	
	The king aros amoreghe,	*the next morning*
	That hadde muchel sorghe;	*sorrow*
845	And Cutberd ros of bedde,	
	With armes he him schredde:	*equipped himself*
	Horn his brunie gan on caste,	*armored corselet put on*
	And lacede hit wel faste,	*laced*
	And cam to the kinge	

850	At his up risinge.	
	"King," he sede, "cum to felde,	
	For to bihelde	
	Hu we fighte schulle,	
	And togare go wulle."	*together will go*
855	Right at prime tide	*six a. m.*
	Hi gunnen ut ride	*They rode out*
	And funden on a grene	*found*
	A geaunt swthe kene,	*giant very bold*
	His feren him biside	*companions beside him*
860	Hore deth to abide.	*Their*
	The ilke bataille	*same battle*
	Cutberd gan asaille:	*wage*
	He yaf dentes inoghe;	*enough blows*
	The knightes felle iswoghe.	*unconscious*
865	His dent he gan withdraghe,	*withhold*
	For hi were negh aslaghe;	*they; nearly slain*
	And sede, "Knights, nu ye reste	*now*
	One while ef you leste."	*For a moment if you desire*
	Hi sede hi nevre nadde	*They never said they had*
870	Of knighte dentes so harde,	*From a knight blows*
	Bote of the King Murry,	*Except from*
	That wes swithe sturdy.	*Who was very (see note)*
	He was of Hornes kunne,	*family*
	Iborn in Suddene.	
875	Horn him gan to agrise,	*shudder*
	And his blod arise.	
	Bivo him sagh he stonde	*Before*
	That driven him of lond	*out of the land*
	And that his fader slogh.	*killed his father*
880	To him his swerd he drogh.	*Against*
	He lokede on his rynge	
	And thoghte on Rymenhilde.	
	He smot him thuregh the herte,	*through*
	That sore him gan to smerte.	*sorely; hurt*
885	The paens that er were so sturne	*pagans; fierce*
	Hi gunne awei urne;	*run*
	Horn and his compaynye	
	Gunne after hem wel swithe highe	*in great haste*

	And sloghen alle the hundes	*killed; hounds*
890	Er hi here schipes funde.	*Before they their; found*
	To dethe he hem alle broghte.	
	His fader deth wel dere hi boghte.	*They paid dearly for his father's death*
	Of alle the kynges knightes	
	Ne scathede wer no wighte,	*harmed; not a one*
895	Bute his sones tweie	*Except for; two*
	Bifore him he sagh deie.	*die*
	The king bigan to grete	*weep*
	And teres for to lete.	*let [fall]*
	Me leiden hem in bare	*Men; funeral bier*
900	And burden hem ful yare.	*buried them right away*
	The king com into halle	
	Among his knightes alle.	
	"Horn," he sede, "I seie thee,	*tell*
	Do as I schal rede thee.	*advise*
905	Aslaghen beth mine heirs,	*Slain are*
	And thu art knight of muchel pris,	*great value*
	And of grete strengthe,	
	And fair o bodie lengthe.	
	Mi rengne thu schalt welde,	*kingdom; rule*
910	And to spuse helde	*receive*
	Reynild, mi doghter,	
	That sitteth on the lofte."	*in the upper room*
	"O Sire King, with wronge	*(see note)*
	Scholte ich hit underfonge,	*accept*
915	Thi doghter, that ye me bede,	*offer*
	Ower rengne for to lede.	*realm; govern*
	Wel more ich schal thee serve,	*Better*
	Sire Kyng, or thu sterve.	*before you die*
	Thi sorwe schal wende	*turn*
920	Or seve yeres ende.	*Before*
	Whanne hit is wente,	*past*
	Sire King, yef me mi rente.	*give; reward*
	Whanne I thi doghter yerne,	*desire*
	Ne shaltu me hire werne."	*Nor shall you refuse me*
925	Cutberd wonede there	*lived*
	Fulle seve yere	
	That to Rymenild he ne sente	*neither sent a message*

	Ne him self ne wente.	*nor returned*
	Rymenild was in Westernesse	
930	With wel muchel sorinesse.	*great sorrow*
	A king ther gan arive	
	That wolde hire have to wyve;	*marry*
	Aton he was with the king	*Agreed*
	Of that ilke wedding.	*very*
935	The daies were schorte,	
	That Rimenhild ne dorste	*dared*
	Leten in none wise.	*Prevent [it]*
	A writ he dude devise;	*she dictated*
	Athulf hit dude write,	*did*
940	That Horn ne luvede noght lite.	*Who loved Horn not a little*
	Heo sende hire sonde	*messenger*
	To evereche londe	*every*
	To seche Horn the knight	
	Ther me him finde mighte.	*Where; men*
945	Horn noght therof ne herde	
	Til o day that he ferde	*one; went*
	To wude for to schete.	*woods; shoot*
	A knave he gan imete.	*servant; met*
	Horn seden, "Leve fere,	*Dear friend*
950	What sechestu here?"	*do you seek*
	"Knight, if beo thi wille,	
	I mai thee sone telle.	
	I seche fram biweste	*the west*
	Horn of Westernesse	
955	For a maiden Rymenhild,	*On behalf of*
	That for him gan wexe wild.	*is going crazy*
	A king hire wile wedde	
	And bringe to his bedde,	
	King Modi of Reynes,	*(i.e., Furness in the northwest of England)*
960	On of Hornes enemis.	
	Ich habbe walke wide,	*far*
	Bi the se side;	
	Nis he nowar ifunde.	*He is not to be found anywhere*
	Walawai the stunde!	*Alas the hour*
965	Wailaway the while!	*time*
	Nu wurth Rymenild bigiled."	*is deceived*

	Horn iherde with his ires,	*heard; ears*
	And spak with bidere tires:	*bitter tears*
	"Knave, wel thee bitide!	*good fortune upon you*
970	Horn stondeth thee biside.	
	Aghen to hure thu turne	*her; return*
	And seie that heo nu murne,	*not be sad*
	For I schal beo ther bitime,	*be there forthwith*
	A Soneday by prime."	*Sunday*
975	The knave was wel blithe	*glad*
	And highede aghen blive.	*hurried [back] again quickly*
	The se bigan to throghe	*sea; toss*
	Under hire woghe.	*wall*
	The knave there gan adrinke:	*was drowned*
980	Rymenhild hit mighte ofthinke.	*regret*
	The see him con ded throwe	*did cast him dead*
	Under hire chambre wowe.	*wall (see note)*
	Rymenhild undude the durepin	*door pin (bolt)*
	Of the hus ther heo was in,	*house where she*
985	To loke with hire ighe	*eyes*
	If heo oght of Horn isighe:	*anything; could see*
	Tho fond heo the knave adrent,	*drowned*
	That heo hadde for Horn isent,	
	And that scholde Horn bringe.	
990	Hire fingres heo gan wringe.	
	Horn cam to Thurston the King	
	And tolde him this tithing.	*news*
	Tho he was iknowe	*Then he [Thurston] was made aware*
	That Rimenhild was his oghe;	*[Horn's] own*
995	Of his gode kenne	*[Horn told him] of; kin*
	The King of Suddenne,	
	And hu he slogh in felde	*how; killed*
	That his fader quelde,	*The one who killed*
	And seide, "King the wise,	
1000	Yeld me mi servise.	*Repay me*
	Rymenhild help me winne,	
	That thu noght ne linne:	*may you not fail me*
	And I schal do to spuse	*bring about the marriage of*
	Thi doghter wel to huse:	*i.e., into a good family*
1005	Heo schal to spuse have	*for a husband*

Athulf, mi gode felaghe, *friend*
God knight mid the beste *Good; among*
And the treweste." *most faithful*
The king sede so stille, *quietly*
1010 "Horn, have nu thi wille."
He dude writes sende *writs*
Into Yrlonde *Ireland*
After knightes lighte, *agile*
Irisse men to fighte. *Irish*
1015 To Horn come inoghe *enough*
That to schupe droghe. *got on board*
Horn dude him in the weie *got underway*
On a god galeie. *good galley*
The wind him gan to blowe
1020 In a litel throghe. *little while*
The se bigan to posse *drive*
Right in to Westernesse.
Hi strike seil and maste *lower sail*
And ankere gunne caste, *anchor dropped*
1025 Or eny day was sprunge *Before another*
Other belle irunge. *Or*
The word bigan to springe *spread*
Of Rymenhilde weddinge.
Horn was in the watere,
1030 Ne mighte he come no latere.
He let his schup stonde, *ship*
And yede to londe. *went*
His folk he dude abide *caused to wait*
Under wude side. *At the edge of the woods*
1035 Horn him yede alone *went*
Also he sprunge of stone. *As if; out of*
A palmere he thar mette *pilgrim*
And faire hine grette: *greeted him*
"Palmere, thu schalt me telle
1040 Al of thine spelle." *news*
He sede upon his tale,
"I come fram o brudale; *bridal feast*
Ich was at o wedding
Of a maide Rymenhild:

1045	Ne mighte heo adrighe	*avoid*
	That heo ne weop with ighe.	*wept; eyes*
	Heo sede that heo nolde	
	Ben ispused with golde.	*wedded; gold [ring]*
	Heo hadde on husbonde	*one*
1050	Thegh he were ut of londe.	*Even if*
	And in strong halle,	
	Bithinne castel walle,	*Within*
	Ther I was atte yate,	*at the gate*
	Nolde hi me in late.	*they; let*
1055	Modi ihote hadde	*commanded*
	To bure that me hire ladde:	*To a chamber; men led her*
	Away I gan glide:	*I snuck away*
	That deol I nolde abide.	*sorrow; endure*
	The bride wepeth sore,	
1060	And that is muche deole."	
	Quath Horn, "So Crist me rede,	*As Christ commands me*
	We schulle chaungi wede.	*exchange clothing*
	Have her clothes myne	*here*
	And tak me thi sclavyne,	*give; cloak*
1065	Today I schal ther drinke	
	That some hit schulle ofthinke."	*So that; regret*
	His sclavyn he dude dun legge,	*lay down*
	And tok hit on his rigge,	*back*
	He tok Horn his clothes:	*[Horn's]*
1070	That nere him noght lothe.	*were not displeasing to him*
	Horn tok burdon and scrippe	*staff; bag*
	And wrong his lippe.	*twisted*
	He makede him a ful chere,	*foul appearance*
	And al bicolmede his swere.	*dirtied; neck*
1075	He makede him unbicomelich	*ugly*
	Hes he nas nevremore ilich.	*As; never before like that*
	He com to the gateward,	*gatekeeper (porter)*
	That him answerede hard:	*said no*
	Horn bad undo softe	*ordered; quietly*
1080	Mani tyme and ofte;	
	Ne mighte he awynne	*succeed*
	That he come therinne.	
	Horn gan to the yate turne	*gate*

	And that wiket unspurne.	*wicket kicked*
1085	The boye hit scholde abugge.	*bastard; pay for it*
	Horn threw him over the brigge	*bridge*
	That his ribbes him tobrake,	*cracked*
	And suthe com in atte gate.	*afterwards*
	He sette him wel loghe	*low*
1090	In beggeres rowe;	*beggars' row (see note)*
	He lokede him abute	*around him*
	With his colmie snute;	*dirty nose*
	He segh Rymenhild sitte	*saw*
	Ase heo were of witte,	*out of her mind*
1095	Sore wepinge and yerne;	*deeply*
	Ne mighte hure no man wurne.	*her; stop*
	He lokede in eche halke;	*corner*
	Ne segh he nowhar walke	*Nor did he see*
	Athulf his felawe,	
1100	That he cuthe knowe.	*As far as he could tell*
	Athulf was in the ture,	*tower*
	Abute for to pure	*look*
	After his comynge,	*For*
	Yef schup him wolde bringe.	*If; ship*
1105	He segh the se flowe	*saw*
	And Horn nowar rowe.	*nowhere*
	He sede upon his songe:	
	"Horn, nu thu ert wel longe.	*now; slow [in coming]*
	Rymenhild thu me toke	*entrusted*
1110	That I scholde loke;	*look after [her]*
	Ich habbe ikept hure evre;	
	Com nu other nevre:	*now or*
	I ne may no leng hure kepe.	*longer; her*
	For soreghe nu I wepe."	*sorrow*
1115	Rymenhild ros of benche,	*off*
	Wyn for to schenche,	*Wine; pour*
	After mete in sale,	*meal; hall*
	Bothe wyn and ale.	
	On horn heo bar anhonde,	*drinking horn; in her hand*
1120	So laghe was in londe.	*As was the law (custom)*
	Knightes and squier	
	Alle dronken of the ber,	*beer*

	Bute Horn alone	
	Nadde therof no mone.	*had no share*
1125	Horn sat upon the grunde;	*ground*
	Him thughte he was ibunde.	*tied up [in emotion]*
	He sede, "Quen so hende,	*Queen; gracious*
	To meward thu wende;	*Towards me turn*
	Thu yef us with the furste;	*give; first*
1130	The beggeres beoth ofthurste."	*very thirsty*
	Hure horn heo leide adun,	*Her vessel she laid down*
	And fulde him of a brun	*filled; from a brown bowl*
	His bolle of a galun;	*bowl; gallon*
	For heo wende he were a glotoun.	*believed; glutton*
1135	Heo seide, "Have this cuppe,	
	And this thing theruppe.	
	Ne sagh ich nevre, so ich wene,	*believe*
	Beggere that were so kene."	*bold*
	Horn tok hit his ifere	*to his companion*
1140	And sede, "Quen so dere,	
	Wyn nelle ich muche ne lite	*desire*
	But of cuppe white.	
	Thu wenest I beo a beggere,	*You think*
	And ich am a fissere,	*But; fisherman*
1145	Wel feor icome by este	*Very far: east*
	For fissen at thi feste.	
	Mi net lith her bi honde,	*lies here at hand*
	Bi a wel fair stronde.	*shore*
	Hit hath ileie there	*lain*
1150	Fulle seve yere.	*seven*
	Ich am icome to loke	
	Ef eni fiss hit toke.	*If*
	Ich am icome to fisse:	
	Drynke null I of dyssh:	*will not from*
1155	Drink to Horn of horne.	
	Feor ich am jorne."	*Far; traveled*
	Rymenhild him gan bihelde;	
	Hire heorte bigan to chelde.	*heart; grow cold*
	Ne knew heo noght his fissing,	*understood*
1160	Ne Horn hymselve nothing.	*did not recognize him*
	Ac wunder hire gan thinke	*But strange she began to*

	Whi he bad to Horn drinke.	*demanded*
	Heo fulde hire horn with wyn	*filled*
	And dronk to the pilegrym.	
1165	Heo sede, "Drink thi fulle,	
	And suthe thu me telle	*truth*
	If thu evre isighe	*saw*
	Horn under wude lighe."	*in the woods*
	Horn dronk of horn a stunde	*awhile*
1170	And threu the ring to grunde.	*threw; bottom [of the vessel]*
	He seyde, "Quen, nou seche	*look at*
	Qwat is in thy drenche."	*What; drink (see note)*
	The Quen yede to bure	*went; bower*
	With hire maidenes foure.	
1175	Tho fond heo what heo wolde,	*There*
	A ring igraven of golde	*engraved*
	That Horn of hure hadde;	*from her*
	Sore hure dradde	*Greatly she feared*
	That Horn isterve were,	*dead*
1180	For the ring was there.	
	Tho sente heo a damesele	*Then*
	After the palmere;	*pilgrim*
	"Palmere," quath heo, "trewe,	*faithful*
	The ring that thu threwe,	
1185	Thu seie whar thu hit nome,	*took*
	And whi thu hider come."	*here*
	He sede, "Bi Seint Gile,	*Giles*
	Ich habbe go mani mile,	*gone*
	Wel feor by yonde weste	*far beyond the west*
1190	To seche my beste.	*seek; fortune*
	I fond Horn child stonde	
	To schupeward in londe. [1]	
	He sede he wolde agesse	*try*
	To arive in Westernesse.	
1195	The schip nam to the flode	*took to the water*
	With me and Horn the gode;	
	Horn was sik and deide,	*died*

[1] Lines 1191–92: *I found Horn in a [certain] land about to go aboard ship*

	And faire he me preide:	*requested*
	'Go with the ringe	
1200	To Rymenhild the yonge.'	*young*
	Ofte he hit custe,	*kissed*
	God yeve his saule reste!"	*give; soul*
	Rymenhild sede at the furste,	*right away*
	"Herte, nu thu berste,	*burst*
1205	For Horn nastu namore,	*you have no more*
	That thee hath pined so sore."	*grieved*
	Heo feol on hire bedde,	*fell*
	Ther heo knif hudde,	*Where; hid*
	To sle with king lothe	*slay the hateful king*
1210	And hureselve bothe	*herself*
	In that ulke nighte,	*same*
	If Horn come ne mighte.	*In case; might not*
	To herte knif heo sette,	
	Ac Horn anon hire kepte.	*But quickly caught her up*
1215	He wipede that blake of his swere,	*dirt; neck*
	And sede, "Quen, so swete and dere,	
	Ich am Horn thin oghe.	*own*
	Ne canstu me noght knowe?	*Cannot you recognize me*
	Ich am Horn of Westernesse;	
1220	In armes thu me cusse."	*kiss*
	Hi custe hem mid ywisse	*each other certainly*
	And makeden muche blisse.	
	"Rymenhild," he sede, "I wende	*will go*
	Adun to the wudes ende:	*down*
1225	Ther beth myne knightes	*are*
	Redi to fighte;	
	Iarmed under clothe,	*Armed; [their] clothing*
	Hi schulle make wrothe	*angry*
	The king and his geste	*guests*
1230	That come to the feste.	
	Today I schal hem teche	
	And sore hem areche."	*strike*
	Horn sprong ut of halle	*out*
	And let his sclavin falle.	*beggar's cloak*
1235	The quen yede to bure	*went; chamber*
	And fond Athulf in ture.	*[watch]tower*

	"Athulf," heo sede, "be blithe	*happy*
	And to Horn thu go wel swithe.	*quickly*
	He is under wude boghe	*forest glade*
1240	And with him knightes inoghe."	
	Athulf bigan to springe	
	For the tithinge.	*Because of the news*
	After Horn he arnde anon,	*ran as quickly*
	Also that hors mighte gon.	*As*
1245	He him overtok ywis;	*indeed*
	Hi makede swithe muchel blis.	*very much*
	Horn tok his preie	*company*
	And dude him in the weie.	*set them on their way*
	He com in wel sone:	
1250	The yates were undone.	*gates*
	Iarmed ful thikke	*Armed; heavily*
	Fram fote to the nekke,	*From foot*
	Alle that were therin	
	Bithute his twelf ferin	*Except for; companions*
1255	And the King Aylmare,	
	He dude hem alle to kare,	*made them all sorry*
	That at the feste were;	
	Here lif hi lete there.	*They forfeited their lives*
	Horn ne dude no wunder	*vengeance*
1260	Of Fikenhildes false tunge.	*On*
	Hi sworen othes holde,	*oaths of allegiance*
	That nevre ne scholde	
	Horn nevre bitraie,	*betray*
	Thegh he at dithe laie.	*Even if; death*
1265	Hi runge the belle	
	The wedlak for to felle;	*wedding; carry out*
	Horn him yede with his	*went with his [men]*
	To the kinges palais,	
	Ther was bridale swete,	*bridal [feast]*
1270	For riche men ther ete.	
	Telle ne mighte tunge	
	That gle that ther was sunge.	*joy*
	Horn sat on chaere,	*[the king's] chair*
	And bad hem alle ihere.	*ordered; to hear*
1275	"King," he sede, "thu luste	*listen to*

	A tale mid the beste.	*among*
	I ne seie hit for no blame:	*blame [towards you]*
	Horn is mi name.	
	Thu me to knight hove,	*raised up*
1280	And knighthod have proved	
	To thee, king, men seide	
	That I thee bitraide;	*betrayed*
	Thu makedest me fleme,	*made me an outlaw*
	And thi lond to reme;	*leave*
1285	Thu wendest that I wroghte	
	That I nevre ne thoghte,	
	Bi Rymenhild for to ligge,	*lie*
	And that I withsegge.	*deny*
	Ne schal ich hit biginne,	
1290	Til I Suddene winne.	
	Thu kep hure a stunde,	*stay; for a while*
	The while that I funde	*While I find my way*
	In to min heritage,	
	And to mi baronage.	
1295	That lond I schal ofreche	*obtain*
	And do mi fader wreche.	*avenge my father*
	I schal beo king of tune,	*town*
	And bere kinges crune;	*crown*
	Thanne schal Rymenhilde	
1300	Ligge bi the kinge."	*Lie*
	Horn gan to schupe draghe	*went to the ship*
	With his Irisse felaghes,	*Irish men*
	Athulf with him, his brother:	
	Nolde he non other.	*he wanted no other*
1305	That schup bigan to crude;	*ship; make its way*
	The wind him bleu lude;	*loudly*
	Bithinne daies five	*Within*
	That schup gan arive	
	Abute middelnighte.	
1310	Horn him yede wel righte;	*went immediately*
	He tok Athulf bi honde	
	And up he yede to londe.	*went*
	Hi founde under schelde	
	A knight hende in felde.	*skilled*

1315 Op the schelde was drawe — *Upon; was drawn*
A crowch of Jhesu Cristes lawe. — *cross; faith (see note)*
The knight him aslepe lay
Al biside the way.
Horn him gan to take — *seize*
1320 And sede, "Knight, awake!
Seie what thu kepest? — *guard*
And whi thu her slepest? — *here*
Me thinkth bi thine crois lighte, — *I think*
That thu longest to ure Drighte. — *belong to our Lord*
1325 Bute thu wule me schewe, — *Unless; will*
I schal thee tohewe." — *hack to pieces*
The gode knight up aros;
Of the wordes him gros. — *he was terrified*
He sede, "Ich serve aghenes my wille — *against*
1330 Payns ful ylle. — *Pagans very evil*
Ich was Cristene a while: — *once*
Tho icom to this ille — *Then came; island*
Sarazins blake,
That dude me forsake. — *made*
1335 On Crist ich wolde bileve. — *would*
On him hi makede me reve — *Against [Horn] they made me a guard*
To kepe this passage — *protect*
Fram Horn that is of age,
That wunieth biweste, — *Who lives in the west (see note)*
1340 Knight with the beste; — *best of knights*
Hi sloghe with here honde — *They slew; their*
The king of this londe,
And with him fele hundred, — *many hundreds*
And therof is wunder — *a marvel*
1345 That he ne cometh to fighte.
God sende him the righte,
And wind him hider drive — *to here*
To bringe hem of live. — *kill them*
He sloghen Kyng Murry, — *They killed*
1350 Hornes fader, king hendy. — *courteous*
Horn hi ut of londe sente; — *They sent Horn out of the land*
Twelf felawes with him wente,
Among hem Athulf the gode,

	Min owene child, my leve fode:	*My own; dear son*
1355	Ef Horn child is hol and sund,	*sound*
	And Athulf bithute wund,	*without wound*
	He luveth him so dere,	
	And is him so stere.	*like a guardian to him*
	Mighte I seon hem tweie,	*them both*
1360	For joie I scholde deie."	
	"Knight, beo thanne blithe	
	Mest of alle sithe;	*Most; times*
	Horn and Athulf his fere	*companion*
	Bothe hi ben here."	
1365	To Horn he gan gon	
	And grette him anon.	*right away*
	Muche joie hi makede there	
	The while hi togadere were.	*together*
	"Childre," he sede, hu habbe ye fare?	*fared*
1370	That ich you segh, hit is ful yare.	*It has been a long time since I saw you*
	Wulle ye this lond winne	
	And sle that ther is inne?"	
	He sede, "Leve Horn child,	
	Yut lyveth thi moder Godhild:	*Yet lives*
1375	Of joie heo miste	*she might [have]*
	If heo thee alive wiste."	
	Horn sede on his rime,	*speech*
	"Iblessed beo the time	*Blessed*
	I com to Suddene	
1380	With mine Irisse menne:	
	We schulle the hundes teche	*hounds*
	To speken ure speche.	*our*
	Alle we hem schulle sle,	
	And al quic hem fle."	*quickly; flay*
1385	Horn gan his horn to blowe;	
	His folk hit gan iknowe;	*knew it*
	Hi comen ut of stere,	*away from the stern (see note)*
	Fram Hornes banere;	*banner*
	Hi sloghen and fughten,	*killed and fought*
1390	The night and the ughten.	*early morning*
	The Sarazins cunde	*kind*
	Ne lefde ther non in th'ende.	*None remained in the end*

	Horn let wurche	*ordered built*
	Chapeles and chirche;	
1395	He let belles ringe	*be rung*
	And masses let singe.	
	He com to his moder halle	*mother's*
	In a roche walle.	*rock*
	Corn he let serie,	*Grain; be carried*
1400	And makede feste merie;	
	Murye lif he wroghte.	*made*
	Rymenhild hit dere boghte.	*paid for it dearly*
	Fikenhild was prut on herte,	*arrogant*
	And that him dude smerte.	*caused him pain*
1405	Yonge he yaf and elde	*[To] young; gave [bribes]*
	Mid him for to helde.	*give allegiance*
	Ston he dude lede,	*Stone; had transported*
	Ther he hopede spede,	*to succeed*
	Strong castel he let sette,	*had built*
1410	Mid see him biflette;	*He filled the moat around the castle with sea water*
	Ther ne mighte lighte	*none might land*
	Bute foghel with flighte.	*Except for birds*
	Bute whanne the se withdrowe,	*drew back*
	Mighte come men ynoghe.	*enough*
1415	Fikenhild gan wende	*intended*
	Rymenhild to schende.	*harm*
	To woghe he gan hure yerne;	*To woo her intensely he began*
	The kyng ne dorste him werne.	*dared; refuse*
	Rymenhild was ful of mode;	*anxiety*
1420	He wep teres of blode.	*She*
	That night Horn gan swete	*began to sweat*
	And hevie for tomete	*heavily to dream*
	Of Rymenhild, his make,	*mate*
	Into schupe was itake.	*Onto the ship [she]; taken*
1425	The schup bigan to blenche:	*lurch*
	His lemman scholde adrenche.	*was about to drown*
	Rymenhild with hire honde	
	Wolde up to londe;	*Wanted [to swim]*
	Fikenhild aghen hire pelte	*pushed her back*
1430	With his swerdes hilte.	*sword's hilt*
	Horn him wok of slape	*woke from sleep*

	So a man that hadde rape.	*Like a man in a hurry*
	"Athulf," he sede, "felaghe,	*comrade*
	To schupe we mote draghe.	*ship; must go*
1435	Fikenhild me hath idon under	*betrayed*
	And Rymenhild to do wunder.	*distress*
	Crist, for his wundes five,	
	Tonight me thuder drive."	*there*
	Horn gan to schupe ride,	
1440	His feren him biside.	*companions beside him*
	Fikenhild, or the dai gan springe,	*before; began*
	Al right he ferde to the kinge,	*Immediately; went*
	After Rymenhild the brighte,	
	To wedden hire bi nighte.	*wed*
1445	He ladde hure bi the derke	*led; at night*
	Into his nywe werke.	*new fortress*
	The feste hi bigunne,	*festivities*
	Er that ros the sunne.	*Before*
	Er thane Horn hit wiste,	*knew*
1450	Tofore the sunne upriste,	*Before; rose*
	His schup stod under ture	*ship; tower*
	At Rymenhilde bure.	*chamber*
	Rymenhild, litel weneth heo	*realizes*
	That Horn thanne alive beo.	*was alive*
1455	The castel thei ne knewe,	
	For he was so nywe.	*it was so new [to them]*
	Horn fond sittinde Arnoldin,	*found sitting*
	That was Athulfes cosin,	*Who; cousin*
	That ther was in that tide,	*time*
1460	Horn for tabide.	*to wait for*
	"Horn knight," he sede, "kinges sone,	
	Wel beo thu to londe icome.	*come*
	Today hath ywedde Fikenhild	
	Thi swete lemman Rymenhild.	
1465	Ne schal I thee lie:	
	He hath giled thee twie.	*deceived; twice*
	This tur he let make	*had built*
	Al for thine sake.	
	Ne mai ther come inne	
1470	Noman with none ginne.	*device*

	Horn, nu Crist thee wisse,	*guide*
	Of Rymenhild that thu ne misse."	*lose*
	Horn cuthe al the liste	*knew; cunning*
	That eni man of wiste.	*knew of*
1475	Harpe he gan schewe,	*bring out*
	And tok felawes fewe,	
	Of knightes swithe snelle	*bold*
	That schrudde hem at wille.[1]	
	Hi yeden bi the gravel	*went; beach*
1480	Toward the castel.	
	Hi gunne murie singe	*merry*
	And makede here gleowinge.	*harping*
	Rymenhild hit gan ihere	*hear*
	And axede what hi were.	*asked who they were*
1485	Hi sede hi weren harpurs	
	And sume were gigours.	*fiddlers*
	He dude Horn in late	*They let*
	Right at halle gate.	
	He sette him on the benche,	
1490	His harpe for to clenche.	*play*
	He makede Rymenhilde lay,	*a song*
	And heo makede walaway.	*made a lament*
	Rymenhild feol yswoghe	*fell swooning*
	Ne was ther non that loughe.	*laughed*
1495	Hit smot to Hornes herte	*hit*
	So bitere that hit smerte.	
	He lokede on the ringe	
	And thoghte on Rymenhilde:	
	He yede up to borde	*went; table*
1500	With gode swerdes orde:	*edge*
	Fikenhildes crune	*crown (head)*
	Ther he fulde adune,	*tumbled*
	And al his men a rowe,	*in order*
	Hi dude adun throwe.	*struck down*
1505	Whanne hi weren aslaghe	*killed*
	Fikenhild hi dude todraghe.	*tear apart*

[1] *Who dressed [i.e., disguised] themselves as they pleased*

	Horn makede Arnoldin thare	
	King after King Aylmare	
	Of al Westernesse	
1510	For his meoknesse.	*meekness*
	The king and his homage	*vassals*
	Yeven Arnoldin trewage.	*tribute*
	Horn tok Rymenhild bi the honde	
	And ladde hure to the stronde,	*shore*
1515	And ladde with him Athelbrus,	
	The gode stward of his hus.	
	The se bigan to flowe,	
	And Horn gan to rowe.	*sail*
	Hi gunne for to arive	*They arrived*
1520	Ther King Modi was sire.	*Where; lord*
	Athelbrus he makede ther king	
	For his gode teching:	
	He yaf alle the knightes ore	*favor*
	For Horn knightes lore.	*Because of knight Horn's advice*
1525	Horn gan for to ride;	*sail away*
	The wind him blew wel wide.	
	He arivede in Yrlonde,	*Ireland*
	Ther he wo fonde,	*sorrow*
	Ther he dude Athulf child	*caused Athulf the knight to*
1530	Wedden maide Reynild.	
	Horn com to Suddenne	
	Among al his kenne;	*family*
	Rymenhild he makede his quene;	
	So hit mighte wel beon.	
1535	Al folk hem mighte rewe	*grieve for*
	That loveden hem so trewe:	
	Nu ben hi bothe dede —	*Now; they*
	Crist to hevene hem lede!	
	Her endeth the tale of Horn	*Here*
1540	That fair was and noght unorn.	*ugly*
	Make we us glade evre among,	*among us*
	For thus him endeth Hornes song.	*Horn's song*
	Jesus, that is of hevene king,	
	Yeve us alle His swete blessing.	*give*
	Amen.	

Notes

Abbreviations: C: Cambridge MS Gg.4.27.2; L: Laud Misc. MS 108; H: Harley MS 2253; F&H: French and Hale.

1–2 A conventional exhortation with strong connections to minstrelsy and oral traditions. Hall suggests that the poem "was apparently sung, or chanted, or recited . . . such a performance might have masked certain metrical irregularities that instantly become evident to a modern prosodist. . ." (p. 33). Because nearly every line of the extant texts contains divergent readings, Allen posits an "exclusive common ancestor" from which all three derive. This ancestor was not the author's version; it is just possible that it was not written down. She offers three reasons for variation in the MS tradition: "1) a later redaction by the author; 2) later additions by performers or unprofessional adaptors; and 3) scribal corruption" (p. 33). William A. Quinn in *Jongleur: A Modified Theory of Oral Improvisation and Its Effects on the Performance and Transmission of Middle English Romances* (Washington: University Press of America, 1982) agrees that *King Horn* and *Havelok* were both performed rather than read to an audience. As in all oral performances, variations occur while the story is being told and metrical irregularities are not as discernible to the ear when there are distractions for the eye.

3 *ich*. C: *ihc*. L: *ich*: H: *ychulle*. There are irregularities in the use of the first-person pronoun. Elsewhere in C it appears as *ich*, but more often as *ihc*. This may indicate a northern influence, perhaps imposed by the scribe. Because there are so many variations among the three MSS, we have been selective. Using C as our base text we have drawn from L and H where emendations seemed appropriate. Our emendations occur where there are omissions in the base text and where textual cruces have been noted by previous editors.

5 Hall suggests that *biweste* is a formality in romance discourse. Direction and precise location are problematic in this poem; among the MSS variation on direction is evident. See notes for lines 1145 and 1339.

6 *So longe so hit laste*. Allen: *Ther whiles that hit yleste*. Hall notes this as a "favorite formula of *Layamon*," though it is also found in other romances.

10 The description of Horn as "fair" is important. More frequently are found superlative descriptions of the romance heroine, though the Horn poet connects Horn with his mother's good looks (lines 7–8). Havelok, too, is extraordinarily handsome.

14–16 *He was bright so the glas; / He was whit so the flur; / Rose red was his colur.* Heroes described this way include *Guy of Warwick* (line 132), *Bevis of Hampton* (line 2675), and *Ipomadon* (line 5021). Hall points out several passages like this used to praise the beauty of women, but has "not found anything quite like it used for a hero of romance" (p. 93). See note to line 319.

17–18 *He was fayr and eke bold, / And of fiftene winter hold.* Lines supplied by L.

27–28 Villains are often placed in opposition to the "good guys" in medieval romance. Thus Athulf is named just before Fikenhild whose name, deriving from OE *ficol*, means "deceitful."

28 *Fikenild.* C: *ffikenheld*; L: *fokenhild*; H: *ffykenyld*. We have emended double f, which appears only occasionally in C.

34 *Rod on his pleing.* Hall notes that "to play almost regularly means to ride out by wood or water" (p. 96). But it could also suggest specific leisure time activities of the aristocracy such as hunting and hawking.

37–38 *With him riden bote two — / Al to fewe ware tho.* C omits these lines. They are supplied here by L.

41 Fifteen is a favorite number for romance writers and probably has numerological significance, i.e., the combination of seven (the number of completion) and eight (a number of new beginning). It could also be a division between stages of life as seems to be suggested by line 18 announcing Horn's age.

42 *Sarazins.* This is a contested term that could apply to many groups of non-Christian invaders. See Diane Speed, "The Saracens of *King Horn*," *Speculum* 65 (1990), 564–95.

43 *hi soght.* L: *isoghte*. We have followed F&H; n.b., similar locutions in lines 603–04.

48 *Crist.* The first mention of the deity, unusual since more often Middle English romances begin with an invocation or prayer. According to Allen in "Some Textual

Cruces in *King Horn*," *Medium Aevum* 53 (1984), 73–77, there are "twenty-seven instances where God or Christ is mentioned in one or more of the three manuscripts and in only five of them is there consensus of agreement in all three" (p. 73).

51 *The king alighte of his stede*. The king's dismounting is curious here. Considering the threat he has just heard, remaining on horseback in a state of combat readiness might be a prudent idea. In later romances hand-to-hand combat takes place only after an opponent is knocked off his horse. Hall thinks this episode harkens back to a pre-Conquest English custom.

68 *The fremde ne the sibbe*. This is a conventional phrase meaning "no manner of men."

77–78 Godhild's retreat under *a roche of stone* may be to a subterranean chamber or cave. Her desire to separate herself from the world is an act reminiscent of the desert saints but also could be an act of self defense. Godhild is an uncommon name in England and is probably derived from the German *Gundihildis*.

105 That Horn is not slain is quite extraordinary given his princely position and the possibility that revenge might occur. The Greeks did not hesitate to kill Hector's son during the Trojan War just for this reason.

115 The *children* (i.e., young knights or squires) are Horn and his companions. At this point, Horn is still considered a "child," not only because of his tender age, but because of his impending social, political, and military obligations. For this reason, Lee C. Ramsey, in *Chivalric Romance: Popular Literature in Medieval England*, classifies *King Horn* as a "child exile" narrative, a story about "growing up in a personal, military, social, and political sense" (p. 26). In line 1529 Athulf is called "child" not in the sense of immaturity, but rather as an indication of his chivalry.

117–30 The boat has been set adrift and becomes subject to the will of God. Tradition held that those exposed in such a manner, just as those subjected to trials by ordeal, would die if guilty of some crime or sin. It could also be construed as a test of faith. Other romance figures were tested in the same ways, most notably Emaré or Custance as she is known in Chaucer's The Man of Law's Tale and Crystabelle with her son Eglamour in the romance bearing his name. Saints were also tested in this way.

120 L fills in four descriptive lines that H & C omit. They are as follows:

Horn yede in to þe shipes bord
Sone at þe firste word
And alle hise feren
Þat ware him lef and dere

121 *The se bigan to flowe.* "The sea reached high tide"; or "The sea began to rise, or surge." See MED *flouen* v. 4a.

142 *Suddene* is a locale contested among scholars. It could be the Isle of Man, between Ireland and Britain, Sussex, Cornwall, South Devon, Roxburgh, and/or the land of Suðdene as in *Beowulf.*

152 *Jesu Cristes.* C: *Jhesucristes*; L: *Ihesu cristes*; H: *ihesu cristes.*

156 *The dent of myne honde.* This line is followed by a couplet in L and three lines in H both describing the weeping of the children as the ship embarks.

210 *Well bruc thu thin evening.* The sense is "bear your name well." As Hall notes, "let your fame be spread wide as is the sound of a horn" (p. 107). Sands notes the puns on the name "Horn," the instrument called a "horn" which resounds literally, just as fame does metaphorically, "Bi dales and bi dune" (p. 22).

212 *Bi dales and bi hulle.* This line is followed by a line describing a journey through each town in L.

224 *fundling.* C: *fundyng.* Horn and his companions are treated as orphans rather than enemies, a sign of their lack of martial prowess and the accoutrements of knighthood. Abandonment and orphanage were serious matters in the Middle Ages. See John Boswell, *The Kindness of Strangers: The Abandonment of Children in Western Europe from Late Antiquity to the Renaissance* (New York: Vintage Books, 1988).

235 *And tech him to harpe.* C: *And tech him to harpe.* L: *Tech him of þe harpe.* H: *Ant toggen oþe harp.* Allen: *To tuchen upon.* Playing the harp with one's fingernails (line 236) is rare in Middle English literature, though not as rare in modern harp playing. Sir Orfeo, for instance, plays with his "wits."

237–38 *Bivore me to kerve, / And of the cupe serve.* Serving at table was customary practice for young boys at court. It taught both courtesy and discipline.

241 *And his feiren.* C: *In his feiren.* L: *His feren.* H: *Ant his feren.* Allen: *And his ifeire.* McKnight: *In his feiren.*

256 *wexe wild.* C: *wexe wild.* L: *wex al wild.* H: line is omitted. Allen: *wexe wode.* The interchangeability of *wild* and *wode*, the Middle English term for "madness," suggests an uncontrollable emotional dimension to love, which the poet emphasizes again in line 300.

258–61 Rymenhild's speechlessness is a symptom of love sickness. Her tongue is "broken," as Sappho might say.

288 Athulf is Horn's sworn brother. The relationship is like that among the four men in *Athelston* and between Amis and Amiloun. In modern terms a sworn brother is synonymous with a "blood brother," though there is usually no exchange of bodily fluid.

300 *wexe wild.* McKnight and Hall note the popularity of this expression. Here it is symptomatic of love sickness and its accompanying loss of reason and self-control. Swooning could also be a symptom of the condition.

303 F&H note that often "beds were the only furniture in most apartments, and hence served as chairs or benches." A maiden's wooing of a man is less usual but may be found in *Amis and Amiloun, Bevis of Hampton*, and *Sir Eglamour.*

318 *fairer.* A scribal error according to Hall, though it anticipates the next line quite well.

319 *Fairer bi one ribbe.* Having one more rib in the same way that (according to the creation story in Genesis) woman has one more rib than man and is also the "fairer" sex. Susan Dannebaum disagrees because "this interpretation has the disadvantage of paralleling Horn's physical excellence to that of women rather than to some masculine ideal" (p. 116). She sees instead a parallel between Adam and Christ, who were conventionally thought by medieval commentators to have had perfect physical bodies. For example, Nicholas Love's *Mirrour of the Blessed Lyf of Jesu Christ* (a translation of St. Bonaventure's *Meditationes Vitae Christi*) sees both Adam and Christ as paragons of masculine beauty. Dannenbaum believes a more typical (or at least male) medieval comparison would link Havelok to these male figures, who

symbolize old and new creation, rather than to Eve, who symbolizes the fall of humanity. See also Liam Purdon, "*King Horn* and the Medieval Trope of Christ the Lover-Knight," *Proceedings of the PMR Conference at Villanova* 10 (1985), 137–47.

349 *With him ye wolden pleie. Pleie* has a range of meanings including those implicating innocent games of "merriment" and "pleasure" as well as more serious games of martial prowess and sexual intercourse. The context here seems to suggest a certain degree of intense sexual interest, something akin to the pleasure of foreplay.

363–64 *On a squieres wise. / Whane the kyng arise.* In C these two lines are reversed.

370 *recche.* C: *recchecche.* Hall and McKnight retain the C reading while F&H and Allen emend to *recche.*

386 Hall notes the paucity of description for Rymenhild. Horn's beauty does indeed seem of more interest. He, not she, illuminates the bedchamber.

403 *gan stonde.* "did stand." *Gan* is an auxiliary verb which simply intensifies the main verb and is indicative of past tense and causative aspect. The H scribe regularly substitutes *con* for *gan.*

405 *Heo sette him on pelle.* According to the MED, *pelle* has a range of meanings including "hide," "skin," "furred skin used as lining or trim on a garment"; it could also refer to a cloak or mantle or a piece of parchment. F&H gloss the term "rich coverlet" (p. 37), with which Hall seems to agree when he calls it the "rich cloth covering the bed" (p. 118). Hall bases his gloss on the use of the term in the *King of Tars*, "on bedde . . . that comelich was isprad with palle" (lines 781–83).

410 Hall detects a lacuna in C. The lines preceding Rymenhild's "are much too abrupt." Both H and L support this with more rhetorical foreplay.

423 *Ich am icome of thralle.* Hall's note illuminates Horn's motive for describing himself as the son of a thrall (peasant): "Horn's statement is dictated by caution and the desire not to compromise his master Athelbrus, who has told him to be careful and true to him" (p. 319).

427–28 The disparity in social status for a marriage alliance such as this in actual life would be subject to disapprobation. Being knighted raises Horn's apparent social status, however, and renders his marriage to a princess possible.

455 *To Aylbrus the stuard.* C: *To Aylbrus & stuard.* L reads *styward.* O: *And beryt houre styward.*

458 *With loveliche speche.* Allen notes that this reading "does not make sense since Rymenhild is begging Athelbrus (through Horn) to make a persuasive appeal to her father to knight her lover." Allen prefers *liþeliche*, which she suggests adds the appropriate touch of graciousness and humility. But Hall's glossing of the term as "loving and affectionate" makes sense too since Rymenhild's appeal to her father is predicated upon a close personal relation (father/daughter) just as much as it is based upon the political relation of king and subject. As any daughter knows, a doting father is easily persuaded with *loveliche speche.*

492 *And after wurth.* C: *And afterward.* L: *And be ny nowne.* H: *Ant be myn oþer.* Allen: *And after wurþe.* The emendation establishes value rather than time.

504–05 A sword, spurs, and a horse are essential items for a knight. Chivalry itself is derived etymologically from *cheval*, the French term for horse; a *chevalier* is one who rides a horse, i.e., a knight. Also, the dubbing signals a transformation in Horn's martial capability because as a thrall he cannot bear arms. Hall notes the oddity of the king's putting the boots and spurs on Horn, a practice usually enacted by knights rather than kings (p. 127).

512 The first request of a newly dubbed knight is usually granted.

524 According to custom, any knight could confer knighthood. Hall notes that "the knighting of Horn's comrades at the same time as himself is in accord with actual custom: the number of persons advanced with the distinguished personage varies with his rank" (p. 127).

548–58 A central requirement of chivalry is for a knight to prove himself worthy of his designated lady's love.

558 *Forthi me stondeth the more rape.* C: *For þe me stondeþ the more rape.* H: *Oþer wyþ wymmon forewart make.* L: *Þerfore me have ich þe forsake.* Allen: *me stont forth rake. Rape* is not to be understood in modern terms, but rather as a ME verb

meaning "haste," "rush," "speed." It is on the basis of the relation of rape to rake that Allen makes her emendation.

567 Medieval romance is filled with magical rings. One of the most memorable is found in Chrétien de Troyes' *Yvain*. Given to the hero by a woman named Lunette, the ring confers invisibility to its wearer, though its true power is to help a knight conquer his fear. Rings could also function as signs of recognition between lovers, as in *Erle of Tolous*, *Sir Eglamour*, *Ipomadon*, and *Floris and Blanchefleur*.

568 Dubbing as ornamentation is unique here. In addition to signifying a ritual conferring knighthood, "dubbing" could also mean "attire," or "adornment," or "finery" according to the MED.

595 The arming of horses seems to have developed in the late twelfth century. The first mention of it in literature is in Wace's *Roman de Rou*. Hall dates the time when the usage became common in England by comparing the Statute of Winchester (1285) with the Statute of 27 Edward I (1298): "The former does not make any mention of armor for the horse, the latter makes it universally obligatory" (p. 132). This is Horn's second steed; the first is white. It is not unusual for literary knights to have three horses of different colors, e.g., *Ipomadon* and *Sir Gowther*.

602 *hethene honde* is a frequently used expression of contempt. Saracens apply it to Christians just as Christians apply it to Saracens and other enemies. See *Sowdone of Babylone* (line 956).

613 *At evreche dunte*. C: *At evreche dunte*, followed by F&H. L: *At the furste dunte*, followed by Allen. Allen's emendation perhaps emphasizes Horn's prowess as he smites off the heads of his opponents at the first attempt. But perhaps he is even more powerful if he succeeds at every attempt.

625 The carrying of an enemy's decapitated head on sword or spear point occurs not only in romance, but is a practice that carried over into real life. During the Rising of 1381, for instance, rebels paraded the heads of the Archbishop of Canterbury and several other government officials through the streets of London before piking them on the city gates. One of their leaders, Wat Tyler, suffered similar retaliatory treatment at the hands of the king's men.

636 *Mid watere al byflowe*. C: *þo hit gan to flowe*. L: *Mid watere al by flowe*. H: *In þe found by flowen*. Allen: *Binne sund bi flowe*.

649 Hall notes the divergence of the MSS and surmises a lost passage in C that would describe Firkenhild's joining the hunting party. Both H and L indicate Firkenhild's presence at the hunt.

650 *The king him rod.* This is an example of a reflexive verb form (as if one were to say "the king took himself out riding").

652 *moder child.* Hall suggests that this use of the phrase in the popular sense, i.e., as every man alive, is comparatively rare in Middle English. Allen notes that *moder* was probably added by the scribe of the lost ancestor she dubs the "exclusive common."

653 *Horn ferde.* C: *Heo ferde.* L: *Horn wente.* H: *Ant to boure wes y gone.* Allen: *Horn wente.* The emendation clarifies this as Horn's action.

654 *To sen aventure.* F&H see *sen* as a blunder for *seie*, meaning recount (p. 44). Allen, on the other hand, emends *sen* to *sechen*, making possible another interpretation.

655 *He saw.* C: *Heo saw.* L and O: *He fond.*

669 *Seint Stevene.* This may refer to one of many saints by the name of Stephen, but a likely candidate would be the deacon and protomartyr whose life first appears in Acts of the Apostles. He was martyred by stoning.

689 *Sture.* Probably the River Mersey, near modern Liverpool.

696 F&H note this baring of the sword as a "magical act" accompanying an oath. Hall sees the practice as more akin to realism: "The practice was of the highest antiquity among all northern nations" (p. 137).

721 A *brunie* was an armored corselet secured to the body with laces.

726 *wyve.* "Wife" should be read as "woman" here. At this point, Horn and Rymenhild are betrothed, but not officially married.

736 Seven years is the regular probationary period for a lover in ballad and romance. It is the measure of apprenticeship. Rymenhild's earlier premonition is fulfilled as will be her dream.

744 *feol to grunde.* The swoon is a trope of medieval romance, though Dante the Pilgrim does it frequently in the *Commedia*, a work not often considered part of the romance tradition. As Allen notes, the episode here is not connected with Rymenhild's previous faint (p. 301).

761–62 *The whyght him gan stonde, / And drof til Hirelonde.* These two lines are supplied by L.

792 *Ne schal hit.* C: *Ne schat hit.* L: *Ne schal hym.* H: *Ne shal þe.* Allen: *Ne schal þe.*

799–804 Editors disagree about the meaning of these lines. F&H think that the glove exchange is a way for Horn and Berild to pledge that they will not compete in love. Sands agrees with Hall when he suggests the following reading, which seems to make sense here: "When you [Berild] go a-wooing, entrust him [Horn] with your glove [i.e., as a symbol that he will not compete with you]; [but if] you intend to marry, he'll drive you away; because of Cutberd's handsomeness, assuredly you'll never succeed [in love]" (p. 36).

805 Exactly the 25th of December.

817–29 The contract made here Hall says is "primitive" in character but seems to represent trial by combat, a practice in which judgment is rendered by whoever wins the battle. Fighting a giant and defeating him is the stuff of which legendary kings are made. (The battle of David and Goliath is one outstanding Scriptural example.) There are many such contests in Arthurian romance, including King Arthur's confrontation with a giant at Mont St. Michel.

851 *cum to felde.* C: *cum to fel.* Both H and L: *felde.* Allen: *felde.* On the basis of this consensus, the emendation is made.

855 *Right at prime tide.* In its original sense, this means something like "6 a.m.," and is a term borrowed from the monastic division of the day into seven prayer-periods (Lauds, Prime, Terce, Sext, None, Vespers, Compline). This comes to mean simply "early in the morning" in secular usage.

863 *He yaf dentes inoghe.* "He gave enough blows," a typical understatement in Old and Middle English battle descriptions.

871–72 *Bote of the King Murry, / That wes swithe sturdy.* These two lines are supplied by H.

889 There are ten lines missing from C. L supplies the following account:

And seyde, "kyng, so þou have reste,
Clep now forþ ofi þi beste,
And sle we þyse hounden,
Here we henne founden."
Þe houndes hye of laucte,
An strokes hye þere kaute.
Faste aȝen hye stode,
Aȝen duntes gode.
Help nauht here wonder;
Cubert hem broute al honder.

894 *Ne scathede wer.* C: *Ne scapede þer.* L: *Þer nas bute few slawe.* Allen: *Ne schaþed bute fawe.*

900 *And burden hem ful yare.* L provides a couplet after this line that does not appear in C. *Into holy kyrke / So man schulde werke.* To leave unburied corpses on the battlefield is a sign of contempt for the enemy.

913 The wording of Horn's reply is confusing. He means something like the following: "Oh king, it would be wrong for me to accept what you are offering — your daughter [in marriage]."

948 *Knave* is often used less pejoratively in the Middle Ages, meaning "boy" or "servant" rather than in more modern usage where it connotes "rascal," "thief," or worse.

959 F&H identify Reynes as Furness, Lancashire (northwestern England).

974 Sunday at six a.m. is probably a significant time of arrival. It marks the sabbath [seventh] day in the Old Law and the first day of creation in the New. The seven-year pattern is thus archetypal.

981–82 *The see him con ded throwe / Under hire chambre wowe.* C: *Þe se bigan to þroghe / Under hire woȝe.* Two lines from H are added here. L omits the detail.

1036 *Also he sprunge of stone.* Sands suggests that this refers to a non-Christian belief that the first humans were fashioned out of stones, and this "stoniness" made them solitary (p. 42). In his *Metamorphoses*, the Roman poet Ovid depicts mythic creation as Pyrrha and Deucalion, the only couple left on earth, sow stones from which a new civilization arises. Hall's note emphasizes a psychosocial dimension of the phrase "which expresses the most complete isolation like that of one who, having come into the world without human parents, is devoid of relations or ties of any sort" (p. 152).

1062 A beggar's disguise is a favorite trope of medieval romance writers. Hall compares this to an episode in the *Gesta Herwardi*, which tells how Hereward on behalf of a friend rescues a Cornish princess. Also, there is a passage in Layamon's *Brut* (lines 30728–30827) which relates how Brian visited the court of Edwine. The motif also recalls Odysseus' entry into Ithaca in Homer's *Odyssey*.

1090 *beggeres rowe*. A place where poor folk were relegated and made to wait for charitable handouts. As a literary trope it appears in romances such as *Sir Gowther*.

1119 The use of an animal horn as a drinking cup is ancient. Pliny, the Roman writer, describes them as vessels of the "barbarians." Other authoritative texts were more favorably disposed, equating specific animal horns with humans of specific social ranks. The ancient Laws of Wales, for instance, relegates the horn of a wild ox to a king, while those of lesser beasts were appropriate for those of lower social status. The English drinking horn was much admired. Decorated drinking horns were prized by kings. Ordericus Vitalis' chronicle of an Easter feast held by William the Conqueror describes the French nobility's appreciation for a beautifully decorated English drinking horn. Henry I and Edward I were known to possess them. Hall finds it curious in light of these references that drinking horns are not mentioned frequently in Middle English literature, though Chaucer's allusion in The Franklin's Tale suggests its currency in the fourteenth century:

> Janus sit by the fyr, with double berd,
> And drynketh of his bugle horn the wyn. (lines 1252–53)

1128–42 F&H note that a few beggars were customarily admitted to wedding feasts and served wine by the bride. Ancient Germanic custom, according to Hall, "required the lady or the daughter of the house to bear the drinking horn or cup round to the guests assembled at the greater feasts" (p. 159). Such is Weoltheow's duty in *Beowulf*.

1136–37 Resigned to what she perceives as the beggar's gluttony, Rymenhild offers him his original cup and the bowl she has just filled as well.

1142 Given the frequency with which the English decorated their drinking horns, the *cuppe white* is probably a horn mounted in silver. F&H disagree on the meaning of the vessel, however: "because drinking horns were made of horns of animals, they were white, while bowls and other pottery were brown" (p. 58).

1144 Horn's disguise is accompanied by his telling of a parable in which he restates Rymenhild's dream to her in an effort to reveal his true identity. The pun on "horn" in line 1155 and the preceding lack of protocol, i.e., his refusal to drink from anything other than the celebratory horn, is designed to spark her memory. He, as a fisherman, has returned to check his net to see whether she has remained true to him.

1145 *by este*. C: *bieste*. L: *by weste*. H: *by wester*. F&H: *bi este*. Allen: *bieste*. If Horn has traveled back to Westernesse from Ireland, east makes more sense geographically than west.

1154 *Drynke null I of dyssh*. C: *Drink to me of disse*. L: *Drynk to me of thy disse*. H: *Drynke null y of dyssh*. Our emendation allows Horn to reject the dish offered to him.

1162 *Whi he bad to Horn drinke*. F&H's capitalization of Horn in this line indicates a reading that explains why in disguise Horn commended Horn in line 1155. Such an expression of celebration would be decidedly inappropriate at a wedding feast acknowledging another man's marriage.

1171–72 *He seyde, "Quen, nou seche / Qwat is in thy drenche."* These two lines derive from L.

1179 *That Horn isterve were*. C: *Þat Horn isteve*. L: *Þat Horn child ded were*. H: *Þat Horn dede were*. Allen: *Þat Horn isterven were*.

1187 St. Giles (or Aegidius) was probably abbot of a Benedictine monastery on the Rhone in Provence; he died in approximately 710. He became very popular as the patron saint of the lame. There was an important shrine of St. Giles at Nimes in southern France. The St. Giles Fair still exists at Oxford.

1269 *Ther was bridale swete*. C: *brid and ale*. L: *bridal swete*. H: *brudale suete*. Allen: *bridale suete*.

1315–16 *Op the schelde was drawe / A crowch of Jhesu Cristes lawe.* These two lines have been supplied by L.

1323 *bi thine crois lighte.* This is "a phrase without parallel" according to Hall, though he points to a similar phrase in *Havelok*: *On his right shuldre swithe brith, / Brithter than gold ageyn the lith* (lines 2140–41).

1329 *Ich serve aghenes my wille.* C: *ihc have ayenes my wille.* L: *hy serve ylle.* H: *Ich servy ille.* Allen: *Ihc serve ille.*

1339 *biweste.* C: *bieste.* This is probably scribal error since both L and H indicate west. L: *He woneþ alby weste.* H: *Þat woneþ her by weste.* Allen concurs with L and H as do we.

1387 *ut of stere.* C: *ut of stere.* H: *out of hurne.* L: *out of scyp sterne.* Allen: *out of herne.* F&H gloss *stere* simply as "boat" while Sands gives the following reading: "They went over the stern [lit. 'rudder'] away from Horn's banner" (p. 51). The other MS readings and Allen's emendation illuminate the scene in greater detail and suggest a third reading. Since ME *hirne* means a corner, nook, or hiding place, it seems reasonable that the Irishmen Horn has brought with him have emerged from a specific place located at the stern of the boat.

1392 A touch of realism is operating in this scene since after foreign invasions, the countryside is left desolate; the native people are left to starve.

1475 Horn's disguise as a minstrel is effective. Like a beggar's disguise it allows him anonymity and freedom of movement through otherwise rigid social barriers.

1502 *he fulde.* C: *ifulde.* L: *leyde þere.* H: *fel þer.* Allen: *he felde.*

1519 *Hi gunne for to arive.* C: *Hi gunne for arive.* H: *eode to ryve.* Omitted in L. Allen: *yede to rive.*

1528 *Ther he wo fonde.* C: *Þer he wo ifulde.* L: *he hadde woned.* H: *couth er fonde.* Allen: *he wonung fonde.*

1529 *Ther he dude Athulf child.* The designation given to Athulf does not suggest immaturity. Rather, he is a knight, having grown into his personal, military, social, and political identity.

The Seal of Grimsby:
HABLOC • GRYEM • GOLDBURGH

Havelok the Dane

Introduction

Most scholars place *Havelok the Dane* at the end of the thirteenth century, between 1280 and 1290, and see it as a reworking of Anglo-Norman sources.[1] *Havelok* opens with the unfortunate childhood of the English princess Goldeboru, Havelok's future wife, orphaned when her father, the good King Athelwold dies, leaving her inadvertently in the hands of a wicked foster parent and protector, Godrich. The scene then shifts to Havelok's own similar childhood in Denmark. When Havelok's father King Birkabein dies, he and his two sisters are left in the care of the treacherous usurper, Godard, who cuts the throats of the two young girls and threatens the life of Havelok. The little boy, in a demonstration of courage well beyond his years, negotiates a promise of fealty in exchange for his life. But instead of accepting Havelok's fealty, Godard hands the boy over to a fisherman, Grim, with instructions to kill him. Bound and gagged, the young prince is then transported to his would-be executioner's hut. Before the deed can be done, however, Grim and his wife see a mysterious light coming from the boy's mouth while he sleeps, and a "kynmerk," the cross-shaped birthmark of a king on his shoulder, which convinces them of Havelok's divinely appointed royal status. Then, in a manner reminiscent of fairy tales, Grim fakes the child's death and then takes his whole family along with the boy to England, where Havelok grows into a young man who earns his bread first as a fisherman and then as a porter.

At this point, Godrich forcibly marries Goldeboru to Havelok, thinking he is a commoner, a misidentification with which Goldeboru concurs until, on their wedding night, the "kynmerk" and the strange light reveal Havelok's true identity. Her misgivings about Havelok's nobility thus assuaged, soon thereafter Goldeboru and Havelok make their way to Denmark, where Havelok poses as a merchant while staying at the house of Ubbe, a Danish earl, only to have his identity as true king affirmed once again by the light

[1] The earliest version is Geoffrei Gaimar's *L'Estoire des Engleis* written around 1140; the *Lai d'Haveloc*, written anonymously, follows shortly thereafter. See Alexander Bell, ed., *L'Estoire des Engleis by Geoffrei Gaimar* (Oxford: Anglo-Norman Text Society, 1960); see also, Alexander Bell, ed., *Le Lai D'Haveloc and Gaimar's Haveloc Episode* (Manchester: University of Manchester Press, 1925). Bell suggests that the writing of *Lai d'Haveloc* may coincide with the incorporation of Grimsby in 1201.

and the birthmark. Havelok avenges the murder of his sisters and wins back the Danish throne from Godard and his forces. Havelok then returns to England with Goldeboru to regain her kingdom from Godrich (who is flayed and hanged at a slow, merciless rate); he arranges the marriages of Grim's two daughters to English noblemen (one of whom is newly elevated from his position as cook), distributes property to his Danish subalterns, and accepts the crown of England which he rules with Goldeboru. To Ubbe, he bequeaths the rulership of Denmark. Together Havelok and Goldeboru have fifteen children — queens and kings all — and live to a comfortable old age.

The Hero's Body

In *Havelok*, as in *Horn* we have another romance hero whose very body is central to the narrative. The most obvious recurring devices — the supernatural light shining from the sleeping hero's mouth, and the cross-shaped birthmark on his shoulder — appear three times at crucial moments in the story: when Grim is about to kill him as a boy; when he has been forcibly married to a very distressed Goldeboru; and when he is staying with Ubbe in Denmark at the commencement of his campaign to win back the land of his birth. Not only is Havelok's body marked by divine authority, but he is noticeably taller than the other men around him. Like the biblical King Saul, he stands out in a crowd: he has a royal bearing that separates him from the ordinary. Havelok also consumes more food than ordinary men, a fact that motivates the hero to seek employment and contribute to the support of his foster family. But in order to avoid calling attention to himself while working among the English locals, he shrouds his body in disguises: at Lincoln he dresses no more remarkably than his foster family in Grimsby does in order to apprentice as a cook. His disguise is akin to that of Sir Gareth, who serves as a "kitchen knave" in Malory's *Le Morte Darthur*.[2] When Havelok arrives in Denmark to visit Ubbe, he presents himself as a merchant; by the end of the poem, he is wearing the crown of England. But whether his body is a *tabula rasa* for a heaven-sent sign, or a frame for clothing from every social stratum, his bodily strength is remarked on consistently throughout his story. He gains the respect of Lincoln locals by winning popular wrestling and stone-throwing contests. He is formidable in battle even when he wields unconventional weapons — from

[2] See Donald G. Hoffman, "Malory's Cinderella Knights and the Notion of Adventure," *Philological Quarterly* 67 (Spring 1988), 145–56. Havelok, as Malory's Gareth, is trained first as a kitchen knave, a lowly position he transcends just as Cinderella does her domestic enslavement. Like many of Malory's knights, Havelok has been recognized as a male Cinderella. See Russell A. Peck, *Cinderella Bibliography*, http://www.lib.rochester.edu/camelot/cinder/cinintro.htm, under male Cinderellas.

an ax to a club or door bar — against opponents more conventionally armed. Just as Horn's beauty is constantly remarked upon and celebrated, so too is Havelok's extraordinary physique and prowess.[3]

Havelok and the Body Politic

If attention to Havelok's body literally underscores the hero's physical attributes and royal status then so too does it represent the political virtues of a potential king. Havelok is a walking metaphor for kingship, literally marked with a sign of royalty. Thus it is no coincidence that the poem begins with the death of the English king, Athelwold, with a description of his rule, followed shortly thereafter by the death of the Danish king, Birkabein, and a similar description. Athelwold, we are told, establishes peace and justice in a realm rife with treachery and violence, an accomplishment for which he is recognized by his subjects — young and old, from every estate — as a wise and effective monarch. Both loved and feared, Athelwold demonstrates compassion in his "gode werkes," while, at the same time, he adjudicates criminal acts to the fullest extent of medieval English law. When the scene shifts to Denmark, we discover that King Birkabein embodies similar personal and political virtues. He too renders equitable justice and secures peace and harmony in the kingdom of Denmark. Each king provides a model of rulership that fosters social and political stability in their respective realms and functions to assure the continuance of the "office" of monarch when the king dies. In this sense, the king has not one body but two: he represents both himself as individual, with a natural body subject to disease, decay, and death, while at the same time he represents the body politic.[4]

Made most famous by John of Salisbury in the *Policraticus*, a twelfth-century treatise on political philosophy, the body politic is a metaphor for hierarchical corporate entities organized with the "head" (the king or prince in this case) at its apex, governing the lower members, construed either as classes of society or particular groups. Each member of the corporate body in this system is expected to contribute to the welfare of the whole organism in order to enhance the quality of communal life. At the center of the body politic, or at its heart, reside the dual laws — divine and positive — by which the organism operates. Just as the king's subjects are obligated to submit to his authority, so too is he obligated by divine law to govern his subjects ethically. Should he fail to honor the

---

[3] Lee C. Ramsey, *Chivalric Romances: Popular Literature in Medieval England* (Bloomington: Indiana University Press, 1983), p. 36.

[4] See Ernst Kantorowicz, *The King's Two Bodies: A Study in Mediaeval Political Theology* (Princeton: Princeton University Press, 1957), for a discussion of the separation between the "office" of monarch and the monarch himself.

precepts under which he rules, the king ceases to function as the site of reason for the corporate body; he ceases to be a just king and instead becomes a tyrant. Given the paradigms of kingship established early in the poem, Havelok's ultimate destiny is to rule the corporate body so that all its members function in a state of health and well-being. His "kynmerk" represents his divinely ordained right to sovereignty.

Havelok **and Social Class**

While the expected romance love-interest appears in Havelok's relationship with Goldeboru, their marriage is born as much of necessity as romantic love; it creates a social and political alliance that confers legitimacy upon their dual cause to reclaim the rightful inheritance of each. In his battle against Godard and Godrich, Havelok exhibits courage and a sense of avenging justice. He dispatches Godard without second thoughts; Godrich requires another strategy, however, since he is an English nobleman given stewardship over Athelwold's daughter by the king himself. No doubt this factors into Havelok's offer of mercy. But when the unrepentant Godrich rejects the gift, he must face the legal consequences of his traitorous acts. Havelok's actions in this regard are not motivated by a romantic code of chivalry, but rather by a desire to protect the social order of his adopted land, and to uphold popular values of English society. This is one reason that the poem seems to express the desires of what J. Halverson calls the upward mobility "of the prosperous, hard-working middle class."[5] Indeed, the work ethic, demonstrated by Havelok's desire to support not only himself, but also his foster family and, subsequently, the larger community, contributes to what Susan Crane describes as "an ideology of cohesion in which all people share an understanding of good and right, and each class' duties contribute to the common purpose of achieving and maintaining social order."[6]

Havelok, probably more than any poem of its time, moves easily from one social class to another, mixing themes of social idealism with the realities of everyday life. We should note here that "bourgeois realism" forms part of the mixed character of the romance mode. Like *King Horn*, *Havelok* shares with other romances the mixture of weird, supernatural events (the birthmark/light-from-the-mouth scenes) and very realistic, and often lower-class, detail: for instance, the dozen types of fish that Grim catches, or the peasant games at Lincoln. Havelok makes himself even lower than bourgeois, and both Godrich and

---

[5] See J. Halverson in "*Havelok the Dane* and Society," *Chaucer Review* 6 (1971), 142–51. John C. Hirsch argues against this view in "*Havelok* 2933: A Problem in Medieval Literary History," *Neuphilologische Mitteilungen* 78 (1977), 339–49.

[6] Susan Crane, *Insular Romance: Politics, Faith, and Culture in Anglo-Norman and Middle English Literature* (Berkeley: University of California Press, 1986), p. 47.

Goldeboru show their disdain for lowly status by their reactions to the prince whom they think to be a churl.[7] These attitudes are not shared by Havelok, however, whose rewards to the loyal and disadvantaged at the end of the poem suggest a movement toward social amelioration. Characters who might otherwise be overlooked — Bertram the cook, the daughters of Grim the fisherman — thus attain noble status by the intervention of a king who has shared their experience.[8] As David Staines so aptly puts it, "Havelok is the embodiment of the ideal king from the point of view of the lower classes."[9] That this late thirteenth-century romance is socially ameliorative is crucial to its tone and uncommon fusion of class values.

Havelok as History and Myth

Havelok seemed as up-to-date and relevant as history to its early readers. Like many other medieval romances, it was even confused with history: one fourteenth-century Anglo-French chronicler, Peter de Langtoft, identifies Havelok with a Danish king named Gunter who made war on Alfred the Great.[10] Another fourteenth-century chronicler, Robert Mannyng of Brunne, corroborates the account in English but stops short when it comes to the question of how Havelok won England for lack of written historical

---

[7] Robert Levine rejects the view that assumes differing literary tastes between the aristocracy and the bourgeoisie. See "Who Composed *Havelok* for Whom?" *Yearbook of English Studies* 22 (1992), 95–104. Levine also criticizes David Staines' "attempt to harmonize the implied political agenda of the poem with its popular appeal" and notes that "the lower classes had more to lose at the hands of a tyrant than the barons did. . . . During the Middle Ages, the nobility and the lower classes certainly found themselves from time to time on the same side, sometimes in opposition to the king, sometimes in opposition to ecclesiastical authority, but which group was more strongly committed to its position seems a moot question" (p. 99).

[8] It is important to point out that the marriages which occur at the end of the poem are a feature only of the English version.

[9] David Staines, in "Havelok the Dane: A Thirteenth-Century Handbook for Princes," *Speculum* 51 (1976), 602–23, especially p. 623, sees numerous parallels between Havelok and Edward I, as do Sheila Delany and Vahan Ishkanian. See "Theocratic and Contractual Kingship in *Havelok the Dane*," *Zeitschrift für Anglistik und Amerikanistik* 22 (1974), 290–302.

[10] According to W. W. Skeat, ed., *The Lay of Havelok the Dane*, second ed., revised by Kenneth Sisam (Oxford: Clarendon Press, 1956), this appears in the Anglo-French Chronicle of Peter de Langtoft, "who died early in the reign of Edward II, and whose Chronicle closes with the death of Edward I. Here the only trace of the story is the mention of 'Gountere le pere Havelok, de Danays Ray clamez' — Gunter, father of Havelok, called king of the Danes. He identifies this Gunter with the Danish invader defeated by Alfred the Great, who in the A. S. Chronicle is called Godrum" (p. xliii).

documentation: "Bot I haf grete ferly that I fynd no man that has writen in story how Havelok this lond wan." Nonetheless, there appears what scholars surmise to be a late interpolation of Havelok's story in Mannyng's chronicle.[11] Mannyng himself points to other kinds of evidence which suggests the existence of a local legend — a stone in Lincoln castle which is said to be the very stone that Havelok threw farther than the other contestants, and a chapel in which Havelok and Goldeboru were married.[12]

There is yet another rather amazing piece of historical evidence to consider: the official thirteenth-century seal of the town of Grimsby, founded, the poem says, by Grim (lines 744–47). As if establishing its own claim to Havelok's fame, the seal of Grimsby depicts its founder along with the hero and his betrothed, Goldeboru (see p. 72 above). Grim's figure, wielding the accoutrements of battle — shield and sword — looms large at the seal's center, while Havelok is depicted in smaller proportions to the left, carrying a battle ax in one hand and a ring in the other; Goldeboru, also a smaller figure than the gigantic Grim, appears to the right, holding a scepter with one hand while her other is extended toward Havelok's ring. Royal diadems hover over the heads of both Havelok and Goldeboru, while a providential hand at the top of the outer circle gestures toward the figures in the center. The seal's inscription, which forms a circular frame for the three central figures, indicates the official status of the incorporation of Grimsby — *Sigillum Comunitatis Grimebye*; all three figures are identified by name. That the seal stands as an emblem of corporate identity is clear. What is less clear is what the seal represents as historical evidence for the existence of Havelok. Perhaps what it ultimately suggests is the less-than-precise boundaries between history and myth.

If the question of defining boundaries between history and myth remains unanswered so too does the question of what a Danish prince is doing in a very English romance. Many scholars suggest that the Anglo-Norman *Lai d'Haveloc* was probably composed in the Northeast Midlands (Lincolnshire/Humberside) where the Danes had once ruled and dominated linguistically. This would explain the persistence of a Danish legend if we assume a direct line of transmission between the Anglo-Norman poem and the English poem, an assumption that has met challenges in recent years. But even if *Havelok* derives from a local oral tradition, as Nancy Mason Bradbury cogently argues, evidence still points to a locale that would have retained Scandinavian linguistic traditions and folkloric

[11] See Idelle Sullens' edition of *Robert Mannyng of Brunne: The Chronicle* (Binghamton: Medieval & Renaissance Texts and Studies, 1996), p. 499. This is known as the Lambeth interpolation.

[12] Other evidence includes a reference to a boundary marker appropriately dubbed "Havelock's Stone," located near Grimsby. See W. W. Skeat, p. liii.

elements well into the late Middle Ages.[13]

In fact, Piero Boitani calls *Havelok* "a folk-tale thinly disguised as a romance." Both W. R. J. Barron and Donald Sands describe the hero as a "male Cinderella."[14] The themes of exile and return, taking revenge, and taking a bride recall similar folktale motifs. To probe a little deeper, a residue of mythology may lie behind certain other aspects of the poem, such as the identity of Grim. Edmund Reiss points out that the name Grímnir in the Old Norse sagas can mean "disguise," and in several sagas Odin disguises himself as a servant or a ferryman. In one version of *Havelok*, Grim is a servant, and in another, a sailor. Digging even deeper, Reiss observes that "just as Odin the ferryman takes the dead heroes to Valhalla, so Grim takes Havelok to a new life." Odin also keeps two ravens, Huginn and Muninn, who advise the god and bring news from around the world; in *Havelok*, one of Grim's sons is named Hugh Raven.[15]

Dating and Provenance

The only complete manuscript of *Havelok* appears in Bodleian MS Laud Misc. 108, dated c. 1300–25. The dialect of the poem seems to be Northeast Midlands, with both Northern and Southern forms.[16] As the introduction to *King Horn* points out, both *Horn* and *Havelok* appear in this manuscript; both poems appear in the same hand. Also appearing are a variety of other writings (seventy all together, by Skeat's count) including hagiography in a fifteenth-century hand, *The Vision of St. Paul*, a *Disputatio inter corpus et animam*, and scientific information in a fifteenth-century hand. Rosamund Allen suggests that scribes who bound together the Laud MS may have included saints' lives

---

[13] Nancy Mason Bradbury, "The Traditional Origins of *Havelok the Dane*," *Studies in Philology* 90 (1993), pp. 117 ff. Indeed, the legend persisted in oral traditions into the seventeenth century, "when Gervase Holles recorded some variant versions of the tale from the townspeople of Grimsby" (p. 125).

[14] Piero Boitani, *English Medieval Narrative in the 13th and 14th Centuries*, trans. Joan Krakover Hall (Cambridge: Cambridge University Press, 1982), p. 51. W. R. J. Barron says of the hero, "this male Cinderella accepts the ashes as his element" (p. 69). Donald Sands, in *Middle English Verse Romances* (New York: Rinehart & Winston, 1966) links the male Cinderella motif to the desires of the poem's humble audience (p. 55). For a comprehensive discussion of male Cinderellas, see Eve Salisbury, "(Re)dressing Cinderella," in *Retelling Tales*, ed. Alan Lupack and Thomas G. Hahn (Rochester: D. S. Brewer, 1997), pp. 275–92.

[15] Edmund Reiss, "*Havelok the Dane* and Norse Mythology," *Modern Language Quarterly* 27 (1966), 115–24.

[16] For further information on the dialect of *Havelok* consult G. V. Smithers, ed., "Introduction" to *Havelok* (Oxford: Clarendon Press, 1987), pp. i–lxxxiii.

because the story of *Havelok* itself is a kind of saint's life, and Horn himself kills Saracen infidels and rebuilds churches; or else, "The empty folios of 228v–237v were filled with saints' legends and moral matter by a fifteenth century compiler who then bound related matter together."[17] As modern readers take the opportunity to read both poems in this volume, they may continue to observe and remark on parallels between the two poems that have often moved critics to consider them together.

---

[17] Rosamund Allen, *King Horn: An Edition Based on Cambridge University Library MS Gg. 4.27* (New York: Garland, 1984), p. 12.

Select Bibliography

Manuscripts

Bodleian Library, Oxford, MS Laud Misc. 108 (c. 1300–25).

Cambridge University Library Add. 4407 (fragments).

Editions

French, Walter Hoyt, and Charles Brockway Hale, eds. *Middle English Metrical Romances*. New York: Prentice-Hall, 1930. [Older edition with textual notes and limited glossary.]

Holthausen, Ferdinand, ed. *Havelok*. London: Sampson Low Marton & Co., 1901. [Brief notes and glossary.]

Madden, Sir Frederic, ed. *Havelok the Dane*. Roxburghe Club. London: W. Nicol, Shakespeare Press, 1828.

Sands, Donald B., ed. *Middle English Verse Romances*. New York: Holt, Rinehart, and Winston, 1966. [An edition with regularized spelling for modern students and scholars; discusses major textual cruces for this audience and updates French and Hale and Skeat.]

Skeat, W. W., ed. *The Lay of Havelok the Dane*. Second ed. Revised by Kenneth Sisam. Oxford: Clarendon Press, 1956. [Early scholarly text with more intensive textual/cultural notes than F&H, but much superseded by later editions.]

———. *The Lay of Havelok the Dane*. EETS e.s. 4. London: N. Trübner & Co., 1868. [Identifies the poem as in no way connected with France, but derived from British or Welsh traditions. Cautions against close association with the lays of Marie de France.]

Smithers, G. V., ed. *Havelok*. Oxford: Clarendon Press, 1987. [Updated edition that includes thorough introduction to the poem's sources, date of composition, dialect and provenance, with commentary on the text. The edition also prints lines connected with the poem from Cambridge University Library MS Add. 4407 which do not appear in Laud MS 108.]

Related Studies

Barron, W. R. J. *English Medieval Romance*. London: Longman, 1987. [Comprehensive general study of generic features, historical contexts, and evolutionary principles.]

Boitani, Piero. *English Medieval Narrative in the 13th and 14th Centuries*. Trans. Joan Krakover Hall. Cambridge: Cambridge University Press, 1982. [Surveys several medieval English literary genres, including religious writing, comic writing, dream visions, and romances, with separate chapters on Gower and Chaucer; compares English with French culture and romance with epic; discusses how Chaucer uses romance.]

Bradbury, Nancy Mason. "The Traditional Origins of *Havelok the Dane*." *Studies in Philology* 90 (1993), 115–42. [Employs folklore methods for tracing oral origins of the Havelok story as presented in the English poem.]

Crane, Susan. *Insular Romance: Politics, Faith, and Culture in Anglo-Norman and Middle English Literature*. Berkeley: University of California Press, 1986. [Sees the exile and return pattern of *Havelok* as a frame for ideological expression of the nobility's interest in land and personal title.]

Delaney, Sheila, and Vahan Ishkanian. "Theocratic and Contractual Kingship in *Havelok the Dane*." *Zeitschrift für Anglistik und Amerikanistik* 22 (1974), 290–302. [Argues for a date in later decades of the thirteenth century and marks parallels between Havelok and Edward I.]

Halverson, J. "*Havelok the Dane* and Society." *Chaucer Review* 6 (1971), 142–51. [Supports the view of a non-noble audience for the poem.]

Hanning, Robert W. "*Havelok the Dane*: Structure, Symbols, Meaning." *Studies in Philology* 64 (1967), 586–605. [Argues that despite its lack of aesthetic beauty, the poem is deserving of commendation for its unified structure, for its consistent use of central symbolic acts or devices, and for the way in which structure and symbols cooperate to establish and clarify the work's central meanings (p. 587).]

Haskin, Dayton. "Food, Clothing and Kingship in *Havelok the Dane*." *American Benedictine Review* 24 (1973), 204–13. [Furthers the discussion of Havelok's kingship "by attending to the hero's interaction with his subjects and his dependence upon them for his eventual truimph, with a view of amplifying our understanding of the poet's vision of the apt ruler" (p. 205).]

Hirsch, John C. "*Havelok* 2933: A Problem in Medieval Literary History." *Neuphilologische Mitteilungen* 78 (1977), 339–49. ["Such romances as *Havelok* tell us not so much what the lower classes thought of the upper, as what the upper classes liked to think the lower classes thought of them" (p. 343).]

Kretzschmar, William A., Jr. "Three Stories in Search of an Author: The Narrative Versions of *Havelok*." *Allegorica* 5 (1980), 21–97. [Compares first 800 lines of Gaimar's *Estoire des Angleis* (c. 1150) with the *Lai d'Haveloc* of the latter half of the twelfth century. Presents complete text and translation of the *Lai*.]

Levine, Robert. "Who Composed *Havelok* for Whom?" *Yearbook of English Studies* 22 (1992), 95–104. [Rejects the characterization of the poem's audience as lower class.]

Liuzza, Roy Michael. "Representation and Readership in the ME *Havelok*." *Journal of English and Germanic Philology* 93 (1994), 504–19. [Sees the catalogue of fish as part of a larger system of economic exchange.]

McIntosh, Angus. "The Language of the Extant Versions of *Havelok the Dane*." *Medium Aevum* 45 (1976), 36–49. [Disputes, by linguistic analysis, the scholarly presumption of Lincolnshire origin; instead, argues Norfolk influence.]

Mills, Maldwyn. "Havelok's Return." *Medium Aevum* 45 (1976), 20–35. [Explores the return scene to shed light on the genesis and unity of the poem.]

———. "Havelok and the Brutal Fisherman." *Medium Aevum* 36 (1967), 219–30. [Argues that Grim is not as good as he seems.]

Pearsall, Derek. "John Capgrave's Life of St. Katharine and Popular Romance Style." *Medievalia et Humanistica* 6 (1975), 121–37. [John Capgrave, a fifteenth-century Augustinian friar, knew and mimicked romance formulae found in *Havelok* in his Life of St. Katharine. The close thematic associations of hagiography and romance are textually manifest as weil.]

Purdon, Liam O. "The Rite of Vassalage in *Havelok the Dane*." *Medievalia et Humanistica* 20 (1993), 25–39. [The rites solidifying the connection between a vassal and his feudal lord combine homage, fealty, and investiture with a fief. These rites, incomplete or bypassed, help to explain the motives and actions of characters in the romance.]

———. "'Na Yaf He Nouth a Stra' in *Havelok.*" *Philological Quarterly* 69 (1990), 377–83. [Argues that the feudal act of renunciation is suggested by the placement, repetition, and language of this particular expression.]

Ramsey, Lee C. *Chivalric Romances: Popular Literature in Medieval England.* Bloomington: Indiana University Press, 1983. [A study of the Middle English romance with a chapter on the child exile story, comparing the characters of the king and traitors and the relation of heroes to heroines in *Havelok* and *King Horn*. Sees royalist sympathies and a concern for the rule of law in thirteenth-century England.]

Reiss, Edmund. "*Havelok the Dane* and Norse Mythology." *Modern Language Quarterly* 27 (1966), 115–24. [Reveals Scandinavian mythological traces in several characters of the poem.]

Scott, Anne. "Language as Convention, Language as Sociolect in *Havelok the Dane.*" *Studies in Philology* 89 (1992), 137–60. [Views formulaic style of *Havelok* as an expression of Havelok's acquisition of "language" or "sociolect" appropriate for a king.]

Smithers, G. V. "The Style of *Havelok.*" *Medium Aevum* 57 (1988), 190–218. [Meticulously detailed study of repetition, periphrasis, apostrophe, simile, hyperbole, and other devices, with comparisons to Anglo-Norman rhetorical practice on which these devices may have depended.]

———. "The Scansion of *Havelok* and the Use of ME *-en* and *-e* in *Havelok* and by Chaucer." In *Middle English Studies Presented to Norman Davis in Honour of His Seventieth Birthday*. Ed. Douglas Gray and E. G. Stanley. Oxford: Clarendon Press, 1983. Pp. 195–234. [Preliminary study of versification for his 1987 edition.]

———. "Four Notes on Havelok." In *So Meny People, Longages and Tonges: Philological Essays in Scots and Mediaeval English Presented to Angus McIntosh*. Ed. Michael Benskin and M. L. Samuels. Edinburgh: Middle English Dialect Project, 1981. Pp. 191–209. [Precedes his 1987 edition with a fuller discussion of certain textual cruces.]

Staines, David. "*Havelok the Dane*: A Thirteenth-Century Handbook for Princes." *Speculum* 51 (1976), 602–23. [Argues that *Havelok* is a mirror for princes with implicit admonitions to treat the lower classes well and observe the rule of law. Sees a number of interesting parallels between Havelok and Edward I.]

Havelok the Dane

	Herkneth to me, gode men —	
	Wives, maydnes, and alle men —	
	Of a tale that ich you wile telle,	
	Wo so it wile here and therto dwelle.	*Whoever; wait*
5	The tale is of Havelok imaked:	
	Whil he was litel, he yede ful naked.	*went around poorly dressed*
	Havelok was a ful god gome —	*a decent guy*
	He was ful god in everi trome;	*company*
	He was the wicteste man at nede	*bravest; in time of need*
10	That thurte riden on ani stede.	*might ride; steed*
	That ye mowen now yhere,	*may; hear*
	And the tale you mowen ylere,	*may learn*
	At the biginnig of ure tale,	*our*
	Fil me a cuppe of ful god ale;	
15	And wile drinken, her I spelle,	*tell a story*
	That Crist us shilde alle fro helle.	*shield*
	Krist late us hevere so for to do	*let; ever*
	That we moten comen Him to;	*may*
	And, witthat it mote ben so,	*in order that; might*
20	*Benedicamus Domino*!	*Let us bless the Lord*
	Here I schal biginnen a rym;	*rhyme*
	Krist us yeve wel god fyn!	*good end*
	The rym is maked of Havelok —	*made*
	A stalworthi man in a flok.	*strong; band*
25	He was the stalwortheste man at nede	
	That may riden on ani stede.	
	It was a king bi are dawes,	*in earlier days*
	That in his time were gode lawes	
	He dede maken and ful wel holden;	
30	Hym lovede yung, him lovede holde —	*Young and old loved him*
	Erl and barun, dreng and thayn,	*vassal; retainer*
	Knict, bondeman, and swain,	*Knight, peasant; commoner*

	Wydues, maydnes, prestes and clerkes,	*widows; clerics*
	And al for hise gode werkes.	*good*
35	He lovede God with al his micth,	*might*
	And Holy Kirke, and soth ant ricth.	*Church; truth and justice*
	Ricthwise men he lovede alle,	*Just*
	And overal made hem for to calle.	*summoned them*
	Wreieres and wrobberes made he falle	*Traitors; informers*
40	And hated hem so man doth galle;	*as; bitter drink*
	Utlawes and theves made he bynde,	*Outlaws*
	Alle that he micte fynde,	
	And heye hengen on galwe-tre —	*high; gallows*
	For hem ne yede gold ne fee!	*took [as a bribe]*
45	In that time a man that bore	
	Wel fifty pund, I wot, or more,	*I suppose*
	Of red gold upon hiis bac,	
	In a male with or blac,	*pouch white or black*
	Ne funde he non that him misseyde,	
50	Ne with ivele on hond leyde.	*evil laid on a hand*
	Thanne micthe chapmen fare	*merchants travel*
	Thuruth Englond wit here ware,	*Throughout; with their*
	And baldelike beye and sellen,	*boldly buy*
	Overal ther he wilen dwellen —	
55	In gode burwes and therfram	*towns; from there*
	Ne funden he non that dede hem sham,	*who caused them shame*
	That he ne weren sone to sorwe brouth,	*they were not soon; brought*
	And pouere maked and browt to nouth.	*made poor; nothing*
	Thanne was Engelond at hayse —	*ease*
60	Michel was swich a king to preyse	*Much; praise*
	That held so Englond in grith!	*peace*
	Krist of hevene was him with —	
	He was Engelondes blome.	*flower*
	Was non so bold louerd to Rome	*lord [as far as]*
65	That durste upon his bringhe	*his [people] bring*
	Hunger ne here — wicke thinghe.	*invasion*
	Hwan he fellede hise foos,	*When he conquered his enemies*
	He made hem lurken and crepen in wros —	*corners*
	The hidden hem alle and helden hem stille,	*They; themselves*
70	And diden al his herte wille.	
	Ricth he lovede of alle thinge —	*Right (Justice); more than all things*

To wronge micht him noman bringe,
Ne for silver ne for gold,
So was he his soule hold. *loyal*
75 To the faderles was he rath — *a help*
Wo so dede hem wrong or lath, *Whoever; harm*
Were it clerc or were it knicth, *knight*
He dede hem sone to haven ricth;
And wo dide widuen wrong, *whoever; widows*
80 Were he nevre knicth so strong,
That he ne made him sone kesten *cast*
In feteres and ful faste festen; *fasten tightly*
And wo so dide maydne shame
Of hire bodi or brouth in blame, *brought*
85 Bute it were bi hire wille, *Unless*
He made him sone of limes spille. *lose limbs*
He was the beste knith at nede
That hevere micthe riden on stede, *ever*
Or wepne wagge or folc ut lede; *wield; company*
90 Of knith ne havede he nevere drede,
That he ne sprong forth so sparke of glede, *spark from coal*
And lete him knawe of hise hand dede, *(see note)*
Hu he couthe with wepne spede;
And other he refte him hors or wede, *clothing*
95 Or made him sone handes sprede
And "Louerd, merci!" loude grede. *Lord; cried*
He was large and no wicth gnede. *generous; not at all stingy*
Havede he non so god brede *good*
Ne on his bord non so god shrede, *shred (morsel)*
100 That he ne wolde thorwit fede
Poure that on fote yede, *The poor who; went*
Forto haven of Him the mede *reward*
That for us wolde on Rode blede — *Cross*
Crist, that al kan wisse and rede *guide; advise*
105 That evere woneth in any thede. *dwelt; country*

The king was hoten Athelwold. *called*
Of word, of wepne, he was bold.
In Engeland was nevre knicth
That betere held the lond to ricth. *justly*

110	Of his bodi ne havede he eyr	*no heir*
	Bute a mayden swithe fayr,	*Except for; very fair*
	That was so yung that sho ne couthee	*did not know how to*
	Gon on fote ne speke wit mouthe.	*Walk; talk*
	Than him tok an ivel strong,	*violent illness*
115	That he wel wiste and underfong	*knew; realized*
	That his deth was comen him on	
	And saide, "Crist, wat shal I don?	*what*
	Louerd, wat shal me to rede?	*what do You advise*
	I wot ful wel ich have mi mede.	*reward*
120	Hw shal now my douhter fare?	*How*
	Of hire have ich michel kare;	*much*
	Sho is mikel in my thouth —	*thoughts*
	Of meself is me rith nowt.	*I think not of myself*
	No selcouth is thou me be wo:	*wonder*
125	Sho ne can speke ne sho kan go.	
	Yif scho couthe on horse ride,	*knew how to*
	And a thousande men bi hire syde,	
	And sho were comen intil helde	*to a proper age*
	And Engelond sho couthe welde,	*rule*
130	And don hem of thar hire were queme,	*pleasing*
	And hire bodi couthe yeme,	*take care of*
	Ne wolde me nevere ivele like,	*Neither; not please me*
	Ne though ich were in heveneriche."	*heaven's realm*
	Quanne he havede this pleinte maked,	*When; made complaint*
135	Therafter stronglike quaked.	*strongly [he]*
	He sende writes sone onon	*writs (notices); very soon*
	After his erles evereichon;	*For; everyone*
	And after hise baruns, riche and poure,	
	Fro Rokesburw al into Dovere,	*Roxburgh*
140	That he shulden comen swithe	*they; quickly*
	Til him, that was ful unblithe,	*To; ill*
	To that stede ther he lay	*place where*
	In harde bondes nicth and day.	*restraints; night*
	He was so faste wit yvel fest	*fastened; fastenings*
145	That he ne mouthe haven no rest,	*might not*
	He ne mouthe no mete hete,	*food eat*
	Ne he ne mouchte no lythe gete,	*comfort*

	Ne non of his ivel that couthe red —	
	Of him ne was nouth buten ded.	*almost dead*
150	Alle that the writes herden	*Everyone who*
	Sorful and sori til him ferden;	*went to him*
	He wrungen hondes and wepen sore	*They; wept bitterly*
	And yerne preyden Cristes hore —	*earnestly; ore (grace)*
	That He wolde turnen him	
155	Ut of that yvel that was so grim.	
	Thanne he weren comen alle	*they*
	Bifor the king into the halle,	
	At Winchestre ther he lay,	*where he*
	"Welcome," he sayde, "be ye ay!	*always*
160	Ful michel thank kan I you	*Very much*
	That ye aren comen to me now."	
	Quanne he weren alle set,	*When they*
	And the king aveden igret,	*had greeted*
	He greten and gouleden and gouven hem ille,	*They mourned; howled; lamented*
165	And he bad hem alle been stille	*quiet*
	And seyde that greting helpeth nouth,	*weeping; not*
	"For al to dede am ich brouth.	*death; brought*
	Bute now ye sen that I shal deye,	
	Now ich wille you alle preye	*beseech*
170	Of mi douther, that shal be	*For my daughter*
	Yure levedi after me,	*[sovereign] lady*
	Wo may yemen hire so longe,	*Who; protect*
	Bothen hire and Engelonde,	
	Til that she be wman of helde	*grown woman*
175	And that she mowe hir yemen and welde?"	*take care of and help*
	He answereden and seyden anon,	*They; quickly*
	Bi Crist and bi Seint Jon,	
	That th erl Godrigh of Cornwayle	
	Was trewe man wituten faile,	
180	Wis man of red, wis man of dede,	*advice*
	And men haveden of him mikel drede —	*great fear*
	"He may hire altherbest yeme,	*best protect*
	Til that she mowe wel ben quene."	

	The king was payed of that rede.	*pleased with; advice*
185	A wol fair cloth bringen he dede,	*(see note)*
	And thereon leyde the messebok,	*missal*
	The caliz, and the pateyn ok,	*chalice; paten also*
	The corporaus, the messe-gere.	*communion cloth; implements of Mass*
	Theron he garte the erl swere	*made*
190	That he sholde yemen hire wel,	*protect*
	Withuten lac, wituten tel,	*fail; reproach*
	Til that she were twelf winter hold	*old*
	And of speche were bold,	
	And that she couthe of curteysye,	
195	Gon and speken of lovedrurye,	*courtship*
	And til that she loven muthe	*might*
	Wom so hire to gode thoucte;	*Whomsoever; seemed*
	And that he shulde hire yeve	*give*
	The beste man that micthe live —	*noblest*
200	The beste, fayreste, the strangest ok;	*strongest also*
	That dede he him sweren on the bok,	
	And thanne shulde he Engelond	
	Al bitechen into hire hond.	*entrust*
	Quanne that was sworn on his wise,	*When; in this way*
205	The king dede the mayden arise,	*compelled*
	And the erl hire bitaucte	*entrusted her to*
	And al the lond he evere awcte —	*owned*
	Engelonde, everi del —	*part*
	And preide he shulde yeme hire wel.	*govern her*
210	The king ne moucte don no more,	*might do*
	But yerne preyede Godes ore,	*earnestly; grace*
	And dede him hoslen wel and shrive,	*himself received the sacrament*
	I wot fif hundred sithes and five,	*I think five*
	And ofte dede him sore swinge	*beat himself hard*
215	And wit hondes smerte dinge	*painfully strike himself*
	So that the blod ran of his fleys,	*from; flesh*
	That tendre was and swithe neys.	*so soft*
	He made his quiste swithe wel	*bequest (will) very*
	And sone gaf it everil del.	*affirmed*
220	Wan it was goven, ne micte men finde	*given*

	So mikel men micte him in winde,	*(see note)*
	Of his in arke ne in chiste,	*coffer; chest*
	In Engelond, that noman wiste;	*knew*
	For al was yoven, faire and wel,	*disposed of*
225	That him was leved no catel.	*left; possession*
	Thanne he havede been ofte swngen,	*beaten*
	Ofte shriven and ofte dungen,	*confessed; beaten*
	"*In manus tuas*, Louerde," he seyde,	*Into your hands, Lord*
	Her that he the speche leyde,	*Here (then at this moment); lay aside*
230	To Jesu Crist bigan to calle	
	And deyede biforn his heymen alle.	*died; noblemen*
	Than he was ded, there micte men se	*When*
	The meste sorwe that micte be:	*greatest*
	Ther was sobbing, siking, and sor,	*sighing; grief*
235	Handes wringing and drawing bi hor.	*pulling out hair*
	Alle greten swithe sore,	*wept very hard*
	Riche and poure that there wore,	*were there*
	And mikel sorwe haveden alle —	
	Levedyes in boure, knictes in halle.	*Ladies; bower*
240	Quan that sorwe was somdel laten	*When; somewhat relieved*
	And he haveden longe graten,	*they; wept*
	Belles deden he sone ringen,	
	Monkes and prestes messe singen;	*mass*
	And sauteres deden he manie reden,	*psalters (psalm books)*
245	That God self shulde his soule leden	
	Into hevene biforn his Sone,	
	And ther wituten hende wone.	*[his soul] should dwell*
	Than he was to the erthe brouth,	*buried*
	The riche erl ne foryat nouth	*forgot not*
250	That he ne dede al Engelond	
	Sone sayse intil his hond,	*seize*
	And in the castels leth he do	*he placed*
	The knictes he mighte tristen to,	*trust in*
	And alle the Englis dede he swere	*he made to swear*
255	That he shulden him ghod fey beren:	*they; good faith*
	He yaf alle men that god thoucte,	*whatever seemed good*
	Liven and deyen til that him moucte,	

	Til that the kinges dowter wore	*would be*
	Twenti winter hold and more.	*old*
260	Thanne he havede taken this oth	*When*
	Of erles, baruns, lef and loth,	*dear; displeasing*
	Of knictes, cherles, fre and thewe,	*commoners; in service*
	Justises dede he maken newe	
	Al Engelond to faren thorw	*travel through*
265	Fro Dovere into Rokesborw.	
	Schireves he sette, bedels, and greyves,	*Sheriffs; beadles; reeves*
	Grith sergeans with longe gleyves,	*Peacekeepers; lances*
	To yemen wilde wodes and pathes	*protect*
	Fro wicke men that wolde don scathes,	*harm*
270	And forto haven alle at his cri,	*beck and call*
	At his wille, at hise merci,	
	That non durste ben him ageyn —	*against him*
	Erl ne barun, knict ne sweyn.	*commoner*
	Wislike for soth was him wel	*Assuredly*
275	Of folc, of wepne, of catel:	*possessions*
	Sothlike, in a lite thrawe	*Truly; while*
	Al Engelond of him stod awe —	*in awe*
	Al Engelond was of him adrad,	*afraid*
	So his the beste fro the gad.	*As is; beast; prod*
280	The kinges douther bigan thrive	
	And wex the fairest wman on live.	*grew into; alive*
	Of alle thewes was she wis	*manners*
	That gode weren and of pris.	*worth*
	The mayden Goldeboru was hoten;	*called*
285	For hire was mani a ter igroten.	*tear wept*
	Quanne the Erl Godrich him herde	*himself*
	Of that mayden — hw wel she ferde,	*how; fared*
	Hw wis sho was, hw chaste, hw fayr,	*how wise she was*
	And that sho was the rithe eyr	*rightful heir*
290	Of Engelond, of al the rike;	*kingdom*
	Tho bigan Godrich to sike,	*sigh*
	And seyde, "Wether she sholde be	*Whether*
	Quen and levedi over me?	*Queen; lady*

	Hwether sho sholde al Engelond	*Whether*
295	And me and mine haven in hire hond?	
	Datheit hwo it hire thave!	*Curses to whomever; tolerates (permits)*
	Shal sho it nevere more have.	
	Sholde ic yeve a fol, a therne,	*I; fool; serving girl*
	Engelond, thou sho it yerne?	*rules*
300	Datheit hwo it hire yeve	*Curses on whomever*
	Evere more hwil I live!	*while*
	She is waxen al to prud,	*grown; proud*
	For gode metes and noble shrud,	*food; clothes*
	That hic have yoven hire to offte;	*I; given; too often*
305	Hic have yemed hire to softe.	*I; guarded*
	Shal it nouth ben als sho thenkes:	*It shall not be*
	Hope maketh fol man ofte blenkes.	*foolish; blind*
	Ich have a sone, a ful fayr knave;	
	He shal Engelond al have!	
310	He shal king, he shal ben sire,	
	So brouke I evere mi blake swire!"	*use; pale neck (see note)*
	Hwan this trayson was al thouth,	*When treason; expressed*
	Of his oth ne was him nouth.	
	He let his oth al overga.	
315	Therof he yaf he nouth a stra,	*straw*
	Bute sone dede hire fete,	*ordered her to be brought*
	Er he wolde heten ani mete,	*Before; eat*
	Fro Winchestre ther sho was,	*where*
	Also a wicke traytur Judas,	*As*
320	And dede leden hire to Dovre,	*ordered her to be led*
	That standeth on the seis oure,	*seashore*
	And therhinne dede hire fede	*keep*
	Pourelike in feble wede.	*Poorly; wretched rags*
	The castel dede he yemen so	*guard*
325	That non ne micte comen hire to	
	Of hire frend, with to speken,	
	That hevere micte hire bale wreken.	*ever might avenge her wrong*
	Of Goldeboru shul we now laten,	*leave off*
	That nouth ne blinneth forto graten	*without ceasing moans*
330	Ther sho liggeth in prisoun.	*Where; lies*
	Jesu Crist, that Lazarun	*who*

	To live broucte fro dede bondes,	*bonds of death*
	He lese hire wit Hise hondes!	*May He loose her*
	And leve sho mote him yse	*permit; him (Godrich) see*
335	Heye hangen on galwe tre	*gallows*
	That hire haved in sorwe brouth,	
	So as sho ne misdede nouth.	*Although; did no wrong*
	Say we now forth in hure spelle!	*our story*
	In that time, so it bifelle,	
340	Was in the lond of Denemark	
	A riche king and swythe stark.	*strong*
	The name of him was Birkabeyn;	
	He havede mani knict and sweyn;	*knights; attendants*
	He was fayr man and wict,	*bold*
345	Of bodi he was the beste knicth	
	That evere micte leden uth here,	*command an army*
	Or stede on ride or handlen spere.	*ride a horse*
	Thre children he havede bi his wif —	
	He hem lovede so his lif.	*as much as*
350	He havede a sone, douhtres two,	*daughters*
	Swithe fayre, as fel it so.	*as it happened*
	He that wile non forbere,	
	Riche ne poure, king ne kaysere,	*caesar*
	Deth him tok than he best wolde	*when*
355	Liven, but hyse dayes were fulde,	*fulfilled (ended)*
	That he ne moucte no more live,	*might not*
	For gold ne silver ne for no gyve.	*gift*
	Hwan he that wiste, rathe he sende	*When; knew, quickly*
	After prestes, fer an hende —	*far and near*
360	Chanounes gode and monkes bothe,	*Canons*
	Him for to wisse and to rede,	*counsel; advice*
	Him for to hoslen an for to shrive,	*confess; absolve*
	Hwil his bodi were on live.	*While; alive*
	Hwan he was hosled and shriven,	*When; given the sacrament*
365	His quiste maked and for him gyven,	*bequest (will)*
	Hise knictes dede he alle site,	
	For thoru hem he wolde wite	*through; know*

	Hwo micte yeme his children yunge	*Who; might look after*
	Til that he kouthen speken wit tunge,	*they knew how to*
370	Speken and gangen, on horse riden,	*walk*
	Knictes and sweynes by here siden.	*attendants at their sides*
	He spoken theroffe and chosen sone	
	A riche man that under mone,	*moon*
	Was the trewest, that he wende —	*thought*
375	Godard, the kinges owne frende —	*friend*
	And seyden he moucthe hem best loke	
	Yif that he hem undertoke,	
	Til hise sone mouthe bere	*might bear*
	Helm on heved and leden ut here,	*Helmet; head; command an army*
380	In his hand a spere stark,	*strong*
	And king been maked of Denemark.	
	He wel trowede that he seyde,	*believed what*
	And on Godard handes leyde;	*laid hands*
	And seyde, "Here biteche I thee	*entrust to*
385	Mine children alle thre,	
	Al Denemark and al mi fe,	*property*
	Til that mi sone of helde be,	*be of age*
	But that ich wille that thou swere	*Except that; want*
	On auter and on messe gere,	*altar; vestments*
390	On the belles that men ringes,	
	On messe bok the prest on singes,	*missal*
	That thou mine children shalt wel yeme,	*protect*
	That hire kin be ful wel queme,	*their kin; approved*
	Til mi sone mowe ben knicth.	
395	Thanne biteche him tho his ricth:	*then his rights*
	Denemark and that ther til longes —	*belongs to it*
	Casteles and tunes, wodes and wonges."	*towns; fields*
	Godard stirt up and swor al that	
	The king him bad, and sithen sat	*commanded; afterwards*
400	Bi the knictes that ther ware,	
	That wepen alle swithe sare	*very sorrowfully*
	For the king that deide sone.	*died soon*
	Jesu Crist, that makede mone	*moon*
	On the mirke nith to shine,	*dark night*
405	Wite his soule fro helle pine;	*Protect; hell's pain*

	And leve that it mote wone	*permit; live*
	In heveneriche with Godes Sone!	*heaven*
	Hwan Birkabeyn was leyd in grave,	
	The erl dede sone take the knave,	*boy*
410	Havelok, that was the eir,	*heir*
	Swanborow, his sister, Helfled, the tother,	*other*
	And in the castel dede he hem do,	*he had them placed*
	Ther non ne micte hem comen to	
	Of here kyn, ther thei sperd were.	*were kept*
415	Ther he greten ofte sore	*they wept; miserably*
	Bothe for hunger and for kold,	
	Or he weren thre winter hold.	*Before; three years old*
	Feblelike he gaf hem clothes;	*wretched clothes*
	He ne yaf a note of hise othes —	*nut*
420	He hem clothede rith ne fedde,	
	Ne hem ne dede richelike bebedde.	*regal bedding*
	Thanne Godard was sikerlike	*surely*
	Under God the moste swike	*greatest traitor*
	That evre in erthe shaped was.	*created*
425	Withuten on, the wike Judas.	*Except for; wicked*
	Have he the malisun today	*curses*
	Of alle that evre speken may —	
	Of patriark and of pope,	*patriarch*
	And of prest with loken kope,	*fastened cloak*
430	Of monekes and hermites bothe,	
	And of the leve Holi Rode	*beloved Holy Cross*
	That God himselve ran on blode!	*bled upon*
	Crist warie him with His mouth!	*curse*
	Waried wrthe he of north and suth,	*Cursed be*
435	Offe alle men that speken kunne,	*can*
	Of Crist that made mone and sunne!	
	Thanne he havede of al the lond	*Nevertheless he (Godard)*
	Al the folk tilled intil his hond,	*subdued*
	And alle haveden sworen him oth,	
440	Riche and poure, lef and loth,	*dear; loathsome*
	That he sholden hise wille freme	*carry out*
	And that he shulde him nouth greme,	*not trouble*
	He thouthe a ful strong trechery,	*designed*

	A trayson and a felony,	
445	Of the children for to make —	*Against*
	The devel of helle him sone take!	
	Hwan that was thouth, onon he ferde	*When; expressed; went*
	To the tour ther he woren sperde,	*tower; they were kept*
	Ther he greten for hunger and cold.	*they wept*
450	The knave, that was sumdel bold,	*boy (Havelok); somewhat*
	Kam him ageyn, on knes him sette,	*Came towards him*
	And Godard ful feyre he ther grette.	*greeted*
	And Godard seyde, "Wat is yw?	*What is the matter*
	Hwi grete ye and goulen now?"	*Why weep; yowl*
455	"For us hungreth swithe sore" —	*badly*
	Seyden he, "we wolden more:	
	We ne have to hete, ne we ne have	*have nothing; eat*
	Her inne neyther knith ne knave	*knight; servant*
	That yeveth us drinke ne no mete,	*gives; food*
460	Halvendel that we moun ete —	*Half the amount; could*
	Wo is us that we weren born!	*Woe*
	Weilawei! nis it no korn	*Alas! is not there any grain*
	That men micte maken of bred?	*make bread from*
	Us hungreth — we aren ney ded!"	*nearly*
465	Godard herde here wa,	*their woe*
	Ther-offe yaf he nouth a stra,	*gave; straw*
	But tok the maydnes bothe samen,	*together*
	Al so it were up on hiis gamen,	*As if; for fun*
	Al so he wolde with hem leyke	*play*
470	That weren for hunger grene and bleike.	*green; pale*
	Of bothen he karf on two here throtes,	*cut; their throats*
	And sithen hem al to grotes.	*then; pieces*
	Ther was sorwe, wo-so it sawe,	
	Hwan the children by the wawe	*wall*
475	Leyen and sprawleden in the blod.	
	Havelok it saw and therbi stod —	*stood by*
	Ful sori was that sely knave.	*innocent*
	Mikel dred he mouthe have,	*Much; might*
	For at hise herte he saw a knif	
480	For to reven him hise lyf.	*rob*
	But the knave, that litel was,	*boy who*

	He knelede bifor that Judas,	
	And seyde, "Louerd, mercy now!	*Lord*
	Manrede, louerd, biddi you:	*Homage; I offer*
485	Al Denemark I wile you yeve,	*give*
	To that forward thu late me live.	*On the condition; you let me live*
	Here hi wile on boke swere	*I will*
	That nevremore ne shal I bere	
	Ayen thee, louerd, sheld ne spere,	*Against; shield*
490	Ne other wepne that may you dere.	*harm*
	Louerd, have merci of me!	
	Today I wile fro Denemark fle,	
	Ne neveremore comen agheyn!	
	Sweren I wole that Bircabein	
495	Nevere yete me ne gat."	*fathered*
	Hwan the devel herde that,	*[Godard] heard*
	Sumdel bigan him for to rewe;	*Somewhat; have pity*
	Withdrow the knif, that was lewe	*warm*
	Of the seli children blod.	*innocent*
500	Ther was miracle fair and god	*good*
	That he the knave nouth ne slou,	*killed*
	But for rewnesse him witdrow —	*pity; withdrew*
	Of Avelok rewede him ful sore,	*Havelok*
	And thoucte he wolde that he ded wore,	*thought he [Godard] wished; were dead*
505	But on that he nouth wit his hend	*would not with his [own] hand*
	Ne drepe him nouth, that fule fend!	*kill; evil demon*
	Thoucte he als he him bi stod,	*stood by*
	Starinde als he were wod,	*Staring; crazy*
	"Yif I late him lives go,	*alive*
510	He micte me wirchen michel wo —	*cause*
	Grith ne get I neveremo;	*Peace*
	He may me waiten for to slo.	*kill*
	And if he were brouct of live,	*killed*
	And mine children wolden thrive,	
515	Louerdinges after me	*Lords*
	Of al Denemark micten he be.	*they*
	God it wite, he shal ben ded —	
	Wile I taken non other red!	*advice*
	I shal do casten him in the she,	*order; sea*
520	Ther I wile that he drench be,	*drowned*

	Abouten his hals an anker god,	*neck; anchor*
	Thad he ne flete in the flod."	*That; float*
	Ther anon he dede sende	*at once*
	After a fishere that he wende	*fisherman; thought*
525	That wolde al his wille do,	
	And sone anon he seyde him to:	
	"Grim, thou wost thu art my thral;	*know; servant*
	Wilte don my wille al	*Will you*
	That I wile bidden thee?	
530	Tomorwen shal maken thee fre,	*[I] make you*
	And aucte thee yeven and riche make,	*property*
	Withthan thu wilt this child take	*Provided that*
	And leden him with thee tonicht,	*you tonight*
	Than thou sest the monelith,	*When; moonlight*
535	Into the se and don him therinne.	*throw*
	Al wile I taken on me the sinne."	
	Grim tok the child and bond him faste,	
	Hwil the bondes micte laste,	*While*
	That weren of ful strong line.	
540	Tho was Havelok in ful strong pine —	*pain*
	Wiste he nevere her wat was wo!	*Knew he never before*
	Jhesu Crist, that makede go	
	The halte and the doumbe speken,	*lame; dumb*
	Havelok, thee of Godard wreke!	*take revenge*
545	Hwan Grim him havede faste bounden,	*When; tightly bound*
	And sithen in an eld cloth wnden,	*then; wound (see note)*
	He thriste in his muth wel faste	*thrust*
	A kevel of clutes ful unwraste,	*gag; rags; filthy*
	That he mouthe speke ne fnaste,	*breathe*
550	Hwere he wolde him bere or lede.	*Wherever*
	Hwan he havede don that dede,	*When*
	Hwat the swike him havede he yede	*What; villain told him he heeded*
	That he shulde him forth lede	
	And him drinchen in the se —	*drown*
555	That forwarde makeden he —	*agreement; they*
	In a poke, ful and blac,	*bag; big; pale*
	Sone he caste him on his bac,	
	Ant bar him hom to hise cleve,	*And; hut*
	And bitaucte him Dame Leve	*entrusted him to*

560	And seyde, "Wite thou this knave,	*Guard*
	Al so thou wit mi lif save!	
	I shal dreinchen him in the se;	*drown*
	For him shole we ben maked fre,	
	Gold haven ynow and other fe:	*enough; possessions*
565	That havet mi louerd bihoten me."	*lord; promised*
	Hwan Dame Leve herde that,	*When*
	Up she stirte and nouth ne sat,	*jumped; did not sit*
	And caste the knave so harde adoun	*down*
	That he crakede ther his croune	
570	Ageyn a gret ston ther it lay.	
	Tho Havelok micte sei, "Weilawei,	*Alas*
	That evere was I kinges bern —	*son*
	That him ne havede grip or ern,	*vulture; eagle*
	Leoun or wlf, wlvine or bere,	*Lion; wolf; she-wolf; bear*
575	Or other best that wolde him dere!"	*beast; harm*
	So lay that child to middel nicth,	*until midnight*
	That Grim bad Leve bringen lict,	*When; light*
	For to don on his clothes:	*put on*
	"Ne thenkestu nowt of mine othes	*Are not you thinking*
580	That ich have mi louerd sworen?	*sworn to my lord*
	Ne wile I nouth be forloren.	*disgraced*
	I shal beren him to the se —	
	Thou wost that hoves me —	*know; behooves*
	And I shal drenchen him therinne;	
585	Ris up swithe an go thu binne,	*at once; inside*
	And blow the fir and lith a kandel."	*stoke; fire; light*
	Als she shulde hise clothes handel	
	On for to don and blawe the fir,	
	She saw therinne a lith ful shir,	*bright*
590	Al so brith so it were day,	*as if*
	Aboute the knave ther he lay.	*Surrounding*
	Of hise mouth it stod a stem	*a ray emerged*
	Als it were a sunnebem;	*sunbeam*
	Al so lith was it therinne	*Just as light*
595	So ther brenden cerges inne.	*As if; burned candles*
	"Jesu Crist!" wat Dame Leve,	*exclaimed*
	"Hwat is that lith in ure cleve?	*our hut*

	Ris up, Grim, and loke wat it menes!	
	Hwat is the lith, as thou wenes?"	*think*
600	He stirten bothe up to the knave	*jumped*
	For man shal god wille have,	
	Unkeveleden him and swithe unbounden,	*Ungagged; quickly*
	And sone anon him funden,	*very quickly*
	Als he tirveden of his serk,	*pulled off; shirt*
605	On hise rith shuldre a kynmerk,	*king's birthmark*
	A swithe brith, a swithe fair.	*bright*
	"Goddot!" quath Grim, "this ure eir,	*God knows; said; heir*
	That shal louerd of Denemark!	*[be] lord*
	He shal ben king, strong and stark;	*mighty*
610	He shal haven in his hand	
	Al Denemark and Engeland.	
	He shal do Godard ful wo;	
	He shal him hangen or quik flo,	*flay alive*
	Or he shal him al quic grave.	*bury alive*
615	Of him shal he no merci have."	
	Thus seide Grim and sore gret,	*greatly wept*
	And sone fel him to the fet,	*[Havelok's] feet*
	And seide, "Louerd, have mercy	
	Of me and Leve, that is me bi!	*next to me*
620	Louerd, we aren bothe thine —	
	Thine cherles, thine hine.	*rustics; servants*
	Louerd, we sholen thee wel fede	*keep*
	Til that thu cone riden on stede,	*Until; know how to*
	Til that thu cone ful wel bere	
625	Helm on heved, sheld and spere.	*head*
	He ne shall nevere wite, sikerlike,	*know, surely*
	Godard, that fule swike.	*foul traitor*
	Thoru other man, louerd, than thoru thee	*Through*
	Shal I nevere freman be.	
630	Thou shalt me, louerd, fre maken,	
	For I shal yemen thee and waken —	*protect and watch over you*
	Thoru thee wile I fredom have."	
	Tho was Haveloc a blithe knave!	*happy boy*
	He sat him up and cravede bred,	*asked for bread*
635	And seide, "Ich am ney ded,	*nearly*
	Hwat for hunger, wat for bondes	*What; ropes*

	That thu leidest on min hondes,	
	And for kevel at the laste,	*[the] gag*
	That in my mouth was thrist faste.	*firmly thrust*
640	I was ther with so harde prangled	*tied up*
	That I was ther with ney strangled!"	*nearly*
	"Wel is me that thou mayth hete!	*eat*
	Goddoth!" quath Leve, "I shal thee fete	*God knows; fetch*
	Bred an chese, butere and milk,	
645	Pastees and flaunes — al with swilk	*such things*
	Shole we sone thee wel fede,	
	Louerd, in this mikel nede.	
	Soth it is that men seyt and swereth:	*True*
	'Ther God wile helpen, nouth ne dereth.'"	*Where; nothing works injury*
650	Thanne sho havede brouth the mete,	
	Haveloc anon bigan to ete	
	Grundlike, and was ful blithe.	*Heartily*
	Couthe he nouth his hunger mithe.	*Could; hide*
	A lof he het, I woth, and more,	*ate; believe*
655	For him hungrede swithe sore.	
	Thre dayes ther biforn, I wene,	*before that time; believe*
	Et he no mete — that was wel sene!	
	Hwan he havede eten and was fed,	*When*
	Grim dede maken a ful fayr bed,	
660	Unclothede him and dede him therinne,	*put*
	And seyde, "Slep, sone, with muchel winne!	*great joy*
	Slep wel faste and dred thee nouth —	*fear not*
	Fro sorwe to joie art thu brouth."	
	Sone so it was lith of day,	*As soon as; light*
665	Grim it undertok the wey	
	To the wicke traitour Godard	*wicked*
	That was of Denemark a stiward	*overseer*
	And saide, "Louerd, don ich have	
	That thou me bede of the knave:	
670	He is drenched in the flod,	
	Abouten his hals an anker god —	*neck*
	He is witerlike ded.	*surely*
	Eteth he nevremore bred:	*He will never eat*
	He lith drenched in the se.	*lies*

675	Yif me gold and other fe,	*Give; possessions*
	That I mowe riche be,	
	And with thi chartre make fre;	
	For thu ful wel bihetet me	*promised*
	Thanne I last spak with thee."	*When*
680	Godard stod and lokede on him	
	Thoruthlike, with eyne grim,	*Thoroughly; eyes*
	And seyde, "Wiltu ben erl?	*Do you want to*
	Go hom swithe, fule drit-cherl;	*base slave*
	Go hethen and be everemore	*hence*
685	Thral and cherl als thou er wore —	*before*
	Shaltu have non other mede;	*You shall have; reward*
	For litel I do thee lede	*slight provocation*
	To the galwes, so God me rede!	*so help me God*
	For thou haves don a wicke dede.	
690	Thou mait stonden her to longe,	*too*
	Bute thou swithe hethen gonge!"	*quickly go hence*
	Grim thoucte to late that he ran	*too*
	Fro that traytour, that wicke man,	
	And thoucte, "Wat shal me to rede?	*How shall I be advised*
695	Wite he him on live he wile bethe	*[If] he knows [Havelok is] alive; both*
	Heye hangen on galwe tre.	
	Betere us is of londe to fle,	*for us out of*
	And berwen bothen ure lives,	*save; our*
	And mine children and mine wives."	*my wife's [life]*
700	Grim solde sone al his corn,	*grain*
	Shep with wolle, neth with horn,	*wool, cattle*
	Hors and swin, geet with berd,	*goats; beard*
	The gees, the hennes of the yerd —	*hens*
	Al he solde that outh douthe,	*was worth anything*
705	That he evre selle moucte;	*might*
	And al he to the peni drou.	*converted to cash*
	Hise ship he greythede wel inow;	*supplied; enough*
	He dede it tere an ful wel pike	*tar; pitch*
	That it ne doutede sond ne krike;	*uncertain sound; creak*
710	Therinne dide a ful god mast,	*installed*
	Stronge kables and ful fast,	
	Ores gode an ful god seyl —	*Oars*

Therinne wantede nouth a nayl, *was needed*
That evere he sholde therinne do. *put*
715 Hwan he havedet greythed so, *had it prepared*
Havelok the yunge he dede therinne, *put*
Him and his wif, hise sones thrinne, *three*
And hise two doutres that faire wore. *daughters; were*
And sone dede he leyn in an ore, *began to steer*
720 And drou him to the heye see, *headed for*
There he mith altherbeste fle. *best of all*
Fro londe woren he bote a mile, *they were*
Ne were it nevere but ane hwile *a short while*
That it ne bigan a wind to rise
725 Out of the north men calleth "bise," *(see note)*
And drof hem intil Engelond, *them*
That al was sithen in his hond, *later; his [Havelok's]*
His, that Havelok was the name;
But or he havede michel shame, *But first; much*
730 Michel sorwe and michel tene, *grief*
And yete he gat it al bidene; *completely*
Als ye shulen now forthward lere, *forthwith learn*
Yf that ye wilen therto here.

In Humber Grim bigan to lende, *land*
735 In Lindeseye, rith at the north ende. *Lincolnshire*
Ther sat his ship upon the sond; *i.e., fishing boat*
But Grim it drou up to the lond;
And there he made a litel cote *cottage*
To him and to hise flote. *For; company*
740 Bigan he there for to erthe, *live*
A litel hus to maken of erthe,
So that he wel thore were *there*
Of here herboru herborwed there. *shelter; sheltered*
And for that Grim that place aute, *owned*
745 The stede of Grim the name laute, *place; took its name*
So that Grimesbi it calleth alle
That theroffe speken alle;
And so shulen men callen it ay, *always*
Bitwene this and Domesday. *now; Judgment Day*

750	Grim was fishere swithe god,	*fisherman*
	And mikel couthe on the flod —	
	Mani god fish therinne he tok,	
	Bothe with neth and with hok.	*nets*
	He tok the sturgiun and the qual,	*sturgeon; whale*
755	And the turbut and lax withal;	*turbot; salmon*
	He tok the sele and the hwel —	*seal; eel*
	He spedde ofte swithe wel.	*succeeded; very*
	Keling he tok and tumberel,	*Cod; porpoise*
	Hering and the makerel,	*mackerel*
760	The butte, the schulle, the thornebake.	*flounder; plaice; skate*
	Gode paniers dede he make,	*baskets*
	On til him and other thrinne	*One for; three*
	Til hise sones to beren fishe inne,	
	Up o londe to selle and fonge —	*On land; collect money*
765	Forbar he neyther tun ne gronge	*Neglected; neither town nor farm*
	That he ne to yede with his ware.	*went*
	Kam he nevere hom hand-bare,	*empty-handed*
	That he ne broucte bred and sowel	*sauce*
	In his shirte or in his cowel,	*hood*
770	In his poke benes and korn —	*bag; grain*
	Hise swink he havede he nowt forlorn.	*work; lost*
	And hwan he took the grete lamprey,	
	Ful wel he couthe the rithe wei	*knew*
	To Lincolne, the gode boru;	*town*
775	Ofte he yede it thoru and thoru,	*traversed; through*
	Til he havede wol wel sold	*wool*
	And therfore the penies told.	*counted*
	Thanne he com thenne he were blithe,	*from there; happy*
	For hom he brouthe fele sithe	*many times*
780	Wastels, simenels with the horn,	*Cakes; horn-shaped bread*
	His pokes fulle of mele and korn,	*bags; flour; grain*
	Netes flesh, shepes and swines;	*Oxens'*
	And hemp to maken of gode lines,	*lines [for fishing]*
	And stronge ropes to hise netes,	*for his nets*
785	In the se weren he ofte setes.	
	Thusgate Grim him fayre ledde:	*bore himself well*
	Him and his genge wel he fedde	*household*

	Wel twelf winter other more.	*or*
	Havelok was war that Grim swank sore	*aware; worked hard*
790	For his mete, and he lay at hom —	*stayed*
	Thouthe, "Ich am now no grom!	*boy*
	Ich am wel waxen and wel may eten	*grown*
	More than evere Grim may geten.	
	Ich ete more, bi God on live,	
795	Than Grim an hise children five!	
	It ne may nouth ben thus longe.	*for long*
	Goddot! I wile with hem gange	*God knows; go*
	For to leren sum god to gete.	*useful thing*
	Swinken ich wolde for my mete —	*Work*
800	It is no shame for to swinken!	
	The man that may wel eten and drinken	
	Thar nouth ne have but on swink long —	
	To liggen at hom it is ful strong.	*stay; wrong*
	God yelde him, ther I ne may,	*reward; since*
805	That haveth me fed to this day!	
	Gladlike I wile the paniers bere —	*baskets*
	Ich woth ne shal it me nouth dere,	*know; harm*
	They ther be inne a birthene gret	*burden*
	Al so hevi als a neth.	*as an ox*
810	Shal ich nevere lengere dwelle —	*stay here*
	Tomorwen shal ich forth pelle."	*hurry forth*
	On the morwen, hwan it was day,	
	He stirt up sone and nouth ne lay,	*started early*
	And cast a panier on his bac,	*basket*
815	With fish giveled als a stac.	*heaped like*
	Al so michel he bar him one,	
	So he foure, bi mine mone!	*As four men, on my word*
	Wel he it bar and solde it wel;	
	The silver he brouthe hom ilk del,	*every bit*
820	Al that he therfore tok —	*for it*
	Withheld he nouth a ferthinges nok.	*trimming of a farthing*
	So yede he forth ilke day	*went; each*
	That he nevere at home lay —	
	So wolde he his mester lere.	*trade learn*
825	Bifel it so a strong dere	*It happened; famine*

Bigan to rise of korn of bred, *grain*
That Grim ne couthe no god red, *plan*
Hw he sholde his meiné fede; *household*
Of Havelok havede he michel drede, *doubt*
830 For he was strong and wel mouthe ete *must*
More thanne evere mouthe be gete; *gotten*
Ne he ne mouthe on the se take *might; sea*
Neyther lenge ne thornbake, *ling; skate*
Ne non other fish that douthe *availed*
835 His meyné feden with he mouthe. *family; might*
Of Havelok he havede kare, *worried*
Hwilgat that he micthe fare. *In what way*
Of his children was him nouth; *he did not think*
On Havelok was al hise thouth, *thought*
840 And seyde, "Havelok, dere sone,
I wene that we deye mone *think; must die*
For hunger, this dere is so strong, *famine*
And hure mete is uten long. *our; long gone*
Betere is that thu henne gonge *from here; go*
845 Than thu here dwelle longe —
Hethen thou mayt gangen to late; *Hence [from here]; must go*
Thou canst ful wel the ricthe gate *know; right way*
To Lincolne, the gode boru — *town*
Thou havest it gon ful ofte thoru.
850 Of me ne is me nouth a slo. *sloeberry (i.e., I am powerless)*
Betere is that thu thider go,
For ther is mani god man inne;
Ther thou mayt thi mete winne. *earn*
But wo is me thou art so naked, *poorly clothed*
855 Of mi seyl I wolde thee were maked *sail*
A cloth thou mithest inne gongen, *Some clothing*
Sone, no cold that thu ne fonge." *Son; endure*

He tok the sheres of the nayl *shears off*
And made him a covel of the sayl, *garment*
860 And Havelok dide it sone on. *put*
Havede he neyther hosen ne shon, *socks; shoes*
Ne none kines other wede: *Nor any kind of other clothes*
To Lincolne barfot he yede. *barefoot; went*

	Hwan he cam ther, he was ful wil —	*perplexed*
865	Ne havede he no frend to gangen til.	*to go to*
	Two dayes ther fastinde he yede,	*fasting*
	That non for his werk wolde him fede.	
	The thridde day herde he calle:	*third*
	"Bermen, bermen, hider forth alle!"	*Porters; here*
870	Poure that on fote yede	*Poor who; went*
	Sprongen forth so sparke on glede,	*Sprang; as spark from burning coal*
	Havelok shof dun nyne or ten	*shoved down*
	Rith amidewarde the fen,	*amidst; mud*
	And stirte forth to the kok,	*toward the cook*
875	Ther the erles mete he tok	
	That he bouthe at the brigge:	*bridge*
	The bermen let he alle ligge,	*porters; stay*
	And bar the mete to the castel,	
	And gat him there a ferthing wastel.	*farthing cake*
880	Thet other day kepte he ok	*also*
	Swithe yerne the erles kok,	
	Til that he say him on the brigge,	*saw*
	And bi him many fishes ligge.	*lie*
	The herles mete havede he bouth	*earl's*
885	Of Cornwalie and kalde oft:	
	"Bermen, bermen, hider swithe!"	*quickly*
	Havelok it herde and was ful blithe	*glad*
	That he herde "bermen" calle.	
	Alle made he hem dun falle	
890	That in his gate yeden and stode —	*way; walked*
	Wel sixtene laddes gode.	
	Als he lep the kok til,	
	He shof hem alle upon an hyl —	*down a hill*
	Astirte til him with his rippe	*Hurried; basket*
895	And bigan the fish to kippe.	*take*
	He bar up wel a carte lode	
	Of segges, laxes, of playces brode,	*squid, salmon; plaice*
	Of grete laumprees and of eles.	*lampreys; eels*
	Sparede he neyther tos ne heles	*toes nor heels (i.e., he ran)*
900	Til that he to the castel cam,	
	That men fro him his birthene nam.	*Where; burden took*
	Than men haveden holpen him doun	

	With the birthene of his croun,	*off; head*
	The kok stod and on him low,	*smiled*
905	And thoute him stalworthe man ynow,	*strong; enough*
	And seyde, "Wiltu ben wit me?	*Will you stay with*
	Gladlike wile ich feden thee:	
	Wel is set the mete thu etes,	*invested*
	And the hire that thu getes!"	*wages*
910	"Goddot!" quoth he, "leve sire,	*said; dear*
	Bidde ich you non other hire,	*Ask; [for] wages*
	But yeveth me inow to ete —	*give*
	Fir and water I wile you fete,	*Firewood; fetch*
	The fir blowe and ful wele maken;	
915	Stickes kan ich breken and kraken,	
	And kindlen ful wel a fyr,	*kindle*
	And maken it to brennen shir.	*brightly*
	Ful wel kan ich cleven shides,	*split sticks*
	Eles to turven of here hides;	*Eels; skin; their*
920	Ful wel kan ich dishes swilen,	*wash*
	And don al that ye evere wilen."	
	Quoth the kok, "Wile I no more!	*Said; I desire*
	Go thu yunder and sit thore,	*there*
	And I shal yeve the ful fair bred,	
925	And made the broys in the led.	*broth; kettle*
	Sit now doun and et ful yerne —	*eagerly*
	Datheit hwo the mete werne!"	*Curse whoever denies you food*
	Havelok sette him dun anon	*at once*
	Al so stille als a ston,	*As still as*
930	Til he havede ful wel eten;	
	Tho havede Havelok fayre geten.	*Then; well made out*
	Hwan he havede eten inow,	
	He kam to the wele, water up drow,	*drew up*
	And filde ther a michel so —	*large tub*
935	Bad he non ageyn him go,	
	But bitwen his hondes he bar it in,	
	Al him one, to the kichin.	*All by himself*
	Bad he non him water to fett,	
	Ne fro brigge to bere the mete.	

940	He bar the turves, he bar the star,	*peat; star grass*
	The wode fro the brigge he bar,	
	Al that evere shulden he nytte,	*use*
	Al he drow and al he citte —	*hauled; cut*
	Wolde he nevere haven rest	*Wanted; to have*
945	More than he were a best.	*Any more than if; beast*
	Of alle men was he mest meke,	*most meek*
	Lauhwinde ay and blithe of speke;	*Laughing; glad*
	Evere he was glad and blithe —	
	His sorwe he couthe ful wel mithe.	*hide*
950	It ne was non so litel knave	*child*
	For to leyken ne for to plawe,	*sport; play*
	That he ne wolde with him pleye.	
	The children that yeden in the weie	*went*
	Of him he deden al here wille,	*their*
955	And with him leykeden here fille.	
	Him loveden alle, stille and bolde,	*shy*
	Knictes, children, yunge and holde —	*old*
	Alle him loveden that him sowen,	*saw*
	Bothen heye men and lowe.	
960	Of him ful wide the word sprong,	*far and wide*
	Hw he was mikel, hw he was strong,	*great*
	Hw fayr man God him havede maked,	
	But on that he was almest naked:	*Except*
	For he ne havede nouth to shride	*nothing; wear*
965	But a kovel ful unride,	*wretched cloak; cumbersome*
	That was ful and swithe wicke;	*foul; very wretched*
	Was it nouth worth a fir-sticke.	*stick of firewood*
	The cok bigan of him to rewe	*take pity*
	And bouthe him clothes al spannewe:	*brand new*
970	He bouthe him bothe hosen and shon,	*socks; shoes*
	And sone dide him dones on.	*made him put them on*
	Hwan he was clothed, osed, and shod,	*hosed*
	Was non so fayr under God,	
	That evere yete in erthe were,	
975	Non that evere moder bere;	
	It was nevere man that yemede	*There; governed*
	In kinneriche that so wel semede	*kingdom*
	King or cayser for to be,	

	Than he was shrid, so semede he;	*clad*
980	For thanne he weren alle samen	*when; together*
	At Lincolne at the gamen,	*games*
	And the erles men woren al thore,	*there*
	Than was Havelok bi the shuldren more	*i.e., taller by a head*
	Than the meste that ther kam:	*greatest*
985	In armes him noman nam	*no one took*
	That he doune sone ne caste.	
	Havelok stod over hem als a mast;	*like*
	Als he was heie, als he was long,	*As; tall*
	He was bothe stark and strong —	
990	In Engelond non hise per	*peer*
	Of strengthe that evere kam him ner.	
	Als he was strong, so was he softe;	*As; gentle*
	They a man him misdede ofte,	*Although; mistreated*
	Neveremore he him misseyde,	*Never; insulted*
995	Ne hond on him with yvele leyde.	*evil intent*
	Of bodi was he mayden clene;	*pure*
	Nevere yete in game, ne in grene,	*sport; sexual desire*
	With hire ne wolde he leyke ne lye,	*her (an attractive woman); sport*
	No more than it were a strie.	*witch*
1000	In that time al Hengelond	*England*
	Th'erl Godrich havede in his hond,	*power*
	And he gart komen into the tun	*made to; town*
	Mani erl and mani barun,	
	And alle that lives were	*alive*
1005	In Englond thanne wer there,	*then*
	That they haveden after sent	
	To ben ther at the parlement.	*assembly*
	With hem com mani chambioun,	*champion*
	Mani with ladde, blac and brown,	*with servants*
1010	And fel it so that yungemen,	
	Wel abouten nine or ten,	
	Bigunnen the for to layke.	*there; sport*
	Thider komen bothe stronge and wayke,	*To that place; weak*
	Thider komen lesse and more	
1015	That in the boru thanne weren thore —	*then*
	Chaunpiouns and starke laddes,	*stalwart youth*
	Bondemen with here gaddes,	*Peasants; cattle prods*

	Als he comen fro the plow.	*As they*
	There was sembling inow;	*enough assembled*
1020	For it ne was non horse-knave,	*there; stable boy*
	Tho thei sholden in honde have,	*be on duty*
	That he ne kam thider, the leyk to se.	*sport; see*
	Biforn here fet thanne lay a tre,	*feet; tree [as a foul line]*
	And pulten with a mikel ston	*heaved; mighty*
1025	The starke laddes, ful god won.	*very large number*
	The ston was mikel and ek gret,	*also*
	And al so hevi so a neth;	*just as; an ox*
	Grundstalwyrthe man he sholde be	*Very strong*
	That mouthe liften it to his kne;	*Who might*
1030	Was ther neyther clerc ne prest,	*nor*
	That mithe liften it to his brest.	
	Therwit putten the chaumpiouns	*With it*
	That thider comen with the barouns.	
	Hwo so mithe putten thore	*Whosoever*
1035	Biforn another an inch or more,	
	Wore he yung, wore he hold,	*Were; old*
	He was for a kempe told.	*outstanding performer counted*
	Al so the stoden and ofte stareden,	*As they*
	The chaumpiouns and ek the ladden,	*also; lads*
1040	And he maden mikel strout	*great dispute*
	Abouten the altherbeste but,	*greatest effort*
	Havelok stod and lokede thertil,	*at that*
	And of puttingge he was ful wil,	*ignorant*
	For nevere yete ne saw he or	*before*
1045	Putten the stone or thanne thor.	*before that time*
	Hise mayster bad him gon therto —	
	Als he couthe therwith do.	
	Tho hise mayster it him bad,	
	He was of him sore adrad.	*himself; doubtful*
1050	Therto he stirte sone anon,	
	And kipte up that hevi ston	*picked*
	That he sholde putten withe;	
	He putte at the firste sithe,	*putted [it]; time*
	Over alle that ther wore	*Farther*
1055	Twelve fote and sumdel more.	*somewhat*
	The chaumpiouns that put sowen;	*shotput saw*

	Shuldreden he ilc other and lowen.	*They shoved each other; laughed*
	Wolden he nomore to putting gange,	*go*
	But seyde, "Thee dwellen her to longe!"	*here too long*
1060	This selkouth mithe nouth ben hyd:	*wonder; hidden*
	Ful sone it was ful loude kid	*made known*
	Of Havelok, hw he warp the ston	*threw*
	Over the laddes everilkon,	*each of them*
	Hw he was fayr, hw he was long,	*tall*
1065	Hw he was with, hw he was strong;	*manly (wight)*
	Thoruth England yede the speche,	*went the rumor*
	Hw he was strong and ek meke;	*also*
	In the castel, up in the halle,	
	The knithes speken therof alle,	
1070	So that Godrich it herde wel:	
	The speken of Havelok, everi del —	*They; everywhere*
	Hw he was strong man and hey,	*tall*
	Hw he was strong, and ek fri,	*skillful*
	And thouthte Godrich, "Thoru this knave	*Through*
1075	Shal ich Engelond al have,	
	And mi sone after me;	
	For so I wile that it be.	*desire*
	The King Athelwald me dide swere	*made me swear*
	Upon al the messe gere	*mass implements*
1080	That I shude his douther yeve	
	The hexte that mithe live,	*greatest (highest)*
	The beste, the fairest, the strangest ok —	*strongest also*
	That gart he me sweren on the bok.	*made*
	Hwere mithe I finden ani so hey,	*Where; tall*
1085	So Havelok is, or so sley?	*skillful*
	Thou I southe hethen into Inde,	*searched from here to India*
	So fayr, so strong, ne mithe I finde.	
	Havelok is that ilke knave	*that very boy*
	That shal Goldeboru have!"	
1090	This thouthe with trechery,	*[he] thought*
	With traysoun, and wit felony;	*with*
	For he wende that Havelok wore	*surmised*
	Sum cherles sone and no more;	*ordinary person (peasant)*
	Ne shulde he haven of Engellond	
1095	Onlepi foru in his hond	*A single furrow; possession*

	With hire that was therof eyr,	*[rightful] heir*
	That bothe was god and swithe fair.	*very*
	He wende that Havelok wer a thral,	*serf (slave)*
	Therthoru he wende haven al	*For this reason; expected*
1100	In Engelond, that hire rith was.	
	He was werse than Sathanas	*Satan*
	That Jhesu Crist in erthe stoc.	*buried*
	Hanged worthe he on an hok!	*Let him be hanged; oak*
	After Goldeboru sone he sende,	*For; soon; sent*
1105	That was bothe fayr and hende,	*courteous*
	And dide hire to Lincolne bringe.	*had her brought*
	Belles dede he ageyn hire ringen,	
	And joie he made hire swithe mikel;	
	But netheless he was ful swikel.	*nonetheless; treacherous*
1110	He saide that he sholde hire yeve	*wed (give)*
	The fayreste man that mithe live.	
	She answerede and saide anon,	
	By Crist and bi Seint Johan,	*Saint John*
	That hire sholde noman wedde	
1115	Ne noman bringen hire to bedde	
	But he were king or kinges eyr,	*Unless; heir*
	Were he nevere man so fayr.	
	Godrich the erl was swithe wroth	*so angry*
	That she swor swilk an oth,	*such*
1120	And saide, "Whether thou wilt be	
	Quen and levedi over me?	
	Thou shalt haven a gadeling —	*rogue*
	Ne shalt thou haven non other king!	
	Thee shal spusen mi cokes knave —	*marry; cook's*
1125	Ne shalt thou non other louered have.	
	Datheit that thee other yeve	
	Everemore hwil I live!	
	Tomorwe ye sholen ben weddeth,	
	And maugre thin togidere beddeth.	*in spite of you*
1130	Goldeboru gret and yaf hire ille;	*wept*
	She wolde ben ded bi hire wille.	
	On the morwen hwan day was sprungen	

And day-belle at kirke rungen, — *church*
After Havelok sente that Judas — *i.e., Godrich*
1135 That werse was thanne Sathanas,
And saide, "Maister, wilte wif?" — *do you want*
"Nay," quoth Havelok, "bi my lif! — *said*
Hwat sholde ich with wif do?
I ne may hire fede ne clothe ne sho. — *shoe*
1140 Wider sholde ich wimman bringe? — *Where*
I ne have none kines thinge —
I ne have hws, I ne have cote, — *house; cottage*
Ne I ne have stikke, I ne have sprote, — *twig [for fuel]*
I ne have neyther bred ne sowel, — *sauce*
1145 Ne cloth but of an hold whit covel. — *clothing except; white cloak*
This clothes that ich onne have — *have on*
Aren the kokes and ich his knave!" — *cook's*
Godrich stirt up and on him dong, — *struck*
With dintes swithe hard and strong, — *blows*
1150 And seyde, "But thou hire take — *Unless*
That I wole yeven thee to make, — *as a mate*
I shal hangen thee ful heye, — *high*
Or I shal thristen uth thin heie." — *thrust out your eye*
Havelok was one and was odrat, — *alone; afraid*
1155 And grauntede him al that he bad. — *ordered*

Tho sende he after hire sone, — *quickly*
The fayrest wymman under mone, — *moon*
And seyde til hire, fals and slike, — *treacherous*
That wicke thrall that foule swike: — *slave; traitor*
1160 "But thu this man understonde, — *Unless; accept*
I shall flemen thee of londe; — *banish you from*
Or thou shal to the galwes renne, — *gallows run*
And ther thou shalt in a fir brenne." — *burn*
Sho was adrad for he so thrette, — *threatened*
1165 And durste nouth the spusing lette; — *dared not; espousal obstruct*
But they hire likede swithe ille, — *even though; very*
Sho thouthe it was Godes wille —
God that makes to growen the korn,
Formede hire wimman to be born. — *woman*
1170 Hwan he havede don him, for drede,

	That he sholde hire spusen and fede,	*espouse*
	And that she sholde til him holde,	*cling*
	Ther weren penies thicke tolde	
	Mikel plenté, upon the bok —	*A very great amount*
1175	He ys hire yaf and she is tok.	*gave her [his]; she took them*
	He weren spused fayre and well,	*They; married*
	The messe he dede, everi del	*every bit*
	That fel to spusing, an god clek —	*dealt with; good clerk*
	The erchebishop uth of Yerk,	*from York*
1180	That kam to the parlement,	*assembly*
	Als God him havede thider sent.	*As; to that place*
	Hwan he weren togidere in Godes lawe,	
	That the folc ful wel it sawe,	
	He ne wisten what he mouthen,	*knew not; might [do]*
1185	Ne he ne wisten what hem douthe,	*would avail them*
	Ther to dwellen, or thenne to gonge.	*Where; go from there*
	Ther ne wolden he dwellen longe,	
	For he wisten and ful wel sawe	*knew*
	That Godrich hem hatede — the devel him hawe!	*seize (possess)*
1190	And if he dwelleden ther outh —	*without security*
	That fel Havelok ful wel on thouth —	*treachery; worried about*
	Men sholde don his leman shame,	*beloved*
	Or elles bringen in wicke blame,	
	That were him levere to ben ded.	*rather*
1195	Forthi he token another red:	*Therefore; counsel*
	That thei sholden thenne fle	
	Til Grim and til hise sone thre —	*to; sons*
	Ther wenden he altherbest to spede,	
	Hem forto clothe and for to fede.	*Themselves*
1200	The lond he token under fote —	
	Ne wisten he non other bote —	*solution*
	And helden ay the rith sti	*always; way*
	Til he komen to Grimesby.	
	Thanne he komen there thanne was Grim ded —	
1205	Of him ne haveden he no red.	*word*
	But hise children alle fyve,	
	Alle weren yet on live,	*alive*
	That ful fayre ayen hem neme	

	Hwan he wisten that he keme,	*When they knew*
1210	And maden joie swithe mikel —	
	Ne weren he nevere ayen hem fikel.	*against; disloyal*
	On knes ful fayre he hem setten	*they set themselves*
	And Havelok swithe fayre gretten,	
	And seyden, "Welkome, louered dere!	*dear lord*
1215	And welkome be thi fayre fere!	*to your; companion*
	Blessed be that ilke thrawe	*that very time*
	That thou hire toke in Godes lawe!	
	Wel is hus we sen thee on live.	*Well is [it for] us; alive*
	Thou mithe us bothe selle and yeve;	*may*
1220	Thou mayt us bothe yeve and selle,	
	With that thou wilt here dwelle.	*If*
	We haven, louerd, alle gode —	*good things*
	Hors, and neth, and ship on flode,	*oxen; sea*
	Gold and silver and michel auchte,	*great possessions*
1225	That Grim ure fader us bitauchte.	*our; bequeathed*
	Gold and silver and other fe	*property*
	Bad he us bitaken thee.	*Told; to entrust you*
	We haven sheep, we haven swin;	*swine*
	Bileve her, louerd, and al be thin!	*Remain; yours*
1230	Tho shalt ben louerd, thou shalt ben syre,	
	And we sholen serven thee and hire;	*her*
	And hure sistres sholen do	*our*
	Al that evere biddes sho:	*she commands*
	He sholen hire clothes washen and wringen,	*They shall*
1235	And to hondes water bringen;	*bring water to her*
	He sholen bedden hire and thee,	*They; put to bed*
	For levedi wile we that she be."	
	Hwan he this joie haveden maked,	*made*
	Sithen stikes broken and kraked,	*Afterwards*
1240	And the fir brouth on brenne;	*stoked*
	Ne was ther spared gos ne henne,	*goose; hen*
	Ne the hende ne the drake:	*duck*
	Mete he deden plenté make;	
	Ne wantede there no god mete,	
1245	Wyn and ale deden he fete,	
	And hem made glade and blithe;	
	Wesseyl ledden he fele sithe.	*i.e., They drank to their health often*

	On the nith als Goldeboru lay,	*During; night; as*
	Sory and sorwful was she ay,	*continually*
1250	For she wende she were biswike,	*thought; deceived*
	That she were yeven unkyndelike.	*given [in marriage] out of her rank*
	O nith saw she therinne a lith,	*One; light*
	A swithe fayr, a swithe bryth —	*so bright*
	Al so brith, all so shir	*bright; shining*
1255	So it were a blase of fir.	*blaze of fire*
	She lokede noth and ek south,	*north*
	And saw it comen ut of his mouth	
	That lay bi hire in the bed.	
	No ferlike thou she were adred!	*wonder that; afraid*
1260	Thouthe she, "What may this bimene?	*mean*
	He beth heyman yet, als I wene:	*nobleman; believe*
	He beth heyman er he be ded!"	
	On hise shuldre, of gold red	*shoulders*
	She saw a swithe noble croiz;	*cross*
1265	Of an angel she herde a voyz:	*voice*
	"Goldeboru, lat thi sorwe be!	*set aside*
	For Havelok, that haveth spuset thee,	*married*
	He, kinges sone and kinges eyr,	
	That bikenneth that croiz so fayr	*betokens*
1270	It bikenneth more — that he shal	*means*
	Denemark haven and Englond al.	
	He shal ben king strong and stark,	
	Of Engelond and Denemark —	
	That shal thu wit thin eyne seen,	*eyes*
1275	And tho shalt quen and levedi ben!"	*lady*
	Thanne she havede herd the stevene	*When; voice*
	Of the angel uth of hevene,	
	She was so fele sithes blithe	*so many times over glad*
	That she ne mithe hire joie mythe,	*might not; hide*
1280	But Havelok sone anon she kiste,	
	And he slep and nouth ne wiste	*knew*
	Hwat that aungel havede seyd.	
	Of his slep anon he brayd,	*out of; started*

And seide, "Lemman, slepes thou? — *Beloved*
1285 A selkuth drem dremede me now — — *wondrous dream; just now*

Herkne now what me haveth met. — *Listen; dreamed*
Me thouthe I was in Denemark set,
But on on the moste hil — *one of the tallest hills*
That evere yete cam I til. — *to*
1290 It was so hey that I wel mouthe — *high*
Al the werd se, als me thouthe. — *world*
Als I sat upon that lowe — *As; hill*
I bigan Denemark for to awe, — *to possess*
The borwes and the castles stronge; — *towns*
1295 And mine armes weren so longe
That I fadmede al at ones, — *embraced; once*
Denemark with mine longe bones; — *i.e., my long body*
And thanne I wolde mine armes drawe
Til me and hom for to have, — *Towards*
1300 Al that evere in Denemark liveden — *Everyone who*
On mine armes faste clyveden; — *clung*
And the stronge castles alle
On knes bigunnen for to falle —
The keyes fellen at mine fet.
1305 Another drem dremede me ek: — *I dreamed also*
That ich fley over the salte se — *fled*
Til Engeland, and al with me
That evere was in Denemark lyves — *alive*
But bondemen and here wives; — *Except serfs; their*
1310 And that ich com til Engelond —
Al closede it intil min hond, — *Enclosed*
And, Goldeborw, I gaf thee. — *[England]*
Deus! lemman, what may this be?" — *God; my dear*
Sho answerede and seyde sone: — *She; quickly*
1315 "Jesu Crist, that made mone, — *moon*
Thine dremes turne to joye . . . — *(see note)*
That wite thu that sittes in trone! — *throne*
Ne non strong, king ne caysere — *caesar*
So thou shalt be, fo thou shalt bere — *for; wear*
1320 In Engelond corune yet. — *crown*
Denemark shal knele to thi fet;

Alle the castles that aren therinne
Shaltou, lemman, ful wel winne.
I woth so wel so ich it sowe, — *saw*
1325 To thee shole comen heye and lowe, — *shall*
And alle that in Denemark wone — — *live*
Em and brother, fader and sone, — *Uncle*
Erl and baroun, dreng and thayn, — *vassal; thane*
Knightes and burgeys and sweyn — — *citizens; attendants*
1330 And mad king heyelike and wel. — *made; solemnly*
Denemark shal be thin evere ilc del — — *every part*
Have thou nouth theroffe douthe, — *nothing to fear*
Nouth the worth of one nouthe; — *value; nut*
Theroffe withinne the firste yer
1335 Shalt thou ben king of evere il del. — *doubt*
But do now als I wile rathe: — *advise*
Nim in wit lithe to Denemark bathe, — *quickly*
And do thou nouth on frest this fare — — *not postpone; journey*
Lith and selthe felawes are.
1340 For shal ich nevere blithe be
Til I with eyen Denemark se, — *eyes*
For ich woth that al the lond — *know*
Shalt thou haven in thin hond.
Prey Grimes sones alle thre, — *Ask*
1345 That he wenden forth with the; — *they; go*
I wot he wilen the nouth werne — — *refuse*
With the wende shulen he yerne, — *go; eagerly*
For he loven thee hertelike. — *they; heartily*
Thou maght til he aren quike, — *may; ready*
1350 Hwore-so he o worde aren; — *Wherever in the world they are*
There ship thou do hem swithe yaren, — *make them quickly prepare*
And loke that thou dwelle nouth — — *delay not*
Dwelling haveth ofte scathe wrouth." — *harm*

Hwan Havelok herde that she radde, — *what; advised*
1355 Sone it was day, sone he him cladde, — *dressed*
And sone to the kirke yede — *church went*
Or he dide any other dede, — *Before*
And bifor the Rode bigan falle, — *in front of; Cross*
"Croiz" and "Crist" bi to kalle, — *Cross; began to call upon*

1360	And seyde, "Louerd, that all weldes —	*who governs*
	Wind and water, wodes and feldes —	
	For the holy milce of you,	*mercy*
	Have merci of me, Louerd, now!	
	And wreke me yet on mi fo	*avenge; enemy*
1365	That ich saw biforn min eyne slo	*eyes kill*
	Mine sistres with a knif,	
	And sithen wolde me mi lyf	
	Have reft, for in the se	*deprived*
	Bad he Grim have drenched me.	*Commanded*
1370	He hath mi lond with mikel unrith,	*great injustice*
	With michel wrong, with mikel plith,	*harm*
	For I ne misdede him nevere nouth,	*mistreated; in any way*
	And haved me to sorwe brouth.	*[he] has*
	He haveth me do mi mete to thigge,	*driven; beg*
1375	And ofte in sorwe and pine ligge.	*pain lie*
	Louerd, have merci of me,	
	And late me wel passe the se —	
	Though ihc have theroffe douthe and kare,	*I*
	Withuten stormes overfare,	
1380	That I ne drenched therine	*drowned*
	Ne forfaren for no sinne,	*lost*
	And bringe me wel to the lond	
	That Godard haldes in his hond,	*holds*
	That is mi rith, everi del —	*right*
1385	Jesu Crist, thou wost it wel!"	*know*
	Thanne he havede his bede seyd,	*prayer*
	His offrende on the auter leyd,	*offering; altar*
	His leve at Jhesu Crist he tok,	*took his leave*
	And at his swete moder ok,	*i.e., the Virgin Mary*
1390	And at the Croiz that he biforn lay;	*Cross*
	Sithen yede sore grotinde awey.	*weeping*
	Hwan he com hom, he wore yare,	*they were ready*
	Grimes sones, for to fare	*to go*
	Into the se, fishes to gete,	
1395	That Havelok mithe wel of ete.	
	But Avelok thoughte al another:	*something else*

First he kalde the heldeste brother, *called; eldest*
Roberd the Rede, bi his name,
Wiliam Wenduth and Huwe Raven,
1400 Grimes sones alle thre —
And seyde, "Lithes now alle to me; *said; Listen*
Louerdinges, ich wile you shewe *Gentlemen*
A thing of me that ye wel knewe.
Mi fader was king of Denshe lond — *Danish*
1405 Denemark was al in his hond
The day that he was quik and ded. *alive*
But thanne havede he wicke red, *advice*
That he me and Denemark al
And mine sistres bitawte a thral; *entrusted to a servant*
1410 A develes lime he hus bitawhte, *limb (i.e., a villain); entrusted us*
And al his lond and al hise authe, *possessions*
For I saw that fule fend *foul fiend*
Mine sistres slo with hise hend:
First he shar a two here throtes, *cut in two their*
1415 And sithen hem al to grotes, *then [chopped] them into small pieces*
And sithen bad in the se *[he] ordered*
Grim, youre fader, drenchen me.
Deplike dede he him swere *Solemnly*
On bok that he sholde me bere
1420 Unto the se and drenchen ine, *in [it]*
And wolde taken on him the sinne.
But Grim was wis and swithe hende — *skillful*
Wolde he nouth his soule shende; *harm*
Levere was him to be forsworen *Preferable; falsely sworn*
1425 Than drenchen me and ben forlorn. *drown; lost*
But sone bigan he forto fle
Fro Denemark for to berthen me. *protect*
For yif ich havede ther ben funden, *if; found*
Havede he ben slayn or harde bunden, *tightly bound*
1430 And heye ben hanged on a tre —
Havede go for him gold ne fe.
Forthi fro Denemark hider he fledde, *Therefore*
And me ful fayre and ful wel fedde,
So that unto this day
1435 Have ich ben fed and fostred ay. *brought up*

But now ich am up to that helde — *age*
Cumen that ich may wepne welde, — *wield weapons*
And I may grete dintes yeve, — *blows give*
Shal I nevere hwil ich lyve
1440 Ben glad til that ich Denemark se!
I preie you that ye wende with me, — *beseech; go*
And ich may mak you riche men;
Ilk of you shal have castles ten, — *Each*
And the lond that thor til longes — — *belongs to it*
1445 Borwes, tunes, wodes, and wonges. — *Boroughs, fields; village*

[Approximately 180 lines are missing here; see note]

1625 "With swilk als ich byen shal. — *such as; buy*
Ther of biseche you now leve — *permission*
Wile ich speke with non other reve — *magistrate*
But with thee, that justise are, — *judge*
That I mithe seken mi ware
1630 In gode borwes up and doun,
And faren ich wile fro tun to tun." — *town*
A gold ring drow he forth anon — — *drew*
An hundred pund was worth the ston —
And yaf it Ubbe for to spede. — *in hope of success*
1635 He was ful wis that first yaf mede; — *shrewd who; gave reward*
And so was Havelok ful wis here:
He solde his gold ring ful dere — — *at a high price*
Was nevere non so dere sold
Fro chapmen, neyther yung ne old. — *merchants*
1640 That sholen ye forthward ful wel heren, — *later; hear*
Yif that ye wile the storie heren. — *If*

Hwan Ubbe havede the gold ring,
Havede he yovenet for no thing, — *given it up*
Nouth for the borw evere ilk del.
1645 Havelok bihel he swithe wel, — *beheld*
Hw he was wel of bones maked,
Brod in the sholdres, ful wel schaped, — *Broad*
Thicke in the brest, of bodi long —
He semede wel to ben wel strong.

1650	"*Deus*!" hwat Ubbe, "Qui ne were he knith?	*God; said; Why; knight*
	I woth that he is swithe with!	*know; very powerful*
	Betere semede him to bere	
	Helm on heved, sheld and spere,	*Helmet; head*
	Thanne to beye and selle ware —	*buy; goods (i.e., be a merchant)*
1655	Allas, that he shal therwith fare!	*get along*
	Goddot! Wile he trowe me,	*If he takes my advice*
	Chaffare shal he late be."	*Trading; leave off*
	Netheles he seyde sone:	*Nonetheless*
	"Havelok, have thi bone!	*request*
1660	And I ful wel rede thee	
	That thou come and ete with me	
	Today, thou and thi fayre wif	
	That thou lovest al so thi lif.	*as much as your life*
	And have thou of hire no drede —	*fear*
1665	Shal hire no man shame bede.	*offer*
	Bi the fey that I owe to thee,	*faith*
	Ther of shal I me self borw be."	*myself; pledge*
	Havelok herde that he bad,	*what he offered*
	And thow was he ful sore drad	*afraid*
1670	With him to ete, for hise wif;	*because of*
	For him wore levere that his lif	
	Him wore reft, than she in blame	
	Felle or lauthe ani shame.	*experienced any*
	Hwanne he havede his wille yat,	*assented*
1675	The stede that he onne sat	*horse; sat on*
	Smot Ubbe with spures faste,	
	And forth awey, but at the laste,	*[went] forth away*
	Or he fro him ferde,	*went*
	Seyde he, that his folk herde:	*so that*
1680	"Loke that ye comen bethe,	*both*
	For ich it wile and ich it rede."	*I; want; advise*
	Havelok ne durste, the he were adrad,	*though he were frightened*
	Nouth withsitten that Ubbe bad.	*oppose what; bade*
	His wif he dide with him lede —	
1685	Unto the heye curt he yede.	*court; went*
	Roberd hire ledde, that was red,	*who (see note)*

	That havede tholed for hire the ded	*would have suffered death*
	Or ani havede hire misseyd,	
	Or hand with ivele onne leyd.	*laid an evil hand on her*
1690	Willam Wendut was that other	
	That hire ledde, Roberdes brother,	
	That was with at alle nedes.	*brave*
	Wel is him that god man fedes!	*i.e., has good retainers*
	Than he weren comen to the halle,	
1695	Biforen Ubbe and hise men alle,	
	Ubbe stirte hem ageyn,	*went towards them*
	And mani a knith and mani a sweyn,	
	Hem for to se and for to shewe.	*inspect*
	Tho stod Havelok als a lowe	*Then; hill*
1700	Aboven that ther inne wore,	*those; were*
	Rith al bi the heved more	*head*
	Thanne ani that ther inne stod.	
	Tho was Ubbe blithe of mod	
	That he saw him so fayr and hende;	*courteous*
1705	Fro him ne mithe his herte wende,	*turn*
	Ne fro him, ne fro his wif —	
	He lovede hem sone so his lif.	*just as much as*
	Weren non in Denemark that him thouthe	
	That he so mikel love mouthe.	*might [have]*
1710	More he lovede Havelok one	*only*
	Than al Denemark, bi mine wone.	*on my word*
	Loke now, hw God helpen kan	
	O mani wise wif and man!	*many [a]*
	Hwan it was comen time to ete,	
1715	Hise wif dede Ubbe sone in fete,	*fetch inside*
	And til hire seyde al on gamen,	*to her; in jest*
	"Dame, thou and Havelok shulen ete samen,	*together*
	And Goldeboru shal ete wit me,	
	That is so fayr so flour on tre.	*Who; as a flower*
1720	In al Denemark is wimman non	*no woman*
	So fayr so sche, by Seint Johan."	*as she*
	Thanne were set and bord leyd,	*table*
	And the beneysun was seyd,	*blessing*
	Biforn hem com the beste mete	

1725	That king or cayser wolde ete:	*emperor; caesar*
	Kranes, swannes, veneysun,	*Cranes, swans, venison*
	Lax, lampreys, and god sturgun,	*Salmon; good sturgeon*
	Pyment to drinke and god claré,	*claret*
	Win hwit and red, ful god plenté —	*Wine white*
1730	Was ther inne no page so lite	*There was; little*
	That evere wolde ale bite.	*request*
	Of the mete forto telle	
	Ne of the win bidde I nout dwelle;	
	That is the storie for to lenge —	*prolong*
1735	It wolde anuye this fayre genge.	*annoy; company*
	But hwan he haveden the kilthing deyled	*each; tippling shared*
	And fele sithe haveden wosseyled,	*toasted*
	With gode drinkes seten longe,	
	And it was time for to gonge,	
1740	Ilk man to ther he cam fro,	*Each*
	Thouthe Ubbe, "If I late hem go,	*let; go*
	Thus one foure, withuten mo,	*four alone*
	So mote ich brouke finger or to,	*use; toe*
	For this wimman bes mikel wo!	*woman; there will be much*
1745	For hire shal men hire louerd slo."	*their lords*
	He tok sone knithes ten,	
	And wel sixti other men	
	Wit gode bowes and with gleives,	*spears*
	And sende hem unto the greyves,	*(see note)*
1750	The beste man of al the toun,	
	That was named Bernard Brun —	
	And bad him als he lovede his lif,	*as*
	Havelok wel yemen and his wif,	*protect*
	And wel do wayten al the nith	*keep watch*
1755	Til the other day that it were lith.	*next; when; light*
	Bernard was trewe and swithe with,	*powerfully strong*
	In al the borw ne was no knith	
	That betere couthe on stede riden,	
	Helm on heved ne swerd bi side.	
1760	Havelok he gladlike understod	
	With mikel love and herte god,	
	And dide greythe a super riche	*prepare a sumptuous supper*
	Al so he was no with chinche	*not a bit stingy*

	To his bihove everil del,	*taste*
1765	That he mithe supe swithe wel.	*eat*
	Al so he seten and sholde soupe,	
	So comes a ladde in a joupe,	*loose jacket*
	And with him sixti other stronge	*strong men*
	With swerdes drawen and knives longe,	
1770	Ilkan in hande a ful god gleive,	*Each one; sword*
	And seyde, "Undo, Bernard the greyve!	*night watchman*
	Undo swithe and lat us in,	
	Or thu art ded, bi Seint Austin!"	*Saint Augustine*
	Bernard stirt up, that was ful big,	*who*
1775	And caste a brinie upon his rig,	*coat of mail; back*
	And grop an ax that was ful god —	*grabbed*
	Lep to the dore so he wore wod,	*as if he were crazy*
	And seyde, "Hwat are ye, that ar ther-oute,	*out there*
	That thus biginnen for to stroute?	*make a ruckus*
1780	Goth henne swithe, fule theves,	*Go hence*
	For, bi the Louerd that man on leves,	*believes*
	Shol ich casten the dore open,	*Should I*
	Summe of you shal ich drepen,	*kill*
	And the othre shal ich kesten	*others; cast*
1785	In feteres and ful faste festen!"	*bind up*
	"Hwat have ye seid?" quoth a ladde,	
	"Wenestu that we ben adradde?	*Do you think; afraid*
	We shole at this dore gonge	*door go*
	Maugre thin, carl, or outh longe."	*Despite all of you, churl, before long*
1790	He gripen sone a bulder ston	*boulder*
	And let it fleye, ful god won,	*fly with great force*
	Agen the dore, that it to-rof.	*broke apart*
	Avelok it saw, and thider drof	*ran*
	And the barre sone ut drow,	*quickly pulled out*
1795	That was unride and gret ynow,	*huge; quite big*
	And caste the dore open wide	
	And seide, "Her shal I now abide!	*Here*
	Comes swithe unto me —	*quickly*
	Datheyt hwo you henne fle!"	*Cursed be any who flee*
1800	"No," quodh on, "that shaltou coupe;"	*one; you will pay*
	And bigan til him to loupe,	*run*

In his hond his swerd ut drawe, — *pulled out*
Havelok he wende thore have slawe,
And with him comen other two
1805 That him wolde of live have do. — *robbed him of life*
Havelok lifte up the dore tre — *door-bar*
And at a dint he slow hem thre. — *with one stroke he killed all three of them*
Was non of hem that hise hernes — *brains*
Ne lay ther ute ageyn the sternes. — *Did not lie open to the stars*
1810 The ferthe that he sithen mette — *fourth*
Wit the barre so he him grette — *greeted*
Bifor the heved that the rith eye — *Upon; head that*
Ut of the hole made he fleye, — *eye socket; fly*
And sithe clapte him on the crune — *hit; head*
1815 So that he stan ded fel thor dune. — *stone dead; there down*
The fifte that he overtok — *fifth*
Gaf he a ful sor dint ok, — *Gave; hard*
Bitween the sholdres ther he stod,
That he spen his herte blod. — *shed*
1820 The sixte wende for to fle, — *turned*
And he clapte him with the tre
Rith in the fule necke so
That he smot hise necke on to. — *in two*
Thanne the sixe weren doun feld, — *felled*
1825 The seventhe brayd ut his swerd — *whipped out*
And wolde Havelok riht in the eye; — *wanted [to hit]*
And Havelok let the barre fleye
And smot him sone agheyn the brest,
That havede he nevere schrifte of prest — *absolution*
1830 For he was ded on lesse hwile — *in less time*
Than men mouthe renne a mile. — *might run*
Alle the othere weren ful kene; — *very tough*
A red they taken hem bitwene — *decision; among themselves*
That he sholde him bihalve, — *They; surround*
1835 And brisen so that wit no salve — *batter [him]*
Ne sholde him helen leche non. — *heal; doctor*
They drowen ut swerdes, ful god won, — *quite a number*
And shoten on him so don on bere — *as do; bear*
Dogges that wolden him to-tere, — *tear apart*
1840 Thanne men doth the bere beyte. — *bear bait*

	The laddes were kaske and teyte	*active; eager*
	And umbiyeden him ilkon.	*surrounded him altogether*
	Sum smot with tre and sum wit ston,	
	Summe putten with gleyve in bac and side	*thrust with sword*
1845	And yeven wundes longe and wide	
	In twenti stedes and wel mo,	*places*
	Fro the croune til the to.	*head to toe*
	Hwan he saw that, he was wod	*crazy*
	And was it ferlik hw he stod!	*amazing that*
1850	For the blod ran of his sides	*off*
	So water that fro the welle glides.	*As*
	But thanne bigan he for to mowe	*mow*
	With the barre, and let hem shewe	*show them*
	Hw he couthe sore smite;	
1855	For was ther non, long ne lite,	
	That he mouthe overtake,	
	That he ne garte his croune krake,	*caused*
	So that on a litel stund,	*in a little while*
	Felde he twenti to the grund.	*felled*
1860	Tho bigan gret dine to rise,	*Then; a great noise*
	For the laddes on ilke wise	*in every way*
	Him asayleden with grete dintes,	*Assailed him*
	Fro fer he sto[n]den him with flintes,	*very far*
	And gleyves schoten him fro ferne,	*swords rushed; from far away*
1865	For drepen him he wolden yerne;	*kill; gladly*
	But dursten he newhen him nomore	*They dared get near*
	Thanne he bor or leun wore.	*Than if; boar; lion*
	Huwe Raven that dine herde,	*Hugh; din*
	And thowthe wel that men misferde	*acted wrongly*
1870	With his louerd for his wif	*Against; lord*
	And grop an ore and a long knif,	*grabbed; oar*
	And thider drof al so an hert,	*as a hart (stag)*
	And cham ther on a litel stert	*came there in a little while*
	And saw how the laddes wode	*angry*
1875	Havelok his louerd umbistode,	*[they] surrounded*
	And beten on him so doth the smith	*as*
	With the hamer on the stith.	*anvil*

	"Allas!" hwat Hwe, "that I was boren!	*said Hugh*
	That evere et ich bred of koren!	*ate; grain*
1880	That ich here this sorwe se!	
	Roberd! Willam! Hware ar ye?	*Where*
	Gripeth ether unker a god tre	*Grab both of you two; cudgel*
	And late we nouth thise doges fle	*allow; not*
	Til ure louerd wreke be.	*Until; avenged*
1885	Cometh swithe, and folwes me:	
	Ich have in honde a ful god ore —	
	Datheit wo ne smite sore!"	*Cursed be [the one] who*
	"Ya! leve, ya!" quod Roberd sone,	*my good boy*
	"We haven ful god lith of the mone."	*good light; moon*
1890	Roberd grop a staf strong and gret,	*grabbed*
	That mouthe ful wel bere a net,	*bear an ox*
	And Willam Wendut grop a tre	
	Mikel grettere than his the,	*Much thicker; thigh*
	And Bernard held his ax ful faste	
1895	I seye was he nouthe the laste!	
	And lopen forth so he weren wode	*rushed; as; frenzied*
	To the laddes ther he stode,	
	And yaf hem wundes swithe grete;	
	Ther mithe men wel se boyes bete,	*knaves*
1900	And ribbes in here sides breke	
	And Havelok on hem wel wreke.	*avenged*
	He broken armes, he broken knes,	
	He broken shankes, he broken thes.	*legs; thighs*
	He dide the blod there renne dune	*caused; run down*
1905	To the fet rith fro the crune,	*feet; crown*
	For was ther spared heved non.	*not one head*
	He leyden on hevedes ful god won,	*quite a number*
	And made croune breke and crake	*crowns*
	Of the broune and of the blake.	*dark; white (OE blāc)*
1910	He maden here backes al so bloute	*be beaten soft*
	Als here wombes and made hem rowte	*As; stomachs; roar*
	Als he weren kradelbarnes —	*babies*
	So dos the child that moder tharnes.	*loses its mother*
	Datheit the recke! For he it servede.	*ruckus; they deserved it*
1915	Hwat dide he thore? Weren he werewed.	*they; mauled*

	So longe haveden he but and bet	*thrust; hit*
	With neves under hernes set	*fists; brains*
	That of tho sixti men and on	*sixty-one*
	Ne wente ther awey lives non.	*No one*
1920	On the morwen, hwan it was day,	
	Ilc on other wirwed lay	*mangled*
	Als it were dogges that weren henged;	*wretches*
	And summe leye in dikes slenget,	*ditches; slung*
	And summe in gripes bi the her	*trenches; hair*
1925	Drawen ware and laten ther.	*left*
	Sket cam tiding intil Ubbe	*Quickly; news to*
	That Havelok havede with a clubbe	
	Of hise slawen sixti and on	
	Sergaunz, the beste that mihten gon.	*Men-at-arms; might have been*
1930	"Deus," quoth Ubbe, "Hwat may this be?	
	Betere is I nime miself and se	*go*
	That this baret on hwat is wold	*what this disturbance means*
	Thanne I sende yunge or old;	
	For yif I sende him unto,	
1935	I wene men sholde him shame do,	
	And that ne wolde ich for no thing.	
	I love him wel, bi Heveneking —	
	Me wore levere I wore lame	*I would prefer*
	Thanne men dide him ani shame	
1940	Or tok or onne handes leyde	
	Unornelike or shame seyde."	*Roughly*
	He lep up on a stede lith,	*lept; horse nimbly*
	And with him mani a noble knith,	
	And ferde forth unto the tun,	*town*
1945	And dide calle Bernard Brun	
	Ut of his hus wan he ther cam;	
	And Bernard sone ageyn nam,	*called*
	Al to-tused and al to-torn,	*cut up; torn to pieces*
	Ner al so naked so he was born	*as*
1950	And al to-brised, bac and the.	*bruised; thigh*
	Quoth Ubbe, "Bernard, hwat is thee?	*what is wrong with you*
	Hwo haves thee thus ille maked,	*Who; treated*
	Thus to-riven and al mad naked?"	*torn to pieces*

	"Louerd, merci," quot he sone,	
1955	"Tonicht, al so ros the mone,	*as the moon rose*
	Comen her mo than sixti theves	
	With lokene copes and wide sleves,	*fastened cloaks*
	Me for to robben and to pine,	*torment*
	And for to drepe me and mine.	*kill*
1960	Mi dore he broken up ful sket,	*quickly*
	And wolde me binden hond and fet.	
	Wan the godemen that sawe,	*people*
	Havelok and he that bi the wowe	*wall*
	Leye, he stirten up sone onon	*right away*
1965	And summe grop tre and sum grop ston	*grabbed*
	And drive hem ut, thei he weren crus,	*out; though they were fierce*
	So dogges ut of milne-hous.	*As; mill*
	Havelok grop the dore-tre,	
	And a dint he slow hem thre.	*with one stroke*
1970	He is the beste man at nede	*in time of need*
	That everemar shal ride stede —	
	Als helpe God, bi mine wone	*in my opinion*
	A thousend men his he worth one!	*alone*
	Yif he ne were, ich were now ded —	*If it were not for him*
1975	So have ich don mi soule red!	*my own soul's counsel*
	But it is of him mikel sinne:	*harm*
	He maden him swilke woundes thrinne	*such; therein*
	That of the altherleste wounde	*very least*
	Were a stede brouht to grunde.	*horse; brought down*
1980	He haves a wunde in the side	
	With a gleyve ful unride;	*sword; very huge*
	And he haves on thoru his arum	*has one through; arm*
	Ther of is full mikel harum;	*harm*
	And he haves on thoru his the —	*one; thigh*
1985	The unrideste that men may se.	*most enormous*
	And othe wundes haves he stronge,	*other*
	Mo than twenti, swithe longe.	*severe*
	But sithen he havede lauth the sor	*since; felt; pain*
	Of the wundes, was nevere bor	*boar*
1990	That so fauth, so he fauth thanne!	*fought*
	Was non that havede the hernepanne	*brain-pan (skull)*
	So hard that he ne dede al to-cruhsse	*utterly crush*

	And al to-shivere and al to-frusshe.	*shiver; smash*
	He folwede hem so hund dos hare —	*as a hound does*
1995	Datheyt on he wolde spare,	*A curse*
	That ne made hem everilkon	*every*
	Ligge stille so doth the ston.	*Lie; as*
	And ther nis he nouth to frie	*he is not to be blamed*
	For other sholde he make hem lye	*either*
2000	Ded, or thei him havede slawen,	*killed*
	Or al to-hewen or al to-drawen.	
	"Louerd, havi nomore plith	*I have; harm*
	Of that ich was grethed tonith.	*troubled*
	Thus wolde the theves me have reft;	*robbed*
2005	But, God thank, he havenet sure keft!	*they have certainly paid for it*
	But it is of him mikel scathe —	
	I woth that he bes ded ful rathe."	*know; will be soon dead*
	Quoth Ubbe, "Bernard, seyst thou soth?"	*truth*
	"Ya, sire, that I ne leye o tooth!	*lie through my teeth*
2010	Yif I, louerd, a word leye,	*[should] tell a lie*
	Tomorwen do me hengen heye."	*hang*
	The burgeys that ther bi stode thore	*citizens; stood by*
	Grundlike and grete othes swore,	*Hearty; solemn*
	Litle and mikle, yunge and holde,	*old*
2015	That was soth that Bernard tolde —	
	Soth was that he wolden him bynde,	
	And trusse al that he mithen fynde	*carry off*
	Of hise in arke or in kiste	*coffer; chest*
	That he mouthe in seckes thriste.	*might in sacks thrust*
2020	"Louerd, he haveden al awey born	
	His thing, and himself al to-torn,	*possessions; torn apart*
	But als God self barw him wel,	*himself preserved*
	That he ne tinte no catel.	*lost no possessions*
	Hwo mithe so mani stonde ageyn	*Who; stand up against*
2025	Bi nither-tale, knith or swein?	*nighttime*
	He weren bi tale sixti and ten —	*tally*
	Starke laddes, stalworthi men,	*Strong*
	And on the mayster of hem alle,	*one*
	That was the name Griffin Galle.	*Who was named*

2030 Hwo mouthe ageyn so mani stonde,
But als this man of ferne londe — *far away*
Haveth hem slawen with a tre? — *killed; beam*
Mikel joie have he!
God yeve him mikel god to welde, — *possessions to control*
2035 Bothe in tun and ek in felde: — *town; country*
Wel is set the mete he etes." — *spent; food*
Quoth Ubbe, "Doth him swithe fete, — *Fetch him quickly*
That I mouthe his woundes se,
If that he mouthen holed be; — *might be made whole*
2040 For if he mouthe covere yet — *recover*
And gangen wel upon hise fet, — *go*
Miself shal dubben him to knith,
Forthi that he is so with. — *Because*
And yif he livede, tho foule theves, — *those*
2045 That weren of Kaym kin and Eves, — *Cain's*
He sholden hange bi the necke — — *They*
Of here ded datheit wo recke, — *their death cursed*
Hwan he yeden thus on nithes — *Since; went; at night*
Tobinde bothe burgmen and knithes! — *citizens*
2050 For bynderes love ich neveremo — — *outlaws; more*
Of hem ne yeve ich nouht a slo." — *sloeberry (i.e., I do not care)*

Havelok was bifore Ubbe browth, — *brought*
That havede for him ful mikel thouth — *concern*
And mikel sorwe in his herte
2055 For hise wundes, that we so smerte. — *were so severe*

But hwan his wundes weren shewed, — *examined*
And a leche havede knawed — *doctor; determined*
That he hem mouthe ful wel hele, — *he (the doctor)*
Wel make him gange and ful wel mele, — *walk; talk*
2060 And wel a palefrey bistride, — *sit on a palfrey*
And wel upon a stede ride, — *charger*
Tho let Ubbe al his care — *Then Ubbe put aside*
And al his sorwe over fare, — *pass over*
And seyde, "Cum now forth with me,
2065 And Goldeboru, thi wif, with thee,
And thine serjaunz alle thre, — *men-at-arms*

	For now wile I youre warant be:	*guarantee*
	Wile I non of here frend	*their friends*
	That thu slowe with thin hend	
2070	Moucte wayte thee to slo	*wait [in ambush]*
	Also thou gange to and fro.	*go*
	I shal lene thee a bowr	*loan; room*
	That is up in the heye tour,	*high tower*
	Til thou mowe ful wel go	*may; get around*
2075	And wel ben hol of al thi wo.	*healed*
	It ne shal nothing ben bitwene	
	Thi bowr and min, al so I wene,	
	But a fayr firrene wowe —	*firwood wall*
	Speke I loude or spek I lowe,	
2080	Thou shalt ful wel heren me,	
	And than thu wilt thou shalt me se.	*whenever you want*
	A rof shal hile us bothe o nith,	*cover; at night*
	That none of mine, clerk ne knith,	
	No sholen thi wif no shame bede	*offer; cause*
2085	No more than min, so God me rede!"	*counsel*
	He dide unto the borw bringe	
	Sone anon, al with joiinge,	*rejoicing*
	His wif and his sergaunz thre,	*men-at-arms*
	The beste men that mouthe be.	
2090	The first nith he lay ther inne,	
	Hise wif and his serganz thrinne,	*three*
	Aboute the middel of the nith	
	Wok Ubbe and saw a mikel lith	*Woke*
	In the bowr thar Havelok lay	*room where*
2095	Al so brith so it were day.	*As bright*
	"*Deus*!" quoth Ubbe, "Hwat may this be?	
	Betere is I go miself and se	
	Hwether he sitten now and wesseylen,	*is partying*
	Or ani sotshipe to deyle,	*foolishness; take part in*
2100	This tid nithes also foles;	*time of night*
	Than birthe men casten hem in poles	*it behooves; pools*
	Or in a grip, or in the fen —	*ditch; mud*
	Now ne sitten none but wicke men,	

	Glotuns, revres, or wicke theves,	*robbers*
2105	Bi Crist that alle folk onne leves!"	*believe in*
	He stod and totede in at a bord	*peered in*
	Her he spak anilepi word	*spoke a single*
	And saw hem slepen faste ilkon	
	And lye stille so the ston;	
2110	And saw al that mikel lith	*light*
	Fro Havelok cam that was so brith.	
	Of his mouth it com il del —	
	That was he war ful swithe wel.	*aware of*
	"*Deus*," quoth he, "Hwat may this mene!"	
2115	He calde bothe arwe men and kene,	*called; shy; bold*
	Knithes and serganz swithe sleie,	*cunning*
	Mo than an hundred, withuten leye,	*More; lie*
	And bad hem alle comen and se	
	Hwat that selcuth mithe be.	*marvel*
2120	Als the knithes were comen alle,	*When*
	Ther Havelok lay ut of the halle,	*out*
	So stod ut of his mouth a glem,	*issued from; gleam*
	Rith al swilk so the sunne-bem,	*Just like*
	That al so lith was thare, bi hevene,	
2125	So ther brenden serges sevene	*As if seven candles burned*
	And an hundred serges ok	*also*
	That durste I sweren on a book!	*they dared*
	He slepen faste, alle five,	*soundly*
	So he weren brouth of live;	*As if; dead*
2130	And Havelok lay on his lift side,	*left*
	In his armes his brithe bride:	
	Bi the pappes he leyen naked —	*Down to the breast*
	So faire two weren nevere maked	
	In a bed to lyen samen.	*together*
2135	The knithes thouth of hem god gamen,	*sport*
	Hem for to shewe and loken to.	*observe*
	Rith al so he stoden alle so,	*Just as*
	And his bac was toward hem wend,	*turned*
	So weren he war of a croiz ful gent	*cross*
2140	On his right shuldre swithe brith,	*so bright*
	Brithter than gold ageyn the lith,	

	So that he wiste, heye and lowe,	*knew*
	That it was kunrik that he sawe.	*mark of exalted birth*
	It sparkede and ful brith shon	*sparkled*
2145	So doth the gode charbuncle ston	*As*
	That men see mouthe se by the lith	
	A peni chesen, so was it brith.	*penny to pick out (choose)*
	Thanne bihelden he him faste,	
	So that he knewen at the laste	
2150	That he was Birkabeynes sone,	
	That was here king, that was hem wone	*Who; their; [to] them wont*
	Wel to yeme and wel were	*govern; protect*
	Ageynes uten-laddes here —	*foreign army*
	"For it was nevere yet a brother	*there was*
2155	In al Denemark so lich another,	*like*
	So this man, that is so fayr,	*As*
	Als Birkabeyn; he is hise eyr."	*As; his heir*
	He fellen sone at hise fet.	*They fell*
	Was non of hem that he ne gret —	*greeted*
2160	Of joye he weren alle so fawen	*glad*
	So he him haveden of erthe drawen.	*As if; risen from the grave*
	Hise fet he kisten an hundred sythes —	*times*
	The tos, the nayles, and the lithes —	*tips*
	So that he bigan to wakne	
2165	And wit hem ful sore to blakne,	*go blank (become pale)*
	For he wende he wolden him slo,	*they*
	Or elles binde him and do wo.	
	Quoth Ubbe, "Louerd, ne dred thee nowth,	
	Me thinkes that I se thi thouth.	
2170	Dere sone, wel is me	
	That I thee with eyn se.	
	Manred, louerd, bede I thee —	*Homage; offer*
	Thi man auht I ful wel to be;	
	For thu art comen of Birkabeyn,	
2175	That havede mani knith and sweyn,	
	And so shalt thou, louerd, have:	
	Thou thou be yet a ful yung knave	
	Thou shalt be King of al Denemark —	

	Was ther inne never non so stark.	*strong [as you]*
2180	Tomorwen shaltu manrede take	*swear fealty*
	Of the brune and of the blake,	*dark; light*
	Of alle that aren in this tun,	*town (fortified place)*
	Bothe of erl and of barun,	
	And of dreng and of thayn	*retainer; vassal*
2185	And of knith and of sweyn.	
	And so shaltu ben mad knith	*knight*
	Wit blisse, for thou art so with."	*strong*
	Tho was Havelok swithe blithe,	*very glad*
	And thankede God ful fele sithe.	*many times*
2190	On the morwen, wan it was lith,	
	And gon was thisternesse of the nith,	*darkness; night*
	Ubbe dide upon a stede	
	A ladde lepe, and thider bede	
	Erles, barouns, drenges, theynes,	*vassals, thanes*
2195	Klerkes, knithes, burgeys, sweynes,	*citizens*
	That he sholden comen anon	
	Biforen him sone everilkon,	*everyone*
	Al so he loven here lives	*their*
	And here children and here wives.	
2200	His bode ne durste he non atsitte	*command; refuse*
	That he ne neme for to wite,	*went; know*
	Sone hwat wolde the justise;	*wanted*
	And bigan anon to rise	
	And seyde sone, "Lithes me,	*Listen to me*
2205	Alle samen, theu and fre,	*together, slave; noble*
	A thing ich wile you here shauwe	
	That ye alle ful wel knawe.	
	Ye witen wel that al this lond	
	Was in Birkabeynes hond	
2210	The day that he was quic and ded,	
	And how that he, bi youre red	*advice*
	Bitauhte hise children thre	*Entrusted*
	Godard to yeme, and al his fe.	*protect; property*
	Havelok his sone he him tauhte	
2215	And hise two douhters and al his auhte.	*possessions*

	Alle herden ye him swere	
	On bok and on messe gere	*vestments*
	That he shulde yemen hem wel,	*protect*
	Withuten lac, withuten tel.	*Without fault; deceit (reproach)*
2220	He let his oth all overgo —	*oath he disregarded*
	Evere wurthe him yvel and wo!	*become him evil*
	For the maydnes here lif	
	Refte he bothen with a knif,	
	And him shulde ok have slawen —	
2225	The knif was at his herte drawen.	
	But God him wolde wel have save:	
	He havede rewnesse of the knave	*pity; boy*
	So that he with his hend	*hands*
	Ne drop him nouth, that sori fend!	*killed; sorry fiend (villain)*
2230	But sone dide he a fishere	*forced; fisherman*
	Swithe grete othes swere,	
	That he sholde drenchen him	*drown*
	In the se, that was ful brim.	*wild*
	Hwan Grim saw that he was so fayr,	
2235	And wiste he was the rith eir,	*knew; rightful heir*
	Fro Denemark ful sone he fledde	
	Intil Englond and ther him fedde	
	Mani winter that til this day	
	Haves he ben fed and fostred ay.	*brought up*
2240	Lokes hware he stondes her!	*Look*
	In al this werd ne haves he per —	*world; peer*
	Non so fayr, ne non so long,	*tall*
	Ne non so mikel, ne non so strong.	*great*
	In this middelerd nis no knith	*earth*
2245	Half so strong ne half so with.	
	Bes of him ful glad and blithe,	*Be*
	And cometh alle hider swithe,	
	Manrede youre louerd for to make,	*Homage to*
	Bothe brune and the blake —	
2250	I shal miself do first the gamen	*ceremonial honor*
	And ye sithen alle samen."	*together*

	O knes ful fayre he him sette —	*On; very*
	Mouthe nothing him ther fro lette,	*Might; from that prevent*
	And bicam is man rith thare,	*became his; there*
2255	That alle sawen that there ware.	*were*
	After him stirt up laddes ten	
	And bicomen hise men,	
	And sithen everilk a baroun	*each*
	That evere weren in al that toun,	
2260	And sithen drenges, and sithen thaynes	*servants*
	And sithen knithes, and sithen sweynes;	
	So that, or that day was gon,	*before; done*
	In al the tun ne was nouth on	*not one*
	That it ne was his man bicomen —	
2265	Manrede of alle havede he nomen.	*Oaths of loyalty; they taken*
	Hwan he havede of hem alle	
	Manrede taken in the halle,	*Fealty*
	Grundlike dide he hem swere	*Solemnly*
	That he sholden him god feyth bere	*faith*
2270	Ageynes alle that woren on live;	*Towards*
	Ther-yen ne wolde never on strive,	*against that never a one would oppose*
	That he ne maden sone that oth —	
	Riche and poure, lef and loth.	
	Hwan that was maked, sone he sende	
2275	Ubbe writes fer and hende,	*writs far and near*
	After alle that castel yemede,	*governed*
	Burwes, tunes, sibbe an fremde	*siblings and kinsmen*
	That thider sholden comen swithe	*immediately*
	Til him and heren tithandes blithe	*To; good news*
2280	That he hem alle shulde telle.	
	Of hem ne wolde nevere on dwelle,	*delay*
	That he ne come sone plattinde;	*hurrying*
	Hwo hors ne havede, com gangande.	*Whoever had no horse; walking*
	So that withinne a fourtenith	*fortnight (two weeks)*
2285	In al Denemark ne was no knith,	
	Ne conestable, ne shireve,	*sheriff*
	That com of Adam and of Eve,	
	That he ne com biforn sire Ubbe —	

	He dredden him so thef doth clubbe.	*They feared; as thief*
2290	Hwan he haveden alle the king gret	*they; greeted*
	And he weren alle dun-set,	*seated*
	Tho seyde Ubbe, "Lokes here	*Look*
	Ure louerd swithe dere,	*Our*
	That shal ben king of al the lond	
2295	And have us alle under hond,	*in control*
	For he is Birkabeynes sone,	
	The king that was umbe stonde wone	*formerly accustomed*
	Us for to yemen and wel were	*govern; defend*
	With sharp swerd and longe spere.	
2300	Lokes now, hw he is fayr:	
	Sikerlike he is hise eyr.	*Surely; heir*
	Falles alle to his fet —	
	Bicomes hise men ful sket."	*quickly*
	He weren for Ubbe swithe adrad	
2305	And dide sone al that he bad.	
	And yet he deden sumdel more:	
	O bok ful grundlike he swore	*On; gravely*
	That he sholde with him halde,	*remain loyal*
	Bothe ageynes stille and bolde	*timid*
2310	That evere wolde his bodi dere.	*harm*
	That dide he hem o boke swere.	
	Hwan he havede manrede and oth	
	Taken of lef and of loth,	*dear ones; hostile ones*
	Ubbe dubbede him to knith	
2315	With a swerd ful swithe brith,	
	And the folk of al the lond	
	Bitauhte him al in his hond,	*Entrusted them*
	The cunnriche everil del	*kingdom*
	And made him king heylike and wel.	*solemnly*
2320	Hwan he was king, ther mouthe men se	
	The moste joye that mouhte be —	
	Buttinge with sharpe speres,	*Thrusting*
	Skirming with talevaces that men beres,	*Fencing; swords*
	Wrastling with laddes, putting of ston,	*shot-putting*
2325	Harping and piping, ful god won,	*a great amount*
	Leyk of mine, of hasard ok,	*Game of backgammon; dice also*

	Romanz reding on the bok.	
	Ther mouthe men here the gestes singe,	*tales*
	The glewmen on the tabour dinge.	*minstrels; drum beat*
2330	Ther moutthe men se the boles beyte,	*bulls baited*
	And the bores, with hundes teyte.	*dogs lively*
	Tho mouhte men se everil glew;	*every type of sport*
	Ther mouthe men se hw grim grew —	*excitement*
	Was nevere yete joye more	
2335	In al this werd than tho was thore.	*world; then*
	Ther was so mikel yeft of clothes	*much giving away*
	That, thou I swore you grete othes,	
	I ne wore nouth ther of trod.	*believed*
	That may I ful wel swere, bi God!	
2340	There was swithe gode metes	
	And of wyn that men fer fetes,	*wine; bring from far away*
	Rith al so mik and gret plenté	*much; abundant*
	So it were water of the se.	
	The feste fourti dawes sat —	*feast; days lasted*
2345	So riche was nevere non so that.	
	The king made Roberd there knith,	
	That was ful strong and ful with,	
	And Willam Wendut hec, his brother,	*also*
	And Huwe Raven, that was that other,	
2350	And made hem barouns alle thre,	
	And yaf hem lond and other fe,	*property*
	So mikel that ilker twenti knihtes	*each one*
	Havede of genge, dayes and nithes.	*Had in his company*
	Hwan that feste was al don,	
2355	A thusand knihtes ful wel o bon	*equipped*
	Withheld the king with him to lede,	
	That ilkan havede ful god stede,	*that each one had*
	Helm and sheld, and brinie brith,	*coat of mail*
	And al the wepne that fel to knith.	*were appropriate*
2360	With hem ek five thusand gode	*good*
	Sergaunz that weren to fyht wode	*eager*
	Withheld he al of his genge —	*company*
	Wile I namore the storie lenge.	*lengthen*
	Yet hwan he havede of al the lond	

2365	The casteles alle in his hond,	
	And conestables don therinne,	*castle wardens; placed*
	He swor he ne sholde never blinne	*stop*
	Til that he were of Godard wreken,	*avenged*
	That ich have of ofte speken.	
2370	Half hundred knithes dede he calle,	
	And hise fif thusand sergaunz alle,	
	And dide sweren on the bok	
	Sone, and on the auter ok,	*altar also*
	That he ne sholde nevere blinne,	*stop*
2375	Ne for love ne for sinne,	
	Til that he haveden Godard funde	
	And brouth biforn him faste bunde.	*bound*
	Thanne he haveden swor this oth,	*When they; sworn*
	Ne leten he nouth, for lef ne loth,	
2380	That he foren swithe rathe	*went very quickly*
	Ther he was, unto the pathe	
	Ther he yet on hunting for,	
	With mikel genge and swithe stor.	*strong retainers; very proud*
	Robert, that was of all the ferd	*army*
2385	Mayster, girt was wit a swerd,	
	And sat upon a ful god stede,	
	That under him rith wolde wede.	*would gallop powerfully*
	He was the firste that with Godard	
	Spak, and seyde, "Hede, cavenard!	*Halt, villain*
2390	Wat dos thu here at this pathe?	
	Cum to the king swithe and rathe!	*soon*
	That sendes he thee word and bedes,	*orders*
	That thu thenke what thou him dedes	
	Whan thu reftes with a knif	*deprived*
2395	Hise sistres here lif	*their lives*
	And sithen bede thou in the se	*ordered*
	Drenchen him — that herde he!	
	He is to thee swithe grim;	*angry*
	Cum nu swithe unto him	
2400	That king is of this kunerike,	*kingdom*
	Thou fule man, thou wicke swike!	*traitor*

And he shal yelde thee thy mede, — *reward*
Bi Crist that wolde on Rode blede!" — *Cross*

Hwan Godard herde that he ther thrette,
2405 With the neve he Robert sette — *fist; struck*
Biforn the teth a dint ful strong. — *teeth; blow*
And Robert kipt ut a knif long — *whipped out*
And smot him thoru the rith arum — — *arm*
Ther of was ful litel harum! — *harm*

2410 Hwan his folk that saw and herde,
Hwou Robert with here louerd ferde, — *their lord fared*
He haveden him wel ner browt of live, — *They [would] have; murdered*
Ne weren his two brethren and othre five — *If it were not for*
Slowen of here laddes ten,
2415 Of Godardes altherbeste men. — *very best*
Hwan the othre sawen that, he fledden, — *others; they*
And Godard swithe loude gredde: — *shouted*
"Mine knithes, hwat do ye?
Sule ye thusgate fro me fle? — *in this way*
2420 Ich have you fed and yet shal fede —
Helpe me nw in this nede — *difficulty*
And late ye nouth mi bodi spille, — *allow; destroy*
Ne Havelok don of me hise wille!
Yif ye it do, ye do you shame — *yourselves*
2425 And bringeth youself in mikel blame!" — *dishonor*
Hwan he that herden, he wenten ageyn, — *they; returned*
And slowen a knit and a sweyn — *knight*
Of the kinges oune men, — *own*
And woundeden abuten ten.
2430 The kinges men, hwan he that sawe,
Scuten on hem, heye and lowe, — *Struck them everywhere*
And everilk fot of hem he slowe, — *everyone*
But Godard one, that he flowe, — *alone whom he flayed*
So the thef men dos henge, — *Like*
2435 Or hund men shole in dike slenge. — *hound; ditch sling*
He bunden him ful swithe faste,
Hwil the bondes wolden laste,
That he rorede als a bole — *roared; bull*

	That wore parred in an hole	*confined*
2440	With dogges forto bite and beite.	*bait*
	Were the bondes nouth to leite —	*not hard to find*
	He bounden him so fele sore	*They; very sorely*
	That he gan crien Godes ore,	*plead for; grace*
	That he sholde of his hend plette;	*cut off*
2445	Wolden he nouht ther fore lette	*stop*
	That he ne bounden hond and fet.	
	Datheit that on that ther fore let!	*Cursed be the one who hinders any of it*
	But dunten him so man doth bere	
	And keste him on a scabbed mere,	*threw; mangy mare*
2450	Hise nese went unto the crice.	*nose; arse*
	So ledden he that ful swike	*they led; traitor*
	Til he biforn Havelok was brouth,	
	That he havede ful wo wrowht,	
	Bothe with hungre and with cold	
2455	Or he were twel winter old,	*Before; twelve*
	And with mani hevi swink,	*much; labor*
	With poure mete and feble drink,	
	And swithe wikke clothes,	*bad*
	For al hise manie grete othes.	
2460	Nu beyes he his holde blame:	*pays for; guilt*
	Old sinne makes newe shame!	
	Wan he was so shamelike	
	Brouth biforn the king, the fule swike!	*When*
	The king dede Ubbe swithe calle	*foul traitor*
2465	Hise erles and hise barouns alle,	
	Dreng and thein, burgeis and knith,	*Vassal; thane*
	And bad he sholden demen him rith,	*judge*
	For he knew the swike dam;	*they; treacherous fellow*
	Everil del God was him gram!	*In every way; [with] him angry*
2470	He setten hem dun bi the wawe,	*They set themselves; wall*
	Riche and pouere, heye and lowe,	
	The helde men and ek the grom,	*old; young*
	And made ther the rithe dom	*judgment*
	And seyden unto the king anon,	
2475	That stille sat so the ston:	
	"We deme that he be al quic flawen	*flayed alive*
	And sithen to the galwes drawe	*then*

At this foule mere tayl, *mare's*
Thoru his fet a ful strong nayl,
2480 And thore ben henged wit two feteres *chains*
And thare be writen thise leteres:
'This is the swike that wende wel *thought*
The king have reft the lond ilk del, *robbed of; every part*
And hise sistres with a knif
2485 Bothe refte here lif.'
This writ shal henge bi him thare.
The dom is demd — seye we namore." *judgment; decided*
Hwan the dom was demd and give,
And he was wit the prestes shrive, *absolved*
2490 And it ne mouhte ben non other, *otherwise*
Ne for fader ne for brother,
But that he sholde tharne lif, *lose*
Sket cam a ladde with a knif *Quickly*
And bigan rith at the to *toe*
2495 For to ritte and for to flo; *cut; flay*
And he bigan tho for to rore *cry out (roar)*
So it were grim or gore, *Because; gory*
That men mithe thethen a mile *from there*
Here him rore, that fule file! *Hear; foul wretch*
2500 The ladde ne let nowith forthi, *stopped no wit*
They he criede, "Merci! Merci!" *Although*
That ne flow him everil del *flayed him every bit*
With knif mad of grunden stel.
Thei garte bringe the mere sone, *had prepared to bring the mare*
2505 Skabbed and ful ivele o bone, *infirm*
And bunden him rith at hire tayl
With a rop of an old seyl *sail*
And drowen him unto the galwes, *dragged*
Nouth bi the gate but over the falwes, *Not; roadway; fields*
2510 And henge him thore bi the hals — *neck*
Datheit hwo recke: he was fals! *Cursed be any who cares*

Thanne he was ded, that Sathanas,
Sket was seysed al that his was *Quickly; seized*
In the kinges hand ilk del — *every bit*
2515 Lond and lith and other catel — *Land; estates; property*

	And the king ful sone it yaf	*gave*
	Ubbe in the hond, wit a fayr staf,	*i.e., into Ubbe's hands*
	And seyde, "Her ich sayse thee	*invest*
	In al the lond, in al the fe . . . ."	*property (see note)*
2520	Tho swor Havelok he sholde make,	
	Al for Grim, of monekes blake	*black monks*
	A priorie to serven in ay	*priory; forever*
	Jhesu Crist, til Domesday,	*Judgment Day*
	For the god he havede him don	
2525	Hwil he was pouere and ivel o bon.	*infirm of body*
	And ther of held he wel his oth,	*promise*
	For he it made, God it woth,	*knows*
	In the tun ther Grim was graven,	*buried*
	That of Grim yet haves the name.	
2530	Of Grim bidde ich namore spelle.	*offer; to tell*
	But wan Godrich herde telle,	*when*
	Of Cornwayle that was erl,	
	That fule traytour, that mixed cherl!	*filthy man*
	That Havelok King was of Denemark,	
2535	And ferde with him, strong and stark	*army*
	Comen Engelond withinne,	*into England*
	Engelond al for to winne;	
	And that she that was so fayr,	*[Goldeboru]*
	That was of Engelond rith eir,	*rightful heir*
2540	Was comen up at Grimesbi,	
	He was ful sorful and sori,	
	And seyde, "Hwat shal me to rathe?	*What is advisable for me to do*
	Goddoth, I shal do slon hem bathe!	*have them both slain*
	I shal don hengen hem ful heye	
2545	So mote ich brouke my rith eie,	*enjoy*
	But yif he of mi londe fle.	*Unless; out of*
	Hwat! Wenden he deserite me?"	*Do they want to disinherit*
	He dide sone ferd ut bidde,	*army called out*
	That al that evere mouhte o stede	*might on horse*
2550	Ride or helm on heved bere,	*helmet on head*
	Brini on bac, and sheld and spere,	*Coat of mail on back*
	Or ani other wepne bere,	
	Hand-ax, sythe, gisarm, or spere,	*Battle axe, scythe, halberd*
	Or aunlaz and god long knif,	*dagger*

2555	That als he lovede leme or lif,	*limb*
	That they sholden comen him to,	
	With ful god wepne yboren, so	*weapons; borne*
	To Lincolne, ther he lay,	
	Of Marz the sevententhe day,	*March*
2560	So that he couthe hem god thank;	*could; well*
	And yif that ani were so rank	*headstrong*
	That he thanne ne come anon,	*they*
	He swor bi Crist and by Seint Johan,	
	That he sholde maken him thral,	*slave*
2565	And al his ofspring forth withal.	*forfeit*
	The Englishe that herde that,	
	Was non that evere his bode sat;	*command resisted*
	For he him dredde swithe sore,	*they feared him*
	So runcy spore, and mikle more.	*As the nag [fears] the spur*
2570	At the day he come sone	
	That he hem sette, ful wel o bone,	*well-equipped*
	To Lincolne with gode stedes,	*warhorses*
	And al the wepne that knith ledes.	*weaponry; carries*
	Hwan he wore come, sket was the erl yare	*eager; to hasten*
2575	Ageynes Denshe men to fare,	*Danish; go*
	And seyde, "Lythes nw alle samen!	*Listen now*
	Have ich gadred you for no gamen,	*gathered; play*
	But ich wile seyen you forthi.	*want to*
	Lokes hware here at Grimesbi	
2580	Hise uten laddes here comen,	*foreigners*
	And haves nu the priorie numen —	*captured*
	Al that evere mithen he finde,	
	He brenne kirkes and prestes binde;	*burns churches*
	He strangleth monkes and nunnes bothe —	
2585	Wat wile ye, frend, her-offe rede?	*advise*
	Yif he regne thusgate longe,	*rules*
	He moun us alle overgange,	*may; overcome*
	He moun us alle quic henge or slo,	*hang alive or kill*
	Or thral maken and do ful wo	
2590	Or elles reve us ure lives	*rob us of our*
	And ure children and ure wives.	
	But dos nw als ich wile you lere,	*teach*

	Als ye wile be with me dere.	*Just as; faithful*
	Nimes nu swithe forth and rathe	*set; indeed*
2595	And helpes me and yuself bathe,	*both*
	And slos upo the dogges swithe.	*strike at; forcefully*
	For shal I nevere more be blithe,	
	Ne hoseled ben ne of prest shriven	*confessed; absolved*
	Til that he ben of londe driven.	*off*
2600	Nime we swithe and do hem fle	*Get going; make them flee*
	And folwes alle faste me!	*follow*
	For ich am he of al the ferd	*army*
	That first shal slo with drawen swerd.	
	Datheyt hwo ne stonde faste	*Cursed be any who do not*
2605	Bi me hwil hise armes laste!"	
	"Ye! lef, ye!" quoth the erl Gunter;	*dear one*
	"Ya!" quoth the Erl of Cestre, Reyner.	*Chester*
	And so dide alle that ther stode	
	And stirte forth so he were wode.	*rushed; as if they; mad*
2610	Tho mouthe men se the brinies brihte	*Then*
	On backes keste and lace rithe,	*thrown; straightened*
	The helmes heye on heved sette.	
	To armes al so swithe plette	*hurried*
	That thei wore on a litel stunde	*time*
2615	Grethet als men mithe telle a pund,	*Equipped; count out a pound*
	And lopen on stedes sone anon;	
	And toward Grimesbi, ful god won,	*forcefully*
	He foren softe bi the sti	*went quietly by the road*
	Til he come ney at Grimesbi.	*near to*
2620	Havelok, that havede spired wel	*learned*
	Of here fare, everil del,	*journey*
	With all his ferd cam hem ageyn.	*army; against them*
	Forbar he nother knith ne sweyn:	*Spared*
	The firste knith that he ther mette	
2625	With the swerd so he him grette,	*thus*
	For his heved of he plette —	*head struck off*
	Wolde he nouth for sinne lette.	*delay*
	Roberd saw that dint so hende —	*skillful*
	Wolde he nevere thethen wende,	*from there; go*
2630	Til that he havede another slawen	

<table>
<tr><td></td><td>With the swerd he held ut drawen.</td><td></td></tr>
<tr><td></td><td>Willam Wendut his swerd ut drow,</td><td></td></tr>
<tr><td></td><td>And the thredde so sore he slow</td><td>third</td></tr>
<tr><td></td><td>That he made upon the feld</td><td></td></tr>
<tr><td>2635</td><td>His lift arm fleye with the swerd.</td><td>left</td></tr>
<tr><td></td><td> Huwe Raven ne forgat nouth</td><td></td></tr>
<tr><td></td><td>The swerd he havede thider brouth.</td><td></td></tr>
<tr><td></td><td>He kipte it up, and smot ful sore</td><td>raised</td></tr>
<tr><td></td><td>An erl that he saw priken thore</td><td>spurring [his horse]</td></tr>
<tr><td>2640</td><td>Ful noblelike upon a stede,</td><td></td></tr>
<tr><td></td><td>That with him wolde al quic wede.</td><td>gallop</td></tr>
<tr><td></td><td>He smot him on the heved so</td><td></td></tr>
<tr><td></td><td>That he the heved clef a two.</td><td>split in two</td></tr>
<tr><td></td><td>And that bi the shudre blade</td><td>shoulder</td></tr>
<tr><td>2645</td><td>The sharpe swerd let wade</td><td>pass</td></tr>
<tr><td></td><td>Thoru the brest unto the herte;</td><td></td></tr>
<tr><td></td><td>The dint bigan ful sore to smerte,</td><td>hurt</td></tr>
<tr><td></td><td>That the erl fel dun anon</td><td></td></tr>
<tr><td></td><td>Al so ded so ani ston.</td><td>as dead as</td></tr>
<tr><td>2650</td><td>Quoth Ubbe, “Nu dwelle ich to longe!”</td><td>hesitate</td></tr>
<tr><td></td><td>And let his stede sone gonge</td><td></td></tr>
<tr><td></td><td>To Godrich, with a god spere,</td><td></td></tr>
<tr><td></td><td>That he saw another bere;</td><td></td></tr>
<tr><td></td><td>And smot Godrich and Godrich him,</td><td></td></tr>
<tr><td>2655</td><td>Hetelike with herte grim,</td><td>Bitterly</td></tr>
<tr><td></td><td>So that he bothe felle dune</td><td>they</td></tr>
<tr><td></td><td>To the erthe, first the croune.</td><td>headfirst</td></tr>
<tr><td></td><td>Thanne he woren fallen dun bothen,</td><td>they</td></tr>
<tr><td></td><td>Grundlike here swerdes he ut drowen,</td><td>Violently</td></tr>
<tr><td>2660</td><td>That weren swithe sharp and gode,</td><td></td></tr>
<tr><td></td><td>And fouhten so thei woren wode</td><td></td></tr>
<tr><td></td><td>That the swot ran fro the crune</td><td>sweat</td></tr>
<tr><td></td><td>To the fet right there adune.</td><td></td></tr>
<tr><td></td><td>Ther mouthe men se to knicthes bete</td><td>two knights</td></tr>
<tr><td>2665</td><td>Ayther on other dintes grete,</td><td></td></tr>
<tr><td></td><td>So that with the altherleste dint</td><td>smallest</td></tr>
<tr><td></td><td>Were al to-shivered a flint.</td><td>Would all be smashed to pieces</td></tr>
<tr><td></td><td>So was bitwenen hem a fiht</td><td></td></tr>
</table>

	Fro the morwen ner to the niht,	
2670	So that thei nouth ne blunne	*ceased*
	Til that to sette bigan the sunne.	
	Tho yaf Godrich thorw the side	
	Ubbe a wunde ful unride,	*ugly*
	So that thorw that ilke wounde	*very*
2675	Havede ben brouth to grunde	*[He] would have*
	And his heved al of slawen,	*cut off*
	Yif God ne were and Huwe Raven,	*were not [there]*
	That drow him fro Godrich awey	*pulled*
	And barw him so that ilke day.	*saved; very*
2680	But er he were fro Godrich drawen,	*before*
	Ther were a thousind knihtes slawen	
	Bi bothe halve and mo ynowe,	*sides; plenty more*
	Ther the ferdes togidere slowe,	*armies; clashed*
	Ther was swilk dreping of the folk	*such killing*
2685	That on the feld was nevere a polk	*pool*
	That it ne stod of blod so ful	
	That the strem ran intil the hul.	*into the hollow (i.e., downhill)*
	Tho tarst bigan Godrich to go	*Then first of all*
	Upon the Danshe and faste to slo	
2690	And forthrith, also leun fares	*as a lion goes*
	That nevere kines best ne spares,	*no kind [of] beast*
	Thanne his gon, for he garte alle	*[the lion] is gone; made*
	The Denshe men biforn him falle.	
	He felde browne, he felde blake,	
2695	That he mouthe overtake.	
	Was nevere non that mouhte thave	*survive*
	Hise dintes, noyther knith ne knave,	
	That he felde so dos the gres	*felled them as; grass*
	Biforn the sythe that ful sharp es.	
2700	Hwan Havelok saw his folk so brittene	*broken*
	And his ferd so swithe littene,	*very much reduced*
	He cam drivende upon a stede,	*charging*
	And bigan til him to grede,	*exhort*
	And seyde, "Godrich, wat is thee,	*how is it with you*
2705	That thou fare thus with me	*do*
	And mine gode knihtes slos?	
	Sikerlike, thou misgos!	*Certainly; do wrong*

	Thou wost ful wel, yif thu wilt wite,	*understand*
	That Athelwold thee dide site	*set*
2710	On knes and sweren on messe bok,	*missal*
	On caliz and on pateyn ok,	*chalice; paten also*
	That thou hise douhter sholdest yelde,	*[to] his; yield*
	Than she were wimman of elde,	*When; age*
	Engelond everil del.	*every part*
2715	Godrich the erl, thou wost it wel!	
	Do nu wel withuten fiht	
	Yeld hire the lond, for that is rith.	
	Wile ich forgive thee the lathe,	*your hatred*
	Al mi dede and al mi wrathe,	*dead [companions]; anger*
2720	For I se thu art so with	*strong*
	And of thi bodi so god knith."	
	"That ne wile ich neveremo,"	
	Quoth erl Godrich, "for ich shal slo	
	Thee, and hire forhenge heye.	*hang high*
2725	I shal thrist ut thy rith eye	*thrust out*
	That thou lokes with on me,	
	But thu swithe hethen fle!"	*Unless; quickly from here*
	He grop the swerd ut sone anon,	
	And hew on Havelok ful god won,	*forcefully*
2730	So that he clef his sheld on two.	*broke; in two*
	Hwan Havelok saw that shame do	
	His bodi ther biforn his ferd,	*army*
	He drow ut sone his gode swerd,	
	And smote him so upon the crune	
2735	That Godrich fel to the erthe adune.	
	But Godrich stirt up swithe sket —	*quickly*
	Lay ne nowth longe at hise fet —	
	And smot him on the sholdre so	
	That he dide thare undo	
2740	Of his brinie ringes mo	
	Than that ich kan tellen fro,	*count up*
	And woundede him rith in the flesh,	
	That tendre was and swithe nesh,	*soft*
	So that the blod ran til his to.	*toe*
2745	Tho was Havelok swithe wo,	*distressed*
	That he havede of him drawen	*[Godrich] should have from*

	Blod and so sore him slawen.	*wounded*
	Hertelike til him he wente	*Vehemently to*
	And Godrich ther fulike shente,	*foully injured*
2750	For his swerd he hof up heye,	*raised*
	And the hand he dide of fleye	*fly off*
	That he smot him with so sore —	
	Hw mithe he don him shame more?	
	Hwan he havede him so shamed,	*When*
2755	His hand of plat and ivele lamed,	*cut off; wickedly*
	He tok him sone bi the necke	
	Als a traitour, datheit who recke!	*As*
	And dide him binde and fetere wel	
	With gode feteres al of stel,	
2760	And to the quen he sende him,	
	That birde wel to him ben grim,	*bride ought; angry*
	And bad she sholde don him gete	*have him guarded*
	And that non ne sholde him bete,	*beat*
	Ne shame do, for he was knith,	
2765	Til knithes haveden demd him rith.	*judged; appropriately*
	Than the Englishe men that sawe,	*saw that*
	That thei wisten, heye and lawe,	*knew; high and low*
	That Goldeboru that was so fayr	
	Was of Engelond rith eyr,	*rightful heir*
2770	And that the king hire havede wedded,	
	And haveden been samen bedded,	
	He comen alle to crie "Merci,"	*They*
	Unto the king at one cri,	*in one voice*
	And beden him sone manrede and oth	*offered; homage*
2775	That he ne sholden, for lef ne loth,	*love; hate*
	Neveremore ageyn him go,	
	Ne ride, for wel ne for wo.	*for weal nor for woe*
	The king ne wolde nouth forsake	*neglect*
	That he ne shulde of hem take	*take from them*
2780	Manrede that he beden and ok	*Homage; they offered; also*
	Hold othes sweren on the bok.	*Loyalty oaths*
	But or bad he that thider were brouth	*commanded*
	The quen for hem swilk was his thouth	*them*

For to se and forto shawe, — *observe*
2785 Yif that he hire wolde knawe — — *recognize*
Thoruth hem witen wolde he — *understand*
Yif that she aucte quen to be. — *ought*

Sixe erles weren sone yare — *eager*
After hire for to fare. — *go*
2790 He nomen onon and comen sone, — *set out immediately*
And brouthen hire, that under mone
In al the werd ne havede per — *peer*
Of hendeleik, fer ne ner. — *courtesy, far or near*
Hwan she was come thider, alle
2795 The Englishe men bigunne falle
O knes, and greten swithe sore, — *on*
And seyden, "Levedi, Kristes ore — *mercy*
And youres! We haven misdo mikel — *done much wrong*
That we ayen you have be fikel, — *against you have been disloyal*
2800 For Englond auhte for to ben — *ought to be*
Youres and we youre men.
Is non of us, yung ne old,
That he ne wot that Athelwold — *Who does not know*
Was king of this kunerike — *kingdom*
2805 And ye his eyr, and that the swike — *traitor*
Haves it halden with mikel wronge — — *held*
God leve him sone to honge!" — *grant; hang*

Quot Havelok, "Hwan that ye it wite, — *Since; understand*
Nu wile ich that ye doune site;
2810 And after Godrich haves wrouht, — *according as; done*
That haves in sorwe himself brouth,
Lokes that ye demen him rith, — *Make sure; judge*
For dom ne spareth clerk ne knith, — *judgment*
And sithen shal ich understonde
2815 Of you, after lawe of londe,
Manrede and holde othes bothe, — *Homage; loyalty oaths*
Yif ye it wilen and ek rothe." — *counsel*
Anon ther dune he hem sette,
For non the dom ne durste lette — *no one; dared prevent*
2820 And demden him to binden faste — *judged*

Upon an asse swithe unwraste, *filthy*
Andelong, nouht overthwert, *Endwise; across*
His nose went unto the stert *turned; tail*
And so to Lincolne lede,
2825 Shamelike in wicke wede, *Shamefully in wretched clothes*
And, hwan he come unto the borw,
Shamelike ben led ther thoru,
Bi southe the borw unto a grene, *south of*
That thare is yet, als I wene, *still; think*
2830 And there be bunden til a stake,
Abouten him ful gret fir make,
And al to dust be brend rith there. *ashes; burned*
And yet demden he ther more,
Other swikes for to warne: *traitors*
2835 That hise children sulde tharne *should lose*
Everemore that eritage *heritage*
That his was, for hise utrage. *crime (outrage)*

Hwan the dom was demd and seyd, *judgment*
Sket was the swike on the asse leyd,
2840 And led him til that ilke grene *to; very*
And brend til asken al bidene. *ashes; right away*
Tho was Goldeboru ful blithe — *then*
She thanked God fele sythe *many times*
That the fule swike was brend *burned*
2845 That wende wel hire bodi have shend; *intended; shamed*
And seyde, "Nu is time to take
Manrede of brune and of blake, *brown*
That ich se ride and go, *Whom; walk*
Nu ich am wreke of mi fo." *avenged upon*

2850 Havelok anon manrede tok
Of alle Englishe on the bok
And dide hem grete othes swere
That he sholden him god feyth bere
Ageyn hem alle that woren lives
2855 And that sholde ben born of wives. *women*

	Thanne he haveden sikernesse	*surety*
	Taken of more and of lesse,	*from high and low (socially)*
	Al at hise wille, so dide he calle	
	The Erl of Cestre and hise men alle,	*Chester*
2860	That was yung knith withuten wif,	*Who*
	And seyde, "Sire erl, bi mi lif,	
	And thou wile mi conseyl tro,	*If; trust*
	Ful wel shal ich with thee do;	*deal*
	For ich shal yeve thee to wive	
2865	The fairest thing that is o live.	*alive*
	That is Gunnild of Grimesby,	
	Grimes douther, bi Seint Davy,	*Grim's daughter*
	That me forth broute and wel fedde,	*brought up*
	And ut of Denemark with me fledde	
2870	Me for to burwe fro mi ded.	*rescue; from; death*
	Sikerlike, thoru his red,	*advice*
	Have ich lived into this day —	
	Blissed worthe his soule ay!	*Blessed be; always*
	I rede that thu hire take	*command*
2875	And spuse and curteyse make,	*espouse*
	For she is fayr and she is fre,	*noble*
	And al so hende so she may be.	*as gracious as*
	Ther tekene, she is wel with me;	*Moreover*
	That shal ich ful wel shewe thee.	
2880	For ich wile give thee a give	*promise*
	That everemore, hwil ich live,	
	For hire shaltu be with me dere,	*Because of; you shall*
	That wile ich that this folc al here."	
	The erl ne wolde nouth ageyn	
2885	The king be, for knith ne sweyn	
	Ne of the spusing seyen nay,	*marriage*
	But spusede that ilke day.	*same*
	That spusinge was in god time maked,	
	For it ne were nevere, clad ne naked,	
2890	In a thede samened two	*land united*
	That cam togidere, livede so	
	So they diden al here live:	*their lives*
	He geten samen sones five,	*They produced*
	That were the beste men at nede	

2895 That mouthe riden on ani stede.
Hwan Gunnild was to Cestre brouth,
Havelok the gode ne forgat nouth
Bertram, that was the erles kok, — *earl's cook*
That he ne dide callen ok, — *also*
2900 And seyde, "Frend, so God me rede,
Nu shaltu have riche mede, — *reward*
For wissing and thi gode dede — *guidance*
That tu me dides in ful gret nede.
For thanne I yede in mi cuvel — *cloak*
2905 And ich ne havede bred ne sowel. — *sauce*
Ne I ne havede no catel,
Thou feddes and claddes me ful wel. — *clothes*
Have nu forthi of Cornwayle — *for that reason*
The erldom ilk del, withuten fayle,
2910 And al the lond that Godrich held,
Bothe in towne and ek in feld;
And ther-to wile ich that thu spuse, — *marry*
And fayre bring hire until huse, — *happily; to*
Grimes douther, Levive the hende, — *gracious*
2915 For thider shal she with thee wende. — *go*
Hire semes curteys for to be,
For she is fayr so flour on tre;
The hew is swilk in hire ler — *hue; face*
So the rose in roser, — *As; rose bush*
2920 Hwan it is fayre sprad ut newe, — *blossomed*
Ageyn the sunne brith and lewe." — *fresh*
And girde him sone with the swerd
Of the erldom, biforn his ferd,
And with his hond he made him knith,
2925 And yaf him armes, for that was rith,
And dide him there sone wedde
Hire that was ful swete in bedde.

After that he spused wore, — *were married*
Wolde the Erl nouth dwelle thore, — *linger*
2930 But sone nam until his lond — *went to*
And seysed it al in his hond — *received*
And livede ther inne, he and his wif,

	An hundred winter in god lif,	
	And gaten mani children samen	*produced*
2935	And liveden ay in blisse and gamen.	*forever; happiness*
	Hwan the maidens were spused bothe,	
	Havelok anon bigan ful rathe	
	His Denshe men to feste wel	*endow*
	Wit riche landes and catel,	*property*
2940	So that he weren alle riche,	
	For he was large and nouth chiche.	*generous; stingy*
	Ther after sone, with his here,	*army*
	For he to Lundone for to bere	*traveled; wear*
	Corune, so that it sawe	*Crown*
2945	Henglishe ant Denshe, heye and lowe,	*and*
	Hwou he it bar with mikel pride,	*How*
	For his barnage that was unride.	*baronry; prolific*
	The feste of his coruning	*at his coronation*
	Lastede with gret joying	
2950	Fourti dawes and sumdel mo.	
	Tho bigunnen the Denshe to go	*Then; Danes*
	Unto the king to aske leve;	*permission to leave*
	And he ne wolde hem nouth greve,	
	For he saw that he woren yare	*were eager*
2955	Into Denemark for to fare;	*travel*
	But gaf hem leve sone anon	
	And bitauhte hem Seint Johan,	*entrusted*
	And bad Ubbe, his justise,	*magistrate*
	That he sholde on ilke wise	*in every way*
2960	Denemark yeme and gete so	*rule; good*
	That no pleynte come him to.	*complaint*
	Hwan he wore parted alle samen,	*they set out*
	Havelok bilefte wit joye and gamen	*stayed behind with*
	In Engelond and was ther-inne	
2965	Sixti winter king with winne,	*joy*
	And Goldeboru Quen, that I wene	
	So mikel love was hem bitwene	
	That al the werd spak of hem two;	*world*

	He lovede hir and she him so	
2970	That neyther owe mithe be	*anywhere*
	Fro other, ne no joye se	*away from*
	But if he were togidere bothe.	*Unless; they*
	Nevere yete no weren he wrothe	*angry at each other*
	For here love was ay newe —	*their; always*
2975	Nevere yete wordes ne grewe	*anger*
	Bitwene hem hwar of ne lathe	*hostile*
	Mithe rise ne no wrathe.	*arise*
	He geten children hem bitwene	
	Sones and doughtres rith fivetene,	*precisely fifteen*
2980	Hwar-of the sones were kinges alle,	*Of whom*
	So wolde God it sholde bifalle,	
	And the douhtres alle quenes:	
	Him stondes wel that god child strenes!	*begets*
	Nu have ye herd the gest al thoru	*story; completely*
2985	Of Havelok and of Goldeboru —	
	Hw he weren boren and hw fedde,	*How they*
	And hwou he woren with wronge ledde	*wrongly*
	In here youthe with trecherie,	
	With tresoun, and with felounye;	*evil*
2990	And hwou the swikes haveden tiht	*traitors; intended*
	Reven hem that was here rith,	*To rob them*
	And hwou he weren wreken wel,	
	Have ich seyd you everil del.	
	Forthi ich wolde biseken you	*Therefore; beseech*
2995	That haven herd the rim nu,	*rhyme now*
	That ilke of you, with gode wille,	
	Saye a Pater Noster stille	*quietly*
	For him that haveth the rym maked,	*rhyme*
	And ther-fore fele nihtes waked,	*kept awake*
3000	That Jesu Crist his soule bringe	*So that*
	Biforn his Fader at his endinge.	*Before; father*

Amen

Notes

We have used the Laud MS (L) as base text, with occasional reference to the fragments found in C. *Abbreviations*: C: Cambridge Add. 4407; L: MS Laud 108; F&H: French and Hale; Ho: Holthausen; Ma: Madden; Sa: Sands; Si: Sisam; Sk: Skeat; Sm: Smithers

1–26 As in the other Middle English romances in this volume, *Havelok* begins with a formal exhortation to its audience. The convention, according to Sm derives from Old French epics and romances and consists of four parts: an exhortation to listen, a statement of subject, praise of the hero, and a prayer. Sa, on the other hand, links the poem to its cultural milieu: "Its Latin subtitle *Incipit vita Hauelok quondam rex anglie et denemarchie* must have matched some sort of popular realization that Englishmen of the North were in blood half-Scandinavian and that they just before the Conquest had actually been part of a dual kingdom of England and Denmark" (p. 55).

20 *Benedicamus Domino*. "Let us bless the Lord." This is a verse in the Mass not often used in literature. The only other literary example known to Sm occurs in Philippe de Thaün's *Bestaire*, in which a pearl is a symbol of Christ.

27–86 Sm notes these lines as an extensive example of a traditional eulogy of kings such as William the Conqueror and Henry I found in the *Anglo-Saxon Chronicle*.

28 *That* refers to the king; thus, construe lines 27–30 as "It was a king in former days who in his time made good laws and upheld them; young people loved him, old people loved him." Note the inverted sentence structure that emphasizes the object "him" twice by giving it syntactical priority.

31 *Dreng* and *thayn* are synonyms for a king's vassals, though connotations may be distinct in other contexts, as Sa suggests when he defines a *dreng* in Northumbria at this time as "a tenant with military obligations" (p. 59).

46 *Wel fifty pund, I wot, or more*. This line is supplied by Ma and F&H. It does not appear in Sm. Ma conjectures this line and indicates that other such liberties have been taken in his edition, many of which Sk follows.

48 *In a male with or blac*. F&H read *with* as *hwit* and translate the term as *white*; the reversal of letters appears in other words, but is not consistent throughout the MS. F&H read the prolific *h's* as "mannerisms in spelling," but it is more likely that the *h's* signify aspiration and point to pronunciation for this dialect. F&H reckon the dialect to be North Midlands with strong Norse influence. Referring to the pouch as "with or black" could mean "white or off-white (pale)," which is a common meaning in ME for "blāc." See MED *blak* n. 6. See also note to line 311.

64 *Was non so bold louerd to Rome*. L: *non so bold lond to rome*. Sm emends *lond* to *louerd* for the sake of sense. Sk emends to: *Was non so bold [þe] lond to rome*, which makes sense too.

65 *upon his bringhe*. L: *upon his bringhe*. Sm emends to *upon his londe bringhe* ostensibly to connect the king's political expertise more definitively to his realm as well as to regularize the meter. Sk reads: *That durste upon his [menie] bringe*.

66 *Hunger ne here*. As noted by Sm, *hunger ne here* is an Old English alliterative phrase used three times by Wulfstan, an Old English writer of homilies.

69 *The*. L: *Þe*. F&H: *Þei*. "They hid themselves and kept themselves still."

74 *his soule hold*. Sm notes this as an unusual expression which occurs in *Ywain and Gawain* (line 887) where it refers to the widow's concern for the soul of her dead husband: *Upon his sawl was sho ful helde*. Athelwold's loyalty to his own soul is not narcissistic, but virtuous.

79 The source for the passage is Psalm 146:9: "The Lord preserveth the stranger; he relieveth the fatherless and widow, but the way of the wicked he turneth upside down."

85 *Bute it were bi hire wille*. This distinguishes rape, which is punishable by medieval English law, from consensual sexual relations, though the issue is complicated in jurisprudence. The most complete articulation of rape laws is found in the Statutes of Westminster in the thirteenth century. Over time secular legislation conflated rape with abduction, shifting it from a crime done to a woman's body to a crime done against the peace of the king.

86 As F&H note "even up to the time of the Commonwealth, mutilation was a legal punishment; it was occasionally forbidden, but continued to be practiced" (p. 77).

Public punishment such as flogging, drawing and quartering, and various forms of mutilation often depicted graphically by romancers were thought to be a deterrent to crime in real life.

87–90 Sm notes the recurrence of these four lines in the account of King Arthur in the *Anonymous Short English Metrical Chronicle of England*. He surmises that *Havelok* was the source for the chronicle repetition and not vice versa.

89 *folc ut lede*. The sense of *folc* is "army."

92 *And lete him knawe of hise hand dede*. L: *And lete him of hise hand dede*. Sm notes that this is the "sole example" of the use of *hand-dede* in post-Conquest English. A relatively ancient word, it implied "violence" and sometimes "criminal violence," or could mean "the actual perpetrator of a crime" and in Middle Dutch "one who perpetrates a criminal or violent act." In *Havelok* the "imputation is of violence" (p. 86). Both Sm and Sk add a verb to this line after *him*, but disagree on what it should be. Sk, followed by F&H and Sa, adds *knawe*, as do we; Sm adds *shewe*.

94 To the victor belong the spoils. The victorious army carried off plunder, particularly valuable horses and armor. As F&H note, "the practice was deplored by moralists as unchristian, but is a matter of course in the romances" (p. 78).

109 *held*. L: *hel*. The emendation is universal.

115 *wel wiste*. L: *we wiste*. The emendation maintains the gravity of Athelwold's perception. The ending consonant is frequently omitted for *wel* in the MS.

120 *Hw shal now my douhter fare*. L: *W shal nou mi douhter fare*. F&H add the consonant presumably to clarify the question.

135 *Therafter stronglike quaked*. F&H note the frequency with which the poet or scribe omits pronouns. They supply them in their edition as does Sk and Ho; Sm frequently does not. Sa regularizes as much as possible.

137 On the dying of a king F&H write: "When a king was dying, the great nobles hastened to the capital, either out of sympathy or a wish to maintain order and look after their interests in arranging for a successor. The romancers made a conventional scene of this" (p. 79). It is important to note that King Athelwold has no male heir to maintain the peace he has established.

139 Roxburgh, a fort on the Scottish border, was often contested by opposing armies and changed hands frequently. Dover, on the southeast coast of England, is famous for its "white cliffs." Traveling from Roxburgh to Dover would mean traversing the whole length of England. See also line 265.

142 *ther he lay.* L: *þe he lay.* Sm and F&H supply the missing consonant. The omission of consonants in various words is a frequent occurrence throughout the MS and unrelated to the common practice of abbreviation.

154 *That He wolde turnen him.* L: *Þat he turned him.* The subjunctive verb — *wolde* — is supplied by all editors.

158 Winchester was the Anglo-Saxon capital of England before the center of government was relocated in London. Important legislation in the poem, however, is enacted in Lincoln, the probable home of the poet.

160 *thank kan I you.* L: *þank kan you.* This is an example of the omission of pronouns by the poet and/or scribe.

174 *that she be wman of helde.* L: *þat she wman of helde.*

175 *And that she mowe hir yemen.* L: *And þa she mowe yemen.* Sk's emendation. F&H emend to: *And tha[t] she mowe [hit] yemen*, followed by Sa. Sm conjectures that the author wrote something like: *and þat she mowe hir-selwe welde.*

177 *Bi Crist and bi Seint Jon.* L: *Bi Crist and bi seint Jon.* Sm: *Bi Jesu Crist and bi seint Johan.* We have followed F&H here by returning to the MS reading.

185 *A wol fair cloth.* L: *A wol fair cloþ.* F&H: *A wel fair cloth.* Sm: *A wol fair cloth.* Sa: *a well fair cloth*; Sk: *a wel fair cloth*; Ho: *a wel fair cloth.* Though a majority of editors read the adjective to describe the beauty of the cloth, it could also modify wool as the cloth's base fabric. Also, there is a distinct rendering of *th* for the *þ* in L.

188 F&H gloss *corporaus* as fine linen cloth. We have placed emphasis on its purpose rather than its fabric by glossing the term as *communion cloth.*

187–88 The missal contains the order of service used in the mass, the principal Christian liturgical rite; the chalice contains the wine used in communion; and the paten holds the bread wafer, called the "Host" (from Latin *hostia*, "victim"). After the bread and wine are consecrated, they are placed on a white linen cloth, the "corporal." All of this "messe-gere" is holy by virtue of its use in the sacred re-enactment of Christ's death that is the Eucharist. Hence, swearing an oath by these instruments is a serious matter.

195 *Gon and speken*. L: *Gon and speken*. F&H: *Don and speken*. Ho: *Gon and speken*; Sk: *Don and speken*; Sm and Ho agree with the MS reading as do we.

199 *beste man*. L: *beste man*; Sk: *hexte man*; F&H: *hexte*; Sm: *heste*.

213–17 Self-flagellation was thought to be an appropriate penance in general, though there is some dispute about whether it was more often a feature of dramatic representation than a realistic feature of life. Frederick Paxon, who charts the development of bedside rites for the dying in *Christianizing Death: The Creation of a Ritual in Process in Early Medieval Europe* (Ithaca: Cornell University Press, 1990), concludes that the earlier focus on the fate of the dying person's soul was replaced with a Germanic/Celtic concern with the needs of the dying person. However, according to the medieval chronicler William of Malmesbury, Henry I confessed, beat his breast, was absolved three times, and received unction before he died.

221–22 *So mikel men micte him in winde, / Of his in arke ne in chiste*. "So much [as a shroud] to wind him in among his possessions, neither in trunk nor chest," since he had already given away so much in his will.

226 *ofte swngen*. L: *ofte swngen*. Ho: *ofte swngen*; Sk: *ofte swungen*; Sm: *ofte swungen*.

228 *Louerde*. L: *Loude*. Preceded by *in manus tuas*, this is a partial quotation of Jesus at the point of death (Luke 23:46): "Into thy hands [I commend my spirit]."

239 The "bower" and "hall" were two fundamental units of a castle or noble dwelling that persisted in some form throughout the Middle Ages. The hall was an open, public space used for dining, entertaining, or convening of nobles; the bower was a relatively more secluded area used for sleeping. The bower, it should be noted, was not necessarily a more private place. Yet the association of bower with ladies and hall with knights is appropriate; while one could find either sex in either place, the bower is associated more with the more intimate love of women, the hall with the masculine world of celebrating achievements and swearing loyalties to comrades.

Compare with *Beowulf*, where the king and queen retire to the burgh while Beowulf and the retainers sleep on and around the same benches where they have feasted.

245 F&H note the subject shift from God to Athelwold's soul in this line. The effect glorifies the king in that God himself should lead his soul into heaven. The attention to the king's soul in line 74 is underscored here.

256 *that god thoucte*. L: *þat god thoucte*. F&H: *þat god him thoucte*.

263 F&H note the use of itinerant justices in Saxon times: "They seem not to have held permanent commission, but to have been appointed in emergencies. Their function was to mitigate the injustice of local courts, which might be dominated by powerful nobles" (p. 84).

265 Sm comments on the significance of the road from Dover to Roxburgh: "The mention of Dover and Roxburgh as marking the extreme limits of England, as in [line] 139, is here in a context of peace-keeping and the king's peace. This is why the AN [Anglo-Norman] *Le Petit Bruit* names a road from *en long de Rokesburg jekis a Dover* as one of *les quatre royales chemyn parmy Engleterre* — the four royal roads were under the king's peace. . ." (p. 99).

266 *Schireves he sette, bedels, and greyves* (Sheriffs, beadles, and reeves). The sheriff, or "shire-reeve," enforced law and order in the shire (county); the beadle was a sort of church police officer; and the grave or "greyve," according to the OED, was a steward placed in charge of property, a reeve. In certain parts of Yorkshire and Lincolnshire, each of a number of administrative officials formerly elected by the inhabitants of a township served this function for a town.

269 Outside the walled cities, protection was difficult and travel hazardous because of marauding thieves. Establishing peace in a violent environment is thus an extraordinary achievement.

282 *Of alle thewes was she wiṣ*. L: *Of alle þewes wshe wis*.

285 The sense here is prophetic, i.e., that many a tear would be wept for Goldeboru's sake.

286 *Quanne the Erl Godrich him herde* (When the Earl Godric heard). "Him" is a reflexive pronoun that would normally be dropped in modern English.

287 *hw wel she ferde*. L: *hw we she ferde.*

288 *hw chaste*. L: *w chaste.*

292 *Wether* (whether) functions as an interrogative particle, which signals that a question is coming.

296 *Datheit* (Curses) is said to be a contraction for *odium Dei habit.*

305 Note the recurrence of the verb *yeme* here. In lines 190 and 206, the dying Athelwold made Godrich promise to "yeme" her "well"; by saying that he has "yemed" her "too softe," Godrich creates perhaps an unconscious double meaning. He is obviously saying (and in his state of jealousy and malice he would naturally mean), "She has grown up to be too pampered," but of course he is to blame because it is he who has not followed the king's dying wish that he guard her "wel."

311 This is perhaps another way of saying, "As long as I have a head on my shoulders." Note that "blake" here probably means "white" (compare French *blanc* or more likely *OE blac* meaning "pale"). See lines 48 and 2165 for a possibly similar usage.

317 Contrast this sort of fasting with King Arthur's refusal to sit down and feast until he had seen some marvel in *Sir Gawain and the Green Knight.*

322 There may be a pun on *fede*, which as a noun can mean "hostility." In its verbal form, to "feed" or "keep," it has a range of meanings both positive and negative. Godrich is probably not interested in comforting or nurturing Goldeboru. Rather, he misconstrues his duties to protect those who cannot protect themselves and holds her captive instead.

328 *Of Goldeboru*. L: *Of Goldeb.*

334 *sho mote*. L: *sho mo.*

352 *He* refers to *deth* in line 354.

353 *kaysere*. A Germanic form of the Latin *caesar.*

354 *Deth him tok than he best wolde*. L: *Deth him tok than he bes wolde.*

360 *Chanounes gode and monkes bothe.* A canon might be a priest of a cathedral church or a member of a particular religious community.

360–61 Sm prefers to maintain the end rhyme in this couplet: *Chanounes gode and monkes baþe / Him for to wisse and to raþe.* To do that he has emended *boþe* to *baþe* and *rede* to *raþe*. There are other such emendations. See lines 693–94 and 1680–81. Sk: *bethe / rede*; Ho: *bothe / rothe.* We follow F&H in retaining the MS reading *bothe / rede.*

373 *under mone.* In other words, "in the whole world." Medieval writers often distinguished between events below and above the moon, as everything beneath the moon's sway was thought to be subject to Fortune.

392 *shalt wel yeme.* L: *shalt we yeme.*

393 *That hire kin be ful wel queme.* The reading here depends on whether the third word in the line should read "kin" ("their relations will indeed be pleased") or is actually a scribal error for "kind" ("type," "nature," "rank"). Sa suggests "that it indeed quite befits their rank" (p. 68).

410 *Havelok, that was the eir.* L: *Havelok that was the eir.* F&H follow Ho's emendation here: *Havelok, that was the brother*, presumably to preserve the end rhyme.

425 For writers of the Middle Ages, Judas, the arch traitor of Christ in the Gospels, was the archetype of treachery and betrayal. Both Godard and Godrich are called by this arch traitor's name, though Godard is called Satan in line 2512. See line 319.

436 *made mone.* L: *maude mone*; Sm: *maude mone*; F&H: *made mone*; Sk: *made mone*; Ho: *made mone.*

456 *Seyden he, "we wolden more.* L: *Seyden he wolden more.* Sm: *Seyden he he wolden more.* F&H: *Seyden hi, we wolden more*; Ho: *Seyden thei withuten more;* Sk: *Seyden he wolden have more.*

476 *Havelok it saw and therbi stod.* L: *Havelok it saw and þe bi stod.*

481 *But the knave.* L: *But þe kave.*

484 Note the pathetic and very ironic scene here: the boy, to save his life, offers feudal homage (*manrede*) to a lord whose last thought is to protect the child.

489 *Ayen thee, louerd, sheld ne spere.* L: *Ayen þe, louerd, shel ne spere.*

496 *Hwan the devel herde that.* L: *Hwan þe devel hede þat.*

502 *witdrow.* L: *þitdrow.* F&H: *witdrow.* Sm: *þit-drow.* Ho: *þith-drow.* Sk: *wit-drow.* Ma: *þit-drow.*

503 *Avelok.* This is the French name to which Havelok is etymologically linked according to Sa. It equates with *OE Anlaf*, a Scandinavian form of Olaf. Sa suggests a historical connection to Olaf Sictricson (p. 57).

512 *He may me waiten.* L: *He may waiten.*

520 *drench.* L: *drench.* Sm: *drenth.* F&H: *drenched.* Ho: *drenched.* Sk: *drenched.* We have returned to the MS reading.

534 *thou sest.* L: *þou se.*

536 *Al wile I taken.* L: *Al wile taken.*

546 The line following this numbered line — *He thriste in his muth wel faste* — is supplied by C and not counted in the line numbering. Sa, Sm, and F&H add the line without counting it. Sk and Ho omit the line altogether.

552 *he yede.* Sm emends to *heþede.* "In the sentence as it stands, a past participle is required; and the final *-e* of *hethede* (if this word is one) is presumably an error. But a rhyme on the unstressed ending of the past participle would be unparalleled in *Hav*" (p. 105).

553 *forth lede.* L: *forth.* F&H: *forth lede.* Sk: *forth lede.* Ho: *forth lede.* Sm: *forth lede.*

558 *Ant bar him.* L: *Ant bar him.* Sk: *And bar him.* Ho: *And bar him.* F&H: *Ant bar him.*

561 *Al so thou wit mi lif save.* L: *Also þou wit my lif have.* Sm: *Also þou wilt mi lif have save.* Ho: *Also þou wilth mi lif save.*

564 *Ynow* means literally "enough," but this typical Middle English stock phrase often understates the situation.

566 *Hwan Dame Leve herde that.* L: *Hwan dame herde þat.* The inclusion of Grim's wife's name adds another foot to the meter and renders her identity clear.

583 *wost that hoves me.* L: *wost þat hoves me.* F&H and Sm: *wost þat bi hoves me.* Ho: *wost that it bi hoveth me.* Sk: *wost that so bihoves me.*

594–95 *Al so lith was it therinne / So ther brenden cerges inne.* "It was as light in there as if candles were burning there." *Al so / so* are correlatives that connect or compare two statements.

601 *For man shal god wille have.* F&H suggest a meaning for this line: "People are naturally kind" (p. 97).

605 *kynmerk.* A king's birthmark attests to royal birth. Sm notes only one other example of the word (slightly modified) in the ME *Emaré*, lines 503–04: "A fayr chyld borne and a godele; / Hadde a dowbyll kyngus marke."

611 *Al Denemark and Engeland.* Grim's prophesy is fulfilled by the poem's end not only by Havelok's reappropriation of his homeland and his victory over Godrich and marriage to Goldeboru, but also by the marriages of Grim's daughters to Englishmen of noble rank.

621 *cherles* often means "villeins," non-free peasants bound to work the land, donating a portion of their produce and labor to the lord of the manor. Because the basic definition of "cherle" is a person from the lowest orders of society, the word is often used as an insult (e.g., line 683), or here, as a label of self-abasement.

645–46 *Pastees* (pasties) are meat pies; *flaunes*, custard, or cheese pies. These are dishes that were an integral part of a professional cook's repertoire. Terence Scully explains in *The Art of Cookery in the Middle Ages* (Woodbridge: Boydell Press, 1995): "What the professional cook dealt with from day to day in the thirteen and fourteen hundreds were menus consisting of well-rounded meals of soups, stews, pies, torts, flans, biscuits, roasts, sauces, jellies and 'desserts'" (p. 3).

667 *That was of Denemark a stiward.* L: *Þat was Denemk a stiward.* The preposition *in* is inserted by F&H. Sk, Ho, and Sm prefer *of.*

675 *Yif me gold and other fe.* L: *Yif me gold other fe.*

677 Villeins (peasants) could be released by their lords and become equals of freeborn men in the eyes of the law.

686 *Shaltu have non other mede.* L: *Shal have non other mede.* F&H: *Shaltu have.* Sk: *Shaltu have.* Ho: *Shaltu have.*

691 *hethen.* L: *ethen.* F&H's emendation.

693 *that wicke man.* L: *þa wicke man.* F&H and Sm emend to provide distinction for the demonstrative adjective.

694–95 *shal me to rede . . . he wile bethe.* The end rhyme in this couplet has been emended by Sm as follows: *And þoucte, wat shal me to raþe / Wite him on live he wile us baþe.* F&H follow L, supplying *[us]* before *beþe.* We have returned to the MS despite the loss of rhyme.

702 *Hors and swin, geet with berd.* L: *Hors and swin with berd.* F&H and Sm add "goats," presumably because neither swine nor horses have beards.

709 Sa suggests the reading "'So that it [should] fear neither sound nor inlet;' *sond* can also be 'sand' with the extended meaning 'shoal water;' but 'sound' seems more appropriate and is quite possible orthographically" (p. 76). F&H translate *sond* and *krike* as bodies of water. Since Grim has just finished placing pitch in the seams of his boat, it is likely that this line refers to the craft's water worthiness. It is sound because it does not creak or leak, for that matter.

723 *Ne were it nevere.* L: *Ne were neuere.*

725 "Bise" appears in Old French works as a common word for the North Wind (see, e.g., *Pelerinage de Charlemagne*, line 354). According to the MED, *Havelok* is the only Middle English romance in which this term appears.

732 *Als ye shulen now forthward lere.* L: *Als ye shulen now forthwar here.* Skeat's emendation.

734–35 The Humber River, now the center of the modern county of Humberside, divides what is considered northern England (Yorkshire and northward to the Scottish border) from the English midlands (Lincolnshire south to London). Lindsay is still a division of the county of Lincoln.

745 The place took its name from Grim (i.e., the present port of Grimsby in Humberside). This line reflects a popular local legend of a fisherman by the name of Grim who founded a town that bears his name. Reputedly the legendary Grim, like the Grim of the poem, befriended an exiled prince. Sm's edition depicts a twelfth-century town seal with three names and figures inscribed on it — Grym, Habloc, and Goldeboru. Robert Mannyng of Brunne tells of a stone that was allegedly thrown by Havelok against his enemies and indicates the chapel where he and Goldeboru were married (p. 78). For an interesting interpretation of Grim, see Maldwyn Mills, "Havelok and the Brutal Fisherman."

754–60 For an interesting interpretation of the catalogue of fish see Roy Michael Liuzza, "Representation and Readership in the ME *Havelok*." Liuzza sees the emphasis on fish as "part of a system of exchange in which money rather than chivalric honor is the source of value" (p. 510). Such exchange systems lend *Havelok* a realism that few romances of the time can claim.

765 *Forbar he neyther tun.* L: *Forbar he neyþe tun.*

772 A lamprey is an eel-like fish with a mouth like a sucker, pouch-like gills, seven spiracles or apertures on each side of the head, and a fistula or opening on the top of the head (OED). F&H's note on the lamprey is interesting in relation to this rather unappetizing description: "A 'great' lamprey weighed as much as five pounds, and sold for three shillings. . . . It was highly prized as a delicacy. Henry I is said to have brought on a fatal illness by partaking too freely of lamprey" (p. 104). His cooks must have prepared the lamprey properly, i.e., soaked it to its death in wine before cooking, then serving it in a gelatinous galantine sauce.

773 *Ful wel.* L: *Ful we.*

776 *wol wel sold.* L: *wol wel sold.* F&H: *al wel sold.* Sm: *wol wel sold.* Grim seems to be selling wool without mention of his keeping sheep, the reason perhaps that F&H emend *wol* to *al*. Sheep are mentioned in line 782, however.

785 *In the se weren he ofte setes.* L: *In the se weren he offte setes.* F&H: *Þat in the se he ofte setes.* Sm: *In the se-weres he ofte setes.* Kevin Gosling in "Sewere in *Havelok* 784," *Notes and Queries* 34 (1987), 151, suggests that this is a compound based on

an ON borrowing in the poet's Lincolnshire dialect. ON *ver* means "station for taking eggs, fishing, catching seals, etc." *Sewere* would then mean "inshore fishing ground." The MS, however, clearly depicts an abbreviation mark above the final *-e* in *sewerē* (*se weren*) rendering verbal force to the suffix. Sm fills in the abbreviation with *s*. We have emended.

791–811 Havelok's insatiable appetite reflects his regal deprivation. Only when he comes fully into his royal estate can his nature be satisfied. His vast appetite becomes a comic send up on his political displacement rather than a sign of gluttony or avarice. In his effort to win his own bread he becomes a lord at all degrees. See also lines 828 ff.; 911–26; and, in the conclusion, line 2986, where his having been fed is deemed a key component of his biographical summary. See note to line 1726.

807 *woth*. Sk emends to *wot*.

819 *ilk del*. L: *il del*. F&H's emendation.

821 *ferthinges nok*. A farthing from medieval to quite modern times was worth a quarter of a penny. A "corner" of a farthing would be a very little bit; the idiom reflects the illegal practice of clipping off bits of coins for the silver, which might, when collected, be sold as bullion.

850 *nouth a slo*. An expression referring to a sloeberry, a fruit of a blackthorn tree used as a metaphor for "something of little value," an "insignificant amount," or to mean "not at all," to "care nothing for."

858 *sheres*. L: *shres*.

861 *Havede he neyther*. L: *Havede neþer*.

862 *other wede*. L: *oþe wede*.

864 *he cam ther*. L: *he cam þe*.

870 *Poure that on fote yede*. This line, supplied by Sk, repeats line 101 and fills in the rhyme scheme.

875 *Ther the erles mete he tok*. This line is supplied by Ma and Sk. Both F&H and Sm agree.

882 *on the brigge*. L: *on þe bigge*.

897 Plaice is a type of European flatfish, often preferred over other species such as salmon, mackerel, and turbot. It is still quite a popular dish in the British Isles.

903 Presumably, Havelok was carrying the load on his head.

908 *Wel is set the mete thu etes*. Echoes the proverb in line 1693: *wel is him that god man fedes*. Here the earl's cook sees an opportunity he cannot refuse.

911 Havelok, as orphaned king's son and kitchen knave, has been referred to as a "male Cinderella." He joins the ranks of a long tradition of male Cinderellas and their stories including a number of Arthurian knights and Horn. See Donald G. Hoffman, "Malory's Cinderella Knights and the Notion of Adventure," *Philological Quarterly* 67 (1988), 145–56. For gender politics in these tales, see Eve Salisbury, "(Re)dressing Cinderella," in *Retelling Tales*, ed. Alan Lupack and Thomas G. Hahn (Rochester: D. S. Brewer, 1997), 275–92. Kitchen drudgery prepares the hero for his future role as king. Analogous to Cinderella's shoe, Havelok's "kynmerk" is a hidden sign of nobility, both of character and of class.

934 *filde ther*. L: *filde þe*.

937 *Al him one*. L: *A him one*.

939 *Ne fro brigge*. L: *Ne fro bigge*.

940 The *turves* were pieces of turf or peat moss cut from the ground and stacked to dry, then used as fuel. Star grass, a name given locally to various coarse seaside grasses and sedges, according to the OED, was used for kindling.

952 *ne wolde with*. L: *ne wode with*. The emendation makes an important distinction between an intransitive subjunctive verb and a noun connoting madness.

961 *mikel*. L: *mike*.

965 *unride*. See Sk's extended discussion of the term as indicative of a large, cumbersome or rough garment; of the body, a deep, wide wound; of metal, something great; of politics, something unwieldy; of sound, something loud or tremendous (p. 164).

966 *That was ful.* L: *Þat ful.* Adding an intransitive verb is followed universally.

971 *dones.* He "dons" them, i.e., puts them on.

983 Havelok's height recalls the biblical King Saul, who was taller than the men around him and admired for his physical beauty. Nobility was presumed to inhere in such men, though giants were often portrayed as outlaws or Philistines (such as Goliath) in Scripture and medieval romance.

988 *als he was long.* L: *al he was long.*

998 *With hire ne wolde he leyke.* L: *Þit hire ne wold leyke.* Sm: *Wit hire.* F&H: *With hore. Hire* could refer to a woman who prostitutes herself for hire, or who is at least a woman of sexual experience. Given the economies of exchange in the poem, sex is another mode of negotiation. The OE *hóre* originally meant adultery, but gradually became more closely associated with female sexuality, perhaps in part because *hire* is a feminine possessive pronoun. Sm rejects the emendation to *hore* on grounds that it is "paleologically very improbable" (p. 119).

1009 *Mani with ladde, blac and brown.* Black could refer to peasants; brown, as F&H suggest (p. 112), can mean "persons of all ranks" or "peasants," since peasant complexions are often described as black or brown, noble faces as red or white. Thus, this phrase may mean "people of every rank" or "the lower classes." See also line 2847, where the metaphor is clearly political, as people of all ranks swear *manrede* to Goldeboru. But see also the note to line 1909, where the idiom "broune or blake" may refer to "dark or fair" complexion, with *broune* meaning dark and *blake* meaning pale or fair.

1024 *And pulten with a mikel ston.* The sport, analogous to shotput, was popular among Germanic peoples, though it is also found in the legends of other cultures. Robert Mannyng of Brunne in Lincolnshire claimed that the stone Havelok throws was preserved in a Lincoln castle in his day (c. 1338). Such chronicle accounts encourage historical identification. (See also lines 1032–37).

1037–39 F&H make a distinction between *chaumpioun* and *kempe.* While the former means "competent athlete, man of valor," the latter means "outstanding performer among many good ones" (p. 113).

1080 *his douther yeve.* L: *his douthe yeve.*

1095 *Onlepi foru.* The aristocratic Godrich imagines Havelok incapable of ever becoming landed by any means.

1102 *erthe stoc.* L: *erthe shop.* While the MS reads *shop* (created), the word neither rhymes nor fits the meaning. Both F&H and Sa substitute *stoc*, which F&H gloss as "shut fast"; Satan resides in hell, the center of the earth in medieval belief.

1120 *Whether* simply introduces a question here. See note to line 292.

1149 *With dintes swithe hard and strong.* This line is supplied by Sk.

1158 *hire, fals and slike.* L: *hire and slike.* F&H: *hire fals and slike.* Sm: *fel and slike.*

1173 *Ther weren penies thicke tolde.* "There were pennies thickly counted," i.e., a lot of them. Mass pennies were given as an offering for the nuptial ceremony.

1175 *He ys hire yaf and she is tok.* L: *she as tok.* F&H emend *as* to *is*, and gloss *ys* as *them*. Their note is helpful here: "Part of the money was the clerk's fee, part was a symbol that the wife was endowed with the husband's worldly goods . . . and part might be payment for the wife's virginity" (p. 118). According to Christopher Brooke in *The Medieval Idea of Marriage* (Oxford: Oxford University Press, 1989): "Each partner is to rehearse his and her consent; the woman's dower is to be confirmed, and some pennies set aside to be distributed among the poor. . . . Marriage from the twelfth to the sixteenth centuries and beyond was a public event, rather than private or clandestine, accompanied by the publication of banns and witnessed by parish or community members" (p. 249). The money is taken by the bride as part of her dowry.

1202 *ay the rith sti.* L: *ay þe rith*; F&H and Sm add *sti.*

1204 *Thanne he komen there thanne was Grim ded.* "Thanne. . . thanne" is a correlative construction linking the clauses: "When they arrived there, [then] Grim was dead." The second "thanne" is best left untranslated in modern English.

1247 *Wesseyl ledden he fele sithe.* "They drank healths (toasted) many times." "Wessail" derives from OE *wes hael* — "be healthy; to your health."

1251 *That she were.* L: *Þat shere.* Sk's emendation, followed by Sm, F&H, and Sa.

1306 *That ich fley over the salte se.* This line could mean: "That I fled over the salty sea" or "That I flew over the salty sea." Given the context, it is a little more likely that "fley" means "fled."

1316 Earlier editors suggest that at least two lines are missing here. Presumably, the first would have a final word rhyming with *joye* of line 1315, while the next would rhyme with *trone* in what is now numbered as 1316.

1337 *Nim in wit lithe to Denemark.* L: *Nim in witl þe to Denemak.* F&H: *Nimen we to Denemark baþe.* Sa: *Nimen wit to Denemark bathe*, where *wit* means "we too." Sm: *Nim in wit liþe to Denemark baþe.* Sm's note on this line is useful: "As an emendation *l[i]the* has the advantage of preserving the *l* in MS *witl* as well as the MS *the*. . . . If *lithe* is interpreted as 'journey' in line 1337, it is necessary to take *wit* as the dual 'we two' and to emend *nim* to *nime*. . . . The line would translate to 'Let's both make the journey to Denmark"' (p. 127).

1343 *thin hond.* L: *þin hon.*

1349 *Thou maght til he aren quike.* Sm emends *til* to *tel* because there is "no known word corresponding in form to *til* that would fit this context" (p. 128). See John Wilson, "*Havelok the Dane*, line 1349: 'til,"' *Notes and Queries* 36 (1989), 150–51.

1370 *He hath mi lond.* L: *He mi lond.* Sm: *He haldes mi lond.* Our emendation agrees with that of F&H.

1377 *And late me wel.* L: *And late wel.*

1397 *he kalde.* L: *he kade.*

1399 *and Huwe Raven.* L: *h aven.* In the *Dictionary of British Surnames*, Percy H. Reaney lists *Raven* as having derived from ON *Hrafn* or OE *Hraefn* or as a nickname from the bird. The surname may also indicate a link to Norse mythology. The trickster god Odin kept two ravens — Huginn and Manimen — to act as advisors and messengers. *Rede*, also Read, Reade, Reed, Red, Redd or Reid, he conjectures, indicates OE *redd* "red" of complexion or hair (p. 292). The closest Reaney comes to *Willam Wenduth* is William Wende, a thirteenth-century listing, derived from OE *wende* meaning "dweller by the bend" (p. 375).

1410 *lime he hus*. L: *lime hus*.

1429 *Havede he ben slayn*. L: *Havede ben*.

1445–1624 At this point in the MS, a whole leaf has been cut away. Ma surmises that approximately 180 lines are missing. The gist of the section, says Sa, "probably was that the three sons agree to follow Havelok; and all the men, together with Goldeboru, sail for Denmark. Ashore, Havelok, William, and Roberd, disguised as peddlers, meet the Danish earl Ubbe and ask permission to sell their wares. Line 1625 opens in the middle of Havelok's plea" (p. 95). F&H's synopsis varies somewhat: "The three sons agree, and exchange some of their property for a peddlar's wares and a fine ring. They sail to Denmark and moor the boat; Hugh Raven remains in it. The others disembark and on the shore meet Ubbe, a Danish earl, who is out riding with his retinue near a town and castle. Havelok asks permission to sell his wares" (p. 127).

1632–34 The jewel in the ring was worth a hundred pounds, an enormous amount of money in the Middle Ages.

1635 *He was ful wis that first yaf mede*. Proverbial. See Bartlett Jere Whiting, *Proverbs, Sentences, and Proverbial Phrases from English Writings Mainly before 1500* (Cambridge, MA: Harvard University Press, 1968), p. 226; entry G78: "He was full wise that first gave gift." Whiting cites similar passages in *Tristrem* 19.626–27, Gower's *Confessio Amantis* V.4720 and V.4798; and Wyntoun VI. 199,6450.

1644 *ilk del*. L: *il del*.

1660 *ful wel rede thee*. L: *ful wel rede þ*.

1680–81 Sm ends the couplet for the sake of the meter and the end rhyme: *Loke that ye comen baþe / For ich it wile and ich it raþe*. Compare lines 694–95 and lines 360–61.

1685 *he yede*. L: *he yde*.

1686 *red*. Sense uncertain. Perhaps *red* means "of ruddy complexion" or "sanguine of disposition"; but more likely the sense is "wise," or "well-advised," or "well-counselled."

1698 *for to shewe.* Sm: *for to shawe.* F&H: *forto shewe.*

1722 *Thanne were set and bord leyd.* F&H and Sm add a pronoun: *Thanne he were set and bord leyd.* The table is the subject, however.

1726 The types of fowl on the menu — cranes and swans — were more common for a medieval feast than they might be now. Cranes, as many other wild fowl, were roasted over an open flame often with a special basting sauce to keep them moist. Presentation was just as important as the dish itself. Swans, peacocks, and other birds of extraordinary plumage underwent an elaborate skinning procedure so that they could be served inside their own skin replete with feathers. The idea was to present the dish as if it were still alive. Food often took on symbolic significance in the Middle Ages. See Robert W. Hanning. For the appetites of medieval romance heroes see Susan E. Farrier, "Hungry Heroes in Medieval Literature," in *Food in the Middle Ages: A Book of Essays*, ed. Melitta Weiss Adamson (New York: Garland, 1995), 145–59.

1728 *Pyment.* Meaning spiced wine, *pyment* differs from *claré*, which is spiced wine mixed with honey, not to be confused with the modern claret, a fine red wine.

1731 Ale is considered a lowly drink, unfit for even a page at such a feast, at least in this poem. In general, however, beer and ale were served and consumed as regular table beverages, preferable even to water. Andrewe Boorde, writing in the mid-fifteenth century, says: "Ale for an Englysshe man is a naturall drynke" (as quoted in Terence Scully, *The Art of Cookery in the Middle Ages* [Woodbridge: Boydell Press, 1995], p. 153.)

1736 *the kilthing deyled.* L: *the kilþing deled.* Sm: *the kilþing deyled.* F&H: *the ilk þing deled.* We concur with Sm's emendation. Sm rejects Sk's "violent emendation," of *kilthing* to *ilk thing*. For Sm it represents "a re-writing that offers no means of accounting for the alleged corruption" (p. 132). Instead, Sm chooses to retain the integrity of the line.

1740 *Ilk man.* L: *Il man.* Sm: *Il man.* F&H: *Ilk man.* Since the distinction is important, we have followed F&H's emendation.

1744 *bes mikel wo.* L: *bes mike wo.*

1749 *greyves*. Not to be confused with shin armor, this term refers to the house of the grave, i.e., the night watchman's place of residence. (See note to line 266.)

1753 *Havelok wel yemen*. L: *Havelok wel ymen*.

1761 *With mikel love*. L: *with mike love*.

1773 *bi Seint Austin*. This could refer to either Augustine, Bishop of Hippo and author of a number of widely read works in the Middle Ages including *Confessions*, or Augustine of Canterbury, the first Archbishop of Canterbury.

1785 *In feteres and ful faste festen*. Notice how the alliteration in this line underscores Bernard's oath.

1794 *barre*. The sliding beam that secures the door.

1798 *Comes swithe unto me*. Armed with his cross beam, Havelok's command strangely echoes Christ's "come unto me." Here the true lord calls with a grim irony; his cross piece will be their death. It is noteworthy that Havelok's "kynmerk" (birthmark) on his shoulder is a cross. See note to lines 2037–45, where his wounds make him more kin of Christ than kin of Cain.

1804 *And with him comen*. L: *And with comen*. The thorn has been replaced by *th* in L.

1827 *Havelok let the barre fleye*. L: *Have le barre fleye*.

1829 *That havede he nevere schrifte of prest*. In other words, he was killed so fast that he did not have time to give his confession to a priest or receive the last rites (quite an understatement).

1840 *bere beyte*. Bear baiting was a cruel sport enjoyed by lovers of violence in England until it was officially banned in 1835. The bear was lugged (chained by his neck or hind leg to a log or something more secure), and dogs were turned loose on the creature. The dogs were often killed or mauled and the bear seriously torn. Detailed accounts may be found in Joseph Strutt, *The Sports and Pastimes of the People of England, from the Earliest Period . . . Illustrated by Reproductions from Ancient Paintings*, 1801; rpt. London: Thomas Tegg, 1834, rev. in a new edition, much enlarged and corrected by J. Charles Cox (London: Methuen & Co., 1903). See especially pp. 204–08 in Cox's revised edition. Though officially banned in 1835 the sport continued illegally for a couple more decades, the last recorded entertainment being in West Derby in 1853. Sometimes the bear was blinded and whipped to add to the sport.

1884 *louerd wreke be.* L: *louerd wreke.*

1890 Romance heroes occasionally use clubs as weapons, though not always with comic effect as in this scene, but rather as a serious demonstration of knightly potential (e.g., Sir Degaré, Sir Perceval).

1909 *of the broune and of the blake.* Sa glosses as "Of the brown and of the fair." *Blake* comes from OE *blǣc*, meaning white. See also lines 1008, 2181, and 2249.

1911 *Als here wombes.* L: *Als hee wombes.*

1941 *or shame seyde.* L: *or same seyde.* F&H: *or shame seyde.* Sm: *or same seyde.*

2009 *leye o tooth.* L: *leye othe.* Si's emendation, followed by F&H and Sa.

2029 *Griffin Galle.* L: *Giffin Galle.* Griffin, a name probably of Breton origin, was used as a nickname for the Middle Welsh *Gruffydd.* Galle was a well-known surname in Lincolnshire in the twelfth and thirteenth centuries. Sm notes that there are other examples combined with "Christian names such as Walter or Arnald. . . . But in *Havelok*, the combination of this surname of Celtic origin with the non-English Griffin is striking" (p. 136). In the *Dictionary of British Surnames*, second ed. (London: Routledge & Kegan, Paul, 1977), Percy H. Reaney comments: "The name in England is found in the counties bordering Wales and also in Lincolnshire where it was of Breton origin. In Brittany where the name was common, it was applied to immigrants from France" (p. 139).

2030 *mouthe ageyn so.* L: *mouthe agey so.*

2036 *Wel is set the mete he etes.* L: *We is set þe mete he etes.* This proverb appears earlier in a variant form in line 908.

2037–45 The beholding of the young lord's wounds is perhaps another allusion to the hero's miraculously redemptive role as opponent to "Kaym kin" (line 2045). See note to line 1798.

2055 *that we so.* L: *þat we so.*

2060 A palfrey was a small saddle-horse used for riding, usually for women or ecclesiastics, and never for war. It would be humiliating for a knight to ride to combat or tournament or even to his execution on a palfrey.

2070 *Moucte wayte thee to slo*. L: *Movcte wayte þe slo*.

2072 *I shal lene thee a bowr*. See note to line 239.

2124 *lith was thare*. L: *lith wa þare*. Sm: *lith was þore*.

2140 *shuldre swithe brith*. L: *shuldre swe brith*. Sk's emendation, followed by F&H and Sa.

2143 Sa remarks that the line means: "'That it was a mark of kingship that they saw'; the word *kunrik* is probably an error for *kynemerk* of line 604" (p. 108). Sm, on the other hand, rejects Sk's emendation on the grounds that *kunrik* is not a noun, but an adjective meaning "of exalted birth" (p. 137).

2145 F&H note the widespread belief that precious stones gave off light at night. The fifteenth-century *Peterborough Lapidary* entry for carbuncle is as follows:

> Carbuncculus is a precios stone, & he schineth as feyre whose chynyngis not overcom by nyght. It chineth in derk places, & it semeth as it were a feyr; & ther bene xii kyndes ther-of, & worthyest ben tho that schynen & send owte leemes as feyre, as Ised. Also it is seyd that the carbunocyl is cleped so in grek, & it is gendryd in libia amonge the tregodites. Of this carnuncul ther is xii maneris of kendes of carbuncles. But thoo ben best that han the coleour of fire & tho ben closed in a wyght veyne. The best carbucul hathe this propirtie: if it is throwene. In the feyre it is qwent as it were amonges dede colis. (*English Mediaeval Lapidaries*, ed. Joan Evans and Mary Serjeantson, EETS o.s. 190 [London: Oxford University Press, 1933; rpt. 1960], p. 82)

2195 *knithes, burgeys, sweynes*. L: *Knighes bugeys sweynes*.

2229 *that sori fend*. L: *þat sor fend*.

2249 *Bothe brune and the blake*. See note to line 1009.

2250 *Gamen* here literally means "fun," "sport," but in a cheerful, jesting way means "ritual [of homage]."

2274 *He* here refers to Ubbe in the next line.

2287 *That com of Adam and of Eve*. I.e., that was born of the human race started by Adam and Eve — in other words, everyone.

2298 *Us for to yemen*. L: *for to yemen*. F&H: *Men for to yemen*. Sm: *Us for to yemen*. Since Ubbe is speaking, his designation of group and self-inclusion make sense.

2310 *evere wolde his*. L: *evere wode his*.

2311 *That dide he hem o boke swere*. L: *Þat dide hem o boke swere*.

2327 Note the reference to romance reading in the context of leisure. Some medieval medical authorities considered reading a good story for the sake of pleasure and the release of emotion and laughter a sound measure for good health. See Glending Olson, *Literature as Recreation in the Middle Ages* (Ithaca: Cornell University Press, 1982).

2331 Bull and boar-baiting were common medieval pastimes. A bull or boar was tied to a stake or set in a pit, and dogs were let loose to annoy and irritate the larger animal. See note to line 1840.

2336 *so mikel yeft of clothes*. L: *so mike yeft of cloþes*.

2352 *ilker twenti knihtes*. L: *ilker twent knihtes*.

2370 *Half hundred*. L: *hal hundred*.

2389 *cavenard*. Sk refers to the term as an error for *caynard*, a term for a scoundrel (see Chaucer's Wife of Bath *CT* III[D] 235). Sa emends to *caynard*.

2404 *that he ther thrette*. L: *þat þer þrette*.

2432 *And everilk fot of hem he slowe*. *Fot* here stands for person — thus, a synecdoche, in which a part of something stands for a whole.

2450 *Hise nese went unto the crice*. He is bound on his steed face down and backwards, with his nose in the cleft between the horse's buttocks.

2453 *he havede ful*. L: *he have ful*.

2458–59 *And swithe wikke clothes, / For al hise manie grete othes*. F&H and Sm emend these lines as follows: *Wan he was brouth so shamelike / Biforn the king, (the fule swike!)*. We have returned to the MS reading.

2470 As F&H explain (p. 158), the wall would have been lined with benches.

2478 *At this foule mere tayl*. Just as riding a palfrey would humiliate a knight, so too would riding a mare. Even more humiliating would be being tied to its befouled tail. F&H note: "Criminals drawn to the gallows were placed on hurdles or a cowhide that they should not be battered to death on the way. The 'foule mere' was an added humiliation, since a knight was usually allowed to ride to his death on a charger. The traces of harness may have been attached to the nail in line 2479. Chains were used to hang for a long time" (p. 158).

2479 *Thoru his fet*. L: *Þoru is fet*.

2483 *ilk*. L: *il*. Sk's emendation, followed by F&H and Sa. So too in line 2514.

2492 *But that he sholde*. L: *Þat he sholde*. F&H and Sm concur on the emendation.

2502 *That ne flow him*. L: *That ne flow everil del*.

2514 *ilk*. L: *il*.

2515 A traitor's estates were confiscated by the Crown.

2518 *sayse*. The appropriate definition of the term here is: "To put in legal possession of."

2519 F&H conjecture the absence of approximately twenty lines: "The copyist omitted a passage, probably about twenty lines long, in which the journey to England is described. The French poems contribute little information; they mention, however, that the expedition disembarks at Grimsby and sends Godrich a demand that he restore England to its rightful owners" (p. 160). Sm and Sa are silent on this alleged omission.

2521 *monekes blak*. The poet may be referring to the Grimsby Abbey monks — Augustinians, founded by Henry I, chartered by Henry II, given to Henry VII, and torn down for a farmhouse. But "black monks" generally refers to Benedictines. Augustinian (Austin) friars were a mendicant order that arrived in England in 1248. Ma's early speculation dated the founding of the house of Austin friars in 1293.

2556 *That* is repeated here from line 2555 for intensifying purposes.

2557 *yboren, so*. L: *ye ber so*. Sk's emendation.

2597 *For shal I*. L: *For shal*.

2615 *Grethet als men mithe telle a pund*. "As men might count out a pound." F&H suggest counting out a pound penny by penny (the only way to make change) would have taken quite a long while. But this meaning, which they accept, does not seem to make sense here, except vaguely as "matter-of-factly" (p. 163).

2629 *nevere thethen*. L: *nevere þeþe*.

2654 *Godrich him*. L: *G-him*.

2663 *To the fet right there adune*. Supplied by Ma's edition and followed by Sk. It echoes line 1905.

2711 *ok*. L: *hok*.

2797 *Kristes*. L: *Kistes*.

2840 *And led him til*. L: *And him til*. Sm: *And led huntil*. F&H: *And led him til*. Sa follows L.

2867 *bi Seint Davy*. St. David, the sixth-century patron saint of Wales whose cult, most evident in the city of the same name, nonetheless spread to other ecclesiastical centers (Sherborne, Glastonbury, and Salisbury). Sm finds it curious that this particular saint should be invoked in this particular English poem and wonders how the poet came to know St. David. The answer, he says, is "to be sought in certain Welsh connections of the cathedral and the monastic community of Lincoln. The prominent Welsh writer and churchman Giraldus Cambrensis, who wrote a *Vita* of St. David, had withdrawn from court life after 1194 to go and study at Lincoln under William of Leicester (then Chancellor of Lincoln), and was there from at least 1196 to 1198. . . . It does not necessarily follow that the author of *Havelok* had read Gerald's *Vita* (or any other). But it does seem likely that he was in some fashion exposed to the ecclesiastical interest in St. David at Lincoln, and therefore he may have lived in Lincoln (as is also suggested by the signs that he knew the city at first hand)" (pp. 154–55).

2888 *was in god time*. L: *was god time*.

2905 *ich ne havede*. L: *ich ne have*.

2909 *ilk del*. L: *il del*.

2933 This line has spawned two theories: (1) that the exemplar of L was a minstrel's copy and (2) that the original poet was probably himself a minstrel. See John C. Hirsh "*Havelok* 2933: A Problem in Medieval Literary History," *Neuphilologische Mitteilungen* 78 (1977), 339–47.

2983 *Him stondes wel that god child strenes*. Proverbial. See Whiting, *Proverbs, Sentences, and Proverbial Phrases*, C224, p. 83.

2993 *Have ich seyd*. L: *Have ich sey*.

2997 A *Pater Noster* (Our Father) is the Lord's Prayer.

Bevis of Hampton

Introduction

Bevis of Hampton (c. 1324) is a romance that has it all: a hero whose exploits take him from callow youth to hard-won maturity to a serene and almost sanctified death; a resourceful and appealing heroine; faithful servants and dynastic intrigue; a parade of interesting villains, foreign and domestic, exotic and local; a geographical sweep which moves back and forth from England to the Near East and through most of western Europe; battles with dragons and giants; forced marriages and episodes of domestic violence; a myriad of disguises and mistaken identities; harsh imprisonments with dramatic escapes, harrowing rescues, violent urban warfare; and, last but not least, a horse of such valor that his death at the end of the poem is at least as tragic as that of the heroine, and almost as tragic as that of Bevis himself. Not surprisingly, however, this much variety makes the poem a difficult one to characterize with any degree of certainty. And several other factors make it a poem which is perhaps easier to enjoy than to evaluate accurately.

The Text of *Bevis*

One of these complicating factors is textual. Unlike the other romances in this volume, which survive in only one or two manuscripts, there are six manuscripts of *Bevis*, and the relationship between them is complex.[1] A. C. Baugh's conclusion is that the six extant manuscripts — descended from a lost earlier Middle English version of the poem, which in turn is descended from the Anglo-Norman *Boeuve de Haumton* — are so different from each other that "[i]nstead of speaking of a single Middle English romance of *Bevis of Hampton* it would be more in accordance with the facts to say that we have at least five versions, each of which is entitled to be considered a separate romance."[2] Our decision to edit the A version (the Auchinleck MS) was not especially problematic; indeed, it was the obvious decision, since this manuscript is recognized as the most complete and also, as

[1] The six manuscripts referred to do not include fragments found in Douce MS 19.

[2] A. C. Baugh, "The Making of *Beves of Hampton*," *Bibliographic Studies in Honor of Rudolf Hirsch*, ed. William E. Miller and Thomas G. Waldman (Philadelphia: University of Pennsylvania Press, 1974), p. 34.

scholarly consensus suggests, the best. Nonetheless, it is important to be forthright in acknowledging that what we have done is present "a" version of *Bevis* rather than "the" definitive version.

The wide variation in manuscripts would certainly seem to be unusual, at least from the point of view of somewhat more "canonical" texts — Biblical and classical — which were held in such awe by medieval authors that they dared not alter them. As Baugh puts it, a "Biblical text was protected by the sanctity of the work, a classical text by the fame of the author. One did not try to improve on Virgil" (p. 17). What happens when a text is protected neither by sanctity nor sufficient authorial fame? Since so many of the Middle English romances survive in only a single manuscript, this is not always a relevant question. But, in the case of an anonymous, non-canonical poem such as *Bevis of Hampton*, its relevance is significant.

Baugh's own explanation for the great differences among the existing manuscripts of *Bevis* is that the written texts represent versions based on oral recitations from minstrels relying on memory and not unwilling to resort to improvisation when memory failed (p. 34). Whether or not one accepts his conclusion, it is clear from a comparison of the *Bevis* manuscripts that the vast textual differences cannot be accounted for by claiming either scribal variation or serendipitous oral performance. Not only are words changed, but entire scenes as well. Bevis' battle with the dragon which likens him to St. George, the patron saint of England, and the descriptive urban war in London, for example, do not appear in the Anglo-Norman version.[3] Likewise, from the textual evidence available, it is also clear that the lost Middle English original from which the Auchinleck manuscript descends was in no sense an attempt to translate literally the French of the Anglo-Norman version. Rather, while retaining fidelity to what Baugh calls "incident and idea," the "author" of the original Middle English text felt free to paraphrase and even to invent.[4]

This brief textual history reminds us that what survives is a *Bevis* tradition rather than a singular *Bevis* text, though it would be an exaggeration to compare it too closely to a *Troilus* tradition, for example. But the way in which the story of *Troilus and Criseyde* is developed by a writer such as Chaucer can at least be suggestive of what we mean here. In composing *Troilus and Criseyde*, Chaucer meticulously translated blocks of narrative from the Italian *Il Filostrato* written by his predecessor Boccaccio. Yet much, if not most of what he does, is something more than a literal translation of his illustrious predecessor, something more aptly described as imaginative recreation. The proportion between

---

[3] See Judith Weiss, "The Major Interpolation in *Sir Beves of Hamtoun*," *Medium Aevum* 48 (1979), 71–79. Laura [Hibbard] Loomis adds a third scene to the two described by Weiss, i.e., the Christmas battle. See *Mediæval Romance in England: A Study in the Source and Analogues of the Non-Cyclic Metrical Romances* (London: Oxford University Press, 1924), p. 116.

[4] On the relationship between *Bevis* and its Anglo-Norman source, see Baugh, pp. 17–23.

imitation and individuality is perhaps reversed in the various versions of *Bevis* — for all their differences, there are still greater similarities in the surviving manuscripts than between Boccaccio and Chaucer — and we are not claiming that anything like the individual genius of Chaucer (or Boccaccio) has put a stamp on any of the later versions of the poem. But the "tradition" of *Bevis* apparently continued to interest a wide number of people over a long period of time, apart from the authority of any individual text. Baugh writes:

> The story's popularity continued on into the sixteenth and even the seventeenth century when various early printed editions appeared. Like the story of Guy of Warwick, it doubtless owed something of its popularity to national pride, but it is a good story in itself and was told three times in French verse, even at great length, to say nothing of versions in Celtic, Old Norse, Dutch, Italian, even in Romanian, Russian, and Yiddish.[5]

Bevis as an Episodic Narrative

A second interesting aspect of *Bevis* concerns the shape of the poem itself, more specifically the verse form. The first 475 lines of the poem are written in six-line tail-rhyme stanzas. Then, for reasons that remain unexplained, there is a switch and the rest of the romance, over 4000 lines, is written in couplets. Rather than attempt to posit another theory to account for this change, perhaps we can do no more than suggest what it points toward, which is the highly episodic nature of the work. Dieter Mehl confidently divides the romance into five parts of almost equal sections of 900 lines each, and suggests the obvious reason for these breaks — ease in recitation at different intervals.[6] These narrative episodes in *Bevis* are largely self-sufficient, without the kind of interlace that is characteristic of, for example, the French romances of Chrétien de Troyes in the twelfth century which are carefully conjoined both structurally and thematically into the larger fabric of the work.[7] Nevertheless, both the dynastic and the personal characteristics of the story are tied up at the end, allowing Mehl to say that *Bevis* is "indeed a unified whole" (p. 216).

While it would be too much even to describe all of the hero's adventures, a brief

---

[5] Baugh, p. 15. See also Laura Hibbard Loomis, *Mediæval Romance in England* (London: Routledge & Kegan Paul), p. 115.

[6] Dieter Mehl, *The Middle English Romances of the Thirteenth and Fourteenth Centuries* (London: Routledge & Kegan Paul, 1968), p. 213.

[7] See Douglas Kelly, *The Art of Medieval French Romance* (Madison: University of Wisconsin Press, 1992).

summary is useful at the outset to provide the reader with the flavor of an episodic plot that is so complex as to challenge even the best of memories.

Episode One:

Like many of the poems of the thirteenth century, this one begins with the death of the hero's father — Guy of Hampton who, in his old age, decides that he needs to produce an heir for his estate. For this purpose he requests marriage to the beautiful young daughter of the King of Scotland, who agrees to the suit without his daughter's consent. Thus arranged, the marriage commences and soon Bevis is born. By the time Bevis is seven years old, however, his mother has become discontent with marriage to a man who spends more time in church than in her boudoir, and she plots his murder. To accomplish the deed she sends a messenger to her former lover, the Emperor of Germany, with an invitation to invade England and murder Sir Guy. Bevis' mother then feigns an illness which requires, as remedy, the blood of a boar that resides at the agreed-upon battle site; persuaded by her imploring rhetoric and her convincing theatrical skill, Sir Guy is duped into combat. Caught by surprise and hopelessly outnumbered by the emperor's army, the hapless earl must beg for mercy; the request is honored by immediate decapitation. Sir Guy's head is then sent to Bevis' mother, who invites the emperor to her bedchamber that very night. Soon the conspirators are married.

This places Bevis in a difficult position, since he is the rightful heir to his father's earldom; for this reason alone the conspirators would kill him. Yet when Bevis, a precocious seven-year-old, calls his mother a "vile whore" and voices his wish to have her executed in the most horrible manner, he unwittingly provides his mother with additional incentive to destroy him. She commands Saber, his teacher, to kill the boy and provide proof of his death. Reluctant to do the deed, however, Saber kills a swine, sprinkles its blood upon the boy's clothes, and vows to send him from harm's way. Bevis takes matters into his own hands; he gains entry into the castle by killing the porter and vehemently attacks his stepfather. Outraged, Bevis' mother requisitions four knights to sell the boy to merchants, and soon Bevis finds himself on a ship headed for the Near East.

Bevis, who seems doomed, finds solace in the Armenian court of King Ermin. When the king hears the boy's woeful story, he welcomes him with the hope that one day he will become a devotee to Mohammed and carry the king's banner in battle. Even when Bevis refuses to convert, the king admires him and arranges that the boy be trained in the manner of all young Armenian warriors. When Bevis turns fifteen, his training has been completed and it is time for his first test of prowess in the field. But before an appropriate venue can be found, Bevis is goaded into a defensive attack by an insult made by one of the king's men. The king is not pleased when he learns that Bevis has annihilated some of his best men; he would hang him for treason but his beautiful daughter, Josian, intercedes, arguing that the novice warrior acted only in self-defense. Showing his grievous wounds Bevis again elicits the king's admiration, and when he reverses his judgment, Josian provides medical aid. This marks the beginning of her love for Bevis.

The episode ends with a battle between Bevis and a vicious, man-eating boar. In a contest that takes all day, Bevis finally makes the kill by inserting his sword in the beast's open mouth and carving its heart in two. He then cuts off the boar's head which he initially plans to present to Josian. Those plans change, however, when Bevis is attacked by an envious steward and several of the king's men. In protecting himself, Bevis slays his attackers and cuts off the steward's head. But rather than take the steward's head to the king to expose the steward's treachery, Bevis delivers the boar's head in its place. Meanwhile, Josian has witnessed the entire event from her tower and falls ever more deeply in love with this amazing young man.

Episode Two:

King Brademond requests Josian's hand in marriage, threatening to destroy Ermin's kingdom should he refuse. The act provokes hostilities and provides Bevis an opportunity to demonstrate his martial prowess which by this time is fully endorsed by Josian. The king agrees to dub the young man and presents him with a special sword named Morgelai and an extraordinary horse named Arondel, both of which prove invaluable during the course of Bevis' career. Thus armed and mobilized, Bevis leads a host of thirty thousand into battle against King Redefoun, Brademond's ally; sixty thousand Saracens are slain. When Brademond witnesses the carnage he flees, only to be caught and challenged to hand-to-hand combat with Bevis himself. When Brademond realizes that this battle could be his last, he cries for mercy. But rather than cut off his head, as the Emperor of Germany had done to his father, Bevis extracts, instead, Brademond's promise of homage to King Ermin.

When Bevis returns to the victory celebration, Josian declares her love for him. But Bevis is taken aback by her assertive behavior and declines her willingness to submit to him in any way. Angry and frustrated at his rejection, she calls him a churl, an insult to which he responds by retreating to the nearest inn. Not easily dissuaded, however, Josian sends her messenger, Bonefas, with an apology. In acknowledgment Bevis sends her a white silk mantle, the extravagance of which compels Josian to seek him out herself. Reluctant to talk with her, however, Bevis feigns sleep, but Josian persists and in a desperate plea for his love, pledges conversion to Christianity. At this magnanimous gesture, Bevis acquiesces and they seal their reconciliation and future together with a kiss. Meanwhile, smoldering with anger and envy, Brademond starts a rumor that Bevis has deflowered Josian; when her father hears it, he orders Bevis to take a letter to Brademond demanding Bevis' death; the newly dubbed knight is ordered to leave his sword and horse at home. Meanwhile, back in England, Saber sends his son, Terri, to find Bevis.

Terri's search takes him all over Europe and the Middle East where he soon meets Bevis while both are seeking repose under a tree one day. Terri, who has never met the man he has been sent to find, does not recognize Bevis. But when he asks this stranger whether he has heard about a child sold to the Saracens, Bevis reveals his identity and a nostalgic scene ensues; it is followed by a brief discussion of the letter Bevis is delivering to Brademond. Bevis knows nothing of its contents and suspects neither the king's betrayal nor Brademond's treacherous motives. Before they part, Bevis requests Terri to take a message to Saber to spread a rumor in England that he is dead. Terri agrees and they separate, going in opposite directions. When Bevis reaches Damascus he commits an impious act against the Saracen gods (throws them in the dirt) before presenting himself to Brademond. When Brademond reads King Ermin's letter of betrayal, he personally restrains the young man while his men subdue him and cast him into a pit twenty fathoms deep. In this deep, dark prison Bevis is bound to a great stone and fed only bread and water.

The scene then switches to Josian who does not know what her father has done. When she asks Bevis' whereabouts, he tells her that her beloved has married an English princess; Josian is grief stricken. This is the point at which King Yvor enters the narrative by proposing a marriage suit that is almost immediately granted by Josian's father. Yvor not only acquires Josian in this deal, but also Arondel, Bevis' wonder horse which Yvor soon discovers can be ridden only by one man. When he is unceremoniously thrown, Yvor commands that Arondel be fettered and chained in a manner reminiscent of Bevis' punishment. Meanwhile, back in his pit, Bevis is attacked by a venomous snake that scars his forehead for life. Now in his seventh year of imprisonment, Bevis is so overwhelmed by despair that in desperation he prays for help; shortly thereafter there appears an opportunity to dispatch his wardens. Another prayer frees him from the great stone and he climbs out of the prison, rearms himself, and finds a horse to make his escape. He dupes the porter into opening the castle gates and rides until he can ride no farther. Then in a state of utter fatigue he falls asleep and dreams that Brademond and seven kings are about to kill him. Startled into wakefulness he rides like a madman until inevitably Brademond's search party catches up with him. One of the kings in the group, King Grander, challenges Bevis to combat and soon loses his life. Bevis quickly confiscates Grander's horse, Trenchefis, and with Brademond's men in hot pursuit, horse and rider leap into the sea and swim for their lives.

Episode Three:

What would seem to be a trivial event launches the third episode — when Trenchefis arises from the sea, shaking himself dry, he inadvertently throws the enervated Bevis to the ground which jars the knight's memory of the horse he left behind. This remembrance spurs him to continue riding until he finds a town that he soon discovers is under siege by a giant, the brother of King Grander. When the giant recognizes Bevis' steed as his brother's, he attacks and accidentally kills his brother's horse. Horseless and wounded, Bevis prevails nonetheless, liberating the townspeople by defeating their oppressor. Grateful, they tend to his wounds until he is ready to continue his journey. On the way he stops off in Jerusalem to visit with a patriarch who tells him to marry no woman unless she is a virgin. This reminds Bevis that he has also left Josian in Armenia, a memory that triggers an adjustment to the purpose of his journey.

When he arrives at the Armenian court he learns that Josian has been married off to King Yvor, who has also acquired Morgelai and Arondel. This triple affront prompts Bevis to press on to Mombraunt, Yvor's stronghold, with intent to recuperate his losses. When he arrives, Yvor is out hunting whereupon Bevis disguises himself as a beggar to gain an audience with Josian, who has already acquired a reputation for generosity toward the needy. When she asks the homeless and transient group before her whether anyone has heard about a man named Bevis, Bevis, in disguise, replies in the affirmative. But before revealing his identity he arranges to see the imprisoned wonder horse. When Arondel shows signs of immediate recognition, Josian realizes who the pilgrim is and reminds Bevis of their tacit betrothal. But since she is already married and presumably not a virgin anymore, Bevis rescinds his commitment. Josian persists in her claim that she has remained a virgin despite her marriage to Yvor and dares him to find anyone to prove otherwise. Meanwhile, her servant Bonefas strongly urges escape since the king is expected back at any moment. Yvor soon arrives but when he is told that his brother, the King of Dabilent, is under siege, he bequeaths guardianship of the city to Garcy, an elderly king, and departs. Bevis and his cohorts drug Garcy in order to escape. But because Garcy is a necromancer he can see in his magic ring where they have gone and instructs a formidable giant named Ascopard to track them and kill Bevis.

Meanwhile, Bevis and company hide in a cave where they soon grow very hungry. When Bevis goes out to hunt, leaving Bonefas and Josian alone, they are attacked by two ferocious lions. The beasts kill Bonefas and his horse, but leave Josian, who is protected by her virginity, unharmed. When Bevis returns, he too is attacked and when Josian offers to help him fight, Bevis refuses for the insult to his masculine pride. He gets wounded in a prolonged fight but finally defeats both lions. Bevis sets Josian upon a mule, and they ride forth. Soon they meet Ascopard whose ambush provokes angry retaliation from Bevis. Josian intercedes successfully this time and recruits Ascopard as Bevis' page before either is killed. Together the three find a ship filled with Saracens whom Ascopard quickly dispatches; he then carries Bevis, Josian and her mule, and Arondel to the ship and they sail away to Cologne. There they meet with Bevis' uncle Saber (not to be confused with his teacher back in England) who is a Florentine bishop. Bevis requests that Josian and Ascopard be baptized into the Christian faith. Josian willingly accepts, but Ascopard rejects the offer, saying that he is too large to fit into the baptismal font.

In Cologne there is a dragon whose origin prompts a minor digression. The dragon is one of two kings magically transformed after a twenty-four-year battle, until a hermit prays for their demise. One then flies to Tuscany where it takes up residence under a cliff at Cologne; the other flies to Rome where every seven years it raises a stench that makes the local folks sick. Before his battle with the beast of Cologne commences, Bevis dreams that he is attacked and covered with its venom. Shaken by the premonition, he asks Ascopard whether they should fight the beast together. At first Ascopard agrees, but when he realizes the dangers of such an endeavor he declines the invitation.

Episode Four:

Bevis' battle with the dragon carries on for days, wearing down the hero's strength. Nearby, however, there is a well made holy, legend says, by the bathing of a virgin. The weary and desperate Bevis drinks from the well and calls on St. George for help. Miraculously, he regains his strength to continue the fight until the dragon spews forth its venom, rendering Bevis' premonitory dream true. His armor bursts; his skin becomes leprous; he cries for divine aid. The third time he is thrown into the well, he recovers his courage, his leprous skin is healed, and as a whole man he assails the dragon again. The hero soon prevails, cuts the dragon's tongue out, and displays it for the liberated townspeople to see. Then in a quiet moment, Bevis seeks counsel from Saber Florentine about his patrimony in England; the bishop advises him to go back and fight. Bevis arranges to leave and assigns Ascopard the task of protecting Josian.

The scene then switches to Josian who has been admired from afar by an earl named Miles. In order to entice Ascopard away from her, the earl sends him a false letter from Bevis and when Ascopard is safely removed, Miles forces Josian into wedlock. Josian, whose will is not to be taken lightly, murders him on their wedding night before the marriage is consummated. The next day her deed is discovered, however, and she is condemned to death. By the time Ascopard breaks away from his imprisonment and gets to Josian, Bevis is already there; he berates the giant for neglecting his guard duties, but after Ascopard offers a rational explanation of events, Bevis' anger is assuaged; together they rescue Josian and sail back to the Isle of Wight.

Bevis enters Hampton disguised as a Frenchman named Gerard and consults with the emperor about procuring military support in a fight against Saber, who by this time has become the emperor's sworn enemy. The cover story works, and a poignant reunion between Bevis and his beloved teacher ensues on the Isle of Wight. Bevis then orders a messenger to return to the emperor to disclose his deception. The emperor is so enraged by the duping that he flings his knife at the messenger and accidentally kills his own son. The messenger then insults the emperor — too much sex has distorted your vision!

During the culminating battle against the emperor, Bevis soon finds himself face to face with his stepfather who is rescued before Bevis can kill him. However, where Bevis fails Ascopard succeeds, and he soon delivers the emperor to Saber's castle where he is thrown into a kettle of molten lead. When Bevis' mother witnesses her husband's gruesome demise, she falls from her tower and breaks her neck. Bevis thus regains his patrimony and sends for Josian and his uncle the bishop to officiate at their wedding. Shortly thereafter, Josian is pregnant with twins.

Bevis requests an audience with the English monarch, King Edgar, in order to gain proper recognition of his reacquired estates. The king, impressed with the courageous man before him, not only renders approbation but also makes Bevis his marshal. The king's son admires Bevis' horse, but Arondel kicks him and the prince dies. King Edgar is very angry and condemns Bevis to death until his barons convince him that only the horse should be put to death. But Bevis would rather relinquish his estates than lose Arondel again. So Bevis, the pregnant Josian, Terri, Ascopard, and Arondel leave for Armenia. When Terri is made Bevis' page, Ascopard begins to plot his betrayal.

Episode Five:

King Yvor receives Ascopard and demands that he abduct Josian. Ascopard, now a traitor, kidnaps Josian immediately after she has given birth to twin sons — Miles and Guy — while Bevis and Terri are off building a hut for her. Her abductors beat her with their swords, bind her hands, and carry her away, leaving her infants unattended. When Bevis and Terri return, they find the boys alone and soon foster them — one to a forester and the other to a fisherman — with instructions to baptize them. Meanwhile, Josian makes herself appear leprous so that the king might be more likely to reject her. The strategy works: he sends her away into the wilderness with Ascopard as her guard.

Bevis and Terri have no idea where Josian has been taken, but come across a tournament being fought for the hand of the princess of Aumbeforce. Bevis and Terri enter and when Bevis demonstrates his prowess the princess wants to marry him. He objects, citing a wife as an impediment to such a marriage, but the persistent princess makes him a deal he cannot refuse. They will live in marital chastity for seven years after which time consummation would occur. Should Josian return before that time, however, the princess agrees to separate from Bevis and wed Terri in his place.

Back in Hampton, Saber dreams that Bevis is on his way to the shrines of St. James and

St. Giles. When Saber's wife interprets the dream — i.e., Bevis has lost either his wife or child — the concerned Saber, with twelve of his knights, initiates another search. They discover the castle in which Ascopard has imprisoned Josian; when she calls to them from the tower they attack. Saber kills Ascopard in battle, then he and Josian alone resume the search for Bevis and Terri. During their wanderings, Saber falls ill and Josian supports them both through her minstrelsy. She prays that Saber will be healed, and finally he is. They continue on their way and eventually find Bevis and Terri. Another poignant reunion takes place.

Josian and Bevis are soon reunited with their children, and Terri is wedded to the princess of Aumbeforce. Together they help King Ermin battle Yvor. Bevis beats Yvor in combat and sends him to Ermin for judgment only to have him ransomed rather than executed. King Ermin dies shortly thereafter making Bevis' son Guy his heir. Together Bevis and Guy convert all of Armenia to Christianity, and Saber goes home to England. A thief from Yvor's court steals Arondel, which prompts another of Saber's premonitory dreams, and compels his return to Armenia to retrieve the horse with several of Yvor's knights in pursuit. Bevis' sons prove themselves in battle and rescue Saber from certain death. A confrontation between Bevis and Yvor takes place on a small nearby island. Inevitably, Yvor is defeated and Bevis is crowned king of Mombraunt in his place. At this point a messenger arrives from England to report that King Edgar has confiscated Saber's son's land, and Bevis promises to aid Saber in a war against the English king. When they arrive, Bevis leaves his army at Hampton, rides to London to make a courteous appeal for restoration of the land. The king receives him and is about to comply with his request when suddenly dissent erupts from his steward. Proclaiming Bevis an outlaw and a traitor, a provocative action indeed, the steward is pursued to Cheapside where an intense street battle commences. News that Bevis has been killed reaches Josian back in Hampton, and she sends her two sons to avenge his death. Instead, Guy rescues his father with his brother's help and victory is proclaimed. Josian is then brought to London for the celebration.

King Edgar offers his only daughter to Miles in marriage. Bevis bequeaths his property and earldom to Saber, and, together, Bevis, Josian, and Guy go back to Armenia where Guy is king. Bevis and Josian continue on to Mombraunt where they live and rule for twenty years until Josian becomes ill. At about the same time Bevis finds Arondel dead in his stall. Soon afterward, Josian and Bevis die together in a poignant embrace. Guy orders that his parents be interred in a newly constructed chapel dedicated to St. Lawrence. He also founds a religious house where songs for their souls and for the soul of the great horse Arondel are to be sung every day.

Realism and the Exotic in *Bevis*

The Anglo-Norman version of *Bevis* is, as Barron suggests, rooted in the need to establish a native ancestry for a new set of rulers.[8] While this dynastic impulse is still surely present in the Middle English versions, with a pre-conquest hero dressed in the garb and the virtues of present-day England, the poem's most characteristic virtues have at least as much to do with adventure as with ideology. The incredible geographic sweep — which gets more and more misty and impressionistic the farther we go from England — is perhaps a way of placing England within the larger rhythms of world history, but it is also a way to have adventure on the grandest possible scale. As in the other romances in this volume, especially *Havelok*, there is an intriguing combination of the exotic and supernatural combined with very realistic detail, local color, and homey touches. In *Bevis,* miraculous escapes from prison are juxtaposed with the naming and the description of actual streets in Cheapside. The final set of battles is one particularly impressive example of using local scenes to energize the story.

Bevis of Hampton was one of the best known and most popular of the Middle English romances (Mehl, p. 211). Yet critical response has not always been kind to our hero, whose story seems in part to be a victim of its own popularity. In the conclusion to *English Medieval Romances*, W. R. J. Barron comes close to damning the poem with only the slightest touch of accompanying faint praise, writing that "[t]he English versions of *Bevis* and *Guy [of Warwick]* are competent but somewhat vulgarized, given to the reduplication of striking effects, paying lip-service to the hero's values while almost wholly preoccupied by their adventures" (p. 233). This characterization of *Bevis* is probably both accurate and at the same time unfair. Bevis is first and foremost an adventure story. But if the values of the hero are not particularly deep, they are nonetheless heartfelt, and expressed with admirable verve. And we should be reluctant to underestimate the value of a good adventure story or the difficulty of producing one. Its energy and its variety, perhaps more than anything, are what enable modern readers to understand its earlier popularity and also to respond to it in the present.

[8] W. R. J. Barron, *English Medieval Romance* (London: Longman, 1987), p. 217.

Bevis of Hampton

Select Bibliography

Manuscripts

Auchinleck MS, fols. 176–201.

University Library, Cambridge Ff. 2.38.

Caius College, Cambridge, Gonville and Caius 175.

Royal Library, Naples, XIII, B 29.

Duke of Sutherland (now Egerton 2862).

Chetham Library, no. 8009, Manchester.

Douce fragments, No. 19.

Early printed text by Wynkyn de Worde.

Edition

Kölbing, Eugen, ed. *The Romance of Sir Beves of Hamtoun*. EETS e.s. 46, 48, 65. London: Kegan Paul, Trench Trübner & Co., 1885–94, rpt. as 1 vol., 1973.

Related Studies

Baldwin, Charles Sears. *Three Medieval Centuries of Literature in England 1100–1400*. New York: Phaeton Press, 1968. Pp. 109–12, 255–56. [Study of several genres in their historical contexts.]

Barron, W. R. J. *English Medieval Romance*. London: Longman, 1987. [Though the analysis of *Bevis* is by no means extensive, references are useful in that they place the work in the larger context of a Middle English romance tradition.]

Baugh, A. C. "The Making of *Beves of Hampton*." *Bibliographical Studies in Honor of Rudolf Hirsch*. Ed. William E. Miller and Thomas G. Waldman. Philadelphia: University of Pennsylvania Press, 1974. Pp. 15–37. [This study is important not only for the textual tradition of *Bevis*, but for its insights with respect to a Middle English romance tradition generally.]

Bennett, J. A. W. *Middle English Literature*. Ed. Douglas Gray. Oxford: Clarendon Press, 1986. Pp. 91, 125–26, 194. [General information.]

Brownrigg, Linda. "The Taymouth Hours and the Romance of *Beves of Hampton*." *English Manuscript Studies 1100–1700* 1 (1989), 222–41. [Looks for stylistic similarities between *Bevis* and one of the outstanding contemporary examples of English MS illumination.]

Burrow, J. A. *Essays on Medieval Literature*. Oxford: Clarendon Press, 1984. Pp. 63, 68, 107. [Argues Chaucer's use of *Bevis* in Sir Thopas.]

Jacobs, Nicolas. "*Sir Degarré, Lay le Freine, Beves of Hamtoun*, and the 'Auchinleck Bookshop.'" *Notes and Queries* 227 (Aug. 1982), 294–301. [Demonstrates the interrelatedness of these Auchinleck romances. Draws parallels between the dragon fight in *Degaré* and that in *Bevis*.]

Kane, George. *Middle English Literature: A Critical Study of the Romances, the Religious Lyrics, Piers Plowman*. London: Methuen, 1951. Pp. 10, 27, 46, 50–51, 58. [Situates *Bevis* in the romance tradition.]

Kinghorn, A. M. *The Chorus of History: Literary-Historical Relations in Renaissance Britain*. New York: Barnes and Noble, Inc., 1971. Pp. 146–47. [Shows the popularity of *Bevis* in MS and printed editions in the fifteenth and sixteenth centuries.]

Loomis, Laura A. [Hibbard]. *Mediæval Romance in England*. London: Oxford University Press, 1924; rpt. New York: Burt Franklin, 1960. [A comprehensive study of sources and analogues.]

Mehl, Dieter. *The Middle English Romances of the Thirteenth and Fourteenth Centuries*. London: Routledge and Kegan Paul, 1968. Pp. 211–21. [A good treatment of the structure of *Bevis*, despite a disconcerting and misleading tendency to call the work a novel.]

Weiss, Judith. "The Major Interpolation in *Sir Beues of Hamtoun*." *Medium Aevum* 48 (1979), 71–76. [Changes made to the Anglo-Norman *Boeve de Haumtone* have the effect of "stamping the ineradicable basic Englishness of its hero firmly on our minds at the close of the romance" (p. 76).]

Bevis of Hampton

	Lordinges, herkneth to me tale!	
	Is merier than the nightingale,	
	That I schel singe;	
	Of a knight ich wile yow roune,	*I will sing to you*
5	Beves a highte of Hamtoune,	*he [is] called*
	Withouten lesing.	*lying*
	Ich wile yow tellen al togadre	*I; together*
	Of that knight and of is fadre,	*his*
	Sire Gii.	
10	Of Hamtoun he was sire	
	And of al that ilche schire,	*same shire*
	To wardi.	*guard*
	Lordinges, this, of whan I telle,	
	Never man of flesch ne felle	*skin*
15	Nas so strong.	*Was not*
	And so he was in ech strive.	*quarrel*
	And ever he levede withouten wive,	*lived*
	Al to late and long.	
	Whan he was fallen in to elde,	*old age*
20	That he ne mighte himself welde,	*control*
	He wolde a wif take;	
	Sone thar after, ich understonde,	
	Him hadde be lever than al this londe	
	Hadde he hire forsake.[1]	
25	An elde a wif he tok an honde,	*elderly man*
	The kinges doughter of Scotlonde,	

[1] Lines 23–24: *It would have been better had he forsaken her than lose all his land*

	So faire and bright.	
	Allas, that he hire ever ches!	*chose*
	For hire love his lif a les	*he lost*
30	With mechel unright.	*much evil*
	This maide ichave of ytold,	*I have*
	Faire maide she was and bold	
	And fre yboren;	*nobly born*
	Of Almayne that emperur	*Germany*
35	Hire hadde loved paramur	*as a mistress*
	Wel thar beforen.	
	Ofte to hire fader a sente	*he*
	And he him selve theder wente	*there (thither)*
	For hire sake;	
40	Ofte gernede hire to wive;	*desired*
	The king for no thing alive	
	Nolde hire him take.[1]	
	Sithe a yaf hire to sire Gii,	*Then he gave*
	A stalword erl and hardi	
45	Of Southhamtoun.	
	Man, whan he falleth in to elde.	*old age*
	Feble a wexeth and unbelde	*Feeble he grew; unbold*
	Thourgh right resoun.	
	So longe thai yede togedres to bedde,	*they went*
50	A knave child betwene hem thai hedde,	
	Beves a het.	*he was called*
	Faire child he was and bolde,	
	He nas boute seve winter olde,	*not quite seven*
	Whan his fader was ded.	
55	The levedi hire misbethoughte	*lady; had evil thoughts*
	And meche aghen the right she wroughte	*much against*
	In hire tour:	*tower*

[1] Lines 41–42: *The king did not wish him to take her away, for anything alive*

	"Me lord is olde and may nought werche,	*work*
	Al dai him is lever at cherche,	*rather*
60	Than in me bour.[1]	
	Hadde ich itaken a yong knight,	
	That ner nought brused in werre and fight,	*was not*
	Also he is,	*As*
	A wolde me loven dai and night,	*He*
65	Cleppen and kissen with al is might	*Embrace; his*
	And make me blis.	
	I nel hit lete for no thinge,	*will not allow it*
	That ich nel him to dethe bringe	*do not*
	With sum braide!"	*trick*
70	Anon right that levedi fer	*Soon; lady fierce*
	To consaile clepede hir masager	*counsel called; messenger*
	And to him saide:	
	"Maseger, do me surté,	*Messenger, promise me*
	That thow nelt nought discure me	*disclose*
75	To no wight!	*person*
	And yif thow wilt, that it so be,	*wish*
	I schel thee yeve gold and fe	*property*
	And make the knight."	
	Thanne answerde the masager —	
80	False a was, that pautener,	*vagabond*
	And wel prut —	*proud*
	"Dame, boute ich do thee nede,	*unless I do your bidding*
	Ich graunte, thow me forbede	*imagine you would forbid me*
	The londe thourgh out."	
85	The levedi thanne was wel fain:	*glad*
	"Go," she seide, "in to Almaine	*Germany*
	Out of me bour!	*chamber*
	Maseger, be yep and snel,	*prompt; swift*

[1] Lines 59–60: *All day he would rather be in church / Than in my bower*

And on min helf thow grete wel — *behalf*
90 That emperur,

And bid, in the ferste dai,
That cometh in the moneth of May,
For love of me,
That he be to fighte prest — *ready*
95 With is ferde in hare forest — *his retinue; our*
Beside the se. — *sea*

Me lord ich wile theder sende
For his love, for to schende — *destroy*
And for to sle; — *kill*
100 Bid him, that hit be nought beleved, — *believed*
That he ne smite of his heved — *cut off; head*
And sende hit me!

And whan he haveth so ydo, — *done*
Me love he schel underfo, — *My; receive*
105 Withouten delai!
Thanne seide that masager:
"Madame, ich wile sone be ther!
Now have gode dai!"

Now that masager him goth.
110 That ilche lord him worthe wroth, — *same; became angry*
That him wroughte!
To schip that masager him wode. — *ship; went*
Allas! The wind was al to gode,
That him over broughte.

115 Tho he com in to Almayne,
Thar a mette with a swain — *he; servant*
And grette him wel.
"Felawe," a seide, "par amur: — *if you please*
Whar mai ich finde th'emperur? — *the emperor*
120 Thow me tel!"

"Ich wile thee telle anon right:
At Rifoun a lai tonight, — *he lay*
Be me swere!" — *by my oath*
The masager him thankede anon
125 And thederwardes he gan gon — *thither*
Withouten demere. — *delay*

Th'empereur thar a fonde; — *he found*
Adoun a knevlede on the grounde, — *he knelt*
Ase hit was right,
130 And seide: "The levedi of South Hamtone
Thee grette wel be Godes sone, — *Greets you; by God's son*
That is so bright,

And bad thee, in the ferste day
That cometh in the moneth o May,
135 How so hit be,
That ye be to fighte prest — *ready*
With your ferde in hare forest — *retinue; her*
Beside the se.

Hire lord she wile theder sende
140 For the love, for to schende, — *kill*
With lite meini; — *With few followers*
Thar aboute thow schost be fouse, — *strenuous*
And thow schelt after her wedde to spouse, — *as*
To thin amy." — *love*

145 "Sai," a seide, "Icham at hire heste: — *he said; command*
Yif me lif hit wile leste, — *If my life will last*
Hit schel be do! — *It shall be done*
Gladder icham for that sawe, — *advice*
Than be fouel, whan hit ginneth dawe, — *Than birds; it begins to dawn*
150 And sai hire so! — *tell her so*

And for thow woldes hire erande bede, — *make known*
An hors icharged with golde rede — *laden with red gold*
Ich schel thee yeve,
And withinne this fourtene night

155	Me self schel dobbe thee to knight,	*dub you knight*
	Yif that ich live."	
	The mesager him thankede yerne;	*earnestly*
	Hom ayen he gan him terne	*Home again*
	To Hamtoun;	
160	The levedi a fond in hire bour,	*he found; chamber*
	And he hire clepede doceamur	*embraced sweetly*
	And gan to roun:	*began to talk secretly*
	"Dame," a seide, "I thee tel:	
	That emperur thee grette wel	*greets you well*
165	With love mest:	*greatest love*
	Glad he is for that tiding,	
	A wile be prest at that fighting	*He will be ready for*
	In that forest.	
	Yif thow ert glad the lord to sle,	*you are happy*
170	Gladder a is for love of thee	*Happier he is*
	Fele sithe!"	*Many times*
	The mesager hath thus isaid,	
	The levedi was right wel apaid	*content*
	And maked hire blithe.	
175	In Mai, in the formeste dai,	*foremost (first)*
	The levedi in hire bedde lai,	
	Ase hit wer nede;	*As though it were a necessity*
	Hire lord she clepede out of halle	*called*
	And seide, that evel was on hire falle,	*evil (sickness)*
180	She wende be ded.	*She thought [she would] be dead*
	That erl for hire hath sorwe ikaught	*earl; sympathetized*
	And askede, yif she disired aught,	*if; desired anything*
	That mighte hire frevre.	*might comfort her*
	"Ye," she seide, "of a wilde bor	*boar*

185	I wene, me mineth, boute for	
	Al of the fevre!"[1]	
	"Madame," a seide, "for love myn,	*my love*
	Whar mai ich finde that wilde swin?	*Where; swine*
	I wolde, thow it hadde!"	
190	And she answerde with tresoun mest,	*treason*
	Be the se in hare forest,	*our*
	Thar a bradde.	*he breeds*
	That erl swor, be Godes grace,	
	In that forest he wolde chace,	
195	That bor to take;	
	And she answerde with tresoun than;	
	"Blessed be thow of alle man	
	For mine sake!"	
	That erl is hors began to stride,	*his; mount*
200	His scheld he heng upon is side,	*shield; his*
	Gert with swerd;	*Armed*
	Moste non armur on him come,	
	Himself was boute the ferthe some	*among a group of four*
	Toward that ferd.	*army*
205	Allas, that he nadde be war	*had not been wary*
	Of is fomen, that weren thar,	*enemies*
	Him forte schende:	*To kill him*
	With tresoun worth he ther islawe	*slain*
	And ibrought of is lif-dawe,	*from his life*
210	Er he hom wende!	*Before*
	Whan he com in to the forest,	
	Th'emperur a fond al prest;	*he found all ready*
	For envi	
	A prikede out before is ost,	*spurred; his host*

[1] Lines 184–86: *"Yes," she said, "from a wild boar I think, if memory serves me right, remedy [will come] for all of the fever"*

215	For pride and for make bost,	*boast*
	And gan to crie:	
	"Aghilt thee, treitour! thow olde dote!	*Surrender; traitor; fool*
	Thow shelt ben hanged be the throte,	
	Thin heved thow schelt lese;	*head; lose*
220	The sone schel anhanged be	*Your son*
	And the wif, that is so fre,	*noble*
	To me lemman I chese!"	*I choose for my lover*
	Th'erl answerde at that sawe:	*The earl; speech*
	"Me thenketh, thow seist ayen the lawe,	*speak against*
225	So God me amende!	
	Me wif and child, that was so fre,	*noble*
	Yif thow thenkest beneme hem me,	*to take them from me*
	Ich schel hem defende!"	*them*
	Tho prikede is stede Sire Gii,	*spurred his horse*
230	A stalword man and hardi,	
	While he was sounde;	*healthy*
	Th'emperur he smot with is spere,	
	Out of is sadel he gan him bere	*his saddle*
	And threw him to grounde.	
235	"Treitour," a seide, "thow ert to bolde!	*too*
	Wenestow, thegh ich bo olde,	*Do you think since I am old*
	To ben afered?	*To be afraid*
	That thow havest no right to me wif,	*my*
	I schel thee kithe be me lif!"	*show*
240	And drough is swerd.	*drew*
	That erl held is swerd adrawe,	*drawn*
	Th'emperur with he hadde slawe,	*would have slain*
	Nadde be sokour:	*Had there not been help*
	Thar come knightes mani and fale,	*many; numerous*
245	Wel ten thosent told be tale,	*thousand tolled by tally*
	To th'emperur.	

	Tho Sire Gii him gan defende,	*himself*
	Thre hondred hevedes of a slende	*heads he struck off*
	With is brond;	*sword*
250	Hadde he ben armed wel, ywis,	*well-armed; I imagine*
	Al the meistré hadde ben his,	*victory*
	Ich understonde.	
	Thre men were slawe, that he ther hadde,	*slain*
	That he with him out ladde	
255	And moste nede;	*and needed the most*
	To have merci, that was is hope;	*his*
	Th'emperur after him is lope	*rode*
	Upon a stede.	*his horse*
	Th'erl knewlede to th'emperur,	*knelt*
260	Merci a bad him and sokour	*succor*
	And is lif:	*his life*
	"Merci, sire, ase thow art fre,	*noble*
	Al that ichave, I graunte thee,	*I have*
	Boute me wif!	*Except*
265	For thine men, that ichave slawe,	*I have slain*
	Have her me swerd idrawe	*here; drawn*
	And al me fe:	*possessions*
	Boute me yonge sone Bef	*Except; Bevis*
	And me wif, that is me lef,	*my beloved*
270	That let thow me!"	
	"For Gode," queth he, "that ich do nelle!"	*will not do*
	Th'emperur to him gan telle,	
	And was agreved,	*angered*
	Anon right is swerd out drough	
275	And the gode knight a slough	*slew*
	And nam is heved.	*took his head*
	A knight a tok the heved an honde:	
	"Have," a seide, "ber this sonde	*take; message*
	Me leve swet!"	*[To] my sweet love*
280	The knight to Hamtoun tho gan gon,	

The levedi thar a fond anon — *he found soon*
And gan hire grete: — *greet*

"Dame," a seide, "to me atende: — *listen to me*
Th'emperur me hider sende — *sent me hither*
285 With is pray!" — *prize*
And she seide: "Blessed mot he be!
To wif a schel wedde me — *he shall*
To morwe in the dai. — *Tomorrow*

Sai him, me swete wight, — *tell; man*
290 That he come yet to night
In to me bour!" — *my bedchamber*
The mesager is wei hath holde, — *held his way*
Al a seide, ase she him tolde, — *All he said*
To th'emperur.

295 Now scholle we of him mone, — *speak*
Of Beves, that was Guis sone, — *Guy's son*
How wo him was: — *sorrowful*
Yerne a wep, is hondes wrong, — *Earnestly he wept, he wrung his hands*
For his fader a seide among: — *repeatedly*
300 "Allas! Allas!"

He cleped is moder and seide is sawe: — *called; speech*
"Vile houre! Thee worst to-drawe — *whore; You should be drawn*
And al to-twight! — *pulled apart*
Me thenketh, ich were ther-of ful fawe, — *I would be very glad*
305 For thow havest me fader slawe — *slain my father*
With mechel unright! — *much injustice*

Allas, moder, thee faire ble! — *complexion*
Evel becometh thee, houre to be, — *Evil becomes you, whore*
To holde bordel, — *manage [a] brothel*
310 And alle wif houren for thee sake, — *all women whore (i.e., work for you)*
The devel of helle ich hii betake, — *I would deliver them*
Flesch and fel! — *skin*

	Ac o thing, moder, I schel thee swere:	*But one*
	Yif ich ever armes bere	
315	And be of elde,	*age*
	Al that hath me fader islawe	*slain*
	And ibrought of is lif dawe,	*dear*
	Ich shel hem yilden!"	*repay*
	The moder hire hath understonde,	
320	That child she smot with hire honde	
	Under is ere.	*his ear*
	The child fel doun and that was scathe,	*pity*
	His meister tok him wel rathe,	*mentor; quickly*
	That highte Saber.	*Who was called*
325	The knight was trewe and of kinde,	*by nature*
	Strenger man ne scholde men finde	
	To ride ne go.	
	A was ibrought in tene and wrake	*He (Saber); harm; injury*
	Ofte for that childes sake	
330	Ase wel ase tho.	*then*
	That childe he nam up be the arm,	*took*
	Wel wo him was for that harm,	
	That he thar hadde.	
	Toward is kourt he him kende;	*showed the way*
335	The levedi after Saber sende	*sent after*
	And to him radde.	*spoke*
	"Saber," she seide, "thow ert me lef,	*love*
	Let sle me yonge sone Bef,	*slay; Bevis*
	That is so bold!	
340	Let him anhange swithe highe,	*very high*
	I ne reche, what deth he dighe,	
	Sithe he be cold!"[1]	

[1] Lines 341–42: *I do not care what kind of death he dies, / As long as he is cold*

	Saber stod stille and was ful wo;	
	Natheles a seide, a wolde do	*Nevertheless*
345	After hire sawe;	*command*
	The child with him hom he nam,	*he took home*
	A swin he tok, whan he hom cam,	*swine*
	And dede hit of dawe.	*killed it*
	The childes clothes, that were gode,	
350	Al a bisprengde with that blode	*sprinkled*
	In many stede,	*places*
	Ase yif the child were to-hewe,	*cut apart*
	A thoughte to his moder hem schewe,	*He; show*
	And so a dede.	*he did*
355	At the laste him gan adrede,	*to be afraid*
	He let clothen in pouer wede	*poor clothes*
	That hende wight,	*gentle person*
	And seide: "Sone, thow most kepe	
	Upon the felde mine schepe	*sheep*
360	This fourte night!	*fortnight (two weeks)*
	And whan the feste is come to th'ende,	
	In to another londe I schel thee sende	
	Fer be southe,	
	To a riche erl, that schel thee gie	*guide you*
365	And teche thee of corteisie	*teach you courtesy*
	In the youthe.	*your*
	And whan thow ert of swich elde,	*such [an] age*
	That thow might the self wilde,	*govern*
	And ert of age,	
370	Thanne scheltow come in te Ingelonde,	*return to England*
	With werre winne in to thin honde	*win back*
	Thin eritage.	*Your heritage*
	I schel thee helpe with alle me might,	*all my*
	With dent of swerd to gete thee right,	*your rights*
375	Be thow of elde!"	*[Until] you are of age*
	The child him thankede and sore wep,	*thanked him; wept*

	And forth a wente with the schep	
	Upon the velde.	*field*
	Beves was herde upon the doun	*shepherd; hill*
380	He lokede homward to the toun,	
	That scholde ben his;	
	He beheld toward the tour,	*tower*
	Trompes he herde and tabour	*Trumpets; drum*
	And meche blis.	*much bliss (celebration)*
385	"Lord," a seide, "on me thow mone!	*remember*
	Ne was ich ones an erles sone	*once; earl's son*
	And now am herde?	*shepherd*
	Mighte ich with that emperur speke,	
	Wel ich wolde me fader awreke	*avenge*
390	For al is ferde!"	*Despite his retinue*
	He nemeth is bat and forth a goth,	*picked up; club*
	Swithe sori and wel wroth,	*Deeply sorry; angry*
	Toward the tour;	
	"Porter!" a sede, "Let me in reke!	*quickly*
395	A lite thing ich ave to speke	*little; have*
	With th'emperur."	
	"Go hom, truant!" the porter sede,	*vagrant*
	"Scherewe houre sone, I thee rede,	*Wicked whore's; command*
	Fro the gate:	*From*
400	Boute thow go hennes also swithe,	*Unless*
	Hit schel thee rewe fele sithe,	
	Thow come ther-ate![1]	
	Sixte the scherewe, "Ho be itte,	*Said; evil man; How*
	A loketh, as a wolde smite	
405	With is bat:	
	Speke he ought meche more,	*If he says anything much more*

[1] Lines 400–02: *Unless you go hence very quickly, / You shall rue it [as] many times / [As] you come there*

	I schel him smite swithe sore	*very sore*
	Upon is hat."	
	"For Gode," queth Beves, "natheles,	
410	An houre sone for soth ich wes,	*A whore's son*
	Wel ich it wot!	
	I nam no truant, be Godes grace!"	
	With that a lefte up is mace	*lifted; club*
	Anon fot hot.	*Quickly*
415	Beves withoute the gate stod.	*outside; stood*
	And smot the porter on the hod,	*hood*
	That he gan falle;	
	His heved he gan al to cleve	*head*
	And forth a wente with that leve	*permission*
420	In to the halle.	
	Al aboute he gan beholde,	
	To th'emperur he spak wordes bolde	
	With meche grame:	*anger*
	"Sire," a sede, "what dostow here?	*are you doing*
425	Whi colles thow aboute the swire	*embraces; neck*
	That ilche dame?	*same*
	Me moder is that thow havest an honde:	
	What dostow her upon me londe	
	Withouten leve?	*permission*
430	Tak me me moder and mi fe,	*Take [from] me my; property*
	Boute thow the rather hennes te,	*Unless; sooner go*
	I schel thee greve!	*make trouble for you*
	Nastow, sire, me fader slawe?	*Have you not; slain*
	Thow schelt ben hanged and to-drawe,	*drawn*
435	Be Godes wille!	
	Aris! Fle hennes, I thee rede!"	*Arise; advise*
	Th'emperur to him sede:	
	"Foul, be stille!"	*Fool*

Beves was nigh wod for grame, *mad; anger*
440 For a clepede him "foul" be name, *called; fool*
And to him a wond; *he turned*
For al that weren in the place,
Thries a smot him with is mace *Three times; club*
And with is honde. *his hand*

445 Thries a smot him on the kroun; *crown (head)*
That emperur fel swowe adoun, *in a swoon*
Thar a sat.
The levedi, is moder, gan to grede: *cry*
"Nemeth that treitour!" she sede, *Seize*
450 "Anon with that!"

Tho dorste Beves no leng abide;
The knightes up in ech a side,
More and lasse,
Wo hem was for the childes sake,
455 Boute non of hem nolde him take *But none of them would take him*
Hii lete him pase. *They; pass*

Beves goth faste ase he mai,
His meister a mette in the wai, *teacher he met*
That highte Saber, *was called*
460 And he him askede with blithe mod: *uplifted spirits*
"Beves!" a seide, "for the Rode, *Cross*
What dostow her?" *are you doing here*

"I schel thee telle al togadre: *at once*
Beten ichave me stifadre *Beaten; stepfather*
465 With me mace;
Thries I smot him in the heved,
Al for ded ich him leved *left*
In the place!"

"Beves," queth Saber, "thow ert to blame:
470 The levedi wile now do me schame *will; shame (harm)*
For thine sake!
Boute thow be me consaile do, *Unless; counsel*

	Thow might now sone bringe us bo	*both*
	In meche wrake!"	*trouble*
475	Saber Beves to his hous ladde,	*led*
	Meche of that levedi him dradde.	*he was very afraid*
	The levedi out of the tour cam,	
	To Saber the wei she nam.	*she made her way*
	"Saber," she seide, "whar is Bef,	
480	That wike treitour, that fule thef?"	*wicked; foul thief*
	"Dame," a seide, "ich dede him of dawe	
	Be thee red and be thee sawe:	*By your advice; by your command*
	This beth his clothe, thow her sixt."	*as you can see*
	The levedi seide: "Saber thow lixt!	*you lie*
485	Boute thow me to him take,	*Unless*
	Thow schelt abegge for is sake."	*pay*
	Beves herde his meister threte;	*teacher (mentor); threatened*
	To hire a spak with hertte grete	
	And seide: "Lo, me her be name!	*Lo, I am here, by name*
490	Do me meister for me no schame!	*Do not shame my teacher on my behalf*
	Yif thow me sext, lo, whar ich am here!"	*call for me; here I am*
	His moder tok him be the ere;	
	Fain she wolde a were of live.	*Eagerly she wished he were dead*
	Foure knightes she clepede blive:	*called quickly*
495	"Wendeth," she seide, "to the stronde:	*Go; shore*
	Yif ye seth schipes of painim londe,	*ships; heathen land*
	Selleth to hem this ilche hyne,	*Sell to them; very boy*
	That ye for no gode ne fine,	*fine possessions*
	Whather ye have for him mor and lesse,	
500	Selleth him right in to hethenesse!"	
	Forth the knightes gonne te,	*began to go*
	Til that hii come to the se,	*they*
	Schipes hii fonde ther stonde	*found standing there*
	Of hethenesse and of fele londe;	*many*
505	The child hii chepeden to sale,	*they offered to sell*
	Marchaundes thai fonde ferli fale	*Merchants; very many*
	And solde that child for mechel aughte	*a good price*
	And to the Sarasins him betaughte.	*delivered*
	Forth thai wente with that child,	
510	Crist of hevene be him mild!	

The childes hertte was wel colde, — *fearful*
For that he was so fer isolde; — *far away sold*
Natheles, though him thoughte eile, — *grief*
Toward painim a moste saile. — *he must*
515 Whan hii rivede out of that strond, — *sailed forth*
The king highte Ermin of that londe; — *was called*
His wif was ded, that highte Morage,
A doughter a hadde of yong age,
Josiane that maide het, — *was named*
520 Hire schon wer gold upon hire fet; — *shoes; feet*
So faire she was and bright of mod, — *mind*
Ase snow upon the rede blod —
Wharto scholde that may discrive? — *To what should she be compared*
Men wiste no fairer thing alive, — *knew*
525 So hende ne wel itaught; — *gentle nor well brought up*
Boute of Cristene lawe she kouthe naught. — *Except; knew nothing*
The marchauns wente an highing — *in haste*
And presente Beves to Ermyn King.
The king thar of was glad and blithe
530 And thankede hem mani a sithe: — *time*
"Mahoun!" a seide, "thee might be proute, — *Mohammed; proud*
And this child wolde to thee aloute; — *If; incline to*
Yif a wolde a Sarasin be, — *If only [he] would be a Saracen*
Yit ich wolde hope, a scholde the! — *As; he should prosper*
535 Be Mahoun, that sit an high, — *By Mohammed*
A fairer child never I ne sigh, — *saw*
Neither a lingthe ne on brade, — *length; breadth*
Ne non, so faire limes hade! — *limbs*
Child," a seide, "whar wer thee bore? — *where were you born*
540 What is thee name? telle me fore!
Yif ich it wiste, hit were me lef." — *It would please me if I knew it*
"For Gode," a seide, "ich hatte Bef; — *am called*
Iborne ich was in Ingelonde, — *I was born; England*
At Hamtoun, be the se stronde. — *seashore*
545 Me fader was erl thar a while,
Me moder him let sle with gile, — *murdered treacherously*
And me she solde in to hethenlonde;
Wikked beth fele wimmen to fonde! — *many; prove to be*
Ac, sire, yif it ever so betide, — *But; happen*

550	That ich mowe an horse ride	*might*
	And armes bere and scheft tobreke,	*lance shatter*
	Me fader deth ich schel wel wreke!"	*avenge*
	The kinges hertte wex wel cold,	*heart grew*
	Whan Beves hadde thus itolde,	
555	And seide: "I nave non eir after me dai,	*have no heir*
	Boute Josian, this faire mai;	*Except; maiden*
	And thow wile thee god forsake	*If you forsake your god*
	And to Apolyn, me lord, take,	
	Hire I schel thee yeve to wive	*give [her] to you to marry*
560	And al me lond after me live!"	*when I die*
	"For Gode!" queth Beves, "that I nolde	*would not*
	For al the selver ne al the golde,	*silver*
	That is under hevene light,	
	Ne for thee doughter, that is so bright.	*Neither*
565	I nolde forsake in none manere	
	Jesu, that boughte me so dere.	*redeemed*
	Al mote thai be doum and deve,	*dumb; deaf*
	That on the false godes beleve!"	
	The king him lovede wel the more,	*loved him*
570	For him ne stod of no man sore,	*endured no other man's sorrow*
	And seide: "Beves, while thow ert swain,	*servant*
	Thow schelt be me chaumberlain,	
	And thow schelt, whan thow ert dobbed knight,	*dubbed*
	Me baner bere in to everi fight!"	*My banner bear*
575	Beves answerde al with skil:	
	"What ye me hoten, don ich wil!"	*command; I will do*
	Beves was ther yer and other,	*a year and a second (two years)*
	The king him lovede also is brother,	*as his*
	And the maide that was so sligh.	*clever*
580	So dede everi man that him sigh.	*saw*
	Be that he was fiftene yer olde,	*By the time*
	Knight ne swain thar nas so bolde,	
	That him dorste ayenes ride	*ride against him (challenge)*
	Ne with wrethe him abide.	*anger tolerate him*
585	His ferste bataile, for soth te say	
	A dede a Cristes messe day;	*He did on Christmas*
	Ase Beves scholde to water ride	

	And fiftene Sarasins be is side,	
	And Beves rod on Arondel,	
590	That was a stede gode and lel.	*loyal*
	A Sarasin began to say	*speak*
	And askede him, what het that day.	*was called*
	Beves seide: "For soth ywis,	
	I not never, what dai it is,	*do not know*
595	For I nas boute seve winter old,	*seven*
	Fro Cristendome ich was isold;	*From*
	Tharfore I ne can telle nought thee,	*cannot tell you*
	What dai that hit mighte be."	
	The Sarasin beheld and lough.	*looked at him; laughed*
600	"This dai," a saide, "I knowe wel inough.	
	This is the ferste dai of Youl,	*Yule*
	Thee God was boren withouten doul;	*Your; pain*
	For thi men maken ther mor blisse	*partake in greater joy*
	Than men do her in hethenesse.	
605	Anoure thee God, so I schel myn,	*Honor*
	Bothe Mahoun and Apolyn!"	
	Beves to that Sarasin said:	
	"Of Cristendom yit ichave abraid,	*partaken*
	Ichave seie on this dai right	
610	Armed mani a gentil knight,	
	Torneande right in the feld	*Tourneying*
	With helmes bright and mani scheld;	*helmets; many [a] shield*
	And were ich alse stith in plas,	*as strong; [my] place*
	Ase ever Gii, me fader was,	
615	Ich wolde for me Lordes love,	
	That sit high in hevene above,	
	Fighte with yow everichon,	*every one*
	Er than ich wolde hennes gon!"	*Before leaving*
	The Sarasin seide to his felawes:	
620	"Lo, brethern, hire ye nought this sawes,	*Listen; these boasts*
	How the yonge Cristene hounde,	
	A saith, a wolde us fellen te grounde.	*He; defeat us*
	Wile we aboute him gon	*Shall*
	And fonde that treitour slon?"	*try; to slay*
625	Al aboute thai gonne thringe,	*press*
	And hard on him thai gonne dinge	*to strike*

And yaf him wondes mani on *wounds*
Thourgh the flesch in to the bon,
Depe wondes and sore,
630 That he mighte sofre namore; *suffer*
Tho his bodi began to smerte, *hurt*
He gan plokken up is hertte, *pluck up his courage*
Ase tid to a Sarasin a wond *Quickly; he turned*
And breide a swerd out of is honde, *took*
635 And fifti Sarasins, in that stonde *place*
Thar with a yaf hem dedli wonde, *them deadly wounds*
And sum he strok of the swire, *some; severed; neck*
That the heved flegh in to the rivere, *head flew*
And sum he clef evene asonder;
640 Here hors is fet thai laine under; *Their horses' feet; they lay*
Ne was ther non, that mighte ascape, *There were none*
So Beues slough hem in a rape. *them hastily*
The stedes hom to stable ran *home*
Withoute kenning of eni man. *guidance from*

645 Beves hom began to ride,
His wondes bledde be ech side;
The stede he graithed up anon, *put into the stable*
In to his chaumber he gan gon
And leide him deueling on the grounde, *himself flat*
650 To kolen his hertte in that stounde. *calm; place*
Tiding com to King Ermyn *Word*
That Beves hadde mad is men tyn; *perish*
The king swor and seide is sawe. *his sentence*
For thi a scholde ben to-drawe. *That he should*
655 Up stod that maide Josian,
And to hire fader she seide than:
"Sire, ich wot wel in me thought, *know; mind*
That thine men ne slough he nought,
Be Mahoun ne be Tervagaunt,
660 Boute hit were himself defendaunt! *Unless he were defending himself*
Ac, fader," she saide, "be me red, *And; advice*
Er thow do Beves to ded, *Before you put; death*
Ich praie, sire, for love o me, *pray*
Do bringe that child before thee!

665 Whan the child, that is so bold,
His owene tale hath itolde,
And thow wite the soth, aplight, — *truth, indeed*
Who hath the wrong, who hath right,
Yef him his dom, that he schel have, — *Render; judgment*
670 Whather thow wilt him slen or save!" — *slay*
King Ermyn seide: "Me doughter fre, — *noble*
Ase thow havest seid, so it schel be!"
Josiane tho anon rightes — *very soon*
Clepede to hire twei knightes: — *Called; two*
675 "To Beves now wende ye — *make your way*
And prai him, that he come to me: — *ask*
Er me fader arise fro his des; — *dais*
Ful wel ich schel maken is pes!" — *peace*
Forth the knightes gonne gon,
680 To Beves chaumber thai come anon
And praide, ase he was gentil man,
Come speke with Josian.
Beves stoutliche in that stounde — *bravely*
Haf up is heved fro the grounde; — *Heaved; head*
685 With stepe eighen and rowe bren — *bright; hairy brows*
So lotheliche he gan on hem sen, — *loathly; looked to them*
The twei knightes, thar thai stode,
Thai were aferde, hii wer nigh wode. — *afraid; confused*
A seide: "Yif ye ner masegers, — *were not messengers*
690 Ich wolde yow sle, losengers! — *cowards*
I nele rise o fot fro the grounde, — *one foot from*
For speke with an hethene hounde:
She is an honde, also be ye, — *heathen as you are*
Out of me chaumber swithe ye fle!" — *Get out quickly*
695 The knightes wenten out in rape, — *haste*
Thai were fain so to ascape. — *eager; escape*
To Josian thai wente as tit — *at once*
And seide: "Of him is gret despit:
Sertes, a clepede thee hethene hound — *Certainly, he called you heathen hound*
700 Thries in a lite stounde — *Three times; short time*
We nolde for al Ermonie — *Armenia*
Eft sones se him with our eie!" — *Again*
"Hardeliche," she seide, "cometh with me, — *Hardily*

	And ich wile your waraunt be!"	*guarantee*
705	Forth thai wente al isame,	*together*
	To Beves chaumber that he came.	
	"Lemman," she seide, "gent and fre,	*Sweetheart*
	For Godes love, spek with me!"	
	She keste him bothe moth and chin	*kissed; mouth*
710	And yaf him confort gode afin,	*throughout*
	So him solaste that mai,	*gave solace; maiden*
	That al is care wente awai,	*his*
	And seide: "Lemman, thin ore!	*mercy*
	Icham iwonded swithe sore!"	*I am wounded very*
715	"Lemman," she seide, "with gode entent	
	Ichave brought an oyniment,	*ointment*
	For make thee bothe hol and fere;	*To make you whole; sound*
	Wende we to me fader dere!"	*Let us go*
	Forth thai wenten an highing	*in haste*
720	Til Ermyn, the riche king,	*To*
	And Beves tolde unto him than,	
	How that stour ended and gan,	*conflict; began*
	And schewed on him in that stounde	*showed; place*
	Fourti grete, grisli wounde.	*Forty; gruesome*
725	Thanne seide King Ermin the hore:	*grayhaired*
	"I nolde, Beves, that thow ded wore	*do not wish*
	For al the londes, that ichave;	
	Ich praie, doughter, that thow him save	
	And prove to hele, ase thow can,	*bring to health*
730	The wondes of that doughti man!"	*brave*
	In to chaumber she gan him take	
	And riche bathes she let him make,	*healthful*
	That withinne a lite stonde	*in a short time*
	He was bothe hol and sonde.	*whole and sound*
735	Thanne was he ase fresch to fight,	
	So was the faukoun to the flight.	*As; falcon*
	His other prowesse who wile lere,	*learn*
	Hende, herkneth, and ye mai here!	*Nobles*
	A wilde bor thar was aboute,	*boar*
740	Ech man of him hadde gret doute.	*fear*
	Man and houndes, that he tok,	
	With his toskes he al toschok.	*tusks; shook to pieces*

	Thei him hontede knightes tene,	*hunted [the boar]; ten*
	Tharof ne yef he nought a bene,	*gave he not a bean (did not care)*
745	At is mouth fif toskes stoden out,	*five*
	Everich was fif enches about,	*Each; inches wide*
	His sides wer hard and strong,	
	His brostles were gret and long,	*bristles*
	Himself was fel and kouthe fighte,	*fierce; knew how to*
750	No man sle him ne mighte.	
	Beves lay in is bedde a night	*his*
	And thoughte, a wolde kethen is might	*dreamed; he would prove his*
	Upon that swin himself one,	*swine; alone*
	That no man scholde with him gone.	
755	A morwe, whan hit was dai cler,	*In the morning*
	Ariseth knight and squier;	
	Beves let sadlen is ronsi,	*saddled; horse*
	That bor a thoughte to honti,	*decided; hunt*
	A gerte him with a gode brond	*armed himself; sword*
760	And tok a spere in is hond,	
	A scheld a heng upon is side,	
	Toward the wode he gan ride.	*forest*
	Josian, that maide, him beheld,	*watched*
	Al hire love to him she feld;	*felt*
765	To hire self she seide, ther she stod:	*as she stood there*
	"Ne kepte I never more gode	
	Ne namore of al this worldes blisse,	
	Thanne Beves with love o time te kisse;	
	In gode time were boren,	
770	That Beves hadde to lemman koren!"	*chosen*
	Tho Beves in to the wode cam,	
	His scheld aboute is nekke a nam	*he took*
	And tide his hors to an hei thorn	*tree*
	And blew a blast with is horn;	
775	Thre motes a blew al arowe,	*notes; in a row*
	That the bor him scholde knowe.	*boar; hear*
	Tho he com to the bor is den,	*Then; boar's den*
	A segh ther bones of dede men,	*saw*
	The bor hadde slawe in the wode,	*slain*
780	Ieten here flesch and dronke her blode.	*Eaten their; drunk their blood*

	"Aris!" queth Beves, "corsede gast,	*cursed spirit*
	And yem me bataile wel in hast!"	*give; right now*
	Sone so the bor him sigh,	*As soon as; saw*
	A rerde is brosteles wel an high	*He raised*
785	And starede on Beves with eien holwe,	*stared at; hungry eyes*
	Also a wolde him have aswolwe;	*As if; swallowed*
	And for the bor yenede so wide,	*when; yawned*
	A spere Beves let to him glide;	
	On the scholder he smot the bor,	
790	His spere barst to pises thore	*pieces there*
	The bor stod stille ayen the dent,	*blow*
	His hyde was harde ase eni flent.	*any flint*
	Now al to-borste is Beves spere,	*broken*
	A drough his swerd, himself to were,	*protect*
795	And faught ayen the bor so grim,	
	A smot the bor and he to him.	
	Thus the bataile gan leste long	
	Til the time of evesong,	*evensong*
	That Beves was so weri of foughte,	*fighting*
800	That of is lif he ne roughte,	*cared*
	And tho the bor was also,	
	Awai fro Beves he gan go,	
	Wile Beves made is praier	*his prayer*
	To God and Mari, is moder dere,	
805	Whather scholde other slen.	
	With that com the bor ayen	
	And bente is brostles up, saunfaile,	*without fail*
	Ayen Beves to yeve bataile;	*Against; give*
	Out at is mouth in aither side	
810	The foim ful ferli gan out glide;	*foam; wondrously*
	And Beves in that ilche veneu,	*very place*
	Thourgh Godes grace and is vertu	*His virtue*
	With swerd out a slinte	*sliced*
	Twei toskes at the ferste dent;	*Two tusks; stroke*
815	A spanne of the groin beforn	*hand's breadth of the snout*
	With is swerd he hath of schoren.	*shorn away*
	Tho the bor so loude cride,	
	Out of the forest wide and side,	*long*
	To the castel thar that lai Ermin,	

820 Men herde the noise of the swin;
And, alse he made that lotheli cri, — *loathly*
His swerd Beves hasteli
In at the mouth gan threste tho — *thrust*
And karf his hertte evene ato — *carved; exactly in two*
825 The swerd a breide ayen fot hot — *brandished again quickly*
And the bor is heved of smot, — *off smote*
And on a tronsoun of is spere — *handle*
That heved a stikede for to bere, — *head; stuck*
Thanne a sette horn to mouthe
830 And blew the pris ase wel kouthe, — *flourish; known*
So glad he was for is honting.
That heved a thoughte Josian bring:
And er he com to that maide fre,
Him com strokes so gret plenté,
835 That fain he was to weren is hed — *eager; defend*
And save himself fro the ded. — *from; death*
A stiward was with King Ermin, — *steward*
That hadde tight to sle that swin; — *Who; hoped*
To Beves a bar gret envie, — *bore*
840 For that he hadde the meistrie; — *mastery*
He dede arme his knightes stoute, — *stout*
Four and twenti in a route,
And ten forsters also he tok
And wente to wode, seith the bok. — *the book says*
845 Thar-of ne wiste Beves nought. — *knew*
Helpe him God, that alle thing wrought! — *who created all things*
In is wei he rit pas for pas. — *rides step for step*
Herkneth now a ferli cas: — *Listen; marvelous event*
A wende pasi in grith and pes, — *He (Bevis) went walking in peace; security*
850 The stiward cride: "Leith on and sles!" — *Attack; strike down*
Beves seigh that hii to him ferde, — *drew*
A wolde drawe to is swerde:
Thanne had he leved it thor, — *left it there*
Thar he hadde slawe the bor. — *Where*
855 He nadde nothing, himself to were, — *defend*
Boute a tronsoun of a spere. — *handle*
Tho was Beves sore desmeid, — *dismayed*
The heved fro the tronsoun a braid, — *took*

	And with the bor is heved a faught	*boar's head he*
860	And wan a swerd of miche maught,	*great power*
	That Morgelai was cleped, aplight.	*was called, indeed*
	Beter swerd bar never knight.	
	Tho Beves hadde that swerd an hond,	*When*
	Among the hethene knightes a wond,	*turned*
865	And sum upon the helm a hitte,	
	In to the sadel he hem slitte,	*them slit*
	And sum knight Beves so ofraughte,	*a certain; reached*
	The heved of at the ferste draughte,	*stroke*
	So harde he gan to lein aboute	*rush*
870	Among the hethene knightes stoute,	
	That non ne pasede hom, aplight;	
	So thourgh the grace of God almight	
	The kinges stiward a hitte so,	
	That is bodi a clef ato.	*he cleft in two*
875	The dede kors a pulte adoun	*corpse; pulled down*
	And lep himself in to the arsoun.	*saddle*
	That strok him thoughte wel iset	*placed*
	For he was horsed meche bet.	*much better*
	He thoughte make pes doun rightes	*wanted to make a certain peace*
880	Of the forsters ase of the knightes;	*With*
	To hem faste he gan ride;	*them*
	Thai gonne schete be ech a side,	*shoot*
	So mani arwes to him thai sende,	*arrows*
	Unnethe a mighte himself defende,	*Scarcely*
885	So tho is a lite stounde	
	The ten forsters wer feld te grounde,	
	And hew hem alle to pices smale:	
	So hit is fonde in Frensche tale.	
	Josian lai in a castel	
890	And segh that sconfit everich del.	*conflict*
	"O Mahoun," she seide, "oure drighte,	*lord*
	What Beves is man of meche mighte!	
	Al this world yif ich it hedde,	*if I had it*
	Ich him yeve me to wedde;	*would wed him*
895	Boute he me love, icham ded.	*Unless*
	Swete Mahoun, what is thee red?	*your advice*
	Lovelonging me hath becought,	*captivated*

Thar-of wot Beves right nought," *knows nothing*
Thus that maide made hire mon, *lament (moan)*
900 Thar she stod in the tour al on, *alone*
And Beves thar the folk beleved *left*
And wente hom with the heved;
That heved of that wilde swin
He presente to King Ermin.
905 The king thar-of was glad and blithe
And thankede him ful mani a sithe, *time*
Ac he ne wiste ther of nowight, *But he did not learn from anyone*
How is stiward to dethe was dight. *was done to death*
Thre yer after that bataile,
910 That Beves the bor gan asaile,
A king ther com in to Ermonie
And thoughte winne with meistrie
Josiane, that maide bright,
That lovede Beves with al hire might. *Who*
915 Brademond cride, ase he wer wod, *crazed*
To King Ermin, thar a stod:
"King," a seide swithe blive, *very quickly*
"Yem me thee doughter to wive! *Give*
Yif thow me wernest, withouten faile, *refuse*
920 I schel winne hire in plein bataile, *all-out combat*
On fele half I schel thee anughe, *many sides; provoke*
And al thee londe I schel destruye *destroy*
And thee sle, so mai betide, *happen*
And lay hire a night be me side,
925 And after I wile thee doughter yeve
To a weine-pain, that is fordrive!" *carter; worn out*
Ermin answerde blive on highe:
"Be Mahoun, sire, thow schelt lighe!" *lie*
Adoun of his tour a went
930 And after al is knightes a sent
And tolde hem how Brademond him asailed hadde,
And askede hem alle, what hii radde. *they advise*
A word thanne spak that maiden bright:
"Be Mahoun, sire! wer Beves a knight,
935 A wolde defende thee wel inough.
Me self I segh, whar he slough

	Your owene stiward, him beset,	*who set upon him*
	Al one in the wode with him a met,	*Alone*
	At wode he hadde his swerd beleved,	*taken away*
940	Thar he smot of the bores heved;	*Where; boar's head*
	He nadde nothing, himself to were,	*defend*
	Boute a tronsoun of is spere,	*handle*
	And your stiward gret peple hadde,	
	Four and twenti knightes a ladde,	*he led*
945	Al y-armed to the teth,	
	And everi hadde swore is deth,	
	And ten forsters of the forest	
	With him a broughte ase prest,	*ready*
	That thoughte him have slawe thore	*there*
950	And take the heved of the bore,	
	And yeve the stiward the renoun.	
	Tho Beves segh that foule tresoun,	
	A leide on with the bor is heved,	*boar's head*
	Til that hii were adoun iweved,	*knocked down*
955	And of the stiward a wan that day	*won*
	His gode swerd Morgelay.	
	The ten forsters also a slough	*slew*
	And hom a pasede wel inough,	
	That he of hem hadde no lothe."	*fear*
960	King Ermyn thanne swor is othe,	*his oath*
	That he scholde be maked knight,	*[Bevis] should be dubbed*
	His baner to bere in that fight.	
	He clepede Beves at that sake	
	And seide: "Knight ich wile thee make.	
965	Thow schelt bere in to bataile	
	Me baner, Brademond to asaile!"	
	Beves answerde with blithe mod:	*enthusiasm*
	"Blethelich," a seide, "be the Rod!"	*Gladly; Cross*
	King Ermin tho anon righte	
970	Dobbede Beves unto knighte	*Dubbed*
	And yaf him a scheld gode and sur	*sure*
	With thre eglen of asur,	*eagles; azure*
	The champe of gold ful wel idight	*field; ornamented*
	With fif lables of selver bright;	*ribbons*
975	Sithe a gerte him with Morgelay,	*Then he armed himself*

A gonfanoun wel stout and gay — *banner*
Josian him broughte for to bere.
Sent of the scheld, I yow swere!
Beves dede on is actoun, — *put on his jacket*
980 Hit was worth mani a toun;
An hauberk him broughte that mai, — *tunic; maiden*
So seiden alle that hit isai: — *viewed it*
Hit was wel iwrought and faire,
Non egge tol mighte it nought paire. — *edge-tool; sever*
985 After that she yaf him a stede, — *horse*
That swithe gode was at nede,
For hit was swift and ernede wel. — *ran*
Me clepede hit Arondel. — *Men called it*
Beves in the sadel lep,
990 His ost him folwede al to hep — *host; in a group*
With baner bright and scheldes schene, — *shining*
Thretti thosent and fiftene, — *Thirty thousand*
The ferste scheld trome Beves nam. — *first shield retinue; took*
Brademond aghenes him cam; — *against*
995 His baner bar the King Redefoun,
That levede on Sire Mahoun. — *Who believed in*
Row he was also a schep, — *Rough; shepherd*
Beves of him nam gode kep. — *took good care*
He smot Arondel with spures of golde;
1000 Thanne thoughte that hors, that he scholde,
Aghen Redefoun Beves gan ride
And smot him thourgh out bothe side,
Hauberk ne scheld ne actoun — *jacket*
Ne vailede him nought worth a botoun, — *availed; button*
1005 That he ne fel ded to the grounde.
"Reste thee," queth Beves, "hethen hounde!
Thee hadde beter atom than here!" — *at home*
"Lay on faste!" a bad his fere. — *he ordered his companions*
Tho laide thai on with eger mod — *Then; eager mood (enthusiastically)*
1010 And slowe Sarsins, as hii wer wod, — *slew; as if they; berserk (see note)*
And Sire Beves, the Cristene knight
Slough ase mani in that fight
With Morgelay himself alone,
Ase thai deden everichone. — *did everyone [else]*

1015 And ever hii were to fighte prest — *ready*
Til that the sonne set in the west.
Beves and is ost withinne a stounde — *moment*
Sexti thosent thai felde to grounde, — *Sixty thousand*
That were out of Dameske isent, — *Damascus*
1020 That never on homward ne went;
Tho Brademond segh is folk islayn, — *When; saw*
A flegh awei with mighte and mayn. — *fled*
Ase he com ride be a cost, — *coast*
Twei knightes a fond of Beves ost; — *host*
1025 Of his stede he gan doun lighte — *dismount*
And bond hem bothe anon righte,
And thoughte hem lede to his prisoun
And have for hem gret raunsoun. — *ransom*
Ase he trosede hem on is stede, — *trussed; steed*
1030 Beves of hem nam gode hede, — *took heed*
And hasteliche in that tide — *time*
After Brademond he gan ride
And seide: "Brademond, olde wreche,
Ertow come Josiane to feche? — *Are you; fetch*
1035 Erst thow schelt pase thourgh min hond — *First*
And thourgh Morgelay, me gode brond!" — *my; sword*
Withouten eni wordes mo — *any; more*
Beves Brademond hitte so
Upon is helm in that stounde, — *place*
1040 That a felde him flat to grounde.
"Merci!" queth Bradmond, "ich me yelde, — *I acknowledge myself*
Recreaunt to thee, in this felde, — *Defeated by*
So harde thee smitest upon me kroun, — *crown*
Ich do me all in the bandoun, — *relinquish; your power*
1045 Sexti cites with castel tour
Thin owen, Beves, to thin onour, — *Your own; honor*
With that thow lete me ascape!" — *Providing that; escape*
Beves answerde tho in rape: — *then in haste*
"Nay!" a seide, "be sein Martyn!
1050 Icham iswore to King Ermin.
Al that ich do, it is his dede; — *for him*
Tharfore, sire, so God me spede,
Thow schelt swere upon the lay, — *law*

Thow schelt werre on him night ne day, *war; [neither] day nor night*
1055 And omage eche yer him yelde *homage*
And al the londe of him helde!"
Brademond answerde anon righte:
"Tharto me treuthe I thee plighte, *Thereto*
That I ne schel never don him dere *harm*
1060 Ne aghen thee, Beves, armes bere!" *Neither against you*
And whan he hadde swore so,
Beves let King Brademond go.
Allas, that he nadde him slawe
And ibrought of is life dawe!
1065 For sithe for al is faire beheste *For later despite all his fair promise*
Mani dai a maked him feste, *feast*
In is prisoun a lai seve yere,
Ase ye may now forthward here. *henceforth hear*
Beves rod hom and gan to singe
1070 And seide to Ermin the Kinge:
"Sire! Brademond, King of Sarasine,
A is become one of thine;
The man a is to thin heste, *command*
While his lif wile leste, *As long as he lives*
1075 Londes and ledes, al that he walt, *people; possesses*
A saith, sire, of thee hem halt!" *He says; holds them for you*
Thanne was King Ermin at that sithe *time*
In is hertte swithe blithe;
A clepede is doughter and saide:
1080 "Josian, the faire maide,
Unarme Beves, he wer at mete, *food (dinner)*
And serve thee self him ther-ate!"
Tho nolde that maide never blinne, *cease*
Til she com to hire inne, *lodging*
1085 Thar she lai hire selve anight:
Thar she sette that gentil knight,
Hire self yaf him water to hond *gave*
And sette before him al is sonde. *servings [of various dishes]*
Tho Beves hadde wel i-ete *eaten*
1090 And on the maidenes bed isete,
That mai, that was so bright of hiwe, *hue (complexion)*
Thoughte she wolde hire consaile schewe, *counsel; show*

	And seide: "Beves, lemman, thin ore!	*my dear; if you please*
	Ichave loved thee ful yore,	*so completely*
1095	Sikerli can I no rede,	*Truly I know no counsel*
	Boute thow me love, icham dede,	*Unless*
	And boute thow with me do thee wille."	*unless you do your will with me*
	"For Gode," queth Beves, "that ich do nelle!	*nothing of the kind*
	Her is," a seide, "min unliche,	*There; unlike me*
1100	Brademond King, that is so riche,	
	In al this world nis ther man,	
	Prinse ne king ne soudan,	*sultan*
	That thee to wive have nolde,	*would not wish to have*
	And he the hadde ones beholde!"	*you have once beheld*
1105	"Merci," she seide, "yet with than	
	Ichavede thee lever to me lemman,	*I would rather have you as my lover*
	Thee bodi in thee scherte naked,	
	Than al the gold, that Crist hath maked,	
	And thow wost with me do thee wille!"	
1110	"For Gode," queth Beves, "that I do nelle!"	*will not do*
	Sche fel adoun and wep right sore:	
	"Thow seidest soth her before:	
	In al this world nis ther man,	
	Prinse ne king ne soudan,	
1115	That me to wive have nolde,	*That would not have me as wife*
	And he me hadde ones beholde,	*If*
	And thow, cherl, me havest forsake;	
	Mahoun thee yeve tene and wrake!	*suffering; injury*
	Beter become the iliche	*the likes [of you]*
1120	For to fowen an olde diche	*clean; ditch*
	Thanne for to be dobbed knight,	*dubbed*
	Te gon among maidenes bright.	
	To other contré thow might fare:	
	Mahoun thee yeve tene and care!"	*pain; suffering*
1125	"Damesele," a seide, "thow seist unright;	*you say wrong*
	Me fader was bothe erl and knight.	
	How mighte ich thanne ben a cherl,	
	Whan me fader was knight and erl?	
	To other contré ich wile te:	*go*
1130	Scheltow me namore ise!	*see*
	Thow yeve me an hors: lo it her!	*[bring] it here*

	I nel namore of thee daunger!"	*will not [endure]; of your threats*
	Forth him wente Sire Bevoun	
	And tok is in in that toun,	*lodging*
1135	Sore aneighed and aschamed,	*annoyed; ashamed*
	For she hadde him so gramed.	*angered*
	Tho Beves was to toun igo,	
	Tho began that maidenes wo;	
	Thanne was hire wo with alle,	
1140	Hire thoughte, the tour wolde on hir falle.	
	She clepede hire chaumberlein Bonefas	
	And tolde to him al hire cas	*troubles*
	And bad him to Beves wende:	
	"And sai him, ich wile amende	*tell; change*
1145	Al togedre of word and dede,	
	Of that ichave him misede!"	*mis-said (spoken falsely)*
	Forth wente Bonefas in that stounde	
	And Beves in is chaumber a founde	
	And seide, she him theder sende,	
1150	And that she wolde alle amende	
	Al togedres to is wille,	
	Bothe loude and eke stille.	
	Thanne answerde Beves the fer:	*valiant*
	"Sai, thow might nought speden her!	
1155	Ac for thow bringest fro hire mesage,	
	I schel thee yeve to the wage	*as payment*
	A mantel whit so melk:	*white as milk*
	The broider is of Tuli selk,	*silk from Toulouse*
	Beten abouten with rede golde,	*Embroidered*
1160	The king to were, thegh a scholde!"	*wear, as he should*
	Bonefas him thankede yerne,	*eagerly*
	Hom aghen he gan terne;	*return*
	A fond that maide in sorwe and care	
	And tolde hire his answare,	
1165	That he ne mighte nought spede	*succeed*
	Aboute hire nede,	
	And seide: "Thow haddest unright,	
	So te misain a noble knight!"	*speak evil of*
	"Who yaf thee this ilche wede?	*very same garment*
1170	"Beves, that hendi knight!" a sede.	*courteous*

"Allas!" she seide, "Ich was to blame,
Whan ich seide him swiche schame,
For hit nas never a cherles dede,
To yeve a maseger swiche a wede!
1175 Whan he nel nought to me come, — *If*
The wei to his chaumber I wil neme, — *take*
And, what ever of me befalle, — *befalls me*
Ich wile wende in to is halle!"
  Beves herde that maide ther-oute.
1180 Ase yif aslep, he gan to route. — *snore*
"Awake, lemman!" she seide, "Awake!
Icham icome, me pes to make. — *my peace*
Lemman, for the corteisie,
Spek with me a word or tweie!" — *two*
1185 "Damesele," queth Beves thanne,
"Let me ligge and go the wei henne! — *lie; go away*
Icham weri of-foughte sore, — *I am weary*
Ich faught for thee, I nel namore."
"Merci," she seide, "lemman, thin ore!" — *if you please*
1190 She fel adoun and wep wel sore:
"Men saith," she seide, "in olde riote, — *sayings*
That wimmannes bolt is sone schote. — *woman's arrow; shot*
Forghem me, that ichave misede, — *Forgive*
And ich wile right now to mede — *as a reward*
1195 Min false godes al forsake — *My*
And Cristendom for thee love take!" — *your*
"In that maner," queth the knight,
"I graunte thee, me swete wight!" — *creature*
And kiste hire at that cordement. — *covenant*
1200 Tharfore he was negh after schent. — *nearly overcome*
  The twei knightes, that he unbond,
That were in Brademondes hond,
He made that on is chaumberlain. — *one*
Him hadde be beter, he hadde hem slein! — *It would have been better*
1205 Thei wente to the king and swor othe: — *oath*
"No wonder, sire, thegh ye be wrothe, — *that you are angry*
No wonder, thegh ye ben agreved,
Whan Beves, scherewe misbeleved, — *wicked infidel*
The doughter he hath now forlain. — *deflowered*

1210	Hit were gode, sire, that he wer slain!"	
	Hii lowe, the scherewes, that him gan wreie.[1]	
	In helle mote thai hongen beie!	
	He dede nothing, boute ones hire kiste,	*kiss her once*
	Nought elles bi hem men ne wiste.	*Nothing else about him; knew*
1215	Tharfore hit is soth isaide	
	And in me rime right wel ilaid.	*my rhyme; placed*
	Delivre a thef fro the galwe,	*gallows*
	He thee hateth after be alle halwe!	*by all saints*
	"Allas!" queth Ermin, the King,	
1220	"Wel sore me reweth that tiding!	
	Sethe he com me ferst to,	*See to it; come to me first*
	So meche he hath for me ido,	*done*
	I ne mighte for al peynim londe,	*pagan*
	That men dede him eni schonde!	*disgrace*
1225	Ac fain ich wolde awreke be,	*eagerly; avenged*
	Boute I ne mighte hit nought ise."	*Unless; see*
	Thanne bespak a Sarasin —	
	Have he Cristes kurs and myn —	*May he have; curse*
	"Sire, she scholle for is sake	
1230	A letter swithe anon do make	
	To Brademond, the stronge king,	
	And do him theder the letter bringe;	*make him*
	And in the letter thee schelt saie,	
	That he hath Josian forlaie!"	*seduced*
1235	Whan the letter was come to th'ende,	
	After Beves the king let sende	
	And seide: "Beves, thow most hanne	*go hence*
	To Brademond, thin owene manne:	
	Al in solas and in delit	
1240	Thow most him bere this ilche scriit!	*very writing*
	Ac yif yow schelt me letter bere,	
	Upon the lai thow schelt me swere,	*law*
	That thow me schelt with no man mele,	*speak*
	To schewe the prente of me sele!"	*imprint; seal*
1245	"I wile," queth Beves ase snel,	*quick*

[1] *The wicked ones who betrayed him were lying*

	"The leter bere treuliche and wel;	*truthfully*
	Have ich Arondel, me stede,	
	Ich wile fare in to that thede,	*country*
	And Morgelai, me gode bronde,	*sword*
1250	Ich wile wende in to that londe!	
	King Ermin seide in is sawe,	*speech*
	That ner no mesager is lawe,	*allowed*
	To ride upon an hevi stede,	*heavy steed (warhorse)*
	That swiftli scholde don is nede.	
1255	"Ac nim a lighter hakenai	*take; hackney*
	And lef her the swerd Morgelai,	*leave here*
	And thow schelt come to Brademonde	
	Sone withinne a lite stounde!"	*a little while*
	Beves an hakenai bestrit	*mounted*
1260	And in his wei forth a rit	*he rode*
	And bereth with him is owene deth,	*own*
	Boute God him helpe, that alle thing seth!	*Unless; sees*
	Terne we aghen, thar we wer er,	*earlier*
	And speke we of is em Saber!	*uncle*
1265	After that Beves was thus sold,	*when*
	For him is hertte was ever cold.	
	A clepede to him his sone Terri	*called*
	And bad him wenden and aspie	*go; search*
	In to everi londe fer and ner,	
1270	Whider him ladde the maroner,	*mariner*
	And seide: "Sone, thow ert min owen,	
	Wel thow canst the lord knowen!	
	Ich hote thee, sone, in alle manere,	*command*
	That thow him seche this seve yer.	*seven*
1275	Ich wile feche him, mowe thow him fynde,	*might*
	Though he be biyende Inde!"	*beyond*
	Terri, is sone, is forth ifare,	*has gone away*
	Beves a soughte everiwhare;	
	In al hethenes nas toun non,	*all pagan lands*
1280	That Cristene man mighte ther in gon,	
	That he ne hath Beves in isought,	
	Ac he ne kouthe finde him nought.	*could*
	So hit be fel upon a cas,	*by chance*
	That Terri com beside Damas;	*Damascus*

1285	And ase he com forth be that stede,	*place*
	A sat and dinede in a wede	*dined; in armor*
	Under a faire medle tre,	*medlar tree*
	That Sire Beves gan of-see.	
	"Sire," queth Terri, "for Sein Juline!	*Saint Julian*
1290	Is it thee wille, come nere and dine!"	*If you would like*
	Beves was of-hongred sore	*very hungry*
	And kouthe him gret thank therfore,	*showed*
	For twei dawes he hadde ride	*days*
	Fastande in that ilche wede.	*Garbed; same clothes*
1295	The palmer nas nought withouten store,	*pilgrim; supplies*
	Inough a leide him before,	
	Bred and flesc out of is male	*Bread; meat; bag*
	And of his flaketes win and ale	*flagons; wine*
	Whan Beves hadde eten gret foisoun	*abundance*
1300	Terri askede at Sire Bevoun,	
	Yif a herde telle yong or olde	*Whether*
	Of a child, that theder was solde.	
	His name was ihote Bevoun	*called*
	Ibore a was at South-Hamtoun.	*Born*
1305	Beves beheld Terri and lough,	*laughed*
	And seide, a knew that child wel inough:	
	"Hit is nought," a seide, "gon longe,	*not; long ago*
	I segh the Sarsins that child anhonge!"	*hang*
	Terri fel ther doun and swough,	*fell down; swooned*
1310	His her, his clothes he al to-drough.	*hair; tore*
	Whan he awok and speke mighte,	
	Sore a wep and sore sighte	*sighed*
	And seide: "Allas, that he was boren!	
	Is me lord Beves forloren!"	*lost*
1315	Beves tok him up at that cas	*event*
	And gan him for to solas:	
	"Wend hom," a seide, "to thee contré!	*Return home*
	Sai the frendes so ichave thee.	*Tell your friends what I have told you*
	Though thow him seche thes seve yer,	*sought; seven*
1320	Thow worst that child never the ner!"	*were; nearer*
	Terri on Beves beheld	
	And segh the boiste with a scheld.	*saw; letter case; seal*
	"Me thenketh, thow ert a masager,	

	That in this londe walkes her;	
1325	Icham a clerk and to scole yede:	*went to school*
	Sire, let me the letter rede,	*read*
	For thow might have gret doute,	*fear*
	Thin owene deth to bere aboute!"	
	Beves seide, ich understonde:	
1330	"He, that me tok this letter an honde,	
	He ne wolde love me non other,	
	Than ich were is owene brother."	*As if*
	Beves him thankede and thus hii delde.	*they parted*
	Terri wente hom and telde	
1335	His fader Saber in the Ilde of Wight,	*Isle; [Man]*
	How him tolde a gentil knight,	
	That Sarsins hadde Beves forfare	*killed*
	And hangede him, while he was thare.	
	Saber wep and made drem.	*lament*
1340	For he was the childes em,	*uncle*
	And ech yer on a dai certaine	
	Upon th'emperur of Almaine	*Germany*
	With a wel gret baronage	
	A cleimede his eritage.	*claimed; heritage*
1345	Let we now ben is em Saber	*Let us now leave*
	And speke of Beves, the maseger!	
	Forth him wente Sire Bevoun	
	Til a com to Dames toun;	*Damascus*
	Aboute the time of middai	
1350	Out of a mameri a sai	*mosque; he saw*
	Sarasins come gret foisoun,	*[in] great abundance*
	That hadde anoured here Mahoun,	*honored their*
	Beves of is palfrei alighte	*palfrey dismounted*
	And ran to her mameri ful righte	*temple*
1355	And slough here prest, that ther was in,	*priest*
	And threw here godes in the fen	*ditch*
	And lough hem alle ther to scorn.	
	On ascapede and at-orn	*escaped; ran fast*
	In at the castel ghete,	
1360	As the king sat at the mete.	*dinner*
	"Sire," seide this man at the frome,	*at once*
	"Her is icome a corsede gome,	*cursed man*

	That throweth our godes in the fen	*gods*
	And sleth al oure men;	
1365	Unnethe I scapede among that thring,	*Scarcely; throng*
	For to bringe thee tiding!"	
	Brademond quakede at the bord	*trembled with fear; table*
	And seide: "That is Beves, me lord!"	
	Beves wente in at the castel ghate,	
1370	His hors he lefte ther-ate	
	And wente forth in to the halle	
	And grete hem in this maner alle:	*greeted them*
	"God, that made this world al ronde,	
	Thee save, Sire King Brademond,	*Save you*
1375	And ek alle thine fere,	*companions*
	That I se now here,	
	And yif that ilche blessing	*very*
	Liketh thee right nothing,	
	Mahoun, that is god thin,	
1380	Tervagaunt and Apolin,	*Termagant*
	Thee blessi and dighte	*bless; save*
	Be alle here mighte!	*their*
	Lo her, the King Ermin	*Look here*
	The sente this letter in parchemin,	*parchment*
1385	And ase the letter thee telleth to,	
	A bad, thow scholdest swithe do!"	*He bade*
	Beves kneueled and nolde nought stonde	*kneeled*
	And yaf up is deth with is owene honde.	*furthered*
	Brademond quakede al for drede,	*fear*
1390	He undede the letter and gan to rede	
	And fond iwriten in that felle,	*hide*
	How that he scholde Beves aquelle.	*kill*
	Thanne seide Brademond to twenti king,	
	That were that dai at is gistning,	*banquet*
1395	A spak with tresoun and with gile:	
	"Ariseth up," he sede "a while,	
	Everich of yow fro the bord,	
	And wolcometh your kende lord!"	*gentle*
	Alle hii gonnen up right stonde,	
1400	And Brademond tok Beves be the honde	
	And held him faste at that sake,	*for that purpose*

That he ne scholde is swerd out take,
And cride, alse he hadde be wod, — *as if he were mad*
To hem alle, aboute him stod:
1405 "Ase ye me loven at this stounde, — *moment*
Bringeth this man swithe to grounde!" — *quickly*
So faste hii gonne aboute him scheve, — *shove*
Ase don ben aboute the heve. — *As bees do around the hive*
So withinne a lite stounde
1410 Beves was ibrought to grounde.
Brademond seide him anon right:
"Yif thow me naddest wonne with fight, — *If you had not beaten me in a fight*
I nolde for nothing hit beleve,
That thow schost be hanged er eve. — *before dark*
1415 Ac ase evel thee schel betide,
In me prisoun thow schelt abide
Under th'erthe twenti teise, — *fathoms*
Thar thow schelt have meche miseise. — *mis-ease (discomfort)*
Ne scheltow have, til thow be ded,
1420 Boute ech a dai quarter of a lof bred; — *loaf of bread*
Yif thow wilt drinke, thegh it be nought swet,
Thee schelt hit take under the fet!"
A dede Beves binde to a ston gret, — *great stone*
That wegh seve quarters of whet, — *wheat*
1425 And het him caste in to prisoun, — *ordered*
That twenti teise was dep adoun. — *fathoms*
At the prisoun dore Beves fond
A tronsoun, that he tok in is hond. — *club*
Tharwith a thoughte were him there — *to protect himself*
1430 Fram wormes, that in prisoun were. — *snakes*
Now is Beves at this petes grounde. — *pit's bottom*
God bringe him up hol and sonde!
Now speke we of Josian, the maide,
That com to hire fader and seide:
1435 "Sire," she seide, "whar Beves be, — *where is Bevis*
That me mighte him nought fern ise?" — *see for a long time*
"Doughter," a seide, "a is ifare — *has gone*
In to his londe and woneth thare, — *dwells*
In to is owene eritage,
1440 And hath a wif of gret parage, — *birth*

	The kinges doughter of Ingelonde,	
	Ase men doth me to understonde."	*tell me*
	Thanne was that maide wo ynough,	*sorrowful*
	In hire chaumber hire her she drogh	*hair she tore out*
1445	And wep and seide ever mo,	*sighed*
	That sum tresoun thar was ydo.	*done*
	"That me ne telde ord and ende,	*did not tell me beginning*
	What dai awai whanne a wolde wende."	
	Of Mombraunt the King Yvor,	
1450	A riche king of gret tresore,	
	Whan he owhar to werre wolde,	*anywhere to make war*
	Fiftene kinges him sewe scholde:	*follow*
	Comen a is Josian to wedde;	
	Aghen hire fader so a spedde,	*Towards; he hastened*
1455	That he hire grauntede to is wive	
	And al is londe after is live.	
	Tho Josian wiste, she scholde be quen,	*she would be queen*
	Hit was nought be hire wille; I wen	*not her will; believe*
	Hire were lever have had lasse	*She would rather; lower station*
1460	And have be Beves is contasse.	*Bevis' countess*
	Natheles, now it is so,	
	Hire fader wil she moste do,	*Her father's will*
	Ac ever she seide: "Bevoun,	
	Hende knight of South Hamtoun,	*Gentle*
1465	Naddestow me never forsake,	*You would never have*
	Yif sum tresoun hit nadde make:	
	Ac for the love, that was so gode,	
	That I lovede ase min hertte blode,	*as my heart's blood*
	Ichave," she seide, "a ring on,	*I have*
1470	That of swiche vertu is the ston:	
	While ichave on that ilche ring,	
	To me schel no man have welling,	*his will*
	And Beves!" she seide, "be God above,	
	I schel it weren for thee love!"	
1475	Whan hit to that time spedde,	*rapidly came closer*
	That Yvor scholde that maide wedde,	
	He let sende withouten ensoine	*delay*
	After the Soudan of Babiloine	*Sultan; Babylon*
	And after the fiftene kinge,	

1480 That him scholde omage bringe, *should bring homage*
And bad hem come lest and meste,
To onoure that meri feste. *honor*
Of that feste nel ich namor telle, *I will not tell anymore*
For to highe with our spelle. *hasten; story*
1485 Whan al the feste to-yede, *finished*
Ech knight wente to is stede,
Men graithede cartes and somers, *prepared; packhorses*
Knightes to horse and squiers,
And Josian with meche care
1490 Theder was brought in hire chare. *Thither; chariot*
King Ermin nom Arondel *took*
And let him sadlen faire and wel,
A wente to Beves chaumber, ther he lay,
And nom his swerd Morgelay;
1495 With Arondel agan it lede *began*
To King Yvor, and thus a sede:
"Sone," a sede, "have this stede, *Son*
The beste fole, that man mai fede, *best horse; feed*
And this swerd of stel broun, *shining*
1500 That was Beves of Hamtoun.
A nolde hit yeve, wer it in is honde, *He (Bevis) would not give it*
Nought for al painim londe!"
"Ne ich," queth the King Yvor, *Nor*
"For al the gold ne the tresor,
1505 That thow might in the cité belouke!" *guard*
"Sone," queth Ermin, "wel mot thee it brouke!" *use*
Yver gan homward te ride
And dede lede Arondel be is side.
Whan he com withoute Mombraunt,
1510 A swor is oth be Tervagaunt,
That he wolde in to his cité ride
Upon Arondel before is bride.
Arondel thar he bestrit; *sat upon*
That hors wel sone underyit, *understands*
1515 That Beves nas nought upon is rigge *back*
The king wel sore scholde hit abegge. *pay for*
He ran over dich and thorn,
Thourgh wode and thourgh thekke korn; *grain*

For no water ne for no londe,
1520 Nowhar nolde that stede astonde; *stop*
At the laste a threw Yvor doun
And al to-brak the kinges kroun, *nearly*
That al is kingdom wel unnethe
Arerede him ther fro the dethe; *Prevented*
1525 And er hii mighte that hors winne, *capture*
Thai laughte him with queinte ginne. *caught; cunning ruse*
A wonderthing now ye may here. *wondrous; hear*
After al that seve yere *seven years*
To rakenteis a stod iteide, *chains*
1530 Nas mete ne drinke before him leid, *No food*
Hey ne oten ne water clere, *Hay; oats; clear*
Boute be a kord of a solere. *Except; cord from a balcony*
No man dorste come him hende, *No one dared approach*
Thar that hors stod in bende. *Where; fetters*
1535 Now is Josian a quene;
Beves in prisoun hath gret tene. *pain*
The romounce telleth, ther a set,
Til the her on is heved grew to is fet; *hair; grew to his feet*
Snakes and euetes and oades fale, *lizards; many toads*
1540 How mani, can I nought telle in tale,
That in the prisoun were with him,
That provede ever with her venim *attempted; their venom*
To sle Beves, that gentil knight,
Oc, thourgh the grace of God Almight, *But*
1545 With the tronsoun, that he to prisoun tok, *club*
A slough hem alle, so saith the bok.
A fleande nadder was in an hole, *flying adder*
For elde blak ase eni cole; *age; coal*
Unto Beves she gan flinge
1550 And in the forehed thoughte him stinge.
Beves was redi with is tronsoun
And smot hire, that she fel adoun.
Upon aghen the nadder rowe *again; adder rose*
And breide awei his right browe; *took away*
1555 Tho was Beves sore agreved
And smot the nadder on the heved; *head*
So harde dent he hire yaf,

	The brein clevede on is staf.	*brain stuck to his*
	Doun fel the nadder, withouten faile,	
1560	And smot so Beves with the taile,	
	That negh a les ther contenaunse,[1]	
	Almest is lif was in balaunse.	
	Whan he awakede of that swough,	*out of; swoon*
	The tronsoun eft to him a drough	
1565	And bet hire al to pises smale,	*beat; small pieces*
	As hit is fonde in Frensche tale.	
	Tho he hadde slawe the foule fendes,	*fiends*
	Be that hadde Beves lein in bendes	*bonds*
	Seve yer in peines grete,	*great pain*
1570	Lite idronke and lasse iete;	*Little; less [he] ate*
	His browe stank for defaut of yeme,	*lack; care*
	That it set after ase a seme,	*scar (seam)*
	Wharthourgh that maide ne kneu him nought,	
	Whan hii were eft togedre brought.	
1575	On a dai, ase he was mad and feint,	*delirious; sick*
	To Jesu Crist he made is pleint	
	And to his moder, seinte Marie,	
	Reuliche he gan to hem crie:	*Mournfully*
	"Lord," a seide, "Hevene King,	
1580	Schepere of erthe and alle thing:	*Maker*
	What have ich so meche misgilt,	*done so wrong*
	That thow sext and tholen wilt,	*see; will allow*
	That Thee wetherwines and Thee fo	*enemies; foes*
	Schel Thee servaunt do this wo?	
1585	Ich bedde Thee, Lord, for Thee pité,	*your*
	That Thow have merci on me	
	And yeve grace, hennes to gange	*hither; go*
	Or sone be drawen other anhange!	*drawn or hanged*
	Me roughte never, what deth to me come,	*I do not care*
1590	With that ich were hennes nome!	*hence taken*
	The gailers, that him scholde yeme,	*jailers; guard*
	Whan hii herde him thus reme,	*cry out*
	"Thef! cherl!" seide that on tho:	*Thief; then*

[1] *That he almost lost his countenance (identifying features) there*

	"Now beth thee lif dawes ydo,	*your life's days are done*
1595	For king ne kaiser ne for no sore	*caesar; sorrow*
	Ne scheltow leve no lenger more."	
	Anon rightes with that word	*Very soon*
	A laumpe he let doun be a cord,	*lamp*
	A swerd a tok be his side,	
1600	And be the cord he gan doun glide	
	And smot him with that other hond,	
	And Beves to the grounde a wond.	*fell*
	"Allas," queth Beves, "that ilche stounde!	*very time of suffering*
	Wo is the man, that lith ybounde	*lies*
1605	Medel bothe fet and honde!	*Middle (waist); feet*
	Tho ich com ferst in to this londe,	
	Hadde ich had me swerd Morgelay	
	And Arondel, me gode palfray,	*saddle horse*
	For Dames, nadde be tresoun,	*Damascus; had it not been for*
1610	I nolde have yeve a botoun,	*give a button (would not care)*
	And now the meste wreche of alle	
	With a strok me doth adoun falle,	
	Bidde ich never with Jesu speke,	
	Boute ich ther-of may ben awreke!"	*avenged*
1615	A smot the gailer with is fest,	*fist*
	That is nekke him to-berst.	*bursts*
	His felawe above gan to crie:	*companion*
	"Highe hider, felawe," queth Beves, "highe!"	*Come*
	"Yif thow most have help," a sede,	
1620	"Ich come to thee with a gode spede!"	
	"Yis!" queth Beves, al for gile,	
	And knette the rop thar while	*knotted*
	Ase high ase a mighte reche.	*reach*
	Tho queth Beves with reuful speche:	*rueful retort*
1625	"For the love of Sein Mahoun,	*Saint Mohammed*
	Be the rop glid blive adoun	*By; glide quickly*
	And help, that this thef wer ded!"	*thief*
	Whan he hadde thus ised,	*said*
	That other gailer no leng abod,	*longer*
1630	Boute by the rop adoun he glod.	*slid*
	Whan the rop failede in is hond,	*missed*
	Beves held up that gode bronde	*weapon*

	And felde to gronde that sori wight,	*man*
	Thourghout is bodi that swerd he pight.	*set*
1635	Now er thai ded, the geilers tweie,	*are they dead*
	And Beves lith to the rakenteie,	*lies in chains*
	His lif him thoughte al to long,	
	Thre daies after he ne et ne drong,	*ate nor drank*
	Tofore that, for soth to sai	
1640	A was woned, ech other dai	*accustomed; every other day*
	Of berelof to have a quarter	*barley-loaf*
	To his mete and to his diner;	*For food; dinner*
	And, for is meisters wer bothe ded,	*keepers*
	Thre daies after he ne et no bred.	
1645	To Jesu Crist he bed a bone,	*prayed a prayer*
	And He him grauntede wel sone;	*granted*
	So yerne he gan to Jesu speke,	*eagerly*
	That his vetres gonne breke	*fetters*
	And of his medel the grete ston.	*off; belly*
1650	Jesu Crist he thankede anon;	
	A wente quik out of prisoun	*He*
	Be the rop the gailer com adoun,	
	And wente in to the castel right,	
	Ac it was aboute the midnight;	*But*
1655	He lokede aboute fer and ner,	*far; near*
	No man wakande ne segh he ther;	
	He beheld forther a lite	
	To a chaunber under a garite,	*watchtower*
	Thar-inne he segh torges ilight;	*torches*
1660	Beves wente theder ful right;	
	Twelf knightes a fond ther aslepe,	*Twelve; found there*
	That hadde the castel for to kepe;	*guard*
	The chaumber dore a fond unsteke,	*unfastened*
	And priveliche he gan in reke	*did indeed go in*
1665	And armede him in yrene wede,	*iron clothes (chain mail)*
	The beste, that he fond at nede,	*best; handy*
	And gerte him with a gode bronde	*girt himself; sword*
	And tok a gode spere in is honde;	
	A scheld aboute is nekke he cast	
1670	And wente out of the chaumber in hast.	
	Forther a herde in a stable	

	Pages fele, withoute fable,	*many*
	Ase thai sete in here raging;	*their wantonness*
	In at the dore Beves gan spring,	
1675	And for thai scholde him nought wrain,	*betray*
	Under his hond he made him plai.	*fight*
	And whan the Sarasins wer islawe,	*slain*
	The beste stede he let forth drawe	
	And sadelede hit and wel adight.	*dressed*
1680	And wente him forth anon right	
	And gan to crie with loude steven	*voice*
	And the porter he gan nevenen:	*did name*
	"Awake!" a seide, "proude felawe,	
	Thow were worthi ben hanged and drawe!	
1685	Highe, the gates wer unsteke,	*Make haste; open*
	Beves is out of prisoun reke,	*escaped*
	And icham sent now for is sake,	*I am*
	The treitour yif ich mighte of-take!"	*capture*
	The porter was al bewaped:	*confused*
1690	"Allas!" queth he, "is Beves ascaped?"	
	Up he caste the gates wide,	
	And Beves bi him gan out ride	
	And tok is wei ful hastelie	
	Toward the londe of Ermonie.	*Armenia*
1695	He nadde ride in is wei	
	Boute seve mile of that contrei,	*away from*
	He wex asleped wondersore,	*got very sleepy*
	He mighte ride no forthermore;	
	He reinede his hors to a chesteine	*tied; chestnut tree*
1700	And felle aslepe upon the pleine;	
	And alse a slẹp, in is swevene	*dream*
	Him thoughte, Brademond and kinges seven	
	Stod over him with swerdes drawe,	
	Al slepande him wolde han slawe.	*have slain*
1705	Of that sweven he was of-drad;	*afraid*
	He lep to hors ase he wer mad,	*crazy*
	Towarde Damas agein, aplight!	*indeed*
	Now reste we her a lite wight,	*short while*
	And speke we scholle of Brademond.	
1710	Amorwe, whan he it hadde ifonde,	

That Beves was ascaped so,
In is hertte him was ful wo.
That time be comin acent — *by common assent*
Thar was comin parlement,
1715 Erles, barouns, lasse and more,
And fiftene kinges were samned thore. — *assembled there*
To hem Brademond tolde thare,
That Beves was fro him ifare, — *gone*
And bad help with might and main,
1720 For to feche Beves again.
A king thar was swithe fer, — *very valiant*
His nam was hote Grander. — *name; called*
An hors he hadde of gret pris, — *worth*
That was icleped Trinchefis:
1725 For him a yaf selver wight, — *weight in silver*
Er he that hors have might.
He armede him in yrene wede,
Seve knightes he gan with him lede
And prikede forth on Trenchefis — *spurred*
1730 And wende wenne meche pris; — *went forth [to] win much honor*
And Beves sone he gan se,
Ase he rod toward the cité.
"Ayilt thee," a seide, "thow fox welp, — *Surrender*
Thee god schel thee nothing help, — *Your god*
1735 For her thourgh min hondes one, — *here; alone*
For sothe, thow schelt thee lif forgon!"
"So helpe me God!" queth Beves tho,
"Hit were no meistri, me to slo, — *mastery; slay*
For this is the ferthe dai agon,
1740 Mete ne drinke ne bot i non: — *have I had neither*
Ac natheles, God it wot, — *God willing*
Yif ich alle nedes mot,
Yit ich wile asaie, — *attempt*
A lite box thee to paie!" — *blow to please (pay) you*
1745 King Grander was of herte grim
And rod to Beves and he to him;
And ase thei bothe togedre mete, — *clashed*
With here launces thei gonne mete,
That hit gonnen al to-drive

1750	And teborsten on pises five.	*burst; pieces*
	Here swerdes drowe knightes stoute	*Their*
	And fighteth faste, it is no doute;	
	The medwe squaughte of her dentes,	*meadow torn [by] their strokes*
	The fur flegh out, so spark o flintes;	*fire flies; from flint*
1755	Thus thai leide on in bothe side	
	Betwene midmorwe and undertide.	*morning; noon*
	King Grander was agremed strong,	*angered greatly*
	That Sire Beves him stod so long,	*withstood*
	And with is swerd a hitte is scheld,	
1760	A quarter fel in to the feld,	
	Hauberk, plate and aktoun,	*armor; quilted jacket*
	In to Beves forther arsoun	*saddlebow*
	Half a fot he karf doun right.	*foot*
	Tho Beves segh that strok of might,	*Then*
1765	A seide: "That dent was wel iset,	*well done*
	Fasten I wile another bet!"	*I will do you one better*
	With that word Beves smot doun	
	Grander is scheld with is fachoun,	*his; falchion*
	And is left honde be the wrest,	*at; wrist*
1770	Hit flegh awei thourgh help of Crist.	
	Tho Grander hadde his scheld ilore,	*taken away*
	He faught ase he wer wode therfore;	
	A yaf Beves strokes that tide,	*time*
	Non ne moste other abide.	
1775	Beves ther-of was agreved	
	And smot of King Grander is heved,	*cut off; his head*
	The dede kors in that throwe	*corpse at that moment*
	Fel out over the sadel bowe.	
	Tho King Grander was islawe,	*When*
1780	The seve knightes of hethen lawe	
	Beves slough that ilche stounde,	
	So hit is in Frensch yfounde.	
	For nought Beves nolde belave,	*would not remain*
	The beter hors a wolde have;	
1785	Beves Trenchefis bestrit,	*bestrode*
	And in is weie forth a rit,	*rode*
	And Brademond with al is ost	*host*
	Com after with meche bost;	

	So longe hii han Beves drive,	
1790	That hii come to the clive,	*cliff*
	Ther the wilde se was.	*sea*
	Harkneth now a wondercas!	
	In to the se a moste, iwis,	*he must [go], certainly*
	Other fighte aghenes al hethenes.	*Or*
1795	To Jesu Crist he bad a bone,	*asked a favor*
	And He him grauntede wel sone:	
	"Lord," a sede, "hevene king,	
	Schepere of erthe and alle thing,	*Maker*
	Thow madest fisch ase wel alse man,	
1800	That nothing of senne ne can,	*know nothing of sin*
	Ne nought of fisches kenne	*kind*
	Never yet ne dede senne,	*sin*
	Of this hethene hounde,	
	That beste Thee and bounde	*That bested you*
1805	And bete Thee body to the dethe,	
	Tharfore ich may alse ethe	*as easily*
	To water fle in this stede,	*on this horse*
	To fisch, that never senne dede,	*sinned*
	Than her daien in londe	*die here*
1810	In al this Sarasines honde!'	
	Beves smot is hors, that it lep	
	In to the se, that was wel dep.	
	Whan he in to the se cam,	
	Over the se, I wot, a swam;	
1815	In a dai and in a night	
	A bar over that gentil knight.	*He*
	Whan he com of that wilde brok,	
	His gode stede him resede and schok,	*raised himself [out of the water]*
	And Beves, for honger in that stounde	*because of hunger; time*
1820	The hors threw him doun to the grounde.	
	"Allas!" queth Beves, whan he doun cam,	
	"Whilom ichadde an erldam	*Once I had; earldom*
	And an hors gode and snel,	*swift*
	That men clepede Arondel;	
1825	Now ich wolde yeve hit kof	*quickly*
	For a schiver of a lof!"	*slice; loaf*
	A restede him ther a lite tide,	

	His gode stede he gan bestride	*mount*
	And rod over dale and doun,	*lowland and upland*
1830	Til he com to a gret toun;	
	The levedi thar-of over the castel lai,	*lady*
	And Beves hire sone of-say	*soon saw her*
	And wende ben al out of care	
	And thoughte wel to spede thare.	
1835	Beves to the castel gate rit	*rode*
	And spak to hire, above him sit:	
	"Dame," a seide, "that sit above,	
	For that ilche lordes love,	
	On wham thin herte is on iset:	
1840	Yeve me today a meles met!"	*meal's measure*
	The levedi answerde him tho:	
	"Boute thow fro the gate go,	*Unless*
	Thee wer beter elleswhar than her;	*elsewhere; here*
	Go, or the tit an evel diner!	*receive*
1845	Me lord," she seide, "is a geaunt	*giant*
	And leveth on Mahoun and Tervagaunt	*believes in*
	And felleth Cristene men to grounde,	
	For he hateth hem ase hounde!"	*like dogs*
	"Be God!" queth Beves, "I swere an othe:	*oath*
1850	Be him lef and be him lothe,	*lovable or loathsome*
	Her ich wile have the mete	
	With love or eighe, whather I mai gete!"	*fear, whichever*
	The levedi swithe wroth with alle	
	Wente hire forth in to the halle	
1855	And tolde hire lord anon fore,	
	How a man hadde iswore,	
	That he nolde fro the ghete,	*would not go from the gate*
	Er he hadde ther the mete.	*Before*
	The geaunt was wonderstrong,	
1860	Rome thretti fote long;	*In length thirty feet*
	He tok a levour in is hond,	*lever (club)*
	And forth to the gate he wond.	
	Of Beves he nam gode hede,	
	Ful wel a knew Beves is stede:	*Bevis' horse*
1865	"Thow ert nome thef, ywis:	*caught thief*
	Whar stele thow stede Trenchefis,	*Where did you steal*

	That thow ridest upon here?	
	Hit was me brotheres Grandere!"	*brother's*
	"Grander," queth Beves, "I yaf hod	*gave [a] cap*
1870	And made him a kroune brod;	
	Tho he was next under me fest,	
	Wel I wot, ich made him prest,	*priest*
	And high dekne ich wile make thee,	*archdeacon*
	Er ich ever fro thee te!"	*go*
1875	Thanne seide the geaunt: "Meister sire,	
	Slough thow me brother Grandere,	
	For al this castel ful of golde	
	A live lete thee ich nolde!"	*I will not let you live*
	"Ne ich thee," queth Beves, "I trowe!"	*Nor I you*
1880	Thus beginneth grim to growe.	*anger*
	The geaunt, that ich spak of er,	
	The staf, that he to fighte ber,	
	Was twenti fote in lengthe be tale,	*by measure (tally)*
	Tharto gret and nothing smale:	
1885	To Sire Beves a smot therwith	
	A sterne strok withouten grith,	*peace*
	Ac a failede of his divis	*But he failed; device (he missed)*
	And in the heved smot Trenchefis,	
	That ded to grounde fel the stede.	
1890	"O," queth Beves, "so God me spede,	
	Thow havest don gret vileinie,	
	Whan thow sparde me bodi	
	And for me gilt min hors aqueld,	*killed*
	Thow witest him, that mai nought weld.[1]	
1895	Be God, I swere thee an oth:	
	Thow schelt nought, whan we tegoth,	*go forth*
	Laughande me wende fram,	*Laughing get away from me*
	Now thow havest mad me gram!"	*made; angry*
	Beves is swerd anon up swapte,	*swept*
1900	He and the geaunt togedre rapte	*rushed*
	And delde strokes mani and fale:	

[1] *You blame him (the horse), who has no control [over the situation]*

	The nombre can I nought telle in tale.	
	The geaunt up is clobbe haf	*heaved*
	And smot to Beves with is staf,	
1905	That his scheld flegh from him thore	*flew*
	Thre akres brede and sumdel more.	*acres across*
	Tho was Beves in strong erur	*wrath*
	And karf ato the grete levour	*cut in two; club (lever)*
	And on the geauntes brest a wonde,	*wound*
1910	That negh a felde him to the grounde.	
	The geaunt thoughte this bataile hard,	
	Anon he drough to him a dart,	*hand spear*
	Thourgh Beves scholder he hit schet,	*hurled*
	The blod ran doun to Beves fet,	
1915	Tho Beves segh is owene blod,	
	Out of is wit he wex negh wod,	*became nearly mad*
	Unto the geaunt ful swithe he ran	
	And kedde that he was doughti man,	*showed; powerful*
	And smot ato his nekke bon:	*in two*
1920	The geaunt fel to grounde anon.	
	Beves wente in at castel gate,	
	The levedi a mette ther-ate.	
	"Dame!" a seide, "go, yeve me mete,	*give me food*
	That ever have thow Cristes hete!"	*hatred*
1925	The levedi, sore adrad with alle,	
	Ladde Beves in to the halle,	
	And of everiche sonde,	*every dish*
	That him com to honde,	*was served*
	A dede hire ete al ther ferst,	
1930	That she ne dede him no berst,	*damage*
	And drinke ferst of the win,	
	That no poisoun was ther-in.	
	Whan Beves hadde ete inough,	
	A keverchef to him a drough	*he drew*
1935	In that ilche stounde,	
	To stope mide is wonde.	*To stop up his wound*
	"Dame, dame," Beves sede,	
	"Let sadele me a gode stede,	
	For hennes ich wile ride,	
1940	I nel lo lenger her abide!"	*here*

	The levedi seide, she wolde fawe;	*joyfully provide*
	A gode stede she let forth drawe	
	And sadeled hit and wel adight,	*appointed*
	And Beves, that hendi knight,	
1945	Into the sadel a lippte,	*he lept*
	That no stirop he ne drippte.	*touched*
	Forth him wente Sire Bevoun,	
	Til he com withoute the toun	
	In to a grene mede.	*meadow*
1950	"Now, loverd Crist," a sede,	*Lord*
	"Yeve it, Brademond the king,	*Grant that*
	He and al is ofspring,	
	Wer right her upon this grene:	
	Now ich wolde of me tene	*pain*
1955	Swithe wel ben awreke,	*avenged*
	Scholde he never go ne speke:	
	Now min honger is me aset,	*satisfied*
	Ne liste me never fighten bet!"	
	Forth a wente be the strem,	
1960	Til a come to Jurisalem;	
	To the patriark a wente cof,	*patriarch; quickly*
	And al his lif he him schrof	*confessed*
	And tolde him how hit was bego,	
	Of is wele and of is wo.	*his weal (success); woe (failure)*
1965	The patriark hadde reuthe	
	Of him and ek of is treuthe	
	And forbed him upon his lif,	
	That he never toke wif,	
	Boute she were clene maide.	*Unless; virgin*
1970	"Nai, for sothe!" Sire Beves saide.	
	On a dai aghenes the eve	*toward evening*
	Of the patriarke he tok is leve;	
	Erliche amorwe, whan it was dai,	*Early*
	Forth a wente in is wai;	
1975	And also a rod himself alone:	
	"Lord," a thoughte, "whar mai I gone?	
	Whar ich in to Ingelonde fare?	
	Nai," a thoughte, "what sholde I thare,	
	Boute yif ichadde ost to gader,	*Unless; an army assembled*

1980	For to sle me stifader?"	*stepfather*
	He thoughte, that he wolde an hie	*hurry on*
	In to the londe of Ermonie,	
	To Ermonie, that was is bane,	*death*
	To his lemman Josiane.	
1985	And also a wente theder right,	
	A mette with a gentil knight,	
	That in the londe of Ermonie	
	Hadde bore him gode companie;	
	Thai kiste hem anon with that	
1990	And ather askede of otheres stat.	*each asked about the other's situation*
	Thanne seide Beves and lough:	*laughed*
	"Ich ave fare hard inough,	*have*
	Sofred bothe honger and chele	*Suffered; chill*
	And other peines mani and fele	*pains*
1995	Thourgh King Ermines gile:	*Through; deceit*
	Yet ich thenke to yelde is while,	*yield; well (a good idea)*
	For he me sente to Brademond,	
	To have slawe me that stonde:	*time*
	God be thanked, a dede nought so,	
2000	Ac in is prisoun with meche wo	
	Ichave leie this seven yare,	
	Ac now icham from him ifare	*far*
	Thourgh Godes grace and min engyn,	*ingenuity*
	Ac al ich wite it King Ermyn,	*credit it all*
2005	And, ne wer is doughter Josiane,	*were it not for his*
	Sertes, ich wolde ben is bane!"	*his slayer*
	"Josiane," queth the knight, "is a wif	
	Aghen hire wille with meche strif.	*Against*
	Seve yer hit is gon and more,	
2010	That the riche King Yvore	
	To Mombraunt hath hire wedde	
	Bothe to bord and to bedde,	
	And hath the swerd Morgelai	
	And Arondel, the gode palfrai:	
2015	Ac sithe the time, that I was bore,	*since*
	Swiche game hadde ich never before,	*amusement*
	Ase ich hadde that ilche tide,	
	Whan I segh King Yvor ride	

Toward Mombraunt on Arondel;
2020 The hors was nought ipaied wel: *contented*
He arnede awai with the king *bolted*
Thourgh felde and wode, withouten lesing, *in truth*
And in a mure don him cast, *mire*
Almest he hadde deied in hast.
2025 Ac er hii wonne the stede,
Ropes in the contré thai leide; *gathered*
Ac never sithe, withoute fable,
Ne com the stede out of the stable,
So sore he was aneied that tide; *[Arondel] annoyed*
2030 Sithe dorste no man on him ride!"
For this tiding Beves was blithe, *happy*
His joie kouthe he no man kithe. *tell*
"Wer Josiane," a thoughte, "ase lele, *as loyal*
Alse is me stede Arondel, *As*
2035 Yet scholde ich come out of wo!"
And at the knight he askede tho:
"Whiderwardes is Mombraunt?" *Yonder*
"Sere," a sede, "be Tervagaunt,
Thow might nought thus wende forth,
2040 Thow most terne al aghen north!"
Beves ternede his stede
And rod north, Gode spede; *God [let him] prosper*
Ever a was pasaunt, *he; moving on*
Til a com to Mombraunt.
2045 Mombraunt is a riche cité;
In al the londe of Sarsine
Nis ther non therto iliche *none like it*
Ne be fele parti so riche.
And whan that hende knight Bevoun
2050 Come withouten the toun,
Tharwith a palmer he mette, *pilgrim*
And swithe faire he him grette:
"Palmer," a sede, "whar is the king?"
"Sire," a seide, "an honting
2055 With kinges fiftene."
"And whar," a seide, "is the quene?"
"Sire," a seide, "in hire bour." *bedchamber*

"Palmer," a seide, "paramour, — *for love's sake*
Yem me thine wede — *Fetch; clothes*
2060 For min and for me stede!"
"God yeve it," queth the palmare,
"We hadde drive that chefare!" — *bargain*
Beves of is palfrei alighte — *dismounted*
And schrede the palmer as a knighte — *clothed*
2065 And yaf him is hors, that he rod in,
For is bordon and is sklavin. — *pilgrim's staff; coat*
The palmer rod forth ase a king,
And Beves went alse a bretheling. — *as a wretched person*
Whan he com to the castel gate,
2070 Anon he fond thar-ate
Mani palmer thar stonde
Of fele kene londe, — *many diverse [kinds of] lands*
And he askede hem in that stede,
What hii alle thar dede.
2075 Thanne seide on, that thar stod:
"We beth icome to have gode, — *goods*
And so thow ert also!"
"Who," queth Beves, "schel it us do?"
"The quene, God hire schilde fro care!
2080 Meche she loveth palmare;
Al that she mai finden here,
Everiche dai in the yere,
Faire she wile hem fede — *feed them*
And yeve hem riche wede
2085 For a knightes love, Bevoun,
That was iboren at Southamtoun;
To a riche man she wolde him bringe,
That kouthe telle of him tiding!"
"Whanne," queth Beves, "schel this be don?"
2090 A seide: "Betwene middai and noun." — *noon*
Beves, hit ful wel he sai, — *saw*
Hit nas boute yong dai; — *early*
A thoughte that he wolde er than — *before then*
Wende aboute the barbican, — *Walk (turn); tower*
2095 For to loke and for to se,
How it mighte best be,

	Yif he the castel wolde breke,	
	Whar a mighte best in reke;	*go in*
	And also a com be a touret,	*turret*
2100	That was in the castel iset,	
	A herde wepe and crie;	
	Thederward he gan him hie.	
	"O allas," she seide, "Bevoun,	
	Hende knight of Southhamtoun,	
2105	Now ichave bide that day,	*lived to see*
	That to the treste I ne may:	*trust*
	That ilche God, that thow of speke,	
	He is fals and thow ert eke!"	*also*
	In al the sevene yer eche dai	
2110	Josiane, that faire mai,	
	Was woned swich del to make,	*wont such mourning*
	Al for Sire Beves sake.	
	The levedi gan to the gate te,	*go*
	The palmeres thar to se;	
2115	And Beves, after anon	
	To the gate he gan gon.	
	The palmers gonne al in threste,	*all pushed forward*
	Beves abod and was the laste;	*remained [behind]*
	And whan the maide segh him thar,	
2120	Of Beves she nas nothing war;	
	"Thee semest," queth she, "man of anour,	*honor*
	Thow schelt this dai be priour	*first*
	And beginne oure deis:	*preside at the feast*
	Thee semest hende and corteis."	*courteous*
2125	Mete and drinke thai hadde afyn,	*throughout*
	Bothe piment and plenté a wyn,	*spiced wine*
	Swithe wel thai hadde ifare;	*So well; partaken*
	Thanne seide the quene to eche palmare:	
	"Herde ever eni of yow telle	
2130	In eni lede or eni spelle,	*people; story*
	Or in feld other in toun,	
	Of a knight, Beves of Hamtoun?"	
	"Nai!" queth al that thar ware.	*who were there*
	"What thow?" she seide, "niwe palmare?"	*new*
2135	Thanne seide Beves and lough:	

"That knight ich knowe wel inough!
Atom," a seide, "in is contré — *At home*
Icham an erl and also is he;
At Rome he made me a spel — *told; story*
2140 Of an hors, men clepede Arondel:
Wide whar ichave iwent
And me warisoun ispent — *treasure*
I sought hit bothe fer and ner,
Men telleth me, that it is her; — *here*
2145 Yif ever lovedestow wel that knight,
Let me of that hors have a sight!"
What helpeth hit, to make fable?
She ladde Beves to the stable:
Josian beheld him before,
2150 She segh his browe to-tore; — *disfigured*
After Bonefas she gan grede, — *Boniface; call*
At stable dore to him she sede;
"Be the moder, that me hath bore, — *By*
Ner this mannes browe to-tore, — *Were not; man's brow all torn*
2155 Me wolde thenke be his fasoun, — *fashion*
That hit were Beves of Hamtoun!"
Whan that hors herde nevene — *speak*
His kende lordes stevene, — *legitimate; voice*
His rakenteis he al terof — *chains; rent asunder*
2160 And wente in to the kourt wel kof — *quickly*
And neide and made miche pride — *neighed*
With gret joie be ech a side.
"Allas!" tho queth Josiane,
"Wel mani a man is bane — *doomed*
2165 To dai he worth ilaught,
Er than this stede ben icaught!"
Thanne seide Beves and lough:
"Ich can take hit wel inough:
Wolde ye," a sede, "yeve me leve, — *permission*
2170 Hit ne scholde no man greve!'
"Take hit thanne," she sede,
"And in to stable thow it lede
And teie it thar it stod, — *tie; where*
And thow schelt have mede gode!" — *reward*

2175 Beves to the hors tegh; *went*
Tho the hors him knew and segh.
He ne wawede no fot, *moved*
Til Beves hadde the stirop;
Beves in to the sadel him threw,
2180 Tharbi that maide him wel knew.
Anon seide Josian with than:
"O Beves, gode lemman, *my dear*
Let me with thee reke *reckon*
In that maner, we han ispeke, *have spoken*
2185 And thenk, thow me to wive tok, *remember*
Whan ich me false godes forsok:
Now thow hast thin hors Arondel,
Thee swerd ich thee fette schel, *fetch*
And let me wende with thee sithe *go; then*
2190 Hom in to thin owene kithe!" *Home; country*
Queth Beves: "Be Godes name,
Ichave for thee sofred meche schame, *suffered*
Lain in prisoun swithe strong:
Yif ich thee lovede, hit were wrong!
2195 The patriark me het upon me lif,
That I ne tok never wif,
Boute she were maide clene; *virgin*
And thow havest seve year ben a quene,
And everi night a king be thee: *by you*
2200 How mightow thanne maide be?"
"Merci," she seide, "lemman fre,
Led me hom to thee contré, *Lead; your*
And boute thee finde me maide wimman, *unless; virgin*
Be that eni man saie can,
2205 Send me aghen to me fon *foes*
Al naked in me smok alon!" *smock alone*
Beves seide: "So I schel,
In that forward I graunte wel!" *agreement*
Bonefas to Sire Beves sede:
2210 "Sire, thee is beter do be rede! *follow [my] advice*
The king cometh sone fro honting
And with him mani a riche king,
Fiftene told al in tale,

	Dukes and erles mani and fale.	*numerous*
2215	Whan hii fonde us alle agon,	*gone away*
	Thai wolde after us everichon	*everyone*
	With wondergret chevalrie,	*horsemanship*
	And do us schame and vileinie;	*harm*
	Ac formeste, sire, withouten fable,	*first; lie*
2220	Led Arondel in to the stable,	
	And ate the gate thow him abide,	*at; wait*
	Til the king cometh bi the ride;	
	A wile thee asken at the frome,	*right then*
	Whider thow schelt and whannes thow come;	*Who are you*
2225	Sai, that thow havest wide iwent,	*traveled widely*
	And thow come be Dabilent,	*from*
	That is hennes four jurné:	*[days'] journey*
	Sai, men wile ther the king sle,	
	Boute him come help of sum other;	*Unless*
2230	And King Yvor is his brother,	
	And whan he hereth that tiding,	
	Theder a wile an highing	*in haste*
	With al is power and is ost:	*host*
	Thanne mai we with lite bost	*effort*
2235	Forth in oure wei go!"	
	Beves seide: "It schel be so!"	
	And Arondel to stable lad,	*led*
	Ase Bonefas him bad;	*bade*
	And to the gate Beves yode	*went*
2240	With other beggers, that ther stode,	
	And pyk and skrippe be is side,	*staff and purse by*
	In a sklavin row and wide;	*pilgrim's cloak rough and unfitted*
	His berd was yelw, to is brest wax	*yellow; [down] to his breast*
	And to his gerdel heng is fax.	*waist; hair*
2245	Al thai seide, that hii ne sighe	
	So faire palmer never with eighe,	*eyes*
	Ne com ther non in that contré:	
	Thus wondred on him that him gan se;	
	And so stod Beves in that thring,	*throng*
2250	Til noun belle began to ring.	*noon*

Fram honting com the King Yvore,
And fiftene kinges him before,
Dukes and erles, barouns how fale — *many*
I can nought telle the righte tale. — *give accurate account*
2255 Mervaile thai hadde of Beves alle. — *Wonder*
Yvor gan Beves to him calle
And seide: "Palmer, thow comst fro ferre: — *afar*
Whar is pes and whar is werre? — *peace; war*
Trewe tales thow canst me sain."
2260 Thanne answerde Beves again:
"Sire, ich come fro Jurisalem
Fro Nazareth and fro Bedlem, — *Bethlehem*
Emauns castel and Synaie; — *Emmaus; Sinai*
Ynde, Erop, and Asie, — *India; Europe; Asia*
2265 Egippte, Grese, and Babiloine,
Tars, Sesile and Sesaoine, — *Tarsus; Sicily; Saxony*
In Fris, in Sodeine and in Tire, — *Friesland; Sidon; Tyre*
In Aufrik and in mani empire,
Ac al is pes thar ichave went, — *wherever*
2270 Save in the lond of Dabilent. — *Except*
In pes mai no man come thare,
Thar is werre, sorwe and care.
Thre kinges and dukes five
His chevalrie adoun ginneth drive,
2275 And meche other peple ischent, — *killed*
Cites itake and tounes ibrent; — *torched*
Him to a castel thai han idrive,
That stant be the se upon a clive, — *cliff*
And al the ost lith him aboute, — *surrounded*
2280 Be this to daie a is in doute,"
King Yvor seide: "Allas, allas,
Lordinges, this is a sori cas! — *situation*
That is me brother, ye witen wel, — *know*
That lith beseged in that castel:
2285 To hors and armes, lasse and more,
In haste swithe, that we wer thore!" — *Immediately; there*
Thai armede hem anon bedene, — *themselves instantly*
Yvor and his kinges fiftene,
And to the Cité of Diablent

2290	Alle samen forth they went.	*together*
	But an old king, that hight Garcy,	
	At home he lefte to kepe the lady.	*guard*
	Thoo seid Beves: "Make yow yare,	*ready*
	Yif that ye wille with me fare!"	*go*
2295	Sir Bonefas answered thoo:	
	"Yif ye wil by my consaile do:	
	Here is an olde king Garcy,	
	That muche can of nygremancy;	*necromancy*
	He may see in his goldryng,	*gold ring*
2300	What any man dooth in alle thing.	
	I know an erbe in the forest.	*herb*
	Now wille I sende therafter prest	*quickly*
	And let brochen Reynessh wyne	*broach (a cask) of Rhenish*
	And do that yerbe anoon therynne,	*herb*
2305	And what he be, that ther-of doth drynke,	
	He shal lerne for to wynke	*nod off*
	And slepe anon after ryght	
	Al a day and al a nyght."	
	Sir Bonefas dide al this thing;	
2310	They resen up in the dawnyng;	
	Inowgh they toke what they wolde,	
	Both of silver and of golde,	
	And other tresoure they toke also,	
	And in hur way they gunne goo.	*on their*
2315	And when they were went away,	
	Garcy awaked a morow day	
	And had wonder swith stronge,	*very*
	That he hadde slept so longe.	
	His ryng he gan to him tee,	*take*
2320	For to loke and for to see;	
	And in his ryng say he thare,	*saw*
	The queene awey with the palmer was fare.	*gone*
	To his men he grad ryght:	*cried out*
	"As armes, lordinges, for to fyght!"	*To arms*
2325	And tolde his folke, verament,	*truly*
	How the queene was awey went.	
	They armed hem in ryche wede	*armor*
	And every knyght lep on his stede,	

	And after went al that route	
2330	And besette hem al aboute.	
	Thenne seide Beves to Bonefas:	
	"Kepe wel Josian at this cas,	
	And I wil wynde to bataile,	*go*
	Garcy and his ost assaile.	
2335	I wil fonde, what I do may,	*try*
	I have rested me moony a day.	*many days*
	Fyght, I will now my fylle	
	And hem overcom by Goddes wille!"	
	Tho Bonefas to him saide:	
2340	"Sir, yow is better do by my reed:	
	Ye shal be in the lasse dout,	
	For I know the contré al about;	
	I can bryng yow in to a cave,	
	There a sheparde with a stave,	*staff*
2345	Theyghe men hadden his deth sworn,	*Though*
	He myght him kepe wel therforn!"	
	Into the cave he hath hem brought;	
	Garcy, the Kyng, hem couth fynde nought,	*could not find them*
	Therfore him was swith woo;	*so angry*
2350	He and his ost bethought hem thoo,	
	Hoom agheyn for to wende	
	And sende Ascopart hem to shende.	*destroy*
	In the cave they were al nyght	
	Withoute mete or drynke, aplyght.	*indeed*
2355	Twoo dayes it was goon,	*passed*
	That mete ne drynke had they noon.	
	Josian was afyngered soore	*starved*
	And told anoon Beves therfore.	
	Beves seid, "How darst thou of me meete crave?	*food [ask for]*
2360	Wel thou wotest, that noon I have."	*you know*
	Josian answered sone anoon	
	And bade Sir Beves to wood goon:	*forest*
	I have herde of savagenes,	*savageness*
	Whenne yonge men were in wyldernes,	
2365	That they toke hert and hinde	*stag; doe*
	And other bestes, that they myght fynde;	
	They slowen hem and soden hem in her hide;	*prepared*

	Thus doon men that in wood abyde.	*live*
	Sir, thou myghtest bestes lyghtly take,	*easily*
2370	For sause good I wyl thee make!"	*sauce*
	Beves seide to Bonefas than:	
	"I pray thee kepe wel Josian,	
	The while I wynde into the forest,	
	For to take sum wylde beest!"	
2375	Forth went Beves in that forest,	
	Beestes to sheete he was ful prest.	*shoot; ready*
	Als sone as he was forth yfare,	
	Two lyouns ther com yn thare,	
	Grennand and rampand with her feet.	*Gnashing; standing (as lions rampant)*
2380	Sir Bonefas then als skeet	*very quickly*
	His hors to him thoo he drowgh	
	And armyd him wel ynowgh	
	And yave the lyouns bataile to fyght;	
	Al to lytel was his myght.	
2385	The twoo lyouns sone had sloon	
	That oon his hors, that other the man.	
	Josian into the cave gan shete,	*shut [herself]*
	And the twoo lyouns at hur feete,	
	Grennand on hur with muche grame,	*ferocity*
2390	But they ne myght do hur no shame,	
	For the kind of lyouns, ywis,	*nature*
	A kynges doughter, that maide is,	*virgin*
	Kinges doughter, quene and maide both,	*queen*
	The lyouns myght do hur noo wroth.	*harm*
2395	Beves com sone fro huntyng	
	With three hertes, without lesyng,	*stags*
	And fonde an hors gnawe to the boon,	*bone*
	And Josian awey was goon.	
	He sowned soone for sorow and thought,	*swooned*
2400	Fro cave to cave he her sought,	
	To wete how that cas myght be,	*understand what happened*
	And in a cave he gan to see,	
	Where Josain sate in grete doute	*fear*
	And twoo lions hur about.	
2405	Too Sir Beves gan she speke:	*To*
	"Sir, thyn help, me to awreke	*avenge*

	Of these two liouns, that thy chamberleyn,	*steward*
	Ryght now han him slayn!"	
	She seide, she wolde that oon hoolde,	
2410	While that he that other quelde.	*killed*
	Aboute the nekke she hent that oon,	*held*
	And Beves bade let him goon,	
	And seide: "Dame, forsoth, ywys,	
	I myght yelp of lytel prys,	*boast; worth*
2415	There I had a lyon quelde,	
	The while a woman another helde!	
	Thow shalt never umbraide me,	*reproach*
	When thou comest hoom to my contré:	
	But thou let hem goo both twoo,	
2420	Have good day, fro thee I goo!"	
	She let hem skip up and doun,	
	And Beves assailed the lyoun.	
	Strenger bataile ne strenger fyght	
	Herde ye never of no knyght	
2425	Byfore this in romaunce telle,	
	Than Beves had of beestes felle.	*cruel*
	Al that herkeneth word and ende,	*listen carefully to the end*
	To hevyn mot her sowles wende!	*may their souls go*
	That oon was a lionesse,	
2430	That Sir Bevis dide grete distresse;	
	At the first begynnyng	
	To Beves hondes she gan spryng	
	And al to peces rent hem there,	
	Or Beves myght ther-of be werre.	*Before; beware*
2435	That other lyon, that Josian gan holde,	
	To fight with Beves was ful bold;	
	He ran to him with grete randon	*vehemently*
	And with his pawes he rent adoun	
	His armour almost to ground,	
2440	And in his thyghe a wel grete wound.	*thigh*
	Tho was Beves in hert grame,	*discouraged*
	For the lioun had do him shame;	
	As he were wood, he gan to fyght;	*mad*
	The lionesse seyghe that sight	
2445	And raught to Beves, without faile,	*rushed*

Both at oones they gan him assaile.
Thoo was Beves, in strong tempestes, — *great trouble*
So strong and egre were these beestes, — *eager*
That nyghe they hadde him there queld; — *nearly; killed*
2450 Unnethe he kept him with his shelde. — *Scarcely he protected himself*
With Morgelay, that wel wold byte,
To the lioun he gan smyte;
His ryght foot he shore asonder, — *sheared*
Sir Beves shilde the Lyoun ranne under
2455 And with his teeth with sory happe — *unfortunately*
He kitte a pece of his lappe,
And Beves that ilke stounde
For anguysse fel to the grounde, — *anguish*
And hastely Beves than up stert,
2460 For he was grevyd in his hert;
He kyd wel tho, he was agrevyd, — *knew*
And clef a twoo the lyon is hevyd, — *split the lion's head in two*
And to his hert the poynt thrast;
Thus the lioun died at the last.
2465 Stoutliche the liounesse than — *Courageously*
Asailede Beves, that doughti man, — *hearty*
And with hire mouth is scheld tok
So sterneliche, saith the bok,
That doun it fel of is left hond.
2470 Tho Josian gan understonde,
That hire lord scholde ben slawe;
Helpe him she wolde fawe. — *gladly*
Anon she hente that lioun: — *seized*
Beves bad hire go sitte adoun,
2475 And swor be God in Trinité,
Boute she lete that lioun be, — *Unless*
A wolde hire sle in that destresse — *would slay her*
Ase fain ase the liounesse. — *As gladly as*
Tho she ne moste him nought helpe fighte,
2480 His scheld she broughte him anon righte
And yede hire sitte adoun, saun faile,
And let him worthe in that bataile.
The liounesse was stout and sterne,
Aghen to Beves she gan erne — *Again; run*

2485	And be the right leg she him grep,	*gripped*
	Ase the wolf doth the schep,	*sheep*
	That negh she braide out is sparlire;	*almost; tore out his calf*
	Tho was Beves in gret yre,	
	And in that ilche selve veneu	*place*
2490	Thourgh Godes grace and is vertu	*His*
	The liounesse so harde he smot	
	With Morgelai, that biter bot	*greviously cut*
	Evene upon the regge an high,	*back*
	That Morgelai in therthe fligh.	*the earth*
2495	Tho was Josian ful fain,	*very glad*
	Tho that hii were bothe slain,	*When they (the lions)*
	And Beves was glad and blithe,	
	His joie ne kouthe he no man kithe,	*could; show*
	And ofte he thankede the king in glori	
2500	Of his grace and is viktori;	*victory*
	Ac wo him was for Bonefas,	
	And tho he segh, non other it nas,	*then; saw*
	A sette Josian upon a mule	
	And ride forth a lite while,	
2505	And metten with a geaunt	*giant*
	With a lotheliche semlaunt.	*loathsome semblance*
	He was wonderliche strong,	
	Rome thretti fote long;	*In length*
	His berd was bothe gret and rowe;	*shaggy*
2510	A space of fot betwene is browe;	*brows*
	His clob was, to yeve a strok,	*club*
	A lite bodi of an ok.	*small trunk; oak*
	Beves hadde of him wonder gret	
	And askede him, what a het,	*he was called*
2515	And yef men of his contré	*whether*
	Were ase meche ase was he.	*large*
	"Me name," a sede, "is Ascopard:	
	Garci me sente hiderward,	
	For to bringe this quene aghen	
2520	And thee, Beves, her of-slen.	*here to slay*
	Icham Garci is chaumpioun	*Garcy's*
	And was idrive out of me toun;	*driven*
	Al for that ich was so lite,	

Everi man me wolde smite;
2525 Ich was so lite and so merugh, — *delicate*
Everi man me clepede dwerugh, — *dwarf*
And now icham in this londe,
Iwoxe mor, ich understonde,
And strengere than other tene, — *stronger; ten others*
2530 And that schel on us be sene;
I schel thee sle her, yif I mai!"
"Thourgh Godes help," queth Beves, "nai!"
Beves prikede Arondel a side, — *spurred Arondel's flanks*
Aghen Ascopard he gan ride — *Against*
2535 And smot him on the scholder an high,
That his spere al to-fligh,
And Ascopard with a retret — *step backward*
Smot after Beves a dent gret,
And with is o fot a slintte — *one foot he slipped*
2540 And fel with is owene dentte.
Beves of is palfrai alighte — *off his*
And drough his swerd anon righte
And wolde have smiten of is heved; — *cut off his head*
Josian besoughte him, it were beleved: — *delayed*
2545 "Sire," she seide, "so God thee save,
Let him liven and ben our knave!" — *servant*
"Dame, a wile us betrai!" — *he will betray us*
"Sire, ich wil ben is bourgh, nai!" — *bail*
Thar a dede Beves omage — *he (Ascopard) did; homage*
2550 And becom is owene page.
Forth thai wenten alle thre,
Til that hii come to the se;
A dromond hii fonde ther stonde, — *fast ship*
That wolde in to hethene londe,
2555 With Sarasines stout and fer, — *fierce*
Boute thai nadde no maroner. — *But they (Saracens); mariner*
Tho hii sighe Ascopard come,
Hii thoughten wel, alle and some,
He wolde hem surliche hem lede,
2560 For he was maroner god at nede. — *good*
Whan he in to the schipe cam,
His gode bat an honde he nam, — *club; took*

A drof hem out and dede hem harm, *them (the Saracens)*
Arondel a bar to schip in is arm, *he bore*
2565 And after in a lite while
Josian and hire mule,
And drowen up saile al so snel *quickly*
And sailede forth faire and wel,
That hii come withouten ensoine *without delay*
2570 To the haven of Coloine. *harbor; Cologne*
Whan he to londe kem,
Men tolde, the bischop was is em, *uncle*
A noble man wis afin *altogether wise*
And highte Saber Florentin.
2575 Beves grete him at that cas *chance*
And tolde him what he was. *who*
The beschop was glad afin
And seide: "Wolkome, leve cosin! *dear*
Gladder I nas, sethe ich was bore,
2580 Ich wende, thow haddest be forlore.
Who is this levedi schene?" *beautiful lady*
"Sire, of hethenesse a quene,
And she wile, for me sake,
Cristendome at thee take." *Be christened by you*
2585 "Who is this with the grete visage?"
"Sire," a sede, "hit is me page
And wile ben icristnede also,
And ich bidde, that ye hit do!"
The nexste dai after than
2590 The beschop cristnede Josian.
For Ascopard was mad a kove; *made; font*
Whan the beschop him scholde in schove,
A lep anon upon the benche
And seide: "Prest, wiltow me drenche?
2595 The devel yeve thee helle pine, *hell's pain*
Icham to meche te be cristine!" *too large; christened*
After Josian is cristing *Josian's christening*
Beves dede a gret fighting,
Swich bataile dede never non
2600 Cristene man of flesch ne bon,
Of a dragoun ther be side,

	That Beves slough ther in that tide,	
	Save Sire Launcelet de Lake,	
	He faught with a fur drake	*firebreathing dragon*
2605	And Wade dede also,	
	And never knightes boute thai to,	*except those two*
	And Gy a Warwik, ich understonde,	
	Slough a dragoun in NorthHomberlonde.	
	How that ilche dragoun com ther,	
2610	Ich wile yow telle, in what maner.	
	Thar was a king in Poyle land	*Apulia*
	And another in Calabre, ich understonde;	*Calabria*
	This twe kinge foughte ifere	*together (i.e., each other)*
	More than foure and twenti yere,	
2615	That hii never pes nolde,	*peace*
	Naither for selver ne for golde,	
	And al the contré, saundoute,	*without doubt*
	Thai distruede hit al aboute;	*destroyed*
	Thai hadde mani mannes kours,	*curse*
2620	Wharthourgh hii ferden wel the wors;	
	Tharfore hii deide in dedli sinne	
	And helle pine thai gan hem winne.	
	After in a lite while	
	Thai become dragouns vile,	*became*
2625	And so thai foughte dragouns ifere	*as dragons together*
	Mor than foure and thretti yere.	
	An ermite was in that londe,	*hermit*
	That was feld of Godes sonde;	*Who had received; mercy*
	To Jesu Crist a bed a bone,	*he requested; favor*
2630	That he dilivre the dragouns sone	*soon*
	Out of that ilche stede,	*very place*
	That hii namore harm ne dede.	*no more*
	And Jesu Crist, that sit in hevene,	
	Wel herde that ermites stevene	*voice*
2635	And grauntede him is praiere.	*his prayer*
	Anon the dragouns bothe ifere	*together*
	Toke here flight and flowe awai,	*flew*
	Thar never eft man hem ne sai.	
	That on flegh anon with than,	*thence*
2640	Til a com to Toscan.	*Tuscany*

	That other dragoun is flight nome	*took his flight*
	To Seinte Peter is brige of Rome;	*Saint Peter's bridge*
	Thar he schel leggen ay,	*lay dormant*
	Til hit come Domes Dai.	*Judgment Day*
2645	And everi seve yer ones,	
	Whan the dragoun moweth is bones,	*moves his*
	Than cometh a roke and a stink	*vapor*
	Out of the water under the brink,	
	That men ther-of taketh the fevere,	
2650	That never after mai he kevere;	*recover*
	And who that nel nought leve me,	*will not believe*
	Wite at pilgrimes that ther hath be,	*Ask; have been there*
	For thai can telle yow, iwis,	
	Of that dragoun how it is.	
2655	That other thanne flegh an highe	*flew*
	Thourgh Toskan and Lombardie,	
	Thourgh Province, withouten ensoine,	*delay*
	Into the londe of Coloyne;	
	Thar the dragoun gan arive	
2660	At Coloyne under a clive.	*cliff*
	His eren were rowe and ek long,	*ears; rough*
	His frount before hard and strong;	*forehead (whole face)*
	Eighte toskes at is mouth stod out,	
	The leste was seventene ench about,	*inches around*
2665	The her, the cholle under the chin,	*hair; throat*
	He was bothe leith and grim;	*loathsome*
	A was imaned ase a stede;	*maned*
	The heved a bar with meche pride,	
	Betwene the scholder and the taile	
2670	Foure and twenti fot, saunfaile.	*without fail*
	His taile was of gret stringethe,	*strength*
	Sextene fot a was a lingthe;	*it was in length*
	His bodi ase a wintonne.	*wine tun*
	Whan hit schon the brighte sonne,	*When the bright sun shone*
2675	His wingges schon so the glas.	*as glass*
	His sides wer hard ase eni bras.	
	His brest was hard ase eni ston;	
	A foulere thing nas never non.	
	Ye, that wile a stounde dwelle,	*[If] you will stay awhile*

2680 Of his stringethe I mai yow telle.
  Beves yede to bedde a night
With torges and with candel light. *torches*
Whan he was in bedde ibrought,
On Jesu Crist was al is thought.
2685 Him thoughte, a king, that was wod, *A vision came to him; mad*
Hadde wonded him ther a stod;
He hadde wonded him biter and sore,
A wende a mighte leve namore, *He thought he might not remain*
And yet him thoughte a virgine *it seemed to him*
2690 Him broughte out of al is pine. *suffering*
Whan he of is slep abraid, *[abruptly] awakened*
Of is swevene he was afraid. *dream*
Thanne a herde a reuli cri, *mournful*
And besoughte Jesu merci:
2695 "For the venim is on me throwe,
Her I legge al to-blowe, *lie; swollen*
And roteth me flesch fro the bon,
Bote ne tit me never non!" *Nor do I have any remedy at all*
And in is cri a seide: "Allas,
2700 That ever yet I maked was!" *ever I was born*
Anon whan hit was dai light,
Beves awakede and askede right, *immediately*
What al that cri mighte ben.
His men him answerde aghen
2705 And seide, that he was a knight,
In bataile he was holden wight; *valiant*
Alse a wente him to plaie *fight*
Aboute her in this contrai,
In this contré aviroun *hereabout*
2710 A mette with a vile dragoun,
And venim he hath on him throwe:
Thar a lith al to-blowe! *he lies; swollen*
"Lord Crist," queth Beves tho,
"Mai eni man the dragoun slo!"
2715 His men answerde, withouten lesing: *lying*
"Thar nis neither emperur ne king,
That come thar the dragoun wore, *where the dragon was*
An hondred thosend men and more,

That he nolde slen hem everichon,
2720 Ne scholde hii never thannes gon."
"Ascopard," a seide, "whar ertow?" *where are you*
"Icham her; what wilte now?" *here; do you want*
"Wile we to the dragoun gon?
Thourgh Godes help we scholle him slo!"
2725 "Ya, sire, so mot I the, *may I prosper*
Bletheliche wile I wende with thee!" *Gladly*
Beves armede him ful wel,
Bothe in yrene and in stel, *steel*
And gerte him with a gode bronde *armed himself; sword*
2730 And tok a spere in is honde.
Out ate gate he gan ride,
And Ascopard be his side.
Alse hii wente in here pleghing,
Hii speke of mani selkouth thing. *wondrous*
2735 That dragoun lai in is den
And segh come the twei men;
A made a cri and a wonder,
Ase hit were a dent of thonder. *As if*
Ascopard was adrad so sore, *afraid*
2740 Forther dorste he go namore;
A seide to Beves, that was is fere: *companion*
"A wonderthing ye mai here!" *marvelous*
Beves saide: "Have thow no doute,
The dragoun lith her aboute; *is close*
2745 Hadde we the dragoun wonne, *defeated*
We hadde the feireste pris under sonne!" *fairest prize*
Ascopard swor, be Sein Jon, *Saint*
A fot ne dorste he forther gon.
Beves answerde and seide tho;
2750 "Ascopard, whi seistow so?
Whi schelt thow afered be
Of thing that thow might nought sen?"
A swor, alse he moste then, *must get away*
He nolde him neither hire ne sen:
2755 "Icham weri, ich mot have reste: *tired; must*
Go now forth and do the beste!"
Thanne seide Beves this wordes fre:

	"Schame hit is, to terne aghe.	*turn back*
	A smot his stede be the side,	
2760	Aghen the dragoun he gan ride,	*Against*
	The dragoun segh, that he cam	
	Yenande aghenes him anan,	*Roaring against him rapidly*
	Yenande and gapande on him so,	*Yawning; gaping*
	Ase he wolde him swolwe tho.	*swallow*
2765	Whan Beves segh that ilche sight,	
	The dragoun of so meche might,	
	Hadde therthe opnede anon,	*the earth*
	For drede a wolde ther in han gon;	
	A spere he let to him glide	
2770	And smot the dragoun on the side;	
	The spere sterte aghen anon,	*jumped back*
	So the hail upon the ston,	*Like; stone*
	And to-barst on pices five.	*burst into*
	His swerd he drough alse blive;	*quickly*
2775	Tho thai foughte, alse I yow sai,	
	Til it was high noun of the dai.	*noon*
	The dragoun was atened stronge,	*greatly irritated*
	That o man him scholde stonde so longe;	*one; withstand*
	The dragoun harde him gan asaile	*fiercely assailed him*
2780	And smot his hors with the taile	
	Right amideward the hed,	*in the middle of*
	That he fel to grounde ded.	
	Now is Beves to grounde brought,	
	Helpe him God, that alle thing wrought!	
2785	Beves was hardi and of gode hert,	
	Aghen the dragoun anon a stert	
	And harde him a gan asaile,	
	And he aghen with strong bataile;	
	So betwene hem leste that fight	*lasted*
2790	Til it was the therke night.	*dark*
	Beves hadde thanne swich thrast,	*thirst*
	Him thoughte his herte to-brast;	*would burst*
	Thanne segh he a water him beside,	
	So hit mighte wel betide,	
2795	Fain a wolde theder flen,	
	He ne dorste fro the dragoun ten;	*go*

	The dragoun asailede him fot hot,	*quickly*
	With is taile on his scheld a smot,	
	That hit clevede hevene ato,	*even in two*
2800	His left scholder dede also.	
	Beves was hardi and of gode hert,	
	Into the welle anon a stert.	
	Lordinges, herkneth to me now:	
	The welle was of swich vertu:	
2805	A virgine wonede in that londe,	*dwelling*
	Hadde bathede in, ich understonde;	
	That water was so holi,	
	That the dragoun, sikerli,	
	Ne dorste neghe the welle aboute	*dared not come near*
2810	Be fourti fote, saundoute.	*forty feet*
	Whan Beves parsevede this,	*perceived*
	Wel glad a was in hertte, iwis;	*indeed*
	A dede of is helm of stel	*He took off his helmet*
	And colede him ther in fraiche wel,	*cooled; pure*
2815	And of is helm a drank thore	*from*
	A large galon other more.	*or*
	A nemenede Sein Gorge, our levedi knight,	*called on; Saint George*
	And sete on his helm, that was bright;	
	And Beves with eger mode	*eager spirit (inspiration)*
2820	Out of the welle sone a yode;	*arose*
	The dragoun harde him asaile gan,	
	He him defendeth ase a man.	
	So betwene hem leste the fight,	*lasted*
	Til hit sprong the dai light,	
2825	Whan Beves mighte aboute sen,	
	Blithe he gan thanne ben;	
	Beves on the dragoun hew,	*cut*
	The dragoun on him venim threw;	
	Al ferde Beves bodi there	*All became (fared)*
2830	A foule mesel alse yif a were;	*foul leper*
	Thar the venim on him felle,	
	His flesch gan ranclen and tebelle,	*rankle; swell*
	Thar the venim was icast,	
	His armes gan al to-brast;	*fall apart*
2835	Al to-brosten is ventaile,	*neck armor*

And of his hauberk a thosend maile. *from his [chain mail] a thousand links*
Thanne Beves, sone an highe
Wel loude he gan to Jesu criye:
"Lord, that rerede the Lazaroun, *raised Lazarus*
2840 Dilivre me fro this fend dragoun!" *fiend*
Tho he segh his hauberk toren, *chain mail*
"Lord!" a seide, "That I was boren!"
That seide Beves, thar a stod, *where he stood*
And leide on, ase he wer wod;
2845 The dragoun harde him gan asaile *fiercely*
And smot on the helm with is taile,
That his helm clevede ato, *helmet; in two*
And his bacinet dede also. *basinet*
Tweies a ros and tweis a fel, *Twice he rose*
2850 The thredde tim overthrew in the wel; *third time*
Thar-inne a lai up right; *he lay face up*
A neste, whather hit was dai other night. *He did not know*
Whan overgon was his smerte *healed; injury*
And rekevred was of is hertte, *recovered; courage*
2855 Beves sette him up anon;
The venim was awei igon;
He was ase hol a man *whole*
Ase he was whan he theder cam.
On is knes he gan to falle,
2860 To Jesu Crist he gan to calle:
"Help," a seide, "Godes sone,
That this dragoun wer overcome!
Boute ich mowe the dragoun slon
Er than ich hennes gon,
2865 Schel hit never aslawe be
For no man in Cristenté!" *Christianity*
To God he made his praiere
And to Marie, his moder dere;
That herde the dragoun, ther a stod,
2870 And flegh awei, ase he wer wod.
Beves ran after, withouten faile,
And the dragoun he gan asaile;
With is swerd, that he out braide, *unsheathed*
On the dragoun wel hard a laide,

2875	And so harde a hew him than,	
	A karf ato his heved pan,	*cut in two; head pan (skull)*
	And hondred dentes a smot that stonde,	*strokes; time*
	Er he mighte kerven a wonder,	
	A hitte him so on the cholle	*throat*
2880	And karf ato the throte bolle.	*throat-ball (Adam's apple)*
	The dragoun lai on is side,	*its*
	On him a yenede swithe wide.	*gaped very*
	Beves thanne with strokes smerte	
	Smot the dragoun to the herte,	
2885	An hondred dentes a smot in on,	
	Er the heved wolde fro the bodi gon,	
	And the gode knight Bevoun	
	The tonge karf of the dragoun;	
	Upon the tronsoun of is spere	*handle*
2890	The tonge a stikede for to bere.	
	A wented tho withouten ensoine	*delay*
	Toward the toun of Coloine.	
	Thanne herde he belles ringe,	
	Prestes, clerkes loude singe;	
2895	A man ther he hath imet,	
	And swithe faire he hath him gret,	*greeted*
	And asked that ilche man tho,	
	Whi thai ronge and songe so.	
	"Sire," a seide, "withouten faile,	
2900	Beves is ded in bataile;	
	Tharfore, for sothe I saie thee:	
	Hit is Beves dirige!"	*dirge*
	"Nai," queth Beves, "be Sein Martin!"	
	And wente to Bischop Florentin.	
2905	Tho the bischop hadde of him a sight,	
	A thankede Jesu ful of might	
	And broughte Beves in to the toun	
	With a faire prosesioun;	
	Thanne al the folk that thar was,	
2910	Thankede Jesu of that gras.	*for; grace*
	On a dai Sire Beves sede:	*One day*
	"Leve em, what is to rede	*Dear uncle; news*
	Of me stifader Devoun	*stepfather Devon*

	That holdeth me londes at Hamtoun?"	
2915	The beschop seide anon right:	
	"Kosin, Saber, thin em, is in Wight,	*uncle*
	And everi yer on a dai certaine	
	Upon th'emperur of Almaine	*Germany*
	He ginneth gret bataile take,	
2920	Beves, al for thine sake;	
	He weneth wel, that thow be ded;	*believes*
	Tharfore, kosin, be me red,	*by; advice*
	An hondred men ich yeve thee wighte,	*I give you manfully*
	Aghen th'emperur to fighte,	*Against*
2925	Stalworde men and fer,	*Stalwart; fierce*
	And thow schelt wende te Saber:	*go to*
	Sai, ich grette him wel ilome!	*many times*
	Yif ye han nede, sendeth to me,	
	Ich wile yow helpe with al me might,	
2930	Aghen th'emperur to fight.	
	While thow dost this ilche tourne,	
	The levedi schel with me sojurne,	
	And the page Ascopard	
	Schel hire bothe wite and ward."	*protect; guard*
2935	Forth wente Beves with than	
	To his lemman Josian:	*lady*
	"Lemman," a seide, "ich wile go	
	And avenge me of me fo,	*my foe*
	Yif ich mighte with eni ginne	*means (device)*
2940	Me kende eritage to winne!"	*My natural heritage*
	"Swete lemman," Josian sede,	
	"Who schel me thanne wisse and rede?"	*guide; advise*
	Beves sede "Lemman min,	
	Min em, the Bischop Florentin,	
2945	And Ascopard, me gode page,	
	Schel thee warde fro damage."	*Protect; harm*
	"Ye, have ich Ascopard," she sede,	*I have*
	Of no man ne stant me drede;	*no man; I dread*
	Ich take thee God and seinte Marie:	*put you [in the hands of]; holy Mary*
2950	Sone so thow might, to me thow highe!"	*As soon as you can; return*
	Beves wente forth anon	
	With is men everichon,	*every one*

That the bischop him hadde yeve. — *given*
So longe thai hadde here wei idrive,
2955 That hii come upon a done, — *hill*
A mile out of South Hamtone.
"Lordinges," to his men a sede,
"Ye scholle do be mine rede! — *take my counsel*
Have ich eni so hardi on, — *anyone so hardy*
2960 That dorre to Hamtoun gon, — *dares*
To th'emperur of Almaine,
And sai: her cometh a vintaine, — *here; division*
Al prest an hondred knighte — *ready*
That fore his love wilen fighte
2965 Both with spere and with launce,
Al fresch icome out of Fraunce!
Ac ever, an erneste and a rage,
Ever speketh Frensche laungage,
And sai, ich hatte Gerard, — *am called*
2970 And fighte ich wile be forward, — *by agreement*
And of the meistri icham sure, — *victory I am confident*
Yif he wile yilde min hure?" — *If; pay my hire*
Forth ther com on redi reke, — *one man readily*
That renabliche kouthe Frensch speke; — *eloquently*
2975 "Sire," a seide, "ich wile gon,
The mesage for to don anon!"
Forth a wente to the castel gate
The porter a mette ther-ate,
To th'emperur he hath him lad,
2980 Al a seide, ase Beves him bad.
  Th'emperur and Beves sete ifere — *together*
That ilche night at the sopere; — *same*
Th'emperur askede him, what a het; — *he was called*
"Gerard!" a seide alse sket — *very quickly*
2985 "Gerard!" a seide, "for soth iwis,
This levedi hadde her er this
An erl to lord, er ich hire wedde,
A sone betwene hem to thai hadde,
A proud wreche and a ying, — *young*
2990 And for sothe a lite gadling; — *impudent*
So was is fader of proud mode, — *spirit*

Icomen of sum lether blode; *evil*
His sone, that was a proud garsoun, *boy*
Men him clepede Bevoun;
2995 Sone he was of age, *As soon as*
A solde me his eritage *inheritance*
And spente his panes in scham and schonde, *money in shame; disgrace*
And sithe flegh out of Ingelonde. *ran away*
Now hath he her an em in Wight, *there; uncle*
3000 Sire Saber, a wel strong knight,
And cometh with gret barnage *baronage*
And cleimeth his eritage,
And ofte me doth her gret gile, *here*
And thow might yilden is while, *stay for a while*
3005 Him to sle with swerd in felde,
Wel ich wolde thin here yelde!" *army pay*
"Sire," queth Beves anon right,
"Ichave knightes of meche might,
That beth unarmed her of wede, *armor*
3010 For we ne mighte non out lede
Over the se withouten aneighe; *difficulty*
Tharfore, sire, swithe an highe *quickly*
Let arme me knightes echon, *each one*
And yef hem gode hors forth enon, *right away*
3015 An hondred men sent thow thee self,
Ase mani ichave be min helf, *on my behalf*
Dight me the schip and thin men bothe, *Prepare*
And I schel swere thee an othe,
That I schel yeve swiche asaut *assault*
3020 On that ilche Sabaaut, *Saber*
That withinne a lite while
Thow schelt here of a queinte gile!" *hear; cunning trick*
Al thus th'emperur hath him dight *supplied*
Bothe hors, armes, and knight,
3025 Tharto schipes with gode vitaile; *victuals*
Forth thai wente and drowe saile.
In the schipe the knightes seten, ywis, *for sure*
On of here, another of his.
Whan thai come amidde the forde,
3030 Ech threw is felawe over the bord;

	Of th'emperures knightes everichon	
	Withinne bord ne levede non.	*left none*
	Saber hem ful wel ysay,	*saw*
	Ase he upon his toure lay,	*tower*
3035	Mani baner he segh arered.	*raised*
	Tho was Saber.sumdel afered,	*somewhat afraid*
	That th'emperur with is ost come,	
	Biker he made wel ylome.	*Fight; many times*
	Beves wiste wel and sede,	
3040	That Saber him wolde drede;	*dread*
	Upon the higheste mast is top there	*mast's top*
	He let sette up a stremere	*banner*
	Of his fader armure,	
	Saber the rather to make sure,	
3045	For mani a time thar beforen	
	He hadde hit in to bataile boren.	*carried it into battle*
	Tho the schip to londe drough,	*drew*
	Saber hit knew wel inough	
	And thoughte and gan to understonde,	
3050	That Beves was come inte Ingelonde.	*into*
	"Lord," a sede, "hered Thow be,	*praised*
	That ich mai me kende lord se:	*lawful*
	That he wer ded, ich was ofdrad,	*afraid*
	Meche sorwe ichave for him had."	
3055	A wente with is knightes blive,	*quickly*
	Thar the schipes scholde arive;	*Where*
	Either other gan to kisse,	*Each began to kiss the other*
	And made meche joie and blisse,	
	And Beves tolde him in a while,	
3060	He hadde do th'emperur a gile.	*done; trick*
	Tho seide Beves with than:	
	"Have ich eni so hardi man,	
	That dorre to Hamtoun gon	*dares*
	Over the water sone anon,	
3065	And sai th'emperur anon right,	
	That I nam no Frensche knight,	
	Ne that I ne hatte nought Gerard,	*I am not named Gerard*
	That made with him the forward,	*agreement*
	And sai him, ich hatte Bevoun,	

3070	And cleymeth the seinori of Hamtoun,	*rule*
	And that is wif is me dame,	*his wife is my mother*
	That schel hem bothe terne to grame;	*anger*
	Now of hem bothe togadre	*together*
	I schel fonde wreke me fadre?"	*try to avenge*
3075	Up thar sterte an hardi on:	*hearty one*
	"Sire," a seide, "ich wile gon,	
	The mesage fordoth hem bothe,	*ruins*
	And maken hem sori and wrothe."	
	Forth a wente ase hot	*at once*
3080	Over the water in a bot,	*boat*
	Forth a wente also whate	*quickly*
	In at the castel gate;	
	At the soper alse a set,	*as he sat*
	Th'emperur he gan thus gret:	
3085	"Sire emperur, I thee bringe	
	A swithe sertaine tiding:	
	Wel the grete that ilche knight,	
	That sopede with thee yerstene night;	*supped*
	A saith a hatte nought Gerard,	*he was not called*
3090	That made with thee the forward;	*agreement*
	A saith, that he hatte Bevoun	
	And cleymeth the seinori of Hamtoun,	
	And is icome with thee to speke,	
	Of his fader deth to ben awreke,	*avenged*
3095	Thee te sle with schame and schonde	*disgrace*
	And for to winne is owene londe."	
	Th'emperur herde of him that word,	
	His sone stod before the bord;	*[the emperor's] son*
	He thoughte with is longe knif	
3100	Bereve that mesageres lif;	*Take away*
	A threw is knif and kouthe nought redi	*aim*
	And smot his sone thourgh the bodi.	
	The mesager spak a gainli word	*suitable*
	Before th'emperur is bord:	*the emperor's table*
3105	"Thow gropedest the wif anight to lowe,	*groped your wife too lowly at night*
	Thow might nought sen aright to throwe;	
	Thow havest so swonke on hire to night,	*worked*
	Thow havest negh forlore the sight:	*almost lost your sight*

	Her thow havest lither haunsel,	*Here; a poor gift*
3110	A worse thee betide schel!"	
	And smot is hors with the spore	*pricked; spur*
	And arnde out at halle dore;	*ran (hightailed)*
	Wel and faire he hath him dight	*conducted himself*
	And com aghen to Beves in Wight	
3115	And tolde a slough is sone for grame;	*he slew [the emperor's] son in anger*
	Beves lough and hadde gode game.	*anger; amusement*
	Lete we with Sire Beves thanne	
	And speke of Josiane,	
	That in Coloine was with Beves em,	*uncle*
3120	Til that he aghen theder kem.	
	In that londe that ilche while	
	Thar wonede an erl, that highte Mile:	*Miles*
	To Josian he hadde his love cast	
	And gan hire to wowen fast,	*woo*
3125	Faire a spak to terne hire thought,	*change her mind*
	And she seide a was aboute nought.	*i.e., "Nothing doing"*
	That erl was wroth in is manere,	*angry*
	For Josian him nolde here,	*Since; would not listen to him*
	And spak to hire with loude gret:	*lamentation*
3130	"For wham," a seide, "scholde ich it lete,	*should I stop it*
	Boute ich mai have of thee me wille?	
	Ich wile," a seide, "who that nille!"[1]	
	She seide: "While ichave Ascopard,	
	Of thee nam ich nothing afard,	
3135	For thee wrethe ne for thin ost,	*anger; army*
	Ne for thee ne for thine bost!"	*threat*
	And tho thoughte that Erl Mile	
	To do Josian a gile:	*trick*
	A leter he let for to write,	
3140	In this maner he dede adite,	*compose*
	That Ascopard come scholde	
	To Beves, thar the letter him tolde,	
	In to a castel in an yle,	*isle*
	The brede of the water thre mile;	*width*

[1] *"I will," he said, "no matter who does not want me to"*

3145	To Ascopard thai come snel;	*quickly*
	Thai seide, Beves him grette wel	
	And besoughte, for is love	
	In haste a scholde to him come.	
	Forth wente Ascopard ase hot	*at once*
3150	Over the water in a bot;	*boat*
	Whan he was over the water come,	
	Hii unlek the ghate at the frome;	*unlocked; start*
	And whan he was comen withinne,	
	Thai sperede him faste with ginne.	*locked him securely; trap*
3155	Aghen to Josiane Miles gan terne:	*return*
	"For wham," a seide, "schel ich it werne?"	*hold back*
	She thoughte for to kepe hire, aplight,	*protect herself, indeed*
	She sente a masager to Wight,	*[Isle of] Wight*
	To Beves, be letter and tolde fore	
3160	Al togedre lasse and more.	
	Miles wolde have is wille	
	And she bed him holde stille:	*bade; stop*
	"Nought, thegh I scholde lese me lif,	
	Boute ich were thee weddede wif;	
3165	Yif eni man me scholde wedde,	
	Thanne mot ich go with him to bedde.	*must*
	I trow, he is nought now here,	
	That schel be me weddefere!"	*husband*
	"I schel thee wedde aghenes thee wille,	
3170	Tomorwe I schel hit fulfille!"	
	And kiste hire anon right	
	And sente after baroun and knight	
	And bed hem come leste and meste,	*ordered them; lowest and highest*
	To anoure that meri feste.	*honor*
3175	The night is gon, that dai comen is,	
	The spusaile don hit is	*espousal*
	With merthe in that toun	
	And joie of erl and baroun.	
	And whan hit drough toward the night,	
3180	Here soper was ther redi dight,	*Their; arrayed*
	And thegh thai richelich weren ifed,	*when*
	That erl wolde ben abed.	
	Josian he het lede to bour,	*commanded [that she be] led to bower*

	To have hire under covertour;	*covers*
3185	Upon hire bedde ther she sat,	
	That erl com to hire with that,	
	With knightes gret compainie	
	With pyment and with spisorie,	*spiced wine; spices*
	With al the gamen that hii hedde,	*tricks*
3190	For to make hire dronke a bedde;	*drunk*
	Ac al another was hire thought,	*But*
	Ne gamnede hire that gle right nought.	*amused; gaiety not at all*
	"Sire," she seide to that erl sone,	
	"Ich bidde thow graunte me a bone,	*favor*
3195	And boute thow graunte me this one,	*unless*
	I ne schel thee never bedde none.	
	Ich bidde thee at the ferste frome,	*very beginning*
	That man ne wimman her in come;	*[neither] man nor; here*
	Belok hem thar-oute for love o me,	*Lock*
3200	That no man se our privité!	*secret things*
	Wimmen beth schamfast in dede	*modest*
	And namliche maidenes," sche sede.	*particularly*
	That erl seide a wolde faine.	*gladly*
	A drof out bothe knight and swaine,	*servants*
3205	Levedies, maidenes, and grome,	*young men*
	That non ne moste ther-in come,	
	And schette the dore with the keie.	*shut; key*
	Litel a wende have be so veie.	*Little he thought; doomed*
	Josian he com aghen to:	
3210	"Lemman," a seide, "ichave ido,	
	Thee bone ichave do with lawe,	*Your boon; in good faith*
	Me schon I mot me self of drawe,	*shoes; take off*
	As I never yet ne dede."	
	Adoun a set him in that stede;	
3215	Thanne was before his bed itight,	*prepared*
	Ase fele han of this gentil knight,	*As many [servants] have done*
	A covertine on raile tre,	*cover; rail-tree*
	For no man scholde on bed ise.	
	Josian bethoughte on highing,	*quickly*
3220	On a towaile she made knotte riding,	*a riding knot (noose)*
	Aboute his nekke she hit threw	
	And on the raile tre she drew;	

	Be the nekke she hath him up tight	
	And let him so ride al the night.	
3225	Josian lai in hire bed.	
	No wonder, though she wer adred.	
	Dai is come in alle wise,	
	A morwe the barouns gonne arise	*In the morning*
	Sum to honten and sum to cherche,	*hunt*
3230	And werkmen gonne for to werche.	*workmen*
	The sonne schon, hit drough to under,	*toward noon*
	The barouns thar-of hadde wonder;	
	That th'erl lai so longe a bed,	
	Gret wonder thar-of he hedde.	
3235	Queth sum: "Let him lie stille!	*Said some*
	Of Josian he hath al is wille."	
	Middai com, hit drough te noune,	*toward noon*
	The barouns speke ther eft soune:	*again*
	Queth the boldeste: "How mai this be?	
3240	Wende ich wile up and ise!"	*I will go up and see*
	That baroun dorste wel speke,	
	To the chaumber he gan reke	*reach*
	And smot the dore with is honde,	
	That al wide opun it wonde.	
3245	"Awake," a seide, "Sire Erl Mile,	
	Thow havest sleped so longe while,	
	Thin heved oweth to ake wel:	*head; ache*
	Dame, let make him a caudel!"	*fortified drink*
	"Nai," queth Josian at that sake,	
3250	"Never eft ne schel his heved ake!	
	Ichave so tyled him for that sore,	*handled; pain*
	Schel hit never eft ake more,	
	Yerstendai he me wedded with wrong	*Yesterday; illegitimately*
	And tonight ichave him honge.	
3255	Doth be me al youre wille,	
	Schel he never eft wimman spille!"	*despoil women*
	Al hii made meche sorwe;	
	Anon rightes in that morwe	
	Sum hire demte thanne	*condemned*
3260	In a tonne for to branne.	*In a barrel; burn*
	Withoute the toun hii pighte a stake,	*Outside; set up*

	Thar the fur was imake,	*There; fire*
	The tonne thai hadde ther iset,	
	Thai fette wode and elet.	*gathered wood and fuel*
3265	Ascopard withinne the castel lay,	
	The tonne and al the folk he say;	*town, saw*
	Ful wel him thoughte that while,	
	That him trokede a gret gile,	*tricked him; deceit*
	For he was in the castel beloke,	*locked*
3270	The castel wal he hath tobroken;	*shattered*
	He was maroner wel gode,	*sailor*
	A stertte in to the salte flode,	*leapt*
	A fischer he segh fot hot,	*fisherman; at once*
	Ever a swam toward the bot.	
3275	The fischer wende, sum fend it were,	*thought; some fiend*
	Out of is bot he flegh for fere.	*flew*
	Ascopard hente the bot an honde	*caught*
	And rew himself to the londe,	
	Toward the fur faste a schok,	*fire; hasten*
3280	Beves com and him oftok:	*overtook*
	"Treitour," a seide, "whar hastow be?	*have you been*
	This dai thow havest betraied me!"	
	"Nai, sire!" Ascopard seide,	
	And tolde, Miles him hadde betraide.	
3285	Toward the fur thai wente blive:	
	The prest, that hire scholde schrive,	*confess*
	Godes blessing mote he fonge,	*receive*
	For that he held Josiane so longe!	
	In hire smok she stod naked,	
3290	Thar the fur was imaked;	
	Ase men scholde hire forbrenne,	
	Beves on Arondel com renne	*came running*
	With is swerd Morgelay;	
	Ascopard com be another way,	
3295	And slowen in that ilche stounde	*killed; very place*
	Al that hii aboute the fur founde,	*found around; fire*
	And that he hadde for is while,	*his effort*
	That proude erl, Sire Mile.	
	A sette Josian on is palfrai,	
3300	And wente forth in here wai;	*their way*

Thai wente to schip anon righte
And sailede forth in to Wighte.
Wel was Saber paid with than
Of Ascopard and of Josian.
3305 Beves and Saber sente here sonde *message*
Wide in to fele londe, *many lands*
And hii sente an hie *in haste*
After gret chevalrie,
Of al the londe the stringeste knighte, *most stalwart*
3310 That hii owhar finde mighte. *anywhere*
That emperur negh daide, *nearly died*
His wif confortede him and saide:
"Sire," she seide, "doute yow nought! *fear not*
Of gode consaile icham bethought: *good counsel*
3315 Ye scholle sende, for sertaine,
After your ost in to Almaine, *host*
And whan your ost is come togadre,
Send to the King of Scotlonde, me fadre;
He wile come to thee an highe *in haste*
3320 With wondergret chevalrie,
That thow derst have no sore *pain*
Of that thef, Saber the hore, *grayhaired*
Ne of Beves, that is me lothe: *loathful to me*
Yit ye schollen hem hangen bothe!"
3325 Tho the letters were yare, *ready*
The masegers wer forth ifare. *gone*
In Mai, whan lef and gras ginth springe, *leaf; begin to*
And the foules merie to singe, *birds*
The King of Scotlonde com to fighte
3330 With thretti thosend of hardi knighte
Of Almaine, is owene barouny,
With wonder-gret chevalry.
"Lordinges," a seide, "ye witeth alle," *know*
Whan hii were before him in the halle,
3335 "That ofte this thef, Saber the hore,
Me hath aneied swithe sore. *annoyed*
Now is him come help to fighte,
Beves of Hamtoun, an hardi knighte,
To Sarasins was solde gon longe; *sold long ago*

3340	Ich wende he hadde ben anhonge.	*wish*
	He me threteth for to slen	
	And for to winne is londe aghen;	
	With him he hath a geaunt brought:	
	Erthliche man semeth he nought,	*Earthly*
3345	Ne no man of flesch ne felle,	*skin*
	Boute a fend stolen out of helle;	*fiend*
	Ascopart men clepeth him ther oute,	
	Of him ichave swithe gret doute.	*fear*
	Ac, lordinges," a seide, "arme ye wel,	
3350	We scholle besege hem in here castel;	
	The Ascopard be strong and sterk,	*Though*
	Mani hondes maketh light werk!"	*hands*
	Forth thai wenten ase snel,	*swiftly*
	Til thai come to the castel	
3355	Thar Saber and Beves weren inne.	
	Thai pighte pavilouns and bente ginne.	*pitched pavilions; field machinery*
	Saber stod on is tour an high,	*tower*
	Al that grete ost a sigh;	*sighted*
	Gret wonder ther of he hade,	
3360	The holi crois before him he made	*cross*
	And swor be his berde hore,	*gray*
	Hit scholde some of hem rewe sore.	*regret*
	Saber doun of his tour went,	
	After al is knightes a sent:	
3365	"Has armes, lordinges!" he gan segge,	*To arms; say*
	"Th'emperur ther oute us wile belegge.	*besiege*
	Make we thre vintaine,	*divisions*
	That be gode and certaine!	
	The ferste ich wile me self out lede,	*lead out*
3370	And thow that other, Beves!" a sede,	
	"And Ascopard the thredde schel have	
	With is gode, grete stave.	
	Be we thre upon the grene,	*field*
	Wel ich wot and nought ne wene:	*know; doubt not*
3375	Mani man is thar oute kete,	*caught*
	This dai schel is lif forlete!"	*be lost*
	Saber is horn began to blowe,	
	That his ost him scholde knowe.	

"Lordinges," a seide, "ne doute yow nought,
3380 Ye scholle this dai be holde so dought, — *brave*
That hem were beter at Rome,
Thanne hii hadde hider icome."
  Tho th'emperur herde in castel blowe,
Tharbi he gan to knowe,
3385 That hii armede hem in the castel;
His knightes he het ase snel: — *called; quickly*
"Has armes, lordinges, to bataile! — *To arms; battle*
Out hii cometh, us to asaile."
Twei ostes thai gonne make,
3390 He of Scotlonde hath on itake,
Th'emperur that other ladde:
His deth that dai ther he hadde.

  Out of the castel cam before
Saber with is berde hore, — *his gray beard*
3395 And in is compainie
Thre hondred knightes hardie.
Sire Morice of Mounclere
His stede smot aghenes Sabere;
His spere was sumdel kene, — *somewhat sharp*
3400 And Saber rod him aghene:
Though is spere wer scharp igrounde,
Saber slough him in that stounde. — *instant*
Out on Arondel tho com Bevoun
And mette with is stifader Devoun, — *stepfather*
3405 And with a dent of gret fors
A bar him doun of his hors; — *knocked; off*
With Morgelay, that wolde wel bite,
He hadde ment is heved of smite; — *meant; his head off*
His ost cam riding him to,
3410 Wel ten thosend other mo; — *or more*
So stronge were tho hii come.
Th'emperur Beves hii benome — *They took the emperor away from Bevis*
And broughte him an horse tho;
Tharfore was Beves swithe wo. — *angry*
3415   Thar com in the thredde part
With is batte Ascopard; — *his club*

	Ever alse he com than,	*as*
	A felde bothe hors and man.	*He struck down*
	Tharwith was Beves wel apaide,	*pleased*
3420	A clepede Ascopard and to him saide:	*called*
	"Ascopard, tak right gode hede:	
	Th'emperur rit on a whit stede;	*rides*
	Thin hure I schel thee yilde wel,	*hire*
	With that thow bringe him to me castel!"	
3425	"Sire," a seide, "I schel for sothe	
	In to the castel bringe him to thee!"	
	Ascopard leide on wel inough,	
	Bothe man and hors he slough;	*slew*
	Thar nas non armur in that londe,	
3430	That mighte the geauntes strok astonde.	*giant's stroke withstand*
	The King of Scotlonde, with is bat	
	A yaf him swiche a sori flat	*slap*
	Upon the helm in that stounde,	*moment*
	That man and hors fel ded to grounde.	
3435	Thanne anon, withoute sojur,	*delay*
	A wente to that emperur,	
	And hasteliche with might and main	
	A hente the hors be the rain;	*grabbed; rein*
	Wolde he, nolde he, faire and wel	*Like it or not*
3440	He bar hors and man to the castel.	*carried*
	Of al that other, siker aplighte,	*yes indeed*
	That were ensemled in that fighte,	*assembled*
	Of Scotlonde and of Almaine,	
	Beves and Saber with might and maine	
3445	With deth is dentes gonne doun drive,	
	That thar ne scapede non alive.	*no one escaped*
	And thus Sire Beves wan the pris	*victory*
	And vengede him of is enemis,	*avenged himself*
	And to the castel thai wente isame	*together*
3450	With gret solas, gle and game,	*satisfaction; joy; mirth*
	And that his stifader wer ded,	*to make certain his stepfather was dead*
	Ase tit he let felle a led	*At once; lead kettle*
	Ful of pich and of bremston,	*pitch; brimstone*
	And hot led let falle ther-on;	*molten lead*
3455	Whan hit alther swither seth,	*all at once seethed*

	Th'emperur thar in a deth,	*in death*
	Thar a lay atenende.	*at his ending*
	Wende his saule, whider it wende!	*soul*
	His moder over the castel lai,	*[Bevis'] mother*
3460	Hire lord sethen in the pich she sai;	*seething; saw*
	So swithe wo hire was for sore,	*very woeful; shock*
	She fel and brak hire nekke therfore.	*broke her neck*
	Alse glad he was of hire,	
	Of his damme, ase of is stipsire,	*mother; stepfather*
3465	And seide: "Damme, forgheve me this gilt,	*Mother, forgive*
	I ne yaf thee nother dent ne pilt!"	*blow nor knock*
	Thanne al the lordes of Hamteschire	*shire of Hampton*
	Made Beves lord and sire	
	And dede him feuté and omage,	*fealty; homage*
3470	Ase hit was lawe and right usage.	*customary*
	Tho was Beves glad and blithe	
	And thankede God ful mani a sithe,	
	That he was wreke wel inough	*avenged*
	Of him, that his father slough.	
3475	Wel hasteliche she let sende	*[Josian]*
	To Coloine after the bischop hende,	
	And spusede Beves and Josiane.	*married*
	Of no joie nas ther wane;	*lack*
	Though ich discrive nought the bredale,	*describe not the wedding*
3480	Ye mai wel wite, hit was riale,	*know; royal*
	That ther was in alle wise	
	Mete and drinke and riche servise.	
	Now hath Beves al is stat;	*estate*
	Tweie children on hir he begat	
3485	In the formeste yere,	*first*
	Whiles that hii were ifere.	*together*
	And Saber him redde thar	*advised*
	Wende to the King Edgar;	*Go*
	Tho with inne a lite stounde	
3490	The king a fond at Lounde.	*London*
	Beves a knes doun him set,	*knelt*
	The king hendeliche a gret;	*courteously he greets*
	The king askede him, what he were	
	And what nedes a wolde there.	

3495 Thanne answerde Bevoun:
"Ichatte Beves of Hamtoun; — *I am called*
Me fader was ther th'erl Gii; — *the earl*
Th'emperur for is levedi — *for his lady*
Out of Almaine com and him slough;
3500 Ichave wreke him wel inough; — *avenged*
Ich bidde before your barnage, — *baronage*
That ye me graunte min eritage!" — *heritage*
"Bletheliche," a seide, "sone min, — *Gladly*
Ich graunte thee, be Sein Martin!" — *Saint*
3505 His marchal he gan beholde: — *marshal*
"Fet me," a seide, "me yerde of golde! — *Bring; staff*
Gii, is fader, was me marchal,
Also Bevis, is sone, schal."
His yerd he gan him ther take:
3510 So thai atonede withoute sake. — *were reconciled; strife*
In somer aboute Whitsontide — *Pentecost*
Whan knightes mest an horse ride,
A gret kours thar was do grede, — *course; prepared*
For to saien here alther stede, — *test all the steeds*
3515 Whiche were swift and strong.
The kours was seve mile long;
Who that come ferst theder, han scholde
A thosand pound of rede golde.
Tharwith was Beves paied wel: — *pleased*
3520 Meche a treste to Arondel. — *trusted*
A morwe, whan hit was dai cler,
Ariseth bothe knight and squier
And lete sadlen here fole. — *horses*
Twei knightes hadde the kours istole, — *stolen (sneaked onto)*
3525 That hii were to mile before, — *two; ahead*
Er eni man hit wiste ybore. — *Before any man knew it was done*
Whan Beves wiste this, fot hot — *learned; immediately*
Arondel with is spures a smot
And is bridel faste a schok; — *shook*
3530 A mide the kours he hem oftok. — *overtook them*
"Arondel," queth Beves tho,
"For me love go bet, go,
And I schel do faire and wel

	For thee love reren a castel!"	*raise*
3535	Whan Arondel herde what he spak,	
	Before the twei knightes he rak,	*reached*
	That he com rather to the tresore,	
	Than hii be half and more.	
	Beves of his palfrai alighte	
3540	And tok the tresore anon righte:	
	With that and with mor catel	*chattel*
	He made the castel of Arondel.	*for*
	Meche men preisede is stede tho,	*Many; praised*
	For he hadde so wel igo;	*run well*
3545	The prince bad, a scholde it him yeve;	*commanded*
	"Nay," queth Beves, "so mot I leve,	
	Though thow wost me take an honde	*Even if; let me*
	Al the hors of Ingelonde!"	*horses*
	Sithe that he him yeve nele,	*Since; not give it to him*
3550	A thoughte, that he it wolde stele.	*steal*
	Hit is lawe of kinges alle,	*custom*
	At mete were croune in halle,	*crowned*
	And thanne everiche marchal	*marshal*
	His yerde an honde bere schal.	*staff; should bear*
3555	While Beves was in that ofice,	*i.e., as marshal*
	The kinges sone, that was so nice,	*foolish*
	What helpeth for to make fable?	*Why tell a lie*
	A yede to Beves stable	*He went*
	And yede Arondel to nighe,	*got too close to*
3560	And also a wolde him untighe,	
	And tho Arondel, fot hot,	*then; immediately*
	With his hint fot he him smot	*hind*
	And todaschte al is brain.	*dashed out*
	Thus was the kinges sone slain.	
3565	Men made del and gret weping	*mourning*
	For sorwe of that ilche thing;	
	The king swor, for that wronge	
	That Beves scholde ben anhonge	
	And to-drawe with wilde fole.	*horses*
3570	The barnage it nolde nought thole	*barons; allow*
	And seide, hii mighte do him no wors,	
	Boute lete hongen is hors;	

	Hii mighte don him namore,	
	For he servede tho the king before.	
3575	"Nai," queth Beves, "for no catele	*property*
	Nel ich lese min hors Arondele,	*lose*
	Ac min hors for to were	*protect*
	Ingelonde ich wile forswere;	
	Min eir ich wile make her	*heir; here*
3580	This gode knight, min em Saber."	
	In that maner hii wer at one,	
	And Beves is to Hamtoun gone;	
	A tolde Josian and Ascopard fore	
	Al togedre, lasse and more.	
3585	Beves lep on is rounci	*horse*
	And made is swein Terri,	*his squire*
	That Saber is sone is;	*Saber's son*
	And whan Ascopard wiste this,	*learned*
	Whiche wei hii wolde take,	
3590	Aghen to Mombraunt he gan schake,	*hasten*
	To betraie Beves, as ye mai se,	*betray*
	For he was falle in poverté,	
	For, whan a man is in poverté falle,	
	He hath fewe frendes with alle.	
3595	To him seide King Yvore:	
	"Treitour, whar hastow be thus yore?"	*where have you been*
	"Sire," a seide, "have sought the quene,	*[I] have*
	And have had for hire miche tene!	*because of her; distress*
	Sire," a seide, "certeine for sothe,	
3600	Yet ich kouthe bringe hire to thee!"	
	"Ich wile thee yeve a kingdom right,	
	Bring yow me that levedi bright!"	
	Queth Ascopart: "Therto I graunt,	*Okay*
	Be Mahoun and be Tervagaunt,	
3605	So that ichave fourti knightes,	
	Stout in armes and strong in fightes;	
	For Beves is ful sterne and stoute,	
	Of him ichave swithe gret doute;	*fear*
	He overcom me ones in bataile:	
3610	Me behoveth help, him to asaile."	*I require*
	King Yvor grauntede anon rightes;	

He let him chese fourti knightes
And armede hem him in yrene wede, — *iron armor*
And forth with Ascopard thai yede.
3615 Now lete we be this Ascopard
And speke of Beves, that rit forthward — *rode*
In is wei til Ermonie — *to Armenia*
Thourgh Fraunce and thourgh Normondie;
And Josiane, Crist here be milde!
3620 In a wode was bestonde of childe — *suddenly in labor*
Beves and Terri doun lighte — *got down*
And with here swerdes a logge pighte; — *hut constructed*
Thai broughte Josiane ther inne,
For hii ne kouthe no beter ginne. — *they knew of no better plan*
3625 Bevis is servise gan hire bede, — *offered her his service*
To helpe hire at that nede.
"For Godes love," she saide, "nai,
Leve sire, thow go thee wai,
God forbede for is pité,
3630 That no wimman is privité
To no man thourgh me be kouthe.
Goth and wendeth hennes nouthe, — *return hence now*
Thow and thee swain Terry,
And let me worthe and Oure Levedy!" — *let me and Our Lady be together*
3635 Forth thai wente bothe ifere,
For hii ne mighte hire paines here. — *So they would not hear her pains*
Allas, that ilche cherre; — *[for] that decorous behavior*
Hii wente from hire alto ferre! — *too far away*
Alse hii wer out of the weie, — *When*
3640 She hadde knave children tweie. — *gave birth to twin boys*
Also she dilivered was, — *As*
Thar com Ascopard goande a pas — *passing by*
And fourti Sarasins, the Frensch seth,
Al iarmede to the teth. — *armed; teeth*
3645 For al hire sorwe and hire wo
Thai made hire with hem te go,
And gret scorning of hire thai maked
And bete hire with swerdes naked. — *beat; swords*
Wo was the levedi in that stounde, — *moment*
3650 That was so beten and ibounde; — *beaten; bound*

	And in here wei ase thai gonne wende,	
	She seide: "Ascopard, freli frende,	*noble*
	For bounté, ich dede thee while	*favor*
	And savede thee fro perile,	
3655	Tho Beves thee wolde han slawe	
	And ibrought of thee lif dawe,	
	Ich was the bourgh, thee schost be trewe.	*guarantee; should*
	Thar fore I praie, on me thee rewe	*take pity*
	And yeve me space a lite wight,	*time*
3660	For wende out of this folkes sight,	
	To do me nedes in privité,	
	For kende hit is, wimman te be	*natural*
	Schamfaste and ful of corteisie,	*Modest*
	And hate dedes of fileinie."	*villainy*
3665	Ascopard answerde hire tho:	
	"Whider thow wilt, dame, thow schelt go,	
	So ichave of thee a sight!"	*As long as*
	Thanne Josiane, anon right	
	Out of the way she gan terne,	
3670	As she wolde do hire dedes derne.	*So that; secret*
	While she was in Ermonie,	
	Bothe fysik and sirgirie	*physic; surgery (medicine)*
	She hadde lerned of meisters grete	*teachers*
	Of Boloyne the gras and of Tulete,	*grass (herbs); Toledo*
3675	That she knew erbes mani and fale,	
	To make bothe boute and bale.	*good; bad (medicines; poisons)*
	On she tok up of the grounde,	
	That was an erbe of meche mounde,	*value*
	To make a man in semlaunt there,	*seem to resemble*
3680	A foule mesel alse if a were.	*leper*
	Whan she hadde ete that erbe, anon	
	To the Sarasines she gan gon,	
	And wente hem forth withoute targing	*tarrying*
	Toward Yvore, the riche king.	
3685	Thai nadde ride in here way	*had not ridden*
	Boute fif mile of that contray,	
	She was in semlaunt and in ble	*appearance; complexion*
	A foule mesel on to se.	
	Tho she was brought to King Yvore,	*When*

3690 To Ascopard a seide thore:
"Who is this wimman, thow hast me brought?"
"What," a seide, "knowest hire nought?
She is Josiane, the Quene.
Ichave had for hire meche tene." *distress*
3695 Thanne seide Yvor: "I praie Mahoun
Tharfore yeve thee is malisoun, *give you his curse*
Swiche a levedi me to bringe,
So foule of sight in alle thinge!
Led hire awai, God yeve yow schame, *Lead*
3700 Thee and hire, bothe isame!" *together*
A castel hadde King Yvor
Fro his paleise fif mile and mor;
Theder Yvor bad hire lede
And finde hire that hire wer nede. *what she needed*
3705 Tho Ascopard withouten dwelling *delaying*
In to that castel gan hire bring,
In wildernesse upon a plaine,
And half a yer a was hire wardaine. *keeper (warden)*
Now lete we be of this levedi
3710 And speke of Beves and of Terri.
Beves, aghen is wei he nam, *took his way*
In to the logge that he cam; *hut*
Fond he ther nother yong ne elder,
Boute twei hethene knave childer, *heathen*
3715 Swithe faire children with alle,
Alse hii were fro the moder falle. *As when they were born*
Beves fel thar doun and swough; *swooned*
Terri wep and him up drough, *raised himself up*
And koursede biter that while *cursed bitterly at that moment*
3720 Ascopard is tresoun and is gile. *Ascopard's; his*
Thei kottede here forers of ermin, *cut; furs; ermine*
The yonge children wonde ther in. *clothed*
Thar nolde hii no long abide,
Thei lope to horse and gonne ride; *leaped*
3725 In the wode a forster thai mette
And swithe faire thai him grette:
"God the blesse, sire!" Beves sede,
"Sighe the eni levedi her forth lede *Did you see*

	Owhar be this ilche way?"	
3730	"Sire, for Gode" a seide, "nay!"	
	"What dones man ertow, bacheler?"	*manner of man are you*
	"Sire," a seide, "a forster!"	
	"Forster, so Crist thee be milde,	*Christ be gentle [with] you*
	Wiltow lete cristen this hethen childe?	*Will you; baptize*
3735	Right, lo, now hit was ibore	
	And yong hit hath is moder forlore.	*abandoned*
	Wilt thow kep it for to min," a sede,	*on my behalf*
	"And I schel quite wel thee mede?"	*pay; reward*
	The forster him grauntede ther,	
3740	To kepe hit al the seven yer.	
	"Sire, what schel it hote yet?"	*be called*
	"Gii," a sede, "ase me fader het.	*Guy; is named*
	Right sone so he is of elde,	*Until; age*
	Tech him bere spere and schelde!"	
3745	That child the forster he betok	
	And forth in is wei a schok.	*he hastened*
	Another man a mette there,	
	That seide, a was a fischere;	*fisherman*
	Ten mark Beves him betok,	*gave*
3750	And that other child to lok,	*look after*
	And he himself, at the cherche stile	
	He let nevene the child Mile.	*had named; Miles*
	Thar nolden lengere abide,	
	Thai lope to hors and gonne ride	
3755	Over dale and over doun,	*hill*
	Til thai come to a gret toun,	
	And at a faire in thai lighte,	*dismounted*
	And riche soper thai gonne hem dighte.	*had prepared for them*
	Beves at a wendowe lokede out	
3760	And segh the strete ful aboute	
	Of stedes wrien and armes bright.	*covered*
	A wonder him thoughte, what it be might;	
	At here ostesse he askede there,	*hostess*
	What al the stoute stedes were.	*places*
3765	"Sire, a seide, "veraiment,	*she; truly*
	Thai ben come for a tornement,	
	That is cride for a maide faire,	*decreed*

A kinges doughter and is air. *heir*
Who that thar be beste knight
3770 And stireth him stoutliche in that fight,
He schel have that maide fre
And Aumbeforce, the faire contré."
Thanne seide Beves unto Terry:
"Wile we tornaie for that levedy?" *tourney; for the sake of*
3775 "Ye, sire," a sede, "be Sein Thomas of Ynde!
Whan were we wonded be byhinde?
We scholle lete for non nede, *refuse*
That we ne scholle manliche forth us bede!"
A morwe the lauerkes songe, *lark's*
3780 Whan that the lighte day was spronge,
Beves and Terry gonne arise
And greithede hem in faire queintise. *ornamented arms*
Here armes were riale of sight,
With thre eglen of asur bright; *eagles; azure*
3785 The chaumpe of gold ful farie Tolede, *field; [made in] Toledo*
Portraid al with rosen rede.
And Terri, Saberes sone of Wight,
In riche armes also was dight.
Ase thai com ride thourgh the toun,
3790 Erles, barouns of renoun
Hadde wonder of here armes slie, *finely made*
In that londe never swich thai sie.
The trompes gonne here bemes blowe; *trumpeters; trumpets*
The knightes riden out in a rowe,
3795 And tho the tornement began, *then*
Thar was samned mani a man, *assembled*
The tornement to beholde,
To se the knightes stout and bolde.
Thai leide on ase hii were wode *clashed; mad*
3800 With swerdes and with maces gode;
Thar nolde no man other knowe,
Thar men mighte se in lite throwe *while*
Knightes out of sadel iboren,
Stedes wonne and stedes loren. *lost*
3805 The kinges sone of Asie *Asia*
Thoughte wenne the meistrie. *Hoped to win*

	Out of the renge he com ride,	*rank*
	And Beves nolde no leng abide;	
	He rod to him with gret randoun,	*violence*
3810	And with Morgelai, is fauchoun,	*falchion*
	The prince a felde in the feld;	*struck down*
	He was boren hom upon is scheld.	*home*
	And also Beves adoun bar	
	A noble duk, that was thar.	*duke*
3815	In Aumbeforce cleped a wes	
	Balam of Nuby, withouten les;	*Nubia; lie*
	Taile over top he made him stoupe	
	And felde him over is horses croupe,	*rump*
	And seven erles he gan doun thrawe,	*did throw down*
3820	Sum iwonded and sum yslawe.	*wounded*
	Saber is sone, that highte Terry,	
	Kedde that he was knight hardy;	
	He leide on, alse he wolde awede,	*rave*
	And wan his lord mani gode stede.	*won*
3825	Alle tho that hii mighte hitte,	
	No man mighte here strokes sitte.	
	So Beves demeinede him that dai,	*bested*
	The maide hit in the tour say.	*tower; saw*
	Hire hertte gan to him acorde,	
3830	That she wolde have him to lorde,	
	Other with love other with strif;	*Either; or*
	And ever a seide, he hath a wif,	
	And seide, she was stolen him fro.	
	Thanne saide the maide: “Now it is so,	
3835	Thow schelt al this seven yere	
	Be me lord in clene manere,	*pure*
	And yif thee wif cometh thee aghen,	
	Terry, the swein, me lord schel ben!”	
	Beves seide: “So I schel;	
3840	In that forward I graunte wel!”	*promise*
	Saber at Hamtoun lai in is bed,	
	Him thoughte, Beves a wonde hed;	*dreamed; wound*
	A way he was, him thoughte that while,	
	Toward Sein Jemes and Sein Gile.	*Saint James; Saint Giles*
3845	Whan he awok, he was afraid,	

	To his wif is swevene a said.	*dream*
	"Sire," she seide, "thow havest wrong,	
	That thow dwellest her so long.	
	Alse ich am wimman ibore,	
3850	Wif or child he hath forlore.	*lost*
	Thourgh Ascopard he hath that gile."	
	Twelf knightes Saber let atile	*equip*
	In palmer is wedes everichon,	*pilgrims' clothes*
	And armede hem right wel anon;	
3855	Here bordones were imaked wel	*pilgrims' staffs*
	With longe pikes of wel gode stel,	
	And whan thai were so idight,	*arrayed*
	To schip thai wente anon right	
	And pasede over the Grikische se;	*Greek sea*
3860	Gode winde and weder hadden he.	*Good; weather*
	Whan thai come to the londe,	
	Faste thai gonne fraine and fonde,	*ask and inquire*
	In what londe were the quene,	
	And men tolde hem al bedene,	*as well*
3865	How the geaunt Ascopard	
	In a castel hire hadde to ward,	*guard*
	In wildernesse al be selve.	
	Tho Saber and is feren twelve,	*companions*
	Thourgh help of God that ilche stounde	*moment*
3870	Sone thai han the castel founde.	
	The castel ase he yede aboute,	
	For to divise the toures stoute,	*survey*
	Josian lay in a tour an high,	
	Saber and felawes she sigh,	*saw*
3875	And to him she gan to crie:	
	"Help, Saber, for love of Marie!"	
	Tho Ascopard herde that stevene,	*voice*
	How she gan Saber to nevene,	*name*
	He wente him out with hertte wroth	
3880	And be Mahoun a swor his oth,	
	To dethe a scholde Saber dighte.	*send*
	His sclavin ech palmer of twighte,	*pilgrim's coat; took off*
	Tho schon here armur wel clere;	
	Tho Saber and his felawes ifere	*together*

3885	Aboute Ascopard thai thringe,	*pressed*
	And harde on him thai gonne dinge	*strike*
	And hew him alle to pices smale	
	And broughte Josian out of bale;	*trouble*
	And hasteliche tho, veraiment,	*truly*
3890	Josian with an oiniment	
	Hire coulur, that was lothli of sight,	*skin*
	She made bothe cler and bright.	
	Tho Saber, that was wis of dede,	
	Josian, hire dighte in palmers wede,	*arrayed; garb*
3895	And forth thai wente hasteli,	
	To seche Beves and sire Terri.	*seek*
	Seve yer togedres thai him sought,	*Seven years*
	Er than hii him finde moughte.	*might*
	In grete Grese, so saith the bok,	*Greece*
3900	Saber gret sikenesse tok,	
	That other half yer in none wise	
	Ne mighte he out of is bed arise,	
	And tresor he nadde namore,	*treasure*
	Than half a mark of olde store.	*provision*
3905	While Josian was in Ermonie,	
	She hadde lerned of minstralcie,	
	Upon a fithele for to play	*fiddle*
	Staumpes, notes, garibles gay;	*Dances; notes; flourishes*
	Tho she kouthe no beter red,	*knew; strategy*
3910	Boute in to the bourgh anon she yed	*went*
	And boughte a fithele, so saith the tale,	
	For fourti panes of one menestrale;	*pence from a minstral*
	And alle the while that Saber lay,	
	Josian everiche a day	*each and every*
3915	Yede aboute the cité withinne,	
	Here sostenaunse for to winne.	*Their sustenance*
	Thus Josian was in swiche destresse,	
	While Saber lai in is siknesse.	
	At that other half yer is ende	
3920	Swiche grace God him gan sende	
	And heled him of his maladie,	
	And forth thai wente hastelie,	
	Beves and Terry for to seche,	

	Wheder that God hem wolde teche.	*show*
3925	So thourgh a toun thai com thringe,	*advance*
	Thar Beves was in also a kinge;	
	A broughte Josian at here inne	
	And wente te toun, here mete to winne.	*food*
	Whan he com to the castel gate,	
3930	Terry, is sone, a mette ther-ate,	
	That was stiward of al that londe,	
	And Saber gan to understonde,	*realized*
	That hit was is sone Terry,	
	And bad him for love of Our Levedy	*Our Lady*
3935	And for the love of the gode Rode	*good Cross*
	Yeve him sumwhat of hire gode.	
	Terry beheld Saber ful blive	*gladly*
	And seide: "Palmer, so mot I thrive,	
	Thow schelt have mete riche	*choice food*
3940	For love of me fader, th'ert iliche!"	*[whom] you are like*
	"So seide thee moder, sone, that I was!"	
	And Terry him in armes las,	*embraced*
	And gonne cleppen and to kisse	*hugged*
	And made meche joie and blisse.	
3945	Saber Josian wel faire gan dighte	*arrayed*
	And broughte hire to the castel righte	
	And tok hire Sire Beves to honde,	
	Ne cam him never lever sonde.	*a more lovely sound*
	"Louerd Crist," queth Josian tho,	*Lord*
3950	"Swithe wel is me bego,	*befallen*
	That ichave me lord ifonde.	
	Hadde ich me children hol and sonde!"	*Would that I; sound*
	That hii were ded, wel she wende.	*thought*
	Beves after hem let sende;	
3955	Than com the fischer and the forster	
	And broughte the children of fair cher.	*countenance*
	Thanne weddede Terry	
	Of that londe the riche levedy;	
	And after mete thar it was,	
3960	The children pleide at the talvas,	*fenced (see note)*

	And to the justes thai gonne ride;	*jousts*
	Thar was joie be everi side.	
	Thanne Sire Beves and Sere Terry	
	Wente hem in til Ermonie,	*to*
3965	And Josiane and Sire Sabere,	
	And Miles and Gii bothe ifere.	
	With that was come King Yvore,	
	To yeve bataile Ermyn the hore;	*grayhaired*
	Ipight he hadde is pavilioun,	*Pitched*
3970	To besege him in that toun.	
	With that com Beves in that tide	
	With gret folk be that other side.	
	Tho was Ermin afered sore,	*sorely afraid*
	For tresoun he hadde don him before.	*Because of the*
3975	Aghen Beves anon a yede	
	And merci cride of his misdede,	
	And Sire Beves tho, veraiment,	
	Foryaf him alle is mautalent	*ill will*
	And seide a wolde anon righte	*he would right away*
3980	Aghen Yvor take the fighte.	
	Out of the cité Beves rod,	
	And al is ost, withouten abod,	*army (host); delay*
	And slowe doun rightes mani and fale,	*slew; many*
	Sixti thosand told in tale;	*in total*
3985	And Beves threw Yvor adoun	
	And sente him Ermin to prisoun.	
	He gan him take be the honde;	
	The King Ermin gan understonde,	
	That he ne schel nought scape awai,	
3990	Withoute gret raunsoun for to pai.	
	Tho swor Yvor to King Ermin	
	Be Mahoun and be Apolyn,	
	That gret raunsoun paie he wolde,	*ransom*
	Sixti pound of rede golde,	
3995	Foure hondred beddes of selk echon,	*beds; silk*
	Quiltes of gold thar upon,	
	Four hondred copes of gold fyn	*cups*
	And ase fele of maslin.	*as many; brass*
	"Ye," seide Beves, "asend it me,	

4000 And wend hom to the contré!"
A masager a sente with main — *strength*
To Tabefor, his chaumberlain,
And he him sente that raunsoun.
Thus com Yvor out of prisoun.
4005 Now let we be of King Yvore
And speke we of Ermin the hore, — *gray*
That in is bedde sike lay.
So hit befel upon a day,
Er he out of this world went,
4010 After Beves children a sent.
He clepede to him Sire Gii
And with is croune gan him crouny — *with his crown crowned him*
And yaf him alle is kenedom. — *kingdom*
Sone thar after hit becom,
4015 That a daide at the ende, — *died*
To hevene mote his saule wende! — *soul*
Thanne Sire Beves and Sire Gii,
Al the lond of Ermony
Hii made Cristen with dent of swerd, — *blows*
4020 Yong and elde, lewed and lered. — *unlearned; learned*
So hit befel upon an eve,
Saber of Beves tok leve,
Hom te wende to his contré,
His wif, his children for to se.
4025 Ne stente never Sire Saber, — *stopped*
Til that he in Ingelonde were;
Wel sore aneighed schel Beves be, — *annoyed*
Er than he Saber eft ise!
The King Yvor hadde a thef. — *thief*
4030 God him yeve evel pref, — *trial*
For that he kouthe so wel stele! — *knew how; to steal*
He stel Beves Arondele — *stole*
With his charmes, that he kouthe, — *knew*
And broughte hit to Mombraunt be southe
4035 And presentede the King Yvore.
The King be Mahoun hath swore
That Beves scholde abegge sore — *pay for*
The raunsoun, that he hadde before.

	Now Sire Beves let we gan	*leave*
4040	And to Sire Saber wile we tan.	*turn*
	Saber at Hamtoun in bedde lay;	
	Him thoughte that he Beves say	*He dreamed; saw*
	In bataile wo begon	
	And al to-heve, flesch and bon.	*cut up*
4045	Tho he abraide out of is swevene,	*started up; dream*
	To his wif a tolde hit ful evene	*exactly*
	Al togedres how him met.	*dreamed*
	"O sire," she seide withouten let,	*delay*
	"Be the swevene ful wel I wat,	*know*
4050	That Beves is in semple stat;	*desperate state*
	He hath forloren Arondel,	*lost*
	And that I wet finliche wel."	*intuit pretty well*
	Saber was wo for that sake;	
	Eft scrippe and bordoun he gan take	*purse; staff*
4055	And tok leve of his wif	
	And to Beves a wente belif.	*with haste*
	Beves was glad, that he was come,	
	And tolde, his hors was him benome:	*taken*
	"A roboun hit stal ful yore	*robber; stole a while ago*
4060	And hath yeve hit to King Yvore."	
	"That," Saber seide, "athenketh me,	*grieves*
	Boute yif ich mighte winne it aye!"	*Unless; again*
	Aghen to Mombraunt wente Saber	
	Thar men watrede the deistrer;	*watered; warhorse*
4065	Thar he stod and abod,	*waited*
	A proud Sarasin ther-on rod;	
	"Mahoun thee save!" seide Saber,	
	"Fro whanne kometh this fair deistrer?	*warhorse*
	Hit haveth brestes thikke and proute.	*strong*
4070	Which is the kroupe terne aboute?"	*rump*
	Aboute he ternde the deistrer;	
	Up behinde lep Saber	
	And smot the Sarasin ded adoun	
	With the pik of his bordoun.	*spike; staff*
4075	To the King Ivor he gan grede:	*did implore*
	"Lo, Arondel ich a wei lede.	
	Ye him stele with envie	

And ich him feche before your eie!" — *eyes*
The King Ivor was swithe wo — *so angry*
4080 And after Saber thai gonne go;
Thre thosend hath Saber beset;
Josian stod in a toret; — *turret*
Al this folk she segh ful wel
And Saber com ride on Arondel;
4085 Out of the tour she wente adoun
And seide: "Beves of Hamtoun,
Her cometh Saber upon thee stede.
Jesu Crist him yilde is mede! — *reward*
Ac he is beset al aboute
4090 With wonderliche grete route; — *host*
Al most he is in point to spille!" — *die*
"Has armes!" Beves cride schille. — *To arms; shrilly*
Ferst smot out the yonge King Gii
And Miles with gret chevalry;
4095 Thai come to Saber at that stour — *attack*
And broughte Saber gode sokour — *help*
And leide on with alle here might — *their*
And slowe Sarasines adoun right. — *slew*
Of al that sewede him so yerne, — *followed; eagerly*
4100 To Mombraunt gonne never on terne, — *return*
That thai ner ded upon the grene, — *nearly died*
Everi moder sone, I wene;
And thus Saber in this wise
Wan Arondel with is queintise. — *cunning*
4105 Now mowe ye here forthormore
Ful strong bataile of King Yvore;
Ac er than we beginne fighte,
Ful us the koppe anon righte! — *Fill; cup*
The King Yvore him ros amorwe,
4110 In his hertte was meche sorwe.
He let of sende an highing — *in haste*
Thretti amirales and ten king. — *emirs*
Thai armede hem in yrene wede,
To Ermonie he gan hem lede.
4115 Hii pighte paviliouns and bente ginne, — *They set up; field artillery*
For to besege hem ther inne,

	And Yvore clepede at that cas	*embraced in his arms*
	Morable and Sire Judos.	*Judas (Iscariot)*
	"Redeth me," a seide, "aright,	*Advise*
4120	Yif ich mai understonde this fight	
	Aghen Beves of Hamtoun,	
	That is so stout a baroun!"	
	"We redeth meintene your parti!"	*company*
	He lep to hors and gan to crie:	
4125	"Sire Beves of Hamtoun," a sede,	
	"Thou havest thar-inne gret ferede,	*company*
	And ich her oute mani stout knight,	*out here*
	Ichave brought with me to fight,	
	And yif we bataile schel abide,	
4130	Gret slaughter worth in either side.	
	Wiltow graunte be then helve,	*on your part*
	That ich and thow mote fighte us selve?	*ourselves*
	Yif thow slest me in bataile,	
	Al min onour, withouten faile,	*honor*
4135	Ich thee graunte thourgh and thourgh,	
	Bothe in cité and in bourgh!"	*borough*
	Here gloven thai gonne up holde	*Their gloves*
	In that forward, that Yvor tolde,	*pledge*
	And armede hem in armes brighte	
4140	And lopen to horse anon righte	
	In an yle under that cité,	*isle*
	Thar that scholde the bataile be.	*Where*
	Over that water thai gonne ride,	
	To hire godes that bede in either side;	*who command*
4145	Beves bad help to Marie sone	*prayed for*
	And King Yvor to Sein Mahoune;	*Saint*
	Ase Beves bad helpe to Marie,	
	To Tervagaunt Yvor gan crie,	
	That he scholde helpe him in that fight,	
4150	Also he was king of meche might.	
	With that hii ride togedres bothe,	
	Ase men, that were in hertte wrothe,	*angry*
	So harde thai gonne togedres mete	
	And with here launces gonne grete,	
4155	That thourgh the scheldes the speres yode;	*went*

	At the breinies the dent withstode.	*coat of mail; blow*
	So harde thai threste togedre tho,	
	That here gerthes borste ato,	*belts; asunder*
	And felle to grounde bothe tho,	
4160	A fote nedes thai moste go.	*On foot*
	Out of here sadles thai gonne springe	
	And with fauchouns to gedere flinge;	*falchions*
	Aither on other strokes set,	*Each*
	Of helm and scheld and bacinet	
4165	The fure brast out so brond ibrent,	*fire erupted as if a torch burned*
	So fel and eger was either dent.	*fierce; stroke*
	Thus togederes thai gonne dinge	*strike*
	Fram prime til underne gan to ringe.	*six in the morning till noon*
	Alle that sighen hem with sight,	
4170	Seide never in none fight	
	So stronge bataile sighe er than	*before*
	Of Sarasin ne of Cristene man.	
	At high midday the King Yvore,	
	To Beves he smot a dent ful sore,	
4175	That sercle of gold and is crestel	*circle; his crest*
	Fer in to the mede fel.	*grass*
	Doun of the helm the swerd gan glace	
	And karf right doun before is face,	
	Doun right the viser with is swerd	
4180	And half the her upon is berd.	*hair*
	Ac thourgh the help of Godes grace	
	His flesch nothing atamed nas.	*pierced*
	Tho cride the Sarasins al at ones:	
	"This Beves with his grete bones	*prayers*
4185	Ful sone worth imaked tame!"	*[will] become tamed*
	Tho wex Beves in gret grame	*grew; anger*
	And thoughte wel with Morgelay	
	Yelden his strok, yif that he may.	*Repay*
	To King Yvor he gan areche	*reach out*
4190	Anon withoute more speche	
	Upon the scholder in that tide,	*time*
	That half a fot hit gan in glide.	
	For smertte Yvor in that stounde	*pain*
	Fel a knes unto the grounde,	

4195	Ac up he sterte in haste than	
	And in wrathe to Beves ran	
	And thoughte han Beves aqueld;	*killed*
	And Beves keppte him with is scheld,	*warded him off with his shield*
	And Yvore with the strok of yre	*anger*
4200	Made fle in to the rivere	*fly*
	A large quarter of his scheld,	
	That never nas atamed in feld.	*tamed*
	Or Ivor mighte his hond withdrawe,	*Before*
	Beves, the knight of Cristene lawe,	
4205	With Morgelay a smot him tho,	
	That his scheld he clef ato,	
	And his left hond, be the wrest	*wrist*
	Hit flegh awei thourgh help of Crist.	
	Whan Ivor hadde his hond lore,	*lost*
4210	He faught, ase he wer wod therfore,	
	And hew to Beves in that tide,	
	No strok ne moste other abide.	*could withstand*
	Tho Beves segh is strokes large,	
	He kepte his strokes with is targe;	*warded off; shield*
4215	Tho Beves to Ivor gan flinge	*rush*
	And thourgh the might of hevene king	
	His right arm and is scholder bon	
	He made fle to gronde anon.	
	With that strok Yvor the Mombraunt	
4220	Cride: "Merci, Tervagaunt,	
	Mahoun, Govin, and Gibiter,	
	Reseve now me saule her,	*Receive; soul*
	For wel ich wot, ich am dede!"	
	Tho Beves herde him so grede,	*cry out*
4225	He seide: "Yvor, let be that cri	
	And clepe to God and to Mari,	
	And let thee cristen, er thee deie,	*let yourself be baptized before you die*
	Or thow schelt go the worsse weie	
	And withouten ende dwelle	
4230	In the stronge peine of helle!"	
	"Nay," queth Yvor, "so mot I then,	*prosper*
	Cristene wile ich never ben,	*Christian*
	For min is wel the beter lawe!"	

	Tho Beves herde that ilche sawe,	*pronouncement*
4235	A felde him doun, withouten faile,	
	And unlacede his ventaile,	*helmet-front*
	And tok him be the heved anon	
	And strok hit fro the scholder bon,	
	And on his spere he hit pighte.	*placed*
4240	And tho the Cristen sighe that sighte,	*when*
	Thai thankede God in alle wise,	
	That Beves hadde wonne the prise.	*contest*
	Thanne al the Sarasins lasse and more,	
	That was ycome with King Yvore,	
4245	Thai sighe her lordes heved arered,	*raised up*
	Sore thai weren alle afered;	
	Toward Mombraunt thei wolde fain,	
	Ac Saber made hem terne again,	
	And Sire Beves and Sire Terry,	
4250	And Sire Miles and Sire Gii	
	Slough hem doun rightes thore,	*there*
	That ther ne scapede lasse ne more.	
	Tho crounede thai Beves king in that lond,	
	That King Yvore held in hond,	
4255	And Josiane bright and schene,	*radiant*
	Now is she ther twies quene.	*twice*
	On a dai thai wente a rivere;	*went hawking*
	Thar com ride a masagere,	
	And ever he askede fer and ner	
4260	After the hende knight Saber.	
	Anon Saber gan forth springe:	
	"Masager," a sede, "what tiding?"	
	"Sire," a sede, "the King Edgare	
	Thee driveth to meche te bismare,	*to infamy*
4265	Desereteth Robaunt, thin eyr!"	*Disinherited; heir*
	"For God," queth Saber, "that is nought feir!"	
	And Sire Saber in haste tho	
	Tok leve of Beves, hom to go;	
	And Sire Beves corteis and hende,	*noble*
4270	A seide a wolde with him wende,	
	And Sire Miles and Sire Gii,	
	And is owene sone Terry.	

Now wendeth Beves in te Ingelonde
With is knightes fel to fonde, *courageous; try*
4275 And Terry with is knightes fale, *many*
Sexty thosend told in tale.
Thai lende over the se belive, *came; in haste*
At Southhamtoun thai gonne up rive. *to land*
Hervebourgh, Saber is wif, *Saber's wife*
4280 And Robaund anon ase blif *quickly*
Aghen Saber come tho; *Toward*
Queth Saber: "How this is igo?"
And thai him tolde at the frome, *beginning*
That Edgar hadde here londes benome. *taken*
4285 Thanne seide Beves: "So mot I the, *thrive*
Thar of ich wile awreke be!" *avenged*
Anon the knight, Sire Bevoun,
His ost he let at Hamtoun, *left*
And toward Londen a wente swithe; *quickly*
4290 His quene a let at Potenhithe; *left; Putney*
He tok with him sex knightes
And wente forth anon rightes,
And in is wei forth a yode *went*
And pasede over Temse flode. *Thames*
4295 To Westmenster whan he com than, *Westminster*
A fond the king and mani man, *found*
And on is knes he him set,
The king wel hendeliche a gret *nobly*
And bad before his barnage, *baronage*
4300 That he him graunte is eritage.
"Bletheliche," a seide, "sone min, *Gladly; my son*
I graunte thee, be Seinte Martin!"
And alle the barouns, that ther were,
On Beves made glade chere,
4305 Boute the stiward of the halle;
He was the worste frend of alle.
The king wolde have yeve him grith, *peace*
The stiward seide nay ther with,
And seide: "This forbanniiste man *banished*
4310 Is come to the land aghan, *returned*
And hath thin owene sone slawe.

	He hath ydon aghenes the lawe,	
	And yif a mot forther gon,	
	A wile us slen everichon!"	
4315	Beves that herde, a was wroth,	
	And lep to hors, withouten oth,	
	And rod to Londen, that cité,	
	With sex knightes in meiné.	*company*
	Whan that he to Londen cam,	
4320	In Tour strete is in he nam	*Tower his lodging*
	And to the mete he gan gon,	*food*
	And is knightes everichon.	
	Let we now Beves be,	
	And of all the stiward telle we,	
4325	That hateth Beves, also is fo.	*as his enemy*
	Sexty knightes he tok and mo,	
	In to Londene sone he cam,	
	And into Chepe the wei he nam	*Cheapside*
	And dede make ther a cri	
4330	Among the peple hasteli,	
	And seide: "Lordinges, veraiment,	
	Hureth the kinges comaundement.	*Hear*
	Sertes, hit is befalle so,	*so happens*
	In your cité he hath a fo,	
4335	Beves, that slough the kinges sone;	
	That tresoun ye oughte to mone.	*remember*
	I comaunde, for the kinges sake,	
	Swithe anon that he be take!"	*Very soon*
	Whan the peple herde that cri,	
4340	Thai gonne hem arme hasteli,	
	And hii that hadde armur non,	*no armor*
	Thai toke staves and gonne gon;	
	Thai schette anon everi gate	
	With the barres, thai founde ther-ate;	*bars*
4345	And sum thai wente to the wal	
	With bowes and with springal;	*catapults*
	Everi lane and everi strete	
	Was do drawe with chaines grete,	*barricaded*
	That, yif Beves wolde awei flen,	
4350	The chaines scholde holde him aghen.	

Boute her of Beves weste nought. *About this; knew not*
Help him God, that alle thing wrought!
Beves at the mete sat,
He beheld and underyat *understood*
4355 Al is fon, that were ther oute; *foes*
He was afered of that route.
He askede at the tavarnere, *tavern*
That armede folk, what it were.
And he answerde him at that sake: *cause*
4360 "Thai ben ycome thee to take!"
Whan Beves herde him speke so,
To a chaumber he gan go,
That he hadde seghe armur inne; *seen*
In haste the dore he gan up winne *open*
4365 And armede ther anon rightes
Bothe he and is sex knightes, *his six*
And gerte him with a gode brond *armed himself; sword*
And tok a spere in is honde,
Aboute his nekke a doble scheld. *double*
4370 He was a knight stout and belde. *bold*
On Arondel a lep that tide,
In to the strete he gan ride.
Thanne seide the stiward to Sire Bef: *Bevis*
"Ayilt thee, treitour, thow foule thef! *Yield*
4375 Thow havest the kinges sone islawe,
Thow schelt ben hanged and to-drawe!"
Beves seide: "Be Sein Jon,
Treitour was I never non.
That I schel kethe hastely, *make known*
4380 Er than ich wende, sikerly!" *certainly*
A spere Beves let to him glide
And smot him under the right side;
Thourgh is bodi wente the dent, *blow*
Ded a fel on the paviment. *Dead he fell*
4385 A sede anon after that dint:
"Treitour! now is the lif itint. *lost*
Thus men schel teche file glotouns, *vile*
That wile misaie gode barouns!" *slander*
The folk com with grete route,

4390 Besette Beves al aboute;
Beves and is sex knightes
Defendede hem with al her mightes,
So that in a lite stounde — *while*
Five hondred thai broughte te gronde.
4395 Beves prikede forth to Chepe, — *galloped; Cheapside*
The folk him folwede al to hepe; — *as a mob*
Thourgh Godes lane he wolde han flowe, — *fled*
Ac sone within a lite throwe
He was beset in bothe side,
4400 That fle ne mighte he nought that tide. — *time*
Tho com ther fotmen mani and fale — *numerous*
With grete clobbes and with smale!
Aboute Beves thai gonne thringe — *throng*
And hard on him thai gonne dinge. — *strike*
4405 Al Beves knightes, in that stounde — *space of time*
Thar hii were feld to grounde
And al to-hewe flesch and bon.
Tho was Beves wobegon, — *woebegone*
For he was on and hii were ded; — *alone*
4410 For sorwe kouthe he no red; — *advice*
That lane was so narw ywrought, — *narrowly built*
That he mighte defende him nought, — *not defend himself*
He ne Arondel, is stede, — *Nor had he; his*
Ne mighte him terne for non nede.
4415 To Jesu he made his praiere
And to Marie, is moder dere,
That he moste pase with is lif, — *escape*
To sen is children and is wif.
Out of the lane a wolde ten, — *go*
4420 The chynes held him faste aghen. — *chains; held him back*
With is swerd he smot the chayne,
That hit fel a peces twayne, — *two pieces*
And forth a wente in to Chepe;
The folk him folwede al to hepe, — *in a mob*
4425 And al thai setten up a cry:
"Ayilt thee, Beves, hastely, — *Yield*
Ayilt thee, Beves, sone anon,
And elles thow schelt thee lif forgon!"

Beves seide: "Ich yelde me
4430 To God, that sit in Trinité!
To non other man I nel me yelde,
While that ich mai me wepne welde!" — *weapon*
Now beginneth the grete bataile
Of Sire Beves, withouten faile,
4435 That he dede ayenes that cité.
Ye that wile here, herkneth to me!
This was aboute the under tide, — *noon*
The cri aros be ech a side
Bothe of lane and of strete;
4440 Aboute him com peple grete,
Al newe and fresch, with him to fight,
Ac Beves stered him ase gode knight, — *comported himself*
So that in a lite thrawe — *while*
Fif thosend thar was islawe
4445 Of the strengeste, that ther wore,
That him hadde yeve dentes sore; — *given painful blows*
Ac ever his stede Arondel
Faste faught with hertte lel, — *loyal*
That fourty fote behinde and forn — *before*
4450 The folk he hath to grounde iborn.
Thus that fight leste longe
Til the time of evesonge. — *evensong*
Tidinge com to Potenhithe, — *Putney*
To Josian also swithe,
4455 That Beves in Londen was islawe
And ibrought of his lif dawe.
Josian thanne fel aswowe, — *swooned*
Gii and Miles hire up drowe — *picked*
And confortede that levedi bright
4460 Hendeliche with alle her might, — *Nobly*
And askede hire, what hire were;
And she tolde hem anon there,
How Beves was in Londen slayn
And his knightes with gret payn:
4465 "Now kethe ye ben noble knightes, — *know*
And wreketh your fader with your mightes!" — *avenge*
Sire Gii and Miles seide than

	To here moder Josian:	*their*
	"Dame, be Him that herwede helle,	*by; harrowed hell*
4470	We scholle his deth wel dere selle!"	*purchase dearly*
	Than Sire Miles and Sire Gii	
	Gonne hem arme hasteli	
	And on here knes set hem doun	
	And bad her moder benesoun.	*mother's blessing*
4475	Sire Gii lep on a rabit,	*Arabian horse*
	That was meche and nothing lite,	
	And tok a spere in is hond,	
	Out at the halle dore a wond	*he departed*
	Toward the cité of Londen toun,	
4480	And Sire Miles with gret randoun	*violence*
	Lep upon a dromedary,	*camel*
	To prike wolde he nought spary,	*spur; spare*
	Whan thai come to Londen gate,	
	Mani man thai fonde ther-ate,	
4485	Wel iarmed to the teth,	
	So the Frensche bok us seth,	
	Aghen the children thei yeve bataile,	
	And hii aghen, withouten faile,	*in return*
	And made of hem so clene werk,	
4490	That thai never spek with prest ne clerk;	
	And afterward, ase ye mai hure,	*hear*
	Londegate thai sette a fure.	*on fire*
	Whan thai come, withouten faile,	
	Tho began a gret bataile	
4495	Betwene Bowe and Londen ston,	
	That time stod us never on.	*not a single one withstood us*
	Thar was a Lombard in the toun,	
	That was scherewed and feloun;	*wicked; villainous*
	He armede him in yrene wede	
4500	And lep upon a sterne stede	*strong*
	And rod forth with gret randoun	*violence*
	And thoughte have slawe Sire Bevoun.	
	With an uge masnel	*huge club*
	Beves a hite on the helm of stel,	
4505	That Beves of Hamtoun, veraiment,	
	Was astoned of the dent;	*dazed*

	What for care and for howe,	*anguish*
	He lenede to his sadelbowe.	
	Thanne com priken is sone Gii,	
4510	To helpe his fader, hastely;	
	With a swerd drawe in is hond	
	To that Lombard sone a wond	*quickly he proceeded*
	And smot him so upon the croun,	
	That man and hors he clevede doun;	*clove*
4515	The poynt fel on the paviment,	
	The fur sprong out after the dent.	*fire*
	Thanne com ride is brother Mile	
	Among the peple in that while;	
	Al tho, that a mighte reche,	
4520	Ne dorste he never aske leche,	*ask for a doctor*
	For to hele ther is wonde,	
	That he ne lai ded upon the grounde.	
	And whan Beves segh that sighte,	
	In hertte he was glad and lighte	
4525	And thankede Jesu, our saviour,	
	That hadde sent him so gode sokour,	*succor*
	And egerliche, withouten faile,	*eagerly*
	The grete peple he gan asaile.	
	So meche folk was slawe and ded,	
4530	That al Temse was blod red;	*Thames*
	The nombre was, veraiment,	
	To and thretti thosent.	*32,000*
	And also sone as hit was night,	
	To the ledene halle thai wente right;	*hall [with the] lead roof*
4535	A fette Josian with faire meiné	*brought; retinue*
	To Londen, to that riche cité,	
	And held a feste fourtene night	
	To al that ever come, aplight!	*indeed*
	Tiding com to King Edgar,	
4540	That Beves hadde his men forfare;	*killed*
	For is borgeis in is cité	*citizens*
	He made del and gret pité	*grief (dole, mourning)*
	And seide: "Ichave leved me lif	*lived*
	Longe withouten werre and strif,	*war*
4545	And now icham so falle in elde,	*old age*

That I ne may min armes welde.
Twei sones Beves hath with him brought,
Tharfore hit is in me thought,
Miles, his sone, me doughter take,
4550 In this maner is pes to make." *peace*
Thai grauntede al with gode entent,
And King Edgar Beves of-sent,
And Sire Saber and Sire Gii,
And Sire Miles and Sire Terry,
4555 And King Edgar Miles gan calle
Before his barouns in the halle
And yaf him is doughter be the honde,
And after is day al Ingelonde,
And pes and love was maked thare
4560 Betwene Beves and King Edgare.
The maide and Miles wer spused same *espoused*
In the toun of Notinghame. *Nottingham*
Ye witeth wel, though I ne telle yow,
The feste was riale inow, *feast; royal enough*
4565 As scholde be at swiche a spusing *spousing (wedding)*
And at the kinges couroning; *crowning*
The feste leste fourtene night
To al that ever come, aplight! *indeed*
And at the fourtene night is ende,
4570 Beves tok leve, hom to wende,
At King Edgar and at Sabere,
And Miles, is sone, a lefte here
And kiste and yaf him is blessing,
And wente to Mombraunt, ther he was king;
4575 And his erldom in Hamteschire *Hampshire*
A yaf to his em Sabere
And schipede at Hamtoun hastely, *sailed from*
And with him wente his sone Gii,
And Terry with is barnage. *baronage*
4580 The wind blew hardde with gret rage
And drof hem in to Ermonie,
Thar belefte his sone Gii
With his barouns gode and hende;
And Terry to Aumberthe gan wende,

4585 And Beves wente withoute dwelling
In to Mombraunt, thar he was king;
With him wente Josian, is quene,
And levede withoute treie and tene — *grief; injury*
Twenti yer, so saith the bok.
4590 Thanne swiche siknesse the levedi tok,
Out of this world she moste wende;
Gii, hire sone, she gan ofsende,
And Terry, the riche king,
For to ben at here parting. — *her passing*
4595 And whan thai were alle thare,
To his stable Beves gan fare;
Arondel a fond thar ded, — *dead*
That ever hadde be gode at nede;
Tharfore him was swithe wo,
4600 In to his chaumber he gan go
And segh Josian drawe to dede.
Him was wo a moste nede,
And er her body began to colde, — *before*
In is armes he gan hire folde,
4605 And thar hii deide bothe ifere. — *died; together*
Here sone ne wolde in non manere, — *son*
That hii in erthe beried were.
Of Sein Lauarauns he let arere — *Saint Lawrence; raise up*
A faire chapel of marbel fin, — *marble fine*
4610 That was ikast with queint engin; — *cast; noble art*
Of gold he made an high cornere
And leide them thar in bothe ifere.
An hous he made of riligioun, — *house of religion (church or monastery)*
For to singe for Sire Bevoun
4615 And ek for Josian the fre: — *noble*
God on here saules have pité! — *souls*
And also for Arondel,
Yif men for eni hors bidde schel, — *pray*
Thus endeth Beves of Hamtoun.
4620 God yeve us alle Is benesoun! — *His*
Amen.

Notes

Abbreviations: A: Auchinleck; Kö: Kölbing; E: Egerton 2862; C: Cambridge University Library MS Ff. 2.38; CC: Caius College MS 175; N: Royal Library, Naples MS XIII, B29; M: Chetham Library, No. 8009

This edition follows the text of the Auchinleck MS (A), fols. 176–201. We have followed Kölbing's edition and used E (Duke of Sutherland, now Egerton 2862) to account for the leaf that is missing in A, for the lines in our edition numbered 2289–2464. Kölbing's emendations to the MS are listed in the notes, both where we have accepted his reading and where we have preferred to follow the MS or made other choices. We should also point out that standard paleographic abbreviations in the MS are presented as emendations in the Kölbing edition, emendations he prints in italics in the text of his edition. In citing his edition in our notes, we have not maintained this distinction.

1 The incipit bears an illustration of a knight standing in full armor holding a lance. Perhaps this is an indication of a wealthy patronage and the making of this collection in a London bookshop. See Laura Hibbard Loomis, "The Auchinleck Manuscript and a Possible London Bookshop of 1330–1340," *PMLA* 57 (1942), 595–609.

11 *schire*. In the Middle Ages a shire was a province or subdivision of a county. Many cities in England retain suffixes that indicate a seat of government. A modern analogue for shire would be county.

15 As the notes to the other romances have reminded us, in Middle English, double and even triple negatives add emphasis. Unlike in modern English a double negative does not constitute an affirmative.

25 *An elde a wif he tok an honde*. A: *An elde wif*. Kö's emendation recognizes the youth of the bride. It is the bridegroom who is overly mature.

34–42 That the emperor of Germany is a former lover as indicated here sets up the unhappy marital relation. The bride, who is never identified except as Bevis' mother, is dissatisfied because her choice of husband has been thwarted by her father's unilateral decision.

62 *fight*. MS hard to read here.

91 *ferste dai*. A: *ferþe*. Kö's emendation is in agreement with E, S, N, and C readings as well as medieval celebrations of May Day, a day dedicated to love.

133 *ferste day*. A: *ferþe*. Kö's emendation is consistent with the emendation in line 91. S, N, and C: *first*.

143 *And thou schelt after her wedde to spouse*. A: *þow schelt after wedde to spouse*. Kö emends by adding *her* as object of the completed quest. Though the lady's desire is known, the emphasis on marriage as a reward is significant.

148 *Gladder icham*. A: *Glad*. E and N: *I am gladder*. The emendation is Kö's based on E and N readings.

173 *levedi was right wel apaid*. A: *levidi riȝt wel apaid*. Kö adds the intransitive verb, based on its presence in C.

190 *tresoun mest*. Treason in the Middle Ages connotes treachery or betrayal of someone to whom one owes loyalty. Treason is thus not only a personal transgression, but a political transgression as well.

203 The earl wears less armor than he would if he knew he were facing a combat situation.

245 The exaggerated number of knights is a convention of medieval romance. Often the hero performs superhuman deeds in battle killing hundreds and thousands of opponents single-handedly. See line 4532 for the extreme instance.

292 The messenger speaks the words he is told to speak, conveying the message verbatim. Messengers play an important role in medieval romance; they not only convey dialogue, but act as narrative links. Oftentimes the messenger takes the brunt of the recipient's anger. Bevis himself will play the role of messenger later in the poem.

302 *Vile houre*. Bevis calls his mother a "vile whore" and wishes her to be drawn to death. Drawing or dragging, usually accompanied by quartering, entailed tying each limb to a separate rope then pulling the body in opposing directions by four horses,

literally tearing the victim's body into four pieces. The punishment was usually reserved for felons of the worst sort.

307 *thee faire ble.* The scribe regularly spells the pronoun *the*. On the assumption that the pronoun was pronounced with a long *ē*, we have transcribed the pronoun *the* as *thee*. Although the poet generally uses *thee* in objective (dative and accusative) situations, possessive and nominative usages are likewise commonplace. For other possessive placements, see, for example, lines 310, 374, 482, 540, 557, 564, 605, 896, 918, 922, 925, 1097, 1107, 1109, 1132, 1196, 1317, 1474, 1736, 2188, 2202, 3164, 3169, 3211, 3628, 3633, 3656, 3738, 3837, 4087, 4428; for nominative use, see lines 531, 1043, 1082, 1103, 1233, 1422, 1843, 2121, 2124, 2188, 2203, 3657, 3658, 4227; and for dative of agency, which we translate with an "it is" syntax, see lines 1007, 2210; or as a reflexive pronoun, see lines 1006, 1733, 3015, 4374, 4426, and 4427. He also uses *me* in all three functions. E.g., see lines 671 and 1043.

310 *alle wif.* Bevis imagines his mother a madame in a brothel.

315 *And be of elde.* A: *ben of elde.* E and N: *be of.* C: *come to.* Kö clarifies the line.

320 *That child she smot with hire honde.* One of many scenes of domestic violence. Not recognized by medieval law, violence among family members was considered a private matter with parents having customary rights to corporal punishment of their children.

322 *The child fel doun and that was scathe.* A: *Þe child fel doun and þat scaþe.* Kö adds an intransitive verb.

323 *meister.* Although Saber is Bevis' uncle he is also his guardian, mentor, or, perhaps, teacher, which is a common gloss on ME *maister.* See also lines 487 ff. where Bevis comes to his "teacher's" defense. Saber's name may have significance (from OE *sigebush*, meaning "victory fortress"); Saber is the faithful keeper of the estate and the faith, throughout Bevis' prolonged absence, and ultimately becomes earl of Hampshire. He is not to be confused with the bishop of Cologne, Saber Florentine, who appears in lines 2926 ff.

325 *The knight was trewe and of kinde.* Kö adds the possessive pronoun *his* before *kinde* to confer a "nature" upon the knight. The emendation is unnecessary.

347 Like the huntsman in Snow White and various other folk narratives, Saber circumvents the commands of a wicked mother by slaying an animal.

395–99 The role of the porter is often stressful in medieval literature since it is he who decides who is worthy of entrance into the city or castle.

398 *Scherewe*. From this term derives "shrew." In the Middle Ages the term connoted "rascal," "rogue," "wicked person," "evil-doer," and "unruly or ill-disciplined child." It could also refer to an overbearing woman.

415–20 Bevis' novel means of entry defies protocol.

443 *a smot him with*. A: *a smot him him wiþ*. This duplication of words is a typical scribal redundancy in A.

454 *Wo hem was for the childes sake*. The knights sympathize with Bevis and let him go. Perhaps, they are also afraid of him.

496 *painim londe*. The term could mean anyplace outside of Christian Europe. *Painim* could refer to any group of people not practicing Christianity.

497 Bevis' mother is participating in an activity that goes well beyond fostering and is reminiscent of the actions of Joseph's brothers when they sell him into slavery in Genesis. Or perhaps Orestes, when Clytemnestra puts him away. Like Orestes, Bevis will return seeking vengeance for the murder of his father. Fortunately for him the mother dies on her own so that he is not compelled to exact justice for her treason. But he does take care of her lover, his stepfather.

499 *mor and lesse*. A: *mor & lesse*. Kö: *mor or lesse*. We have retained the MS reading as a commonplace idiom implying "all."

510 *be him mild*. A: *be us mild*. E: *him*. Kö capitalizes Him, as if to ask Christ's mercy for Bevis rather than for "us," as in A.

515 The trip is given short shrift. In the course of two lines, they have sailed out of England and arrived in the Middle East. The land, as indicated in other MSS, is called Ermony, which usually refers to Armenia.

520–22 The contrast between snow and blood as well as the attention to the shoes on Josian's feet recall fairy tale motifs such as those of Cinderella, Snow White, and Rose Red. The allusion would not be farfetched since fairy tales and folk tales, then as now, were present in virtually every culture in the world. Both genres are integrally related to medieval romance.

531 *Mahoun* was a common name for Mohammed in Middle English. In the standard Middle English treatment of the Islamic people (most often called Saracens in Middle English), he is treated as one of many "pagan" gods, rather than as the historical prophet of the one God, whose Arabic name is Allah.

548 *Wikked beth fele wimmen to fonde.* Proverbial, though not cited in Whiting or Tilley. The sense is "Many women prove to be wicked."

558 *Apolyn* is another of the "pagan" gods of the Saracens according to medieval understanding. This treatment of Islam is commonplace in English romances, especially the English Charlemagne romances. See Alan Lupack, ed., *Three Middle English Charlemagne Romances* (Kalamazoo: Medieval Institute Publications, 1990).

594 *I not never, what.* A: *I no never.* C: *never not.*

599 The Saracen finds Bevis' ignorance laughable because even he knows the significance of the day.

688 *Thai were aferde, hii wer nigh wode.* A: *Þai were hii wer niȝ wode. Aferde* is omitted in A. Kölbing emends on the basis of other MSS' readings.

690 *losengers.* According to the MED this term has a range of meaning including: "one who curries favor," "a flatterer," "liar," "backbiter," "calumniator," "hypocrite," "traitorous counselor," "rascal," "coward."

707 *Lemman.* A term of endearment usually reserved for one's beloved. Bevis' response to Josian's declaration suggests an epiphany born of love.

844 *seith the bok.* The poet uses a convention of medieval romance to lend authority to his narrative. Often the "book" is French. Here it may be more than convention since this poem has a French source.

860 *maught.* Though the usual sense is "might" or "strength," when used to describe a weapon the sense may be "power," "craftsmanship," or "virtue."

861 The naming of a sword is commonplace in medieval romance and epic: Arthur's Excalibur, Gawain's Galantyne, Beowulf's Hrunting, Roland's Durandal, Oliver's Glorious, and Siegfried's Griel are a few.

885 *So tho is a lite stounde.* Kö: *And tho*, on the basis of E.

897 Josian's equation of love-longing as captivation is a feature of medieval ideas of courtly love. Love captures its victim with a hook or arrow and causes pain and suffering. As Andreas Capellanus explains in the *Art of Courtly Love*: "love is like an inborn suffering."

899 *Thus that maide made.* A: *Þus that maide maide her mon.* Kö transforms a noun to a verb for the sake of clarity.

904 Bevis' decision to take the decapitated head of the boar to the king rather than to Josian (see line 832) is no doubt related to the attack of the envious steward. He needs to prove his deed, i.e., the slaying of the beast. The steward's plan to steal the boar's head away from Bevis in order to claim his own prowess is thwarted when Bevis, in the process of defending himself, kills the steward and his accomplices. He then has an opportunity to bring the head of the steward to the king but decides against it. He has already been charged with treason once. Should the king misconstrue Bevis' story, he could face another charge of treason. Josian, who witnesses the whole scene, discloses Bevis' act later as an endorsement of his candidacy for knighthood.

924 Brademond threatens to deflower Josian and pass her on to a member of the lower classes, a serious threat indeed, given the value placed upon female virginity and social ranking in the Middle Ages.

931 *And tolde hem how Brademond him asailed hadde.* A: *And Brademond him asailed hadde.* Because A omits the first clause in the line, Kö emends following E and N: *And tolde hem how.*

945 *to the teth.* A: *to the deþ.* To be "armed to the teeth" is a familiar aphorism. See also lines 3644 and 4485. To be "armed to the death" makes little sense.

993 *ferste scheld trome. trome* (from OE *truma*) is a rank of warriors, a body of armed men; the *ferste scheld* is the vanguard, the first ward. Bevis leads his choice retainers into battle, a gesture to which the enemy instantly responds. In E the equivalent gesture is contained in the line *Beues gan than his horne blowe*, to which the enemy responds.

1010 *wod.* We have borrowed the anachronistic gloss "berserk" from Scott's nineteenth-century usage (OED) to describe the "wodness" of medieval battle frenzy. Scott's neologism provides a useful modern term for which there is no better equivalent.

1016 *sonne set in the west.* A: *sonne set riȝt.* E and N: *sonne in the west.* Kö's emendation which completes the rhyme and mends the breech in material.

1041 *"Merci!" queth Bradmond, "ich me yelde.* A: *Merci! queþ, ich me yelde.* Kö confers the speech upon Brademond, which clarifies the textual confusion.

1049 St. Martin, probably of Tours (316–97), was a soldier who later became a monk and bishop in Gaul. While Martin was still a soldier, he came upon a naked beggar near Amiens in Northern France and cut his cloak in half to give the poor man something to wear. Later Martin dreamed that Christ himself was the beggar. Martin's life and frequent miracles were popular legend in the Middle Ages. His feast day, 8 November, became known in England as Martinmas. See David Hugh Farmer, *Oxford Dictionary of Saints* (Oxford: Oxford University Press, 1982), pp. 265–66.

1051 *Al that ich do, it is his dede.* A: *Al þat ich do, it is dede.* Kö: *it is his dede.* The emendation is based on E and N.

1054 *Thow schelt werre.* E, N, and C add a negative adjective, i.e., *never* to *warre*, which is consistent with the oath Bevis demands from Brademond.

1066 *Mani dai a maked him feste.* E and N: *a wykked fest.* Kö retains A. The implication is that had Bevis known what Brademond would do to him he would/should have killed him rather than show mercy.

1098 *"For Gode," queth Beves, "that ich do nelle!* A: *For gode, queth, þat ich do nelle!* Here Kö confers speech upon Bevis. Also see line 1110.

1108 *Than al the gold.* EN: *good.*

1110 *"For Gode," queth Beves.* A: *For gode, queþ he.* Kö's emendation confers Bevis with direct address as in line 1098.

1132 *daunger.* This term is often related to the practices of courtly love, wherein a would-be lover could act in an aloof and distant manner. According to the MED it could also mean "domination, power, control, or possession" and "threaten to cause difficulty or damage" as Josian seems to here, at least in Bevis' perception of her declamation of love.

1166 *Aboute hire nede.* This is a very short line, lengthened in C: *Of þat y went about your nede.*

1168 *So te misain.* A: *So te misin.* Kö: *So te misain a.* Kö silently emends A here. But his reading improves the line.

1192 *wimmannes bolt is sone schote.* Proverbial; not in Tilley or Whiting. The proverb implies lack of discretion, *sone* suggesting "haste" or "carelessness." Compare Malory's *The Great Tournament*, where the huntress shoots *anone* and misses the hind but hits Lancelot's buttocks.

1210 *Hit were gode, sire.* A: *Hit gode, sire, þat he were slain.* Kö: *It were gode, sire.* Kö emends on the strength of N and C.

1239 *Al in solas and in delit.* A: *Al in solas in delit.* Kö: *Al in solas and in delit* on the basis of C.

1288 *That Sire Beves gan of-see.* A: *Beves gan of.* Kö's emendation.

1289 St. Julian is the patron saint of hospitality.

1331 *He ne wolde love me non other.* A: *He ne wolde me non oþer.* Kö adds "love" to the line.

1344 *A cleimede his eritage.* To claim a heritage is to assert a legal right to something, to demand title to something.

1380 *Tervagaunt* (usually Termagant) is another member of the Saracen pantheon.

1398 *kende*. We have glossed the term as "gentle," which seems to be closest to the primary sense of the term in this unctuous usage; "noble," "lordly," "spirited," "courageous," "brave," "dutiful," or "loyal" might do as well. See MED *kinde* (adj.) 4 and 5.

1412–18 Though a scoundrel, Brademond has some sense of honor; since Bevis once defeated him but did not kill him, Brademond will imprison Bevis rather than execute him. Had Bevis not previously shown his prowess, Brademond says that he would have executed him before sundown.

1422 *under the fet*. The point is that Bevis will no longer eat from a table. His prison is a pit twenty fathoms deep. Food and drink are dropped to him. That the stench would be suffocating is no harder to imagine than it would be to endure. Entrance and egress is by rope, which later proves to be his salvation. See lines 1537 ff.

1424 A quarter was an actual unit of measurement for grain. According to the OED it was equal to eight bushels of wheat.

1448 *What dai awai whanne a wolde wende*. A: *What dai whanne*. Kö adds *awai*.

1468 *That I lovede ase min hertte blode*. Josian's expression of love is intensified by the anatomical reference.

1469–72 Magic rings are commonplace in romance traditions. Lunette gives one to Yvain in Chrétien de Troyes' *Yvain: The Knight with the Lion* to protect him from harm. Rings are also used as means of identification or for signifying a courtly relation. Lapidary was a subject of great interest in the Middle Ages and gemstones often had symbolic meaning as proof of their power.

1483 *Of that feste*. A: *If þat feste*. Kö: *Of þat feste*. In the MS, the "I" is one of the large decorated initials.

1487 *Men graithede cartes and somers*. A: *Men graicede cartes and somers*. Kö: *graiþede*.

1571 *His browe stank*. Apparently the wound on his forehead putrifies before forming the scar.

1584 The suffering servant motif seems to be operating here. Exegetical tradition holds Christ to be the prototype. Bevis' descent and eventual ascent may mark him as a Christ figure or at the very least a mythic hero in Northrop Frye's sense of the term. See *The Secular Scripture*.

1612 *With a strok me doth adoun falle*. A: *Wiþ a strok me adoun falle*. Kö's emendation is based on E and N.

1614 *ther-of may ben awreke*. A: *þer of ben me awreke*. Kö's emendation is based on C.

1630 *by the rop*. A: *be rop*. Kö's emendation based on N.

1733 *fox welp*. An insult equivalent to *heathen hound*.

1756 *undertide*. A: *undetide*. Kö's emendation. The time designated by this term is noon, thought to be a particularly significant moment during the day, i.e., the time at which demons could tempt vulnerable humans. See John Block Friedman, "Eurydice, Heurodis, and the Noon-day Demon," *Speculum* 41 (1996), 22–29.

1799 *ase wel alse man*. Kö adds the *wel*.

1800 In this somewhat convoluted comparison, a contrast is made between the innocence of fish, who as creatures lacking reason are not able to sin, and the perfidy of Saracens, who are thought by implication to be guilty of the death of Christ.

1872 Bevis is making a grim and ironic joke about the tonsure, the "close shave" that identified medieval clerics.

1951–53 The sense is "if King Brademond and all his offspring were right there."

2058–66 The beggar's or pilgrim's disguise is a popular practice in medieval romance as well as epic poems such as Homer's *Odyssey*. An effective strategy for entering a hostile city, it suggests the "invisibility" of those members of society at the bottom of the social ladder.

2128 *quene to eche palmare*. A: *quene to palmare*. Kö adds *eche* to maintain the meter as well as to indicate direct, individual contact since the noun is singular.

2161 *made miche pride*. A: *made made miche pride*. Kö deletes the redundant verb.

2164–66 Perhaps the sense is that "it is many a man's bane to be laughed at today before the steed is caught," that is, many will try and fail (before Bevis comes along).

2203–06 The sense here is that if in England anyone can testify that Josian is married, she will return to her homeland with nothing but the smock on her back. She is suggesting that the marriage is unconsummated, which would render the relation invalid.

2210 *do be rede*. Kö emends to *do be me rede* on the authority of E and N. In so doing he clarifies Bonefas' directive, i.e., to take his advice on an escape strategy, though emendation may not be necessary.

2217 *chevalrie*. The term might be glossed as "chivalry," but in the sense of "horsemanship" rather than "courtesy," which subsequently displaces the earlier meaning.

2286 *that we wer thore*. A: *þat were þore*. Kö's emendation; the first-person plural pronoun clarifies the line.

2289 *Cité of Diablent*. From here to line 2464 the narrative is missing in A. We follow Kö's usage and use E for the intervening lines. The E scribe has a propensity for capitalization which has been emended here according to modern usage.

2352 *Ascopart*. Giants enjoy a long and varied history in Scripture and medieval romance. They are depicted usually as villains, apostates, arrogant, threatening monsters, and descendants of Cain (e.g., Nimrod, Goliath, Grendel, and the giants of Rabelais). There is at least one exception to the negative portrayal of giants through the ages: St. Christopher, a benevolent giant, is said to have carried the Christ child across a treacherous river. In *Bevis*, Ascopard is remarkable in that he falls in between.

2379 The lions seem to be in a rampant position similar to how they would appear in heraldry.

2390–94 A commonplace of medieval lore was that virginity could confer invulnerability. Also, the taming of wild beasts occurs through their recognition of the virgin queen. Only a female virgin could lure the wild unicorn into her presence. In iconography the unicorn lies blissfully with its head in the virgin's lap.

2485 *And be the right leg she him grep*. A: *he him grep*. Kö restores gender to the lion grabbing Bevis by the right leg.

2503 *upon a mule*. Where this mule comes from is not explained. It simply appears when needed as the knight and his lady set out. Given the recent fact of Josian's conversion, the trope perhaps suggests female virtue. Compare Gower's Constance in *Confessio Amantis* as she rides out to meet her father "Upon a Mule whyt amblaunt" (II.1506) and Una's mount as she sets out with Redcrosse Knight in the *Faerie Queene*, I.i.29 Or it may simply be an appropriate mount for a royal woman as in *King Alexander*, where Cleopatra "rod on a mule white so milk" (line 1031). Religious connotations are also possible as seen in Jesus' entrance into Jerusalem; riding on an ass rather than a warhorse denotes him as the Prince of Peace, not a conquering military hero. The Virgin Mary is also depicted in iconography riding an ass toward Jerusalem to give birth, then later during the flight into Egypt. The "wild ass" was associated with Ishmael and became a symbol of conversion.

2569–70 *come withouten ensoine / To the haven of Coloine*. Compare *Richard the Lion Hearted*, ed. Brunner (1913): *Fforþ þey wenten wiþuten ensoyne / To þe cyte off Coloyne*, as cited by MED *ensoine* (n.). That MS dates from c. 1475. Not many words rhyme with *ensoine* (or *Coloine*), which may be a factor. See also lines 2657–58 and 2891–92, where the words are rhymed.

2585 *Who is this with the grete visage*. The bishop is referring to Ascopard.

2601 *dragoun*. The dragon ("drake" or serpent) is one of the most vivid beasts created by the medieval European imagination. As serpent it represents the archetype of temptation in the Garden of Eden. In its more imaginative manifestations it becomes the beast of *Revelation*, a symbol of pure evil, who opposes the archangel Michael and his angelic forces. Its presence in medieval romance usually points to the hero's extraordinary prowess.

2603–07 Wade, Lancelot, and Guy of Warwick are great heroes in the romance tradition. By comparing Bevis' exploits to theirs, the author is authenticating Bevis' credentials as a hero of the first rank, and is also exemplifying the fact that the romance is a self-conscious genre, with individual romances constantly referring to characters and incidents in other romances and to their own sources. Notice, for example, the number of times in *Bevis* that we are given lines such as "as the book saith," or "as the French book saith." Such lines also remind us that medieval writers held written authority in high esteem. A reference to an earlier book is not simply a footnote, but a validation from an "auctor." (This Latin word means both author and authority at the same time.)

2611 Apulia is in Southern Italy, as is Calabria. One of the distinguishing features of *Bevis* is a kind of geographical sweep. Italy here joins with Germany, the near east, and many parts of England as part of that sweep.

2637 *Toke here flight.* A: *To here fliȝ t.* Kö restores the appropriate verb.

2640 Tuscany is in north-central Italy. It is the region of such cities as Florence, Siena, and Pisa.

2665 The *cholle* is that part of a dragon's anatomy which extends from the chin to the throat and from ear to ear.

2673 *wintonne.* A wine tun is a wine barrel.

2693 *Thanne a herde.* Bevis' vision comes in two phases: first a vision of one wounded by a mad king who is saved by a virgin; and second of one swollen with venom from a dragon. Both visions pertain to his own precarious situation.

2698 *me never non.* A: *me never mo.* Kö's emendation which improves the sense and rhyme.

2747 There are many saints named John. Perhaps the invocation is to John of Patmos, who, in the Middle Ages, is often credited with the writing of the *Book of Revelation.* The apocalyptic, cosmic battle depicted there features a fierce, seven-headed dragon.

2749 *Beves answerde.* A: *Beves answede.* Kö clarifies the action.

2762 *anan.* A: *anan.* More usually *anon*, this may be scribal error. Kö retains the variance, nonetheless, and so have we.

2802 Bevis' taking of refuge in the healing well as he fights the dragon is echoed in Redcrosse Knight's retreat to the well of virginal virtue after the first and second days of fighting in Spenser's *Faerie Queene.* Note Bevis' second venture in the well in lines 2850 ff. It is not mere coincidence that in line 2817 Bevis calls upon St. George for strength. See note to line 2817.

2815 *of is helm a drank thore.* The line is perhaps echoed in Chaucer's Tale of Sir Thopas (*CT* VII.15), though there the parallel is attributed to "sire Percyvell."

2817 St. George is the martyr and patron of England. The story of George and the dragon was immensely popular, disseminated through the twelfth-century *Golden Legend* of Jacobus de Voragine which was then translated by William Caxton in the fifteenth century. But, according to the *Oxford Dictionary of Saints*, the story was known in England as early as the seventh century. Edmund Spenser's portrayal of Redcrosse Knight in the *Fairie Queene* reiterates St. George's status as patron saint of England.

2838–39 The story of Jesus' raising of Lazarus from the dead is told in the Gospel according to John, ch. 11. Because it was considered one of Jesus' definitive miracles, it is often used when asking God's help in extremely precarious, not to say seemingly hopeless, situations.

2848 *bacinet*. A basinet is a supplementary cap worn under the helmet.

2852 *dai other night*. A: *dai the niȝt*.

2879 See note to line 2665.

2882 *yenede swithe wide*. Because of its armor plate the only way that Bevis can get to the dragon's heart is through its throat; thus the dragon's wide-mouthed gasp proves fatal to the beast.

2897 *And asked that*. A: *And asked at*. Kö replaces the thorn.

2967 *Ac ever, an erneste and a rage*. Perhaps this suggests that he was not only serious, but angry as well.

2976 *mesage for to don anon*. A: *message for don anon*. Kö adds *to don anon* on the basis of M.

2985–06 Note the irony of giving Bevis a version of his own history.

3105–08 The sense of this passage seems to be that because the emperor has sex with his wife too frequently, his aim has been affected. Distorted vision, thought to be an effect of sexual excess, is also used as a metaphor by some medieval writers.

3180 *Here soper was ther redi dight*. A: *Here soper wer redi diȝt*. Kö restores the meter on the evidence of E and N.

3187 ff. It was not unusual for witnesses to observe a newly married couple in bed in order to validate the marriage. The issue of whether consent or sexual intercourse were necessary for a valid marriage was vexed in the Middle Ages. David Herlihy writes: "The most common opinion was that consent alone was sufficient, but some experts continued to affirm that physical union perfected the marriage and rendered it binding" (*Medieval Households* [Cambridge: Harvard University Press, 1985], p. 80).

3217 Kö provides the following explanation of "rail-tree": "On bed curtains, see *Our English Home*, p. 101: 'Bed-curtains hung upon rails of 'tre' or metal were in use [at this time] . . ." (p. 323).

3244 *That al wide opun it wonde.* A: *upon.* Kö: *opun* on the basis of N.

3248 A caudle is a drink, often taken for medicinal purposes, consisting of thin gruel, wine, and spices.

3289 *In hire smok.* A: *In hire hire smok.* Kö eliminates the redundant pronoun.

3340 *Ich wende he hadde ben anhonge.* A: *Ich wende hadde ben anhonge.* Kö adds *he* for the sake of clarity.

3352 *Mani hondes maketh light werk.* Whiting cites *Bevis* (c. 1300) as the earliest recorded instance of this proverb.

3356 A pitched battle is a particular strategy in medieval warfare.

3362 *Hit scholde some of hem rewe sore.* A: *some of rewe sore.* Kö adds *hem* to restore the meter.

3391 *that other ladde.* A: *þat oþe ladde.*

3392 As Kö notes, the King of Scotland dies later at the hands of Ascopard. According to the French text, Saber murders the Scottish king.

3453 *Ful of pich and of bremston.* A: *Ful of bich.* Kö emends the pitch based on the other MSS.

3511 Whitsunday is the English name for Pentecost, the Christian feast, coming fifty days after Easter, which celebrates the descent of the Holy Spirit to the Apostles and is considered the "birthday" of the Christian church. It is described in Acts of the Apostles, ch. 2.

3513–42 Horse races for the accumulation of wealth are not often found in medieval romance. But they were common in practice. See, for example, *The Voyage of Ohtere*, where the one with the swiiftest horse gets the most. Here the race functions as a demonstration of Arondel's "horsepower."

3590 Ascopard's betrayal is ostensibly caused by Bevis' fall into poverty, but is just as likely a jealous response. The proclivities of fairweather friends appear in other Middle English romances. See, for instance, *Sir Cleges* in *Middle English Breton Lays*, ed. Anne Laskaya and Eve Salisbury (Kalamazoo: Medieval Institute Publications, 1995). Nonetheless, Ascopard does have trouble maintaining credibility, despite his good deeds.

3622 *swerdes a logge pighte*. A: *swerdes logge piȝte*. Kö's emendation based on other MSS.

3629 *God forbede*. A: *For for bed*. Kö restores the deity based on E, N, C, and M: *God for-bede*.

3630–31 Childbirth was strictly the provenance of women in the Middle Ages. Josian's rejection of male interference reflects that custom. Also, the birth of twins is notable since medieval folklore sometimes held that multiple births were the consequence of many fathers rather than one. Often, because of the social stigma the birth of twins accrued, one twin could be subject to death or exile. See *Lay le Freine*, for instance.

3634 Josian is invoking the Virgin's help in childbirth.

3640–50 The abduction of the heroine is particularly violent. Other abductions such as that of Guenevere have not been depicted as brutally as this scene. Adding to the brutality is the fact of Josian's recent parturition and the abandonment of her twins.

3714 "Heathen" seems to be a curious way to describe the children. As we find out a few lines later (line 3734), however, it refers to the fact that they have not yet been baptized, a condition that is swiftly remedied.

3749 A mark was an accounting measure (not an actual coin) used in medieval England, equal to thirteen shillings fourpence.

3772 Though it is not clear whether *Aumbeforce* is a real or an imagined place from the text, A. C. Baugh points out that in the Anglo-Norman original Aumberforce is the city of Seville (p. 21).

3775 St. Thomas of India is actually one of the twelve original apostles, most famous as "doubting Thomas," because of the story in John's Gospel (ch. 20) in which he refuses to believe the resurrection of Christ until he can put his fingers in Christ's wounds. According to ancient tradition he brought the gospel to India, where he was martyred.

3776 Terri's answer to Bevis is a way of saying that they have never been cowards, that is, they have never been afraid to fight face to face.

3785 The Spanish city of Toledo was famous for the manufacture of steel and weapons. The form of the word is French, indicating the influence of the Anglo-Norman version of *Bevis*.

3844 St. James and St. Giles are both important pilgrimage saints. James, one of the twelve original apostles, was thought to have preached in Spain. Santiago de Compostela, in northwestern Spain, where his body was thought to be found, was one of the most important pilgrimage centers of the Middle Ages, the most important in western Europe. Giles, a hermit from either the sixth or eighth century, is the patron saint of cripples and beggars. His shrine — Saint-Gilles, in Provence — was also an important pilgrimage center in the Middle Ages.

3859 This probably refers to the entire eastern Mediterranean, rather than to anything more specific.

3871 *ase he yede aboute.* A: *ase yhe yede aboute.* Kö's emendation clarifies gender.

3910 Josian's entrepreneurial activity, i.e., "as a minstrel," recalls an episode in the romance of *Apollonius of Tyre* in which Apollonius' abducted daughter escapes service in a foreign brothel by thwarting the desire of those seeking her services by her rhetoric. Once out, she takes up harp playing and pedagogy to support herself.

3960 *pleide at the talvas*. A *talevas* is a round shield, or buckler. To play at the talevas is an idiom for fencing. See MED *talevard.*

3978 *mautalent.* A: *mauntalent,* with the *n* by abbreviation. MED ignores the *n* but cites the passage as an "erroneous" spelling of the term.

3990 This refers to a king's ransom. By comparison Chaucer was ransomed for £16 when he was captured by the French during the Hundred Years War. This was considered a significant amount of money in the fourteenth century.

4028 *Er than he Saber eft ise.* A: *Er than he Beves eft ise.* Kö restores Saber to his role.

4034 *And broughte hit to Mombraunt be southe.* A: *And brouȝt it Mombraunt.* Kö's preposition restores clarity and meter.

4037 *That Beves scholde abegge sore.* A: *abegged sore.* Kö maintains a sensible verb tense: *abegge sore.*

4040 *tan.* A northern form of *taken*, the sense being to "turn attention to" (MED *taken* 23a); "to embrace," "consider," "pick up," "proceed," "perceive a course," "assent," "apply ourselves," or "follow counsel," "take up the thread," or "deliberate."

4054 The purse and staff here signify that Saber is going in the guise of a pilgrim.

4082 *Josian stod in a toret.* A: *Josian stond.*

4088 *Jesu Crist him yilde is mede.* A: *him yilde him his mede.*

4091 *he is in point to spille.* A: *he is point to spille.* Kö's emendation.

4168 As the notes to the earlier romances indicate, time was usually measured according to the monastic offices or prayer services. Prime is the first of the monastic offices, which takes place at 6 a.m. Prime can thus refer specifically to 6 a.m. or to the time between 6 and 9 a.m. Undern refers to the time between 9 a.m. and 1 p.m., or sometimes noon to 3 p.m..

4185 The sense of this is that Bevis' prayers have tamed the valor of Yvor.

4266 *"For God," queth Saber, "that is nought feir."* A: *For god, queþ, that is nought feir.* Other MSS assign the quotation to Saber.

4272 *is owene sone Terry.* That is to say, we are back talking about Saber's own son, not Bevis' sons, who are mentioned in the previous verse.

4437 See note for line 4168.

4453 *Tidinge com to Potenhithe.* A: *Tidynge to potenhiþe.* Kö's emendation.

4469 The Harrowing of Hell is the medieval English term for Christ's descent into hell after His death to defeat the powers of evil. This is also one of the most widely depicted scenes in medieval literature, art, and drama, often vividly presenting Christ opening the jaws of hell-mouth and leading the Old Testament patriarchs and prophets to salvation. See, for example, William Langland's *Piers Plowman* B.XVIII.270 ff. (Skeat 1.538–40) for a powerful Middle English version of this event.

4490 This seems to be an especially roundabout way of saying that they killed them.

4522 ff. *That he ne lai ded upon the grounde. / And whan Beves segh that sighte, / In hertte he was glad and lighte.* The order here is difficult and convoluted. Perhaps it goes something like this: "So that he might get there [without delay], he did not dare ask for a doctor to heal his wound so that he should not lie dead on the ground." The final line here starts to move off on a tangent.

4534 *ledene halle.* Kö capitalizes *Ledene.* MED does cite *Ledynhall* as a specific place name, noting that the place was also called Laurence Hall.

4608 *Sein Lauarauns.* Saint Lawrence died as a deacon and martyr in Rome in 258 A.D. He is usually depicted with a gridiron, on which he was reputed to have been executed by roasting. Relics of St. Lawrence were sent from Rome to King Oswin of Northumbria in the seventh century.

Athelston

Introduction

It would seem that *Athelston*, a relatively brief romance of 812 lines dating from the late fourteenth century, should pose few problems for the modern editor, existing as it does without any known direct source and surviving in only one manuscript. But that is not the case. Rather, this short romance perhaps even more than the longer romances presented in this volume raises a number of questions about historical backgrounds, sources and analogues, the poet's agenda, as well as textual and aesthetic matters. Early scholars, for instance, have seen in it references to events ranging in date from the tenth to the late fourteenth centuries, including the struggle between Henry II and Thomas Becket and the challenge of the barons to Richard II.[1] Still others point to a historical Wymound, found guilty of simony in 1102, or to the events taking place during the reign of King John. The poem's source is also contested. A. M. Trounce claims repeatedly that there is a French original lurking in the archival shadows, despite the obvious local colors, place names, and details of English custom and law.[2] Laura Hibbard Loomis argues that the poem's origin resides in the legend of Queen Emma and the Ploughshares, a story of the mother of Edward the Confessor.[3] A frequently mentioned literary analogue is the Middle English *Amis and Amiloun*, but several of the poem's motifs are common to other works. The diversity of scholarly views on these matters suggests the presence of an amazingly complex intertextuality and interpretive potential for this seemingly simple romance.

Neither is the plot as straightforward as it appears to be at first. Rather, the poem's unfolding of betrayal and treachery is brought to a happy resolution only after a series of deferrals and unveilings, made more suspenseful by the intensified action and heightened

---

[1]In *Athelston: A Middle English Romance*, EETS o.s. 224 (London: Oxford University Press, 1951) A. McI. Trounce argues that Alryke resembles Stephen Langton more than Thomas Becket but also sees a strong historical resemblance between Alryke and William Bateman of Norwich (1344–53).

[2] See also Kurt Beug, "Die Sage von König Athelstan," *Archiv* 148 (1925), 181–95, for a discussion of the relevance of the Queen Emma legend and the existence of a historical Wymound found guilty of simony in 1102.

[3] See Laura Hibbard Loomis, *Mediæval Romance in England: A Study of the Sources and Analogues of the Non-Cycle Metrical Romances* (New York: Burt Franklin, 1960), pp. 143–46.

psychological intrigue, an effect the poet gains by mirroring characters' identities and constructing vivid and dramatic narrative events. The poem begins simply enough: four men, described as messengers, swear an oath of brotherhood and truth to each other. One of them, Athelston, becomes king when the king his cousin dies. Athelston then makes two of his sworn brothers earls and the third Archbishop of Canterbury. Here is where the intrigue begins with something akin to sibling rivalry. One of these earls, the Earl of Stone, remains true to him; the other, however, the Earl of Dover, is false, betraying his brother by accusing him of treachery to the king. The king believes the Earl of Dover, and resolves to kill the alleged traitor and his family, but before he does the queen sends a messenger to the Archbishop who comes to London to plead for the life of his friend. The king first refuses to listen, and there follows a fierce struggle between the king and the archbishop. It seems as though the king is going to win, but he relents when the archbishop gains support from the people. An ordeal by fire establishes the innocence of the Earl of Stone and the guilt of the traitor; the romance ends with the spectacle of the traitor's death.

In his introduction to his edition Donald Sands implies that *Athelston* has an overly high reputation. He suggests that the poem is indeed very impressive on first reading but that the closer one looks, the less one sees.[4] As an introduction to the poem, this is not a bad characterization, suggesting as it does that the poem depends on a kind of surface attraction, which is surely there. But it is probably not an altogether just estimation. Sands is no doubt correct when he states that one will not find overly subtle character portraits in the work, though the credulity of the king, the resoluteness of the archbishop, and the villainy of the traitor all show touches which go beyond simple fairy tale opposition between good and evil. Dieter Mehl is not wrong when he says that the characters are both memorable and individualized.[5]

Not only are the four main characters — Athelston the King, the Earls of Dover and Stone, and the Archbishop — memorable for their powerful positions, personalities, and confrontations with one another, but the supporting characters are also unforgettably drawn. The messenger, who is employed by the king, the queen, and several earls, is described early in the poem as a "foundling" but later, as a "noble man," stands in stark contrast, even acts as an alter-ego, to the king whose name he bears.[6] His stalwart endurance and professional integrity in delivering messages to the right people at the right time despite the grueling distances between stops exposes the lack of steadfastness in the

[4] Donald B. Sands, ed., *Middle English Verse Romances* (New York: Holt, Rinehart, and Winston, 1966), p. 130.

[5] Dieter Mehl, *The Middle English Romances of the Thirteenth and Fourteenth Centuries* (London: Routledge and Kegan Paul, 1968), p. 148.

[6] A. Inskip Dickerson, "The Subplot of the Messenger in *Athelston*," *Papers on Language and Literature* 12 (1976), 121.

king. The messenger does not waiver in his moral obligations — the king does. The very office of messenger resonates with the four main characters; described as messengers from "dyvers cuntré" they come into England to fulfill the obligations of their profession — one of which is the necessity for conveying the truth, the very oath they swear to seal their bond of brotherhood. A subsequent elevation in status — a result of Athelston's fortuitous rise to kingship — confers political power on those who otherwise would not have it and prepares the way for testing the integrity of their oath to one another. The inevitable corruptive forces accompanying such a quick rise in prestige follow, as Wymound soon falls prey to envy; true nobility is not associated with rank and social status, but rather with moral character.

The typical tail-rhyme stanza in *Athelston* consists of four rhymed couplets, each of which is followed by a tail rhyme which remains constant throughout the stanza, so that the rhyme scheme of the twelve-line stanza in the poem is *aab ccb ddb eeb*. Perhaps taking his cue from Chaucer's parody of romance in The Tale of Sir Thopas, Sands is also critical of the rhyme scheme of the work, objecting both to what he sees as the monotony of tail rhyme and also to the apparent inconsistency of several irregular stanzas. Here too his judgment is probably overly harsh. Kevin Kiernan contends that this stanzaic structure helps account for the integrated character of the work and that variations in the poem are purposeful. He stretches his point, perhaps, when he says that the poem is more closely knit than *Sir Gawain and the Green Knight*, but he nonetheless makes a convincing case for the artistry of the work.[7] A. M. Trounce sees tail rhyme as an opportunity to exercise the imagination; poetic diction often generates a number of interpretative possibilities. The tail-rhyme poets also have a flare for the dramatic — the scene of cruelty to the queen, the unrobing and extended trial by ordeal, including the testing of the earl's two sons and pregnant wife, the birth of St. Edmund immediately following the ordeal, the spectacular execution of Wymound, a traitor every bit as treacherous as Ganelon or Judas. His body, singed by fire, hanged, and left dangling by decree, marks the point at which the poet makes his conventional exit.

Like the noble messenger, the female characters are models of integrity and perseverance. Dame Edyff, awaiting the impending birth of a third child when Wymound's false message arrives, refuses to stay at home where safe delivery would be more certain. Rather, she decides to accompany her husband and sons to London in order to witness what she expects to be a great honor. Instead, the entire family is taken into custody at the order of a king whose good judgment, by this time, has been transformed by Wymound's treachery. Despite the hardship of captivity, however, Dame Edyff not only manages to

---

[7] Kevin S. Kiernan, "*Athelston* and the Rhyme of the English Romances," *Modern Language Quarterly* 36 (1975), 340–41.

survive but shortly thereafter endures the onset of labor in the midst of the ordeal by fire. It is only after she has successfully walked over the burning ploughshares that she gives birth to another son, the child-saint Edmund. Just as the deeds of the noble messenger reveal the lack of integrity in Wymound, the birth of Edmund recalls the cruelty of the king to his pregnant wife and her subsequent miscarriage of the rightful heir to the throne. Like Edyff, the queen endures great suffering. Unlike Edyff, however, her purpose in the narrative is to dramatize the extent to which the king has fallen from rational judgment. As Elizabeth Ashman Rowe argues, the queen's miscarriage signifies beyond the tragedy of the event itself; it points directly to the king's miscarriage of justice.[8]

In the struggle between the king and the archbishop, an English audience would no doubt be reminded of the encounter between Henry II and Thomas Becket, the famous conflict which ended with the murder of Becket in 1170. Other probable historical analogues in the poem would include the name Athelston itself (hero of the battle of Brunanburh), and the reference to the birth of St. Edmund (of East Anglia) at the end of the poem. Rowe locates the poem in a specific fourteenth-century context. For Athelston the King we may substitute the tyrannical Richard II, who dispensed with due process for his rivals, whom he then unlawfully imprisoned, exiled, or executed.[9] The specificity of these historical allusions should not allow us to overlook the larger issues which the poem embodies. Indeed, one of the signal strengths of the poem is that the legendary material out of which it is constructed has become the vehicle for embodying some of the large concerns of the Middle Ages. Clearly the most central of these is the relationship between the secular and the ecclesiastical spheres. This struggle provides the central dramatic conflict in the poem in its vivid and energetic presentation of threat and counter threat by king and bishop. Its implications are far wider than the probable specific allusion to the Becket controversy, however much it may follow the contours of that controversy in insisting on distinct limits to royal power and in seeing ecclesiastical privilege as a check on royal tyranny. As W. R. J. Barron has pointed out, the defiance of tyranny in the name of brotherhood and the importance of the rule of law emerge as key themes in the work.[10]

Another of the larger issues is contained in the way the poem handles the question of good and evil. The poem provides a clear statement of the cause of the betrayal of King Athelston and the Earl of Stone. The Earl of Dover committed his sin not out of greed, but out of envy. As he poignantly tells us immediately before his death (speaking of the king's relationship to the Earl of Stone and to himself): "He lovyd him to mekyl and me to

---

[8] Elizabeth Ashman Rowe, "The Female Body Politic and the Miscarriage of Justice in *Athelston*," *Studies in the Age of Chaucer* 17 (1995), 79–98.

[9] Rowe, p. 88.

[10] W. R. J. Barron, *English Medieval Romance* (London: Longman, 1987), p. 81.

lyte; / Therfore envye I hadde" (lines 799–800). At this point, the moral implications are more important than the political ones, or perhaps to put it in slightly different terms, this ending shows us how, as in most significant medieval narratives, the moral and the political cannot be meaningfully separated from each other.

Sands states that the audience of *Athelston* must have been made up of small tradesmen, "very conscious of the history of their country, very well aware of its traditions, and very sensitive to the authoritarian habit of kings."[11] It is not necessary to be quite this restrictive in recreating the audience of *Athelston*, especially since the poem is one of many poems written in English for an emerging, influential middle-class.[12] There is, in fact, some evidence of a middle-class perspective, particularly if we look to the amusing presentation of the hard-working messenger. Of all the characters a middle-class audience might identify with in the poem, he is the most probable, since the king himself, in his rashness, gullibility, and stubbornness, is not especially sympathetic.[13] Whether or not we want to accept this parallel, it should at least open us to the possibility of a work which is very carefully structured and whose structure, like many medieval romances, is dependent on the careful paralleling of large and small units of meaning.

---

[11] Sands, p. 131.

[12] See Derek Pearsall, "The Development of Middle English Romances," *Medieval Studies* 27 (1965), 91–116.

[13] Dickerson, p. 121.

Athelston

Select Bibliography

Manuscript

Caius College Library, Cambridge MS 175. Fols. 120r–31r. [The MS also contains *Richard Coeur de Lyon, Sir Isumbras*, the *Life of St. Catherine*, a short work entitled *Matutinas de cruce, Beves of Hampton*, and *De Spiritu Gurydonis*. *Athelston* appears before *Beves of Hampton*.]

Editions

French, Walter Hoyt, and Charles Brockway Hale, eds. *Middle English Metrical Romances*. New York: Prentice Hall, 1930. Pp. 179–205.

Hartshorne, C. H., ed. "King Athelstone." In *Ancient Metrical Tales*. London: W. Pickering, 1829. Pp. 1–34.

Hervey, Lord Francis, ed. *Corolla Sancti Edmundi: The Garland of Saint Edmund King and Martyr*. New York: E. P. Dutton & Co., 1907. Pp. 525–55.

Sands, Donald B., ed. *Middle English Verse Romances*. New York: Holt, Rinehart, and Winston, 1966. Pp. 130–53.

Trounce, A. McI., ed. *Athelston: A Middle English Romance*. EETS o.s. 224. London: Oxford University Press, 1951. [A critical edition, including comprehensive notes and introductory materials.]

Wright, T., and J. O. Halliwell. *Reliquiae Antiquae*. Vol. 2. London: J. R. Smith, 1845. Pp. 85–103.

Zupitza, J. "Die Romanze von Athelston." *Englische Studien* 13 (1883), 331–414.

Translation

Rickert, Edith. *Early English Romances in Verse*. The New Medieval Library. Vol. 8. New York: Cooper Square Publishers, 1966. Pp. 67–85.

Related Studies

Bennett, J. A. W. "*Havelok; Gamelyn; Athelston; Sir Amadace; Libeaus Desconus.*" In *Middle English Literature*. Ed. Douglas Gray. Oxford: Clarendon Press, 1986. Pp. 154–69.

Beug, Kurt. "Die Sage von König Athelstan." *Archiv* 148 (1925), 181–95. [Admits the relevance of the Queen Emma legend, but points to a historical Wymound, who was found guilty of simony by a Westminster council in 1102.]

Dickerson, A. Inskip. "The Subplot of the Messenger in *Athelston*." *Papers on Language and Literature* 12 (1976), 115–24. [An analysis of the importance of the messenger — intriguingly named Athelston — who provides a kind of moral center to the work, since he stands in contrast to his namesake Athelston the king, who is easily duped and not easily dissuaded from his folly. As a middle-class character, the messenger thus provides the focus for a middle-class audience critical of abuses of royal prerogatives and power.]

Gerould, Gordon Hall. "Social and Historical Reminiscences in the Middle English *Athelston*." *Englische Studien* 36 (1906), 193–208. [Argues that the historical reminiscence is to the famous dispute between Henry II and Thomas Becket, which ended in Becket's death and his subsequent beatification. Becket's cult was widespread by the fourteenth century.]

Hibbard, Laura A. [Loomis]. "*Athelston*, A Westminster Legend." *PMLA* 36 (1921), 223–44. [Argues that the source for the romance is the legendary *Queen Emma and the Ploughshare*, a story disseminated by monastic writers.]

———. *Mediæval Romance in England*. New York: Burt Franklin, 1960. Pp. 143–46. [Places *Athelston* among "legendary English heroes," arguing a strong connection between the fictional hero and the historical Athelstan, King of England from 925–39, conqueror at the Battle of Brunanburh, and the "storied king for whom Guy of Warwick fought with the Danish giant Colbrand."]

Kiernan, Kevin S. "*Athelston* and the Rhyme of the English Romances." *Modern Language Quarterly* 36 (1975), 338–53. [Focuses on the artistry of the tail-rhyme stanza and argues that irregularities in the stanzaic structure in *Athelston* are purposeful, deliberate attempts to marry form and content in the work. Concludes that the work is among the most closely knit of Middle English romances.]

Mehl, Dieter. *The Middle English Romances of the Thirteenth and Fourteenth Centuries*. London: Routledge and Kegan Paul, 1968. Pp. 146–52. [Places *Athelston* within the category of "homiletic romances," and in an analysis which focuses on both the specific details of the romance and on short comparisons with a great many other works in Middle English, concludes that it is "one of the most impressive of the homiletic romances" (p. 152).]

Pearsall, Derek. "The Development of Middle English Romances." *Medieval Studies* 27 (1965), 91–116. [Discusses the "grammar" of romance: formal and literary conventions, social contexts, popular, non-courtly perspectives, and newly emergent bourgeois audience.]

Pigg, Daniel. "The Implications of Realist Poetics in the Middle English *Athelston*." *English Language Notes* 32 (1994), 1–8. [Considers the importance of realist — as opposed to nominalist — sign theory in relation to feudal monarchy. The Earl of Dover's false accusations threaten both the realist understanding of sign and referent and the feudal institutions that such a system of signs upholds.]

Rowe, Elizabeth Ashman. "The Female Body Politic and the Miscarriage of Justice in *Athelston*." *Studies in the Age of Chaucer* 17 (1995), 79–98. [Argues that the poem attacks the tyranny of Richard II, but not monarchy itself; the poem may thus date as late as 1399. Furthermore, *Athelston* uses a female/maternal metaphor for the body politic itself, which becomes silenced within the romance.]

Schmidt, A. V. C., and Nicholas Jacobs. *Medieval English Romances, Part One*. New York: Holmes & Meier, 1980. Pp. 123–50. [General study of select romances.]

Taylor, George. "Notes on *Athelston*." *Leeds SE* 3 (1934), 24–25. [Challenges several emendations made by previous editors.]

Athelston

Lord that is off myghtys most, *powers greatest*
Fadyr and Sone and Holy Gost,
Bryng us out of synne
And lene us grace so for to wyrke *grant*
5 To love bothe God and Holy Kyrke *Church*
That we may hevene wynne.
Lystnes, lordyngys, that ben hende, *gracious*
Of falsnesse, hou it wil ende *will bring about an end to*
A man that ledes hym therin. *a man [who] leads himself*
10 Of foure weddyd bretheryn I wole yow tell *sworn*
That wolden yn Yngelond go dwel,
That sybbe were nought of kyn. *relative; family*

And all foure messangeres they were,
That wolden yn Yngelond lettrys bere,
15 As it wes here kynde. *their occupation*
By a forest gan they mete *did; meet*
With a cros, stood in a strete *by a road*
Be leff undyr a lynde, *By a leaf; linden (tree)*
And, as the story telles me,
20 Ylke man was of dyvers cuntré, *Each; different*
In book iwreten we fynde — *(see note)*
For love of here metyng thare, *their*
They swoor hem weddyd bretheryn for evermare, *themselves*
In trewthe trewely dede hem bynde. *an oath*

25 The eldeste of hem ylkon, *them all*
He was hyght Athelston, *called*
The kyngys cosyn dere;
He was of the kyngys blood, *a [blood] relative*
Hys eemes sone, I undyrstood; *uncle's*
30 Therefore he neyghyd hym nere. *approached*
And at the laste, weel and fayr, *well*

	The kyng him dyyd withouten ayr.	*died; heir*
	Thenne was ther non hys pere	*equal*
	But Athelston, hys eemes sone;	*uncle's*
35	To make hym kyng wolde they nought schone,	*refuse (shun)*
	To corowne hym with gold so clere.	
	Now was he kyng semely to se:	*handsome*
	He sendes afftyr his bretheryn thre	*[sworn] brothers*
	And gaff hem here warysoun.	*them their reward*
40	The eldest brothir he made Eerl of Dovere —	
	And thus the pore man gan covere —	*recover*
	Lord of tour and toun.	*tower*
	That other brother he made Eerl of Stane —	*Stone*
	Egelond was hys name,	
45	A man of gret renoun —	
	And gaff him tyl hys weddyd wyff	*to be*
	Hys owne sustyr, Dame Edyff,	
	With gret devocyoun.	
	The ferthe brothir was a clerk,	*fourth; cleric*
50	Mekyl he cowde of Goddys werk.	*Much; knew*
	Hys name it was Alryke.	
	Cauntyrbury was vacant	
	And fel into that kyngys hand;	
	He gaff it hym that wyke,	*office*
55	And made hym bysschop of that stede,	*place*
	That noble clerk, on book cowde rede —	
	In the world was non hym lyche.	*like*
	Thus avaunsyd he hys brother thorwgh Goddys gras,	*advanced; grace*
	And Athelston hymselven was	
60	A good kyng and a ryche.	*powerful*
	And he that was Eerl of Stane —	
	Sere Egeland was hys name —	
	Was trewe, as ye schal here.	
	Thorwgh the myght off Goddys gras,	*grace*
65	He gat upon the countas	*begat; countess*
	Twoo knave-chyldren dere.	*boys*
	That on was fyfftene wyntyr old,	*years*

	That other thryttene, as men me told:	
	In the world was non here pere —	*their equal*
70	Also whyt so lylye-flour,	*As white as [a] lily flower*
	Red as rose off here colour,	
	As bryght as blosme on brere.	*briar*
	Bothe the Eerl and hys wyff,	
	The kyng hem lovede as hys lyff,	
75	And here sones twoo;	*their*
	And offtensythe he gan hem calle	*often-times*
	Bothe to boure and to halle,	*inner chamber*
	To counsayl whenne they scholde goo.	
	Therat Sere Wymound hadde gret envye,	
80	That Eerle of Dovere, wyttyrlye.	*certainly*
	In herte he was ful woo.	*aggrieved*
	He thoughte al for here sake	*on their account*
	False lesyngys on hem to make,	*lies*
	To don hem brenne and sloo.	*cause them [to be] burned and slain*
85	And thanne Sere Wymound hym bethoughte:	*thought to himself*
	"Here love thus endure may noughte;	*Their*
	Thorwgh wurd oure werk may sprynge."	*Through word; advance*
	He bad hys men maken hem yare;	*ready*
	Unto Londone wolde he fare	*go*
90	To speke with the kynge.	
	Whenne that he to Londone come,	
	He mette with the kyng ful sone.	*right away*
	He sayde, "Welcome, my derelyng."	*friend*
	The kyng hym fraynyd seone anon,	*questioned soon*
95	By what way he hadde igon,	
	Withouten ony dwellyng.	*delaying*
	"Come thou ought by Cauntyrbury,	
	There the clerkys syngen mery	*Where*
	Bothe erly and late?	
100	Hou faryth that noble clerk,	
	That mekyl can on Goddys werk?	*much knows of*
	Knowest thou ought hys state?	*what his condition is*
	And come thou ought be the Eerl of Stane,	*by*

That wurthy lord in hys wane? *residence*
105 Wente thou ought that gate? *out of; way*
Hou fares that noble knyght,
And hys sones fayr and bryght
My sustyr, yiff that thou wate?" *if; know*

"Sere," thanne he sayde, "withouten les, *falsehood*
110 Be Cauntyrbery my way I ches; *chose*
There spak I with that dere. *Where; dear [person]*
Ryght weel gretes thee that noble clerk,
That mykyl can of Goddys werk; *knows much*
In the world is non hys pere. *equal*
115 And also be Stane my way I drowgh; *took*
With Egelond I spak inowgh, *enough*
And with the countesse so clere. *beautiful*
They fare weel, is nought to layne, *well; nothing to conceal*
And bothe here sones." The king was fayne *their; happy*
120 And in his herte made glad chere.

"Sere kyng," he saide, "yiff it be thi wille
To chaumbyr that thou woldest wenden tylle, *go to*
Consayl for to here,
I schal thee telle a swete tydande, *report*
125 There comen nevere non swyche in this lande *such*
Of all this hundryd yere."
The kyngys herte than was ful woo *sad*
With that traytour for to goo;
They wente bothe forth in fere; *together*
130 And whenne that they were the chaumbyr withinne,
False lesyngys he gan begynne *lies; began*
On hys weddyd brother dere.

"Sere kyng," he saide, "woo were me,
Ded that I scholde see thee, *Dead; [it] should*
135 So moot I have my lyff! *As I may*
For by Hym that al this worl wan, *world redeemed*
Thou has makyd me a man,
And iholpe me for to thryff. *helped; thrive*
For in thy land, sere, is a fals traytour.

140 He wole doo thee mykyl dyshonour — *much*
And brynge thee of lyve. — *kill you*
He wole deposen thee slyly, — *depose you*
Sodaynly than schalt thou dy — *Suddenly*
By Chrystys woundys fyve!"

145 Thenne sayde the kyng, "So moot thou the, — *might; thrive*
Knowe I that man, and I hym see? — *if I*
His name thou me telle."
"Nay," says that traytour, "that wole I nought
For al the gold that evere was wrought —
150 Be masse-book and belle —
But yiff thou me thy trowthe will plyght — *Unless; vow; pledge*
That thou schalt nevere bewreye the knyght — *betray*
That thee the tale schal telle." — *[to] you*
Thanne the kyng his hand up raughte, — *raised*
155 That false man his trowthe betaughte, — *faith entrusted*
He was a devyl of helle!

"Sere kyng," he sayde, "thou madyst me knyght,
And now thou hast thy trowthe me plyght — *pledged*
Oure counsayl for to layne: — *conceal*
160 Sertaynly, it is non othir
But Egelane, thy weddyd brothir —
He wolde that thou were slayne; — *wishes*
He dos thy sustyr to undyrstand
He wole be kyng of thy lande,
165 And thus he begynnes here trayne. — *to lead her astray*
He wole thee poysoun ryght slyly;
Sodaynly thanne schalt thou dy,
By Him that suffryd payne."

Thanne swoor the kyng be Cros and Roode: — *Cross*
170 "Meete ne drynk schal do me goode — *[Neither] food*
Tyl that he be dede;
Bothe he and hys wyf, hys soones twoo,
Schole they nevere be no moo
In Yngelond on that stede." — *place*
175 "Nay," says the traytour, "so moot I the, — *thrive*

Ded wole I nought my brother se;
  But do thy beste rede." *advice*
No lengere there then wolde he lende; *remain*
He takes hys leve, to Dovere gan wende. *began to go*
180 God geve hym schame and dede! *death*

Now is that traytour hom iwent.
A messanger was afftyr sent *afterward*
  To speke with the kyng.
I wene he bar his owne name: *believe; bore*
185 He was hoten Athelstane; *called*
  He was foundelyng. *a foundling*
The lettrys were imaad fullyche thare, *fully there*
Unto Stane for to fare *go*
  Withouten ony dwellyng, *delaying*
190 To fette the eerl and his sones twoo, *fetch*
And the countasse alsoo,
  Dame Edyve, that swete thyng.

And in the lettre yit was it tolde, *also*
That the kyng the eerlys sones wolde
195 Make hem bothe knyght;
And therto his seel he sette. *seal*
The messanger wolde nought lette; *delay*
  The way he rydes ful ryght.

The messanger, the noble man,
200 Takes hys hors and forth he wan, *went*
  And hyes a ful good spede. *hastens*
The eerl in hys halle he fande; *found*
He took hym the lettre in his hande
  Anon he bad hym rede: *bade*
205 "Sere," he sayde also swythe, *quickly*
"This lettre oughte to make thee blythe: *glad*
  Thertoo thou take good hede. *heed*
The kyng wole for the cuntas sake *countess'*
Bothe thy sones knyghtes make —
210 To London I rede thee spede. *advise; hurry*

	The kyng wole for the cuntas sake	
	Bothe thy sones knyghtes make,	
	The blythere thou may be.	*happier*
	Thy fayre wyff with thee thou bryng —	
215	And ther be ryght no lettyng —	*delaying*
	That syghte that sche may see."	
	Thenne sayde that eerl with herte mylde,	
	"My wyff goth ryght gret with chylde,	
	And forthynkes me,	*I regret [that]*
220	Sche may nought out of chaumbyr wyn,	*go*
	To speke with non ende of here kyn	*no part*
	Tyl sche delyveryd be."	
	But into chaumbyr they gunne wende,	*began to go*
	To rede the lettrys before that hende	*courteous lady*
225	And tydingys tolde here soone.	
	Thanne sayde the cuntasse, "So moot I the,	*thrive*
	I wil nought lette tyl I there be,	*stop*
	Tomorwen or it be noone.	*before*
	To see hem knyghtes, my sones fre,	*noble*
230	I wole nought lette tyl I there be;	
	I schal no lengere dwelle.	*delay*
	Cryst foryelde my lord the kyng,	*requite*
	That has grauntyd hem here dubbyng.	*their dubbing*
	Myn herte is gladyd welle."	
235	The eerl hys men bad make hem yare;	*ready*
	He and hys wyff forth gunne they fare,	*began to go*
	To London faste they wente.	
	At Westemynstyr was the kyngys wone;	*dwelling*
	There they mette with Athelstone,	
240	That afftyr hem hadde sente.	*Who*
	The goode eerl soone was hent	*seized*
	And feteryd faste, verrayment,	*chained; truly*
	And hys sones twoo.	
	Ful lowde the countasse gan to crye,	
245	And sayde, "Goode brothir, mercy!	

Why wole ye us sloo? — *slay*
What have we ayens yow done, — *against*
That ye wole have us ded so soone?
Me thynkith ye arn ourn foo." — *enemy*
250 The kyng as wood ferde in that stede; — *insane behaved; place*
He garte hys sustyr to presoun lede — — *ordered*
In herte he was ful woo.

Thenne a squyer, was the countasses frende, — *friend*
To the qwene he gan wende, — *did go*
255 And tydyngys tolde here soone.
Gerlondes of chyryes off sche caste, — *Garlands of cherries; off*
Into the halle sche come at the laste,
Longe or it were noone. — *before*
"Sere kyng, I am before thee come
260 With a child, doughtyr or a sone.
Graunte me my bone, — *request*
My brothir and sustyr that I may borwe — *act as surety for*
Tyl the nexte day at morwe,
Out of here paynys stronge; — *pain*

265 That we mowe wete by comoun sent — *might know by unanimous assent*
In the playne parlement."
"Dame," he saide, "goo fro me!
Thy bone shall nought igraunted be, — *request (boon)*
I doo thee to undyrstande.
270 For, be Hym that weres the corowne of thorn, — *by; wears*
They schole be drawen and hangyd tomorn,
Yyff I be kyng of lande!"

And whenne the qwene these wurdes herde,
As sche hadde be beten with yerde, — *been; stick*
275 The teeres sche leet doun falle. — *let*
Sertaynly, as I yow telle,
On here bare knees doun she felle,
And prayde yit for hem alle.
"A, dame," he sayde, "verrayment — *truly*
280 Hast thou broke my comaundement — *[If] you have broken*
Abyyd ful dere thou schalle." — *Pay for*

	With hys foot — he wolde nought wonde —	*refrain*
	He slowgh the chyld ryght in here wombe;	*slew; her*
	She swownyd amonges hem alle.	*swooned*
285	Ladyys and maydenys that there were,	
	The qwene to here chaumbyr bere,	*bore*
	And there was dool inowgh.	*dole (sorrow) enough*
	Soone withinne a lytyl spase	*space of time*
	A knave-chyld iborn ther wase,	*miscarried*
290	As bryght as blosme on bowgh.	
	He was bothe whyt and red;	
	Of that dynt was he ded —	*From that blow; dead*
	His owne fadyr hym slowgh!	*slew*
	Thus may a traytour baret rayse	*strife raise*
295	And make manye men ful evele at ayse,	*ill at ease*
	Hymselff nought afftyr it lowgh.	*after; laughed (see note)*
	But yit the qwene, as ye schole here,	
	Sche callyd upon a messangere,	
	Bad hym a lettre fonge.	*take*
300	And bad hym wende to Cauntyrbery,	*go*
	There the clerkys syngen mery	*Where*
	Bothe masse and evensonge.	
	"This lettre thou the bysschop take,	
	And praye hym for Goddys sake,	
305	Come borewe hem out off here bande.	*rescue; bonds*
	He wole doo more for hym, I wene,	*believe*
	Thanne for me, though I be qwene —	
	I doo thee to undyrstande.	
	An eerldom in Spayne I have of land;	
310	Al I sese into thyn hand,	*give as a possession*
	Trewely, as I thee hyght,	*promise*
	And hundryd besauntys of gold red.	*besant (a coin)*
	Thou may save hem from the ded,	*death*
	Yyff that thyn hors be wyght."	*valiant*
315	"Madame, brouke weel thy moregeve,	*use; morning gift*
	Also longe as thou may leve.	*live*
	Therto have I no ryght.	

But of thy gold and of thy fee, *property*
Cryst in hevene foryelde it thee; *reward*
320 I wole be there tonyght.

Madame, thrytty myles of hard way *thirty miles*
I have reden syth it was day. *since*
Ful sore I gan me swynke; *work*
And for to ryde now fyve and twenti thertoo
325 An hard thyng it were to doo,
Forsothe, ryght as me thynke.
Madame, it is nerhande passyd prime, *nearly past six a.m.*
And me behoves al for to dyne,
Bothe wyn and ale to drynke.
330 Whenne I have dynyd, thenne wole I fare.
God may covere hem of here care, *relieve; their*
Or that I slepe a wynke." *Before*

Whenne he hadde dynyd, he wente his way,
Also faste as that he may,
335 He rod be Charynge-cross *Charing Cross*
And entryd into Flete-strete *Fleet Street*
And sithen thorwgh Londone, I yow hete, *promise*
Upon a noble hors.
The messanger, that noble man,
340 On Loundone-brygge sone he wan — *London bridge; reached*
For his travayle he hadde no los — *work; praise (fame)*
From Stone into Steppyngebourne,
Forsothe, his way nolde he nought tourne; *not alter*
Sparyd he nought for myre ne mos. *mud nor bog*

345 And thus hys way wendes he
Fro Osprynge to the Blee.
Thenne myghte he see the toun
Of Cauntyrbery, that noble wyke, *place*
Therin lay that bysschop ryke, *powerful*
350 That lord of gret renoun.

And whenne they runggen undernbelle, *morning bell*
He rod in Londone, as I yow telle:

He was non er redy; *earlier*
And yit to Cauntyrbery he wan, *reached*
355 Longe or evensong began; *before six p.m.*
He rod mylys fyffty. *fifty miles*

The messanger nothing abod; *delayed*
Into the palays forth he rod,
There that the bysschop was inne.
360 Ryght welcome was the messanger,
That was come from the qwene so cleer, *radiant*
Was of so noble kynne.
He took hym a lettre ful good speed *such*
And saide, "Sere bysschop, have this and reed," *take; read*
365 And bad hym come with hym.
Or he the lettre hadde halff iredde, *Before; read*
For dool, hym thoughte hys herte bledde; *sorrow*
The teeres fyl ovyr hys chyn. *chin*

The bysschop bad sadele hys palfray:
370 "Also faste as thay may, *As*
Bydde my men make hem yare; *themselves ready*
And wendes before," the bysschop dede say, *go before*
"To my maneres in the way; *manors*
For nothyng that ye spare,
375 And loke at ylke fyve mylys ende *each*
A fresch hors that I fynde,
Schod and nothing bare; *Shod*
Blythe schal I nevere be,
Tyl I my weddyd brother see,
380 To kevere hym out of care." *recover*

On nyne palfrays the bysschop sprong, *nine*
Ar it was day, from evensong — *Before*
In romaunce as we rede.
Sertaynly, as I yow telle,
385 On Londone-brygge ded doun felle *dead*
The messangeres stede. *messenger's horse*
"Allas," he sayde, "that I was born!
Now is my goode hors forlorn, *utterly lost*

	Was good at ylke a nede;	*at each need*
390	Yistyrday upon the grounde,	
	He was wurth an hundryd pounde,	
	Ony kyng to lede."	
	Thenne bespak the erchebysschop.	*archbishop*
	Oure gostly fadyr undyr God,	*spiritual*
395	Unto the messangere:	
	"Lat be thy menyng of thy stede,	*Desist your lamenting; horse*
	And thynk upon oure mykyl nede,	*great need*
	The whylys that we ben here;	
	For yiff that I may my brother borwe	*save*
400	And bryngen hym out off mekyl sorwe,	*great*
	Thou may make glad chere;	
	And thy warysoun I schal thee geve,	*reward (see note)*
	And God have grauntyd thee to leve	*Even if*
	Unto an hundryd yere."	
405	The bysschop thenne nought ne bod:	*remained no longer*
	He took hys hors, and forth he rod	
	Into Westemynstyr so lyght;	*nimbly*
	The messanger on his foot alsoo:	
	With the bysschop come no moo,	*no others*
410	Nether squyer ne knyght.	
	Upon the morwen the kyng aros,	
	And takes the way, to the kyrke he gos,	*church*
	As man of mekyl myght.	
	With hym wente bothe preest and clerk,	
415	That mykyl cowde of Goddys werk,	*Who knew much*
	To praye God for the ryght.	
	Whenne that he to the kyrke com;	
	Tofore the Rode he knelyd anon,	*Cross*
	And on hys knees he felle:	
420	"God, that syt in Trynyté	
	A bone that thou graunte me,	*boon (i.e., favor)*
	Lord, as Thou harewyd helle —	*harrowed*
	Gyltless men yiff thay be,	*Guiltless; if they*
	That are in my presoun free,	

425 Forcursyd there to yelle, — *Condemned; shriek*
Of the gylt and thay be clene, — *if; innocent*
Leve it moot on hem be sene, — *Grant; seen [by them]*
That garte hem there to dwelle." — *Who made them to dwell there*

And whenne he hadde maad his prayer,
430 He lokyd up into the qweer; — *choir*
The erchebysschop sawgh he stande.
He was forwondryd of that caas, — *astonished at; situation*
And to hym he wente apas, — *quickly*
And took hym be the hande. — *by; hand*
435 "Welcome," he sayde, "thou erchebysschop,
Oure gostly fadyr undyr God." — *spiritual*
He swoor be God levande, — *by; living*
"Weddyd brother, weel moot thou spede, — *prosper*
For I hadde nevere so mekyl nede,
440 Sith I took cros on hande. — *Since*

Goode weddyd brother, now turne thy rede; — *change your mind*
Doo nought thyn owne blood to dede — *[cause] to die*
But yiff it wurthy were. — *Unless*
For Hym that weres the corowne of thorn,
445 Lat me borwe hem tyl tomorn, — *be surety for*
That we mowe enquere, — *might have an inquiry*
And weten alle be comoun asent — *know; agreement*
In the playne parlement — *full*
Who is wurthy be schent. — *punished*
450 And, but yiff ye wole graunte my bone,
It schal us rewe bothe or none, — *grieve us both; before noon*
Be God that alle thyng lent." — *gave*

Thanne the kyng wax wrothe as wynde, — *grew angry; wind*
A wodere man myghte no man fynde — *An angrier*
455 Than he began to bee:
He swoor othis be sunne and mone: — *oaths by; moon*
"They scholen be drawen and hongyd or none — — *before noon*
With eyen thou schalt see! — *eyes*
Lay doun thy cros and thy staff,
460 Thy mytyr and thy ryng that I thee gaff; — *mitre*

Out of my land thou flee!
Hyghe thee faste out of my syght! *Get*
Wher I thee mete, thy deth is dyght; *decided*
Non othir then schal it bee!"

465 Thenne bespak that erchebysschop,
Oure gostly fadyr undyr God, *spiritual*
Smertly to the kyng: *Sharply*
"Weel I wot that thou me gaff *know*
Bothe the cros and the staff,
470 The mytyr and eke the ryng; *also*
My bysschopryche thou reves me, *bishopric; deny*
And Crystyndom forbede I thee! *forbid*
Preest schal ther non syngge;
Neyther maydynchyld ne knave *girl; boy*
475 Crystyndom schal ther non have;
To care I schal thee brynge.

I schal gare crye thorwgh ylke a toun *proclaim*
That kyrkys schole be broken doun *churches*
And stoken agayn with thorn. *stuck*
480 And thou shalt lygge in an old dyke, *lie; ditch*
As it were an heretyke, *if you; heretic*
Allas that thou were born!

Yiff thou be ded, that I may see,
Assoylyd schalt thou nevere bee; *Absolved*
485 Thanne is thy soule in sorwe.
And I schal wende in uncouthe lond, *go; unknown*
And gete me stronge men of hond;
My brothir yit schal I borwe. *save*
I schal brynge upon thy lond
490 Hungyr and thyrst ful strong,
Cold, drougthe, and sorwe;
I schal nought leve on thy lond *leave*
Wurth the gloves on thy hond *Worth*
To begge ne to borwe."

495	The bysschop has his leve tan.	*leave taken*
	By that his men were comen ylkan:	*each one*
	They sayden, "Sere, have good day."	
	He entryd into Flete-strete;	
	With lordys of Yngelond gan he mete	
500	Upon a noble aray.	
	On here knees they kneleden adoun,	
	And prayden hym of hys benysoun,	*blessing*
	He nykkyd hem with nay.	*refused them by saying no*
	Neyther of cros neyther of ryng	
505	Hadde they non kyns wetyng;	*kind of knowing*
	And thanne a knyght gan say.	*began to speak*
	A knyght thanne spak with mylde voys:	*mild voice*
	"Sere, where is thy ryng? Where is thy croys?	*cross*
	Is it fro thee tan?"	*taken*
510	Thanne he sayde, "Youre cursyd kyng	
	Hath me refft of al my thyng,	*bereft*
	And of al my worldly wan;	*goods*
	And I have entyrdytyd Yngelond:	*interdicted England*
	Ther schal no preest synge Masse with hond,	*celebrate Mass*
515	Chyld schal be crystenyd non,	*No child shall be christened*
	But yiff he graunte me that knyght,	*Unless; release to me*
	His wyff and chyldryn fayr and bryght:	
	He wolde with wrong hem slon."	*slay*
	The knyght sayde, "Bysschop, turne agayn;	
520	Of thy body we are ful fayn;	*glad*
	Thy brothir yit schole we borwe.	*rescue*
	And, but he graunte us oure bone,	
	Hys presoun schal be broken soone,	*violated*
	Hymselff to mekyl sorwe.	*[driven] to great*
525	We schole drawe doun both halle and boures,	*chambers*
	Bothe hys castelles and hys toures,	
	They schole lygge lowe and holewe.	*razed*
	Though he be kyng and were the corown,	*wear*
	We scholen hym sette in a deep dunjoun:	*dungeon*
530	Oure Crystyndom we wole folewe."	

	Thanne, as they spoken of this thyng,	
	Ther comen twoo knyghtes from the kyng,	
	And sayden, "Bysschop, abyde,	*wait*
	And have thy cros and thy ryng,	
535	And welcome whyl that thou wylt lyng,	*stay*
	It is nought for to hyde.	
	Here he grauntys thee the knyght,	
	Hys wyff and chyldryn fayr and bryght;	
	Again I rede thou ryde.	*advise you return*
540	He prayes thee pur charyté	*by pure charity*
	That he myghte asoylyd be,	*absolved*
	And Yngelond long and wyde."	
	Hereof the bysschop was ful fayn,	*Of this; eager*
	And turnys hys brydyl and wendes agayn —	
545	Barouns gunne with hym ryde —	*did*
	Unto the Brokene-cros of ston;	
	Thedyr com the kyng ful soone anon,	
	And there he gan abyde.	
	Upon hys knees he knelyd adoun,	
550	And prayde the bysschop of benysoun,	*for blessing*
	And he gaff hym that tyde.	*gave it to him*
	With holy watyr and orysoun,	*prayer*
	He asoylyd the kyng that weryd the coroun,	*absolved; who wore*
	And Yngelond long and wyde.	
555	Than sayde the kyng anon ryght:	
	"Here I graunte thee that knyght,	
	And hys sones free,	*noble*
	And my sustyr hende in halle.	*courteous*
	Thou hast savyd here lyvys alle:	*their lives*
560	Iblessyd moot thou bee."	
	Thenne sayde the bysschop also soone:	
	"And I schal geven swylke a dome —	*judgment*
	With eyen that thou schalt see!	*your own eyes*
	Yiff thay be gylty off that dede,	
565	Sorrere the doome thay may drede,	*More grievous*
	Thanne schewe here schame to me."	

	Whanne the bysschop hadde sayd soo,	
	A gret fyr was maad ryght thoo,	*fire; immediately*
	In romaunce as we rede —	
570	It was set, that men myghte knawe,	*know*
	Nyne plowgh-lengthe on rawe,	*ploughshares; in a row*
	As red as ony glede.	*coal*
	Thanne sayde the kyng: "What may this mene?"	
	"Sere, of gylt and thay be clene,	*from; if; innocent*
575	This doom hem thar nought drede."	*ordeal; need not fear*
	Thanne sayde the good Kyng Athelston:	
	"An hard doome now is this on:	*judgment; one*
	God graunte us alle weel to spede."	*succeed*
	They fetten forth Sere Egelan —	*fetched*
580	A trewere eerl was ther nan —	*truer; none*
	Before the fyr so bryght.	
	From hym they token the rede scarlet,	
	Bothe hosyn and schoon that weren hym met,	*hose; shoes; suitable*
	That fel al for a knyght.	*were appropriate*
585	Nyne sythe the bysschop halewid the way	*times; consecrated*
	That his weddyd brother scholde goo that day,	
	To praye God for the ryght.	
	He was unblemeschyd foot and hand;	
	That sawgh the lordes of the land,	
590	And thankyd God of Hys myght.	
	They offeryd him with mylde chere	*gentle bearing*
	Unto Saint Powlys heyghe awtere,	*Paul's; altar*
	That mekyl was of myght.	
	Doun upon hys knees he felle,	
595	And thankyd God that harewede helle	*harrowed*
	And Hys modyr so bryght.	
	And yit the bysschop tho gan say:	*then*
	"Now schal the chyldryn gon the way	
	That the fadyr yede."	*went*
600	Fro hem they tooke the rede scarlete,	
	The hosen and schoon that weren hem mete,	*shoes; fit*
	And al here worldly wede.	*clothes*

	The fyr was bothe hydous and rede,	*hideous*
	The chyldryn swownyd as they were ded;	*as if*
605	The bysschop tyl hem yede;	*to them went*
	With careful herte on hem gan look;	
	Be hys hand he hem up took:	
	"Chyldryn, have ye no drede."	*fear*
	Thanne the chyldryn stood and lowgh:	*laughed*
610	"Sere, the fyr is cold inowgh."	
	Thorwghout they wente apase.	*quickly*
	They weren unblemeschyd foot and hand:	
	That sawgh the lordys of the land,	
	And thankyd God of His grace.	
615	They offeryd hem with mylde chere	
	To Seynt Poulys hyghe awtere	
	This myracle schewyd was there.	*miracle*
	And yit the bysschop efft gan say:	*again*
	"Now schal the countasse goo the way	
620	There that the chyldryn were."	
	They fetten forth the lady mylde;	*fetched*
	Sche was ful gret igon with chylde	*very pregnant*
	In romaunce as we rede —	
	Before the fyr whan that sche come,	
625	To Jesu Cryst he prayde a bone,	*favor*
	That leet His woundys blede:	
	"Now, God lat nevere the kyngys foo	
	Quyk out of the fyr goo."	*Alive*
	Therof hadde sche no drede.	
630	Whenne sche hadde maad here prayer,	
	Sche was brought before the feer,	*fire*
	That brennyd bothe fayr and lyght.	*burned*
	Sche wente fro the lengthe into the thrydde;	*end; third [ploughshare]*
	Stylle sche stood the fyr amydde,	
635	And callyd it merye and bryght.	
	Hard schourys thenne took here stronge	*[labor] pains*
	Bothe in bak and eke in wombe;	*back; also*
	And sithen it fell at syght.	*(see note)*

Whenne that here paynys slakyd was, *After; pain abated*
640 And sche hadde passyd that hydous pas, *walk*
Here nose barst on bloode. *burst*
Sche was unblemeschyd foot and hand:
That sawgh the lordys of the land,
And thankyd God on Rode. *Cross*
645 They comaundyd men here away to drawe, *move away from here*
As it was the landys lawe; *law of the land (customary)*
And ladyys thanne tyl here yode. *to her went*
She knelyd doun upon the ground
And there was born Seynt Edemound:
650 Iblessed be that foode! *child*

And whanne this chyld iborn was,
It was brought into the plas; *place*
It was bothe hool and sound *whole (healthy)*
Bothe the kyng and bysschop free *noble*
655 They crystnyd the chyld, that men myght see, *christened*
And callyd it Edemound. *Edmund*
"Halff my land," he sayde, "I thee geve,
Also longe as I may leve, *As*
With markys and with pounde; *marks*
660 And al afftyr my dede — *death*
Yngelond to wysse and rede." *guide; advise*
Now iblessyd be that stounde! *time*

Thanne sayde the bysschop to the Kyng:
"Sere, who made this grete lesyng, *lie*
665 And who wroughte al this bale?" *evil*
Thanne sayde the kyng, "So moot I thee, *thrive*
That schalt thou nevere wete for me, *know*
In burgh neyther in sale; *town; hall*
For I have sworn be Seynt Anne
670 That I schal nevere bewreye that manne, *betray*
That me gan telle that tale.
They arn savyd thorwgh thy red; *are; counsel*
Now lat al this be ded, *dead*
And kepe this counseyl hale." *hold (keep secret); entirely*

675 Thenne swoor the bysschop, "So moot I the,	*thrive*
Now I have power and dignyté	
For to asoyle thee as clene	*absolve; guiltless*
As thou were hoven off the fount-ston.	*lifted from; baptismal font*
Trustly trowe thou therupon,	*Truly believe*
680 And holde it for no wene:	*guess*
I swere bothe be book and belle,	
But yiff thou me his name telle,	*Unless*
The ryght doom schal I deme:	*judgment; pronounce*
Thyselff schalt goo the ryghte way	
685 That thy brother wente today,	
Though it thee evele beseme."	*ill befits you*
Thenne sayde the kyng, "So moot I the,	*thrive*
Be schryffte of mouthe telle I it thee;	*By confession*
Therto I am unblyve.	*reluctant*
690 Sertaynly, it is non othir	
But Wymound, oure weddyd brother;	*sworn*
He wole nevere thryve."	
"Allas," sayde the bysschop than,	
I wende he were the treweste man,	*thought*
695 That evere yit levyd on lyve.	
And he with this ateynt may bee,	*If; guilty*
He schal be hongyd on trees three,	
And drawen with hors fyve."	*horses*
And whenne that the bysschop the sothe hade	*truth*
700 That that traytour that lesyng made,	*lie*
He callyd a messangere,	
Bad hym to Dovere that he scholde founde,	*hasten*
For to fette that Eerl Wymounde:	*fetch*
(That traytour has no pere!)	
705 Sey Egelane and hys sones be slawe,	
Bothe ihangyd and to-drawe.	
(Doo as I thee lere!)	*teach*
The countasse is in presoun done;	
Schal sche nevere out of presoun come,	
710 But yiff it be on bere."	*Unless; bier*

	Now with the messanger was no badde;	*delay*
	He took his hors, as the bysschop radde,	*commanded*
	To Dovere tyl that he come.	
	The eerl in hys halle he fand:	*found*
715	He took hym the lettre in his hand	
	On hygh, wolde he nought wone:	*In haste; delay*
	"Sere Egelane and his sones be slawe,	
	Bothe ihangyd and to-drawe:	
	Thou getyst that eerldome.	
720	The countasse is in presoun done;	
	Schal sche nevere more out come,	
	Ne see neyther sunne ne mone."	
	Thanne that eerl made hym glade,	
	And thankyd God that lesyng was made:	*lie*
725	"It hath gete me this eerldome."	
	He sayde, "Felawe, ryght weel thou bee!	
	Have here besauntys good plenté	*besants (coins)*
	For thyn hedyr-come."	*coming hither*
	Thanne the messanger made his mon:	*complaint*
730	"Sere, of youre goode hors lende me on:	*one*
	Now graunte me my bone;	
	For yystyrday deyde my nobyl stede,	*died*
	On youre arende as I yede,	*business; went*
	Be the way as I come."	
735	"Myn hors be fatte and cornfed,	
	And of thy lyff I am adred."	*anxious*
	That eerl sayde to him than,	
	"Thanne yiff min hors sholde thee sloo,	*slay*
	My lord the kyng wolde be ful woo	
740	To lese swylk a man."	*lose; such*
	The messanger yit he broughte a stede,	
	On of the beste at ylke a nede	*One; this very need*
	That evere on grounde dede gange,	*go*
	Sadelyd and brydelyd at the beste.	
745	The messanger was ful preste,	*ready*
	Wyghtly on hym he sprange.	*With agility*

"Sere," he sayde, "have good day;
Thou schalt come whan thou may;
I schal make the kyng at hande." — *aware*
750 With sporys faste he strook the stede; — *spurs; struck*
To Gravysende he come good spede,
Is fourty myle to fande. — *travel*

There the messanger the traytour abood, — *awaited*
And sethyn bothe insame they rod — *then; together*
755 To Westemynstyr wone. — *town*
In the palays there thay lyght; — *alighted*
Into the halle they come ful ryght, — *immediately*
And mette with Athelstone.
He wolde have kyssyd his lord swete.
760 He sayde: "Traytour, nought yit! lete! — *[allow] it not! desist!*
Be God and be Seynt Jhon! — *John*
For thy falsnesse and thy lesyng — *Because of*
I slowgh myn heyr, scholde have ben kyng, — *heir*
When my lyf hadde ben gon."

765 There he denyyd faste the kyng, — *strongly denied*
That he made nevere that lesyng, — *ever made that lie*
Among hys peres alle.
The bysschop has hym be the hand tan; — *taken*
Forth insame they are gan — *together*
770 Into the wyde halle.
Myghte he nevere with crafft ne gynne, — *trick*
Gare hym shryven of hys synne, — *Have himself absolved*
For nought that myghte befalle.
Thenne sayde the goode Kyng Athelston:
775 "Lat hym to the fyr gon,
To preve the trewthe with alle."

Whenne the kyng hadde sayd soo,
A gret fyr was maad thoo, — *then*
In romaunce as we rede.
780 It was set, that men myghten knawe,
Nyne plowgh-lenge on rawe, — *lengths; row*
As red as ony glede. — *coal*

	Nyne sythis the bysschop halewes the way	*times; blessed*
	That that traytour schole goo that day:	
785	The wers him gan to spede.	*worse; happened*
	He wente fro the lengthe into the thrydde,	
	And doun he fell the fyr amydde:	
	Hys eyen wolde hym nought lede.	*lead (guide)*
	Than the eerlys chyldryn were war ful smerte,	*fully aware*
790	And wyghtly to the traytour sterte,	*quickly; ran*
	And out of the fyr him hade;	
	And sworen bothe be book and belle:	
	"Or that thou deye, thou schalt telle	*Before*
	Why thou that lesyng made."	*made that lie*
795	"Certayn, I can non other red,	*know no other*
	Now I wot I am but ded:	*nearly dead*
	I telle yow nothyng gladde —	*reluctantly (without joy)*
	Certayn, ther was non other wyte:	*injury*
	He lovyd him to mekyl and me to lyte;	*much; little*
800	Therfore envye I hadde."	
	Whenne that traytour so hadde sayde,	
	Fyve good hors to hym were tayde,	*tied*
	Alle men myghten see with yghe —	*eye*
	They drowen him thorwgh ylke a strete,	*drew; each*
805	And sethyn to the Elmes, I yow hete,	*then; assure*
	And hongyd him ful hyghe.	
	Was ther nevere man so hardy,	*bold*
	That durste felle hys false body:	*dared take down*
	This hadde he for hys lye.	
810	Now Jesu, that is Hevene-kyng,	
	Leve nevere traytour have betere endyng,	*better*
	But swych dome for to dye.	*judgment*

Explicit

Notes

Abbreviations: C: Caius College Library, Cambridge, MS 175; F&H: French and Hale; Tr: Trounce; Sa: Sands; Z: Zupitza

1–6 The invocation is typical of tail-rhyme romances. Tr notes the similarity in two ME Breton lays — *Sir Gowther* and *Emaré*. Chaucer's The Tale of Sir Thopas offers an amusing send up of exhortations to pay attention.

6 *That we may hevene wynne*. C: *That may heven wynne*. Z adds *we*; Tr follows, as do F&H. The addition maintains the integrity of the meter and heals a headless clause.

8 *Of*. C: *Off*. F&H note that the copyist is "prodigal with the letter F, frequently doubling it after a long vowel (*wyff*), and using it initially when no capital could have been intended" (p. 179). But he also does so after short vowels as in *affter* and *gyff*. We have reduced double *ff* to simple *f* in all instances of *of*, to clarify the distinction between *of* and *off*, which in C are spelled the same way.

9 *A man that ledes hym therin*. As Tr notes, *man* is dative, *hym* reflexive. Thus the invocation requests listeners to pay attention to the consequences of disloyalty, a theme that is central to the poem.

10 *weddyd bretheryn*. Sworn brotherhood or "blood" brotherhood, as it is sometimes called, is an ancient custom, whereby men bound themselves with an oath to be faithful to each other till death. Herodotus reports, for example, that the Scythians participated in a ritual whereby they cut their fingers, let the blood run into a chalice, dipped the tips of their swords in the blood, and drank it (see John Boswell, *Same Sex Unions in Pre-Modern Europe* [New York: Villard Books, 1994], p. 94). Tr notes that this bond among men was "superior to the marriage tie," evidence of which appears in lines 306–07 when the calumniated queen expresses the disparity between these two oaths of loyalty, expecting that the bishop will honor the king before he will honor her: *He wole doo more for hym, I wene, / Thanne for me, though I be qwene*.

John Boswell also notes the multiple meanings for the term: in fact, the relationships called "blood brotherhood," "sworn-brotherhood," "spiritual brotherhood" and so on, vary enormously from culture to culture (and sometimes within a single society) in their mode of formation, in their social, legal, and religious significance, and in their personal (e.g., affective) aspects" (p. 272). Sworn brotherhood is also a central theme in *Amis and Amiloun*, the analogue Tr considers so closely related to *Athelston*. Elizabeth Ashman Rowe sees the phrase "sworn brother" as a cynical substitution for an "opportunistic brotherhood" who "join in pursuit of political opportunity rather than economic profit" (p. 81). Rowe compares this alliance to the false brotherhood of Chaucer's The Pardoner's Tale.

11 *That wolden yn Yngelond go dwel.* Z emends to *wilen yn Yngelond gon dwel.* Tr rejects Z's emendation on the grounds that the "phrase 'of dyvers cuntre' [in line] 20 strengthens the idea of strangers from widely separated parts meeting and joining themselves in brotherhood" (pp. 93–94). Because sworn-brotherhood is a central theme of the poem, Tr's return to the MS has been retained. George Taylor, "Notes on *Athelston*," suggests that *wilen* is preferred in line 11, while *wolden* is preferable for line 14: "to assume that the messengers were foreigners, as does T[rounce] only leads to further difficulties" (p. 20).

17 Wayside crosses were common in the Middle Ages, though here there is undoubtedly added religious significance, since the poem is preoccupied with ecclesiastical authority, *Goddys werk*, and the phenomenon of miracle.

21 *In book iwreten we fynde.* A conventional phrase often repeated in the poem in variant forms, that is a probable reason scholars still seek a lost source.

26 *Athelston.* The name could allude to at least three historical persons: Athelstan I, an obscure king of East Anglia and Kent in the ninth century, Athelstan II, the Danish prince Guthrum conquered by King Alfred and renamed Athelstan at baptism, and Athelstan III, victor at the Battle of Brunanburh in the year 937. (See Laura A. Hibbard, "*Athelston*, A Westminster Legend," *PMLA* 36 [1921], 223–44.)

30 *neyghyd hym nere.* The usual meaning of *neyghyd*, "to approach," makes "sound sense" according to George Taylor: "Athelston, being the king's cousin, considered it advantageous to be about the Court, and his expectation was realised as we see in the vv. following where he succeeds his cousin" (p. 20).

40 *Eerl of Dovere.* Just as Egeland is given the castle at Stone, Wymound is given the castle at Dover, a strategically important site.

43 Stone is on the road from London to Canterbury. As F&H point out, nearly all the place names mentioned in the poem are on this road.

47 *Edyff.* The name may suggest a tenth-century Anglo-Saxon saint whose veneration continued into the fourteenth century. The name might also allude to Edward the Confessor's wife.

56 *That noble clerk, on book cowde rede.* Literacy in late medieval England meant those who could read Latin, i.e., members of the clergy.

67 Tr draws a parallel between the precocious growth of the children in *Amis and Amiloun* and that of the children here, all of which seems to suggest nobility. The growth of the hero in *Sir Gowther* is also precocious, but is considered an effect of demonic paternity.

77 *to boure and to halle.* F&H suggest that the meaning is "both to public and to private counsel." The bower was a relatively secluded area used for sleeping. For a more complete explanation, see the explanatory note for *Havelok*, line 239.

84 *To don hem brenne and sloo.* Tr notes that this is a "conventional punishment, especially of women, in the French *chansons de geste*, and, since it differs from the drawing and hanging with which offenders are later threatened, it may point to confusion of an old tale with a newer one" (pp. 98–100).

97–98 F&H's comment that "the monks of St. Augustine's in Canterbury were reputed to be gay fellows and good singers" is challenged by Tr who asserts that the merry monks are not engaged in frivolity, but rather are experiencing the "pleasant effect of the chanting of the services" (p. 182).

99 *erly and late.* A tag meaning throughout the day or perhaps, like line 302, suggesting matins and evensong.

101 *on Goddys werk.* Tr notes the variation between this line and line 50, *of Goddys werk.* The terms are interchangeable, but *Goddys werk* may be a specific reference to the Benedictine Rule.

136 *worl.* Tr notes the probable meaning (world) as correct. Z shows a parallel in *Layamon* in line 23081.

139 *For in thy land, sere, is a fals traytour.* The omission of *sere* in this line would improve the meter. Tr notes the many times this expression appears in *Bevis of Hampton* as well as in *Athelston.*

142 *deposen.* Tr retains as do F&H. Z's emendation to *poysoun*, in Taylor's opinion, is to be preferred.

145 *So moot thou the.* This phrase, repeated regularly throughout the text, has something of the force of the modern "So help me God."

149–50 Tr determines these lines to constitute "padding"; similar expressions may be found in the well-padded *Bevis of Hampton* and virtually all other English verse romances.

154 *Thanne the kyng his hand up raughte.* The raising of the hand, usually the right hand, indicates an ancient ritual of oathtaking that originally involved placing the right hand on a sacred object, sometimes a sword, while speaking the oath.

155 Several lines in the poem indict and, according to Tr, vilify the "false man," a "constant habit of medieval narrative, including Chaucer" (p. 105).

166 Tr notes that despite the popularity of poisoning in literature as well as in life, "it seems to have been less used in England than elsewhere" (p. 105).

172–74 Tr attributes what seems to be gratuitous punishment of wife and children to ordeal stories derived from German and Scandinavian sources. Laura Hibbard Loomis, on the other hand, sees the *Queen Emma and the Ploughshare* story as indigenous to England, which suggests that such cruelty is not always culturally bound.

176 Wymound's attitude, fostered by envy, is typical of literary traitors. Tr notes that the name Wymound connotes "rascality." He points to the third executioner in a York Mystery play with the same name. Also, in a poem in the *Reliquiae Antiquae* the "wimorant" is a pejorative term for the rascally rabbit. George Taylor sees connotations in ME *wighel*, "deceit," *wicke*, "wicked," and *wik-hals* "rogue" (see "Notes on *Athelston*," p. 20).

184–85 *I wene he bar his owne name: / He was hoten Athelstane.* The messenger is also named Athelston. This practice of reduplicating names is evident in Celtic tradition. Sa suggests that this is a possible indication of a lost source.

208–09 *The kyng wole for the cuntas sake . . . knyghtes make.* The couplet is repeated in lines 211–12, a linking strategy frequently found in tail-rhyme romance.

238 *Westemynstyr.* A feature of the poet's attempt to adapt the narrative to an English environment, says Tr, who assumes a French source.

256 According to Thomas Wright's *Domestic Manners and Sentiments in England during the Middle Ages* (London: Chapman and Hall, 1862), cherries "appeared to have been one of the most popular fruits in England during the Middle Ages" (p. 299). In romances such as *Sir Cleges*, the fruit is miraculous and instrumental in restoring Cleges' status in the world.

266 *playne parlement.* At this point Tr and others have noted a lacuna occurring similar to another at line 448, where the phrase appears again and the rhyme scheme and the sense of the poem are disrupted. See Kevin Kiernan's article listed in the bibliography. George Taylor's explanation for the break is that "the scribe was beginning a new page" (p. 22). Because the poem exists in a single MS, such defects are difficult to verify.

281 *Abyyd.* Z notes that this early example of ME *abye* "to pay for" leads to confusion with *abyde*, "to abide" (p. 22).

282–83 Many critics have commented on the cruelty in this passage. Gordon Hall Gerould suggests that the behavior is Angevin in nature; he looks for a source in Walter Map. Tr remarks at the commonplace of this sort of treatment of women in the Middle Ages. As Elizabeth Ashman Rowe argues, "Despite its appearance to modern eyes, Athelston's kicking his wife would not have been a crime in fourteenth-century England, and the resulting death of his child was not one for which he would have been likely to have been convicted" (p. 87). See Select Bibliography.

288–89 *Soone withinne a lytle spase / A knave-chyld iborn ther wase.* The end rhyme in this couplet is a favorite of East Midlands romance.

291 *He was bothe whyt and red.* A curious class distinction is made by F&H who suggest that white and red, conventional descriptions of flesh and blood, are "colors of the aristocracy," and therefore distinct from the *blac and brown* used in *Havelok* (line 1009) to describe the lower classes. Tr points out other uses of the latter term in his rejection of F&H's determination.

294 *baret*. Tr notes that this is a word found frequently in West Midlands poems. He offers no explanation for its presence here, suggesting the difficulty of locating poems within specific dialect areas.

296 The implication here is that he will be paid back in the end.

309 The mention of *Spayne* in this line has led to speculation among scholars concerning a historical model for Edyff. Among those considered are Eleanor of Castile, wife of Edward I, and Constance of Castile, second wife of John of Gaunt, despite the fact that she was never a queen. Tr insists that this is evidence of a French original since in the *chansons* dealing with the "enfances of Charlemagne, his wife whom he ill-treats and who needs a rescuer, is a Spanish princess" (p. 110).

312 *besauntys*. A bezant (*byzantium nummus*) was a gold coin of the Byzantine Empire in widespread circulation in medieval Europe through the fifteenth century.

315 *moregeve*. A gift given a bride by the groom on the morning after the wedding. It is not part of a dowry, which would be provided by the bride's family as a gift to her husband. Rather, it is proferred directly to the bride by her husband.

324 *fyve and twenti thertoo*. Tr conjectures that the five and twenty added to thirty miles announced in line 321 equals the distance from Canterbury to London.

327–30 Around 6 a.m., or less exactly, very early in the morning. For a more complete explanation, see the explanatory note for *Horn*, line 855. Tr makes a curious comment in response to the messenger's putting his personal needs before duty: "John Bull wants his dinner" (p. 110).

335 *Charynge-cross*. Charing Cross is an area between modern Whitehall and Trafalgar Square now lending its name to a nearby London commuter train station. One of a series of thirteen memorial crosses erected by command of Edward I along the funeral procession route of his wife, Eleanor of Castile, in 1291. The route began and ended at Westminster Abbey.

336 *Flete-strete*. Named from the Fleet River, first recorded in 1280, it became a center of journalism in the modern era until most British newspapers moved to outlying areas of London.

340 *Loundone-brygge*. The original bridge was built in 994 A. D., but is now found in Lake Havesu, Arizona. Tr notes that this is the bridge over which Wat Tyler and his followers entered the city during the Rising of 1381. He dates the poem to about that time, though according to A. V. C. Schmidt and Nicolas Jacobs, it could have been written as late as 1399. Elizabeth Ashman Rowe concurs, suggesting that the poem points to Richard II and his troubled reign.

341 *los*. Tr rejects the F&H gloss on *los* as "praise" because it "gives no sense; whereas 'loss' provides us with just such an expression as medieval popular poets loved — the restatement of a fact in a negative form" (p. 111). But to our way of thinking "praise," "glory," or "repute" makes much better sense than loss in that the messenger loses — his time, his horse, and his effort — neither can he get any recognition from the church or aristocracy for this hard work. His perpetual frustration is a key part of the bourgeois humor of the poem.

342 *Stone into Steppyngebourne*. Stone Castle was a resting place for the bishops of Rochester on their journeys to and from London. *Steppyngebourne* is probably Sittingbourne.

344 *Sparyd he nought for myre ne mos*. Tr omits *nought* for the meter. We have retained it for the sense.

346 *Fro Osprynge to the Blee*. Ospringe is a resting place on the Canterbury pilgrim route. *Blee* refers to the ancient forest of Blean on the plain above Canterbury.

349 *bysschop ryke*. Z suggests that *ryke* be understood as an adjective rather than as a suffix for *bysschop*.

364 *have this and reed*. Recalls the famous *tolle lege* passage in Book 8 of Augustine's *Confessions* exhorting the Bishop of Hippo to take and read a Scriptural passage that subsequently changes his life (8.12.29). The archbishop's tearful response here makes the allusion all the more probable.

369 For more on *palfray*, see the explanatory note to *Havelok*, line 2060.

391 A horse worth a hundred pounds would be very valuable in the Middle Ages. Perhaps the messenger is given to exaggeration.

394 *Oure gostly fadyr undyr God.* Tr points out the similarity of this expression with what Becket says in the *Early South-English Legendary* (EETS o.s. 87 [London: Trübner, 1887], p. 136): "Also dignete of the preost, herre than the kyngus is, and is gostliche fader ich am."

402–04 *And thy warysoun I schal thee geve . . . hundryd yere.* Tr would like to omit *and* to improve the meter and logic of the passage. We have retained it because it is unlikely to have been an inadvertent insertion by a minstrel or copyist as Tr contends. *Warysoun* is an interesting term here. The archbishop tantalizes the messenger with more than a simple reward or payment, implying that he will be permitted to enjoy it even though he lives to a very old age. Perhaps it is a pension of some sort that is implied, or an annuity, or a land holding which would be in his name until death.

407 *so lyght.* The phrase could signify the bright illumination of Westminster in the morning sun.

412 *kyrke.* Probably the chapel within Westminster Abbey.

423 *Gyltless men yiff thay be.* The MS shows a word replacement — *yiff* for *that* — which is crossed out. We have retained the scribal correction.

424 *presoun free.* Tr disagrees with F&H who suggests that this term means "on parole." Instead, Tr believes that it means "strong prison," which would make it more consistent with the following line and an earlier reference to fettering.

437 *He swoor be God levande.* There is a disagreement over who is swearing by God. While Z says that *he* refers to the king, Tr prefers to assign the gesture to the archibishop, which is more in keeping with the office and the urgency of the matter. S agrees with Tr.

448 *In the playne parlement.* As in line 266, a lacuna is suspected here.

456 Edith Rickert refers to *Kyng Alisaunder* (line 1750) — *He laughwith and swerith by the sonne* — as evidence of pre-Christian influence on oath taking.

459–60 See note for line 470.

465 Tr makes a lengthy comparison between Alryke and Bishop William Bateman who was a champion of the church and an opponent of the king's power.

469–70 The cross, staff, miter, and ring are symbols of the archbishop's office. The king is implying that since he gave these symbols to the archbishop, he also has the right to take them away. The struggle over the right to invest a bishop with the symbols of his office in the Middle Ages was called the Investiture Controversy — an extremely important power struggle between ecclesiastical and secular authority.

472 The archbishop is talking here about the formal process of Interdiction, in which the sacraments of the church were forbidden to those under its ban. The medieval church used the Interdict as a weapon in its struggles with secular authority, sometimes applying it to whole countries.

480 Heretics were denied burial in consecrated ground, as were criminals and prostitutes.

483–94 Tr notes an unusual repetition of the same rhymes in this stanza.

513 *entyrdytyd*. Tr suggests *entyrdyt* to improve the meter.

516–17 *But yiff he graunte me that knyght, / His wyff and chyldryn fayr and bryght*. These lines repeat in lines 537–38. Such repetition is not uncommon in ME romance. See, for example, *Emaré*, line 45.

546 *Brokene-cros*. The history of this important landmark has been a source for determining the poem's date. The landmark acquired its name in 1379 and was removed in 1390. Despite this fact Schmidt and Jacobs contend that the poem could have been written "during or after the deposition crisis of 1399 and still have referred to a famous landmark removed a mere ten years or so previously" (*Medieval English Romances*, p. 194). Elizabeth Ashman Rowe notes that "neither Trounce nor Schmidt and Jacobs read Taylor's 'Notes on *Athelston*,' which revives Z's identification of the cross with the Chester Cross. Not only was the Chester Cross located in the correct place (it was in the Strand, which lies between Fleet Street and Westminster) but it also marked the bounds of Westminster and the liberty belonging to the house of Lancaster, making it a suitable place for the Archbishop of Canterbury to wait for the king" (p. 95). Rowe also notes that nothing known about Chester Cross contributes to the dating of the poem.

571 The ordeal by ploughshare leads Laura A. Hibbard [Loomis] to conclude that the source for the poem resides in a Westminster legend of Queen Emma, mother of Edward the Confessor. The story is told in the *Annales of Wintonia* as follows:

In 1042 Emma, once known as the Flower of Normandy and the widow successively of the English king, Athelred the Redeless (978–1016), and of the Danish conqueror, Canute, was living at Winchester. She was possessed of great treasures many of which she gave to the great church of Saint Swithin whose bishop Alwyn was her most familiar friend. To her English sons, Athelred, Alfred and Edward, later known as the Confessor, she had given little or nothing, all her favor having been lavished on Harthacnut, her son by Canute. When, therefore, Edward came to the throne in 1042, he showed her no honour. Instead he surrounded himself with those Norman friends who had aided him in his long exile, and among them he especially honoured Robert of Jumieges whom he made Bishop of London and afterwards Archbishop of Canterbury. The king was a man of wonderful simplicity and at last he would believe Robert even if the latter told him a black crow was white. In time Robert poisoned Edward's mind against the good bishop Alwyn and Queen Emma.

The queen, who was imprisoned at Wherwell, promptly wrote a letter to those bishops whom she could trust and begged them to persuade the king that she might clear herself by an ordeal to take place at Saint Swithin's. In a long speech which uninvited he made to the bishops, Robert accused the queen not only of evil conduct with Alwyn but of having consented to the murder of Alfred, the king's brother, and of having planned to poison the king himself.

On the day of the trial a great concourse of people gathered in Saint Swithin's church where in a row were placed nine red hot plough-shares. The queen, who had passed the previous night in prayer before the shrine of Saint Swithin and had been comforted by beholding the saint in a dream, walked forth bravely. Having cast off her mantle she closed her eyes and was led by two bishops across the burning metal while the people cried aloud: "Swithune, Sancte Swithune, tu illam adjuva!" Unconscious that she had passed the ordeal the queen opened her eyes and beheld the miracle. She prayed to be taken to the king who, overwhelmed with holy penitence, lay prostrate on the floor. Willingly he confessed his fault, willingly he restored Bishop Alwyn to highest favor. Joyous was the tumult of the people.

From Dover, where he had waited to hear the result of the ordeal, Robert fled to Jumieges where presently he died. In Winchester king and queen and bishop vied with each other in giving treasure and manors to the church of the holy saint who had saved them all. (As quoted in Laura A. Hibbard, "Athelston, A Westminster Legend," pp. 227–28)

575 The *doom*, or ordeal, was a method of testing guilt or innocence by means of direct physical trial. The accused was "subject to some physical test, such as the plunging of a hand into boiling water" (OED). The result was thought to represent the immediate judgment of God. Trial by ordeal was no longer used by the time *Athelston* was written, but it continued to be an important literary convention. One thinks of a work such as Gottfried von Strassburg's *Tristan*, where Isolde's ordeal is one of the central episodes in the narrative.

582–83 It was customary to remove the clothes of ordeal victims, though here the queen retains her garments.

592 The high altar of St. Paul's was famous for its elaborate adornment. Sa suggests that the offering may be part of the ordeal ceremony.

611 *Thorwghout they wente apase.* C: *Þorwghout he went apase.* Z's emendation is followed universally.

617 *schewyd.* Often used in relation to miracles, it indicates the suspension of natural phenomena by God, here to demonstrate innocence. Divine intervention is usually initiated by prayer in medieval romance.

625 *To Jesu Cryst he prayde a bone.* On general grounds this should be a prayer uttered by the queen. Tr argues that *he* refers to the archbishop.

638 *And sithen it fell at syght.* Tr notes that he can make nothing of this line. Sa also finds the line a mystery. Z, on the other hand, translates "It came to pass that she sighed." Taylor suggests that the scribe may have mistook "sighed" for "sight" (p. 25). But it may mean that the baby has dropped into the birthing position.

646 *As it was the landys lawe.* This may refer to the custom whereby women had exclusive rights to witness and participate in the birthing process. Only under extra-ordinary circumstances would a man be allowed to intervene. A similar expression for privacy in birth is spoken by Josian in *Bevis of Hampton* (lines 3627–31).

649 The St. Edmund mentioned here is St. Edmund of East Anglia. Born of Saxons, raised a Christian, he became king of the East Angles in the ninth century. During a Viking raid he was killed either by scourging or shot with arrows as tradition relates, or by being offered to the gods in accord with Viking ritual practices. His body, later found to be incorrupt, was transferred to Bedricsworth (Bury St. Edmunds). In 925 King Athelstan founded a community of priests and deacons to take care of the shrine. One of the most famous representations of Edmund is in the Wilton Diptypch where he and Edward the Confessor are depicted as two royal patrons of England. Together they present King Richard II to the Virgin and Child. His traditional emblem is the arrow, the instrument of his passion, but he is occasionally depicted with a wolf, believed to have guarded his head after death. See the *Oxford Dictionary of Saints*, pp. 120–21; also see Lord Francis Hervey, *Corolla*

Sancti Eadmundi: The Garland of Saint Edmund King and Martyr (New York: E. P. Dutton & Co., 1907).

652 *into the plas*. Edith Rickert and F&H take this to mean "open square." Tr thinks it means simply "thither," just as *in that plas* is used for "there."

669 *Seynt Anne*. The traditional name of the mother of the Virgin Mary; St. Anne does not appear in the Gospels, but her cult is popular in late medieval England. She is also the patron saint of childbirth. (See Kathleen Ashley and Pamela Sheingorn, eds. *Interpreting Cultural Symbols: Saint Anne in Late Medieval Society* [Athens: University of Georgia Press, 1990.])

676–78 From what has the king to be absolved? Z suggests that the king's sin is breaking his oath to his sworn brother. The rhetorical question posed by Tr is thus answered since he agrees with Z. But perhaps the absolution is necessary to eradicate his participation in the death of his unborn son. Though the act would not be considered criminal, it could be construed as immoral.

697–98 *trees three . . . hors fyve*. F&H suggest that "trees three" refers to the two uprights and crossbar of the gallows. *Fyve*, Tr remarks, is nothing more than a "popular number [used] as a rhyme word" (p. 130). Legal dragging usually required only one horse. Taylor suggests a relation to an incident involving Thomas Becket as described in L. F. Salzman's *English Trade in the Middle Ages* (Oxford: Clarendon Press, 1931):

> When Thomas Becket went to Paris in 1158, as Chancellor and Ambassador of Henry II, it is true that twelve well-appointed pack-horses formed part of his imposing Cavalcade, but there were also eight splendid chariots each drawn by five horses no less strong and shapely than war-horses. (p. 204)

705 *Sey*. Z: *Sere*; Tr: *Sere*.

733 *youre arende*. The messenger's journey to Canterbury and back is his "business" in a double sense according to Tr, concerning both Egeland's imprisonment and Wymound's trial by ordeal.

751 *Gravysende*. The town of Gravesend on the road from London to Dover.

760 *nought yit! lete!* Sa remarks on the king's imperious retort. "[E]ssentially it says something like 'Do not indeed allow,' to which we might add 'yourself familiarities with me'" (p. 152).

776 *To preve the trewthe with alle.* C: *To preve the trewþe in dede.* Z emends to maintain the meter. Tr adopts the emendation "because it is convenient for the text and is a pleasant example of his [Z's] unfailing ingenuity" (p. 134). We have maintained Z's emendation for the sake of the rhyme.

784 *schole.* Z alters to *scholde*; Tr rejects it, as do we.

803 *Alle men.* I.e., the citizens of London.

805 *the Elmes.* Thought to be west of Smithfield, a place where many elm trees grew. It was also a place of execution; such luminaries as William Wallace and Roger Mortimer met their fate there. Tr argues that Tyburn is a more likely site and the reference to the Elmes is based upon an OF phrase — *juges de dessous l'orme* (judges without tribunal) — as well as the frequent use of elm trees for hanging.

Glossary

This is a select glossary, designed to help readers with words not always glossed in the margins. It is also intended to help with words which, in particular contexts, need to be distinguished from synonyms, homonyms, and words with similar spellings.

a *a; he; all; to*
abide *wait*
aboute (n), abuten *around, at about, approximately, regarding*
aboven *towering above*
ac *but*
adoun, adune *down*
adrad, adradde, adred *afraid*
afin *altogether*
ageyn, ayeyn *again; against; back, facing, reflecting; towards, to meet*
ageyn-come *come to meet, encounter*
ageynes *against*
ageyne stonde *resist*
aghen *again; against*
altherbeste *best of all, very best*
altherleste *slightest of all*
and *and; if*
andelong *lengthways, the length of*
anilepi, onlepi *a single*
anuye *bore*
are-dawes *days of yore*
arke *coffer*
arwe *timorous*
asken *ashes*
astirte *leap*
atsitte *oppose*
auhte *property, possessions*
aunlaz *a dagger*
auter *altar*
awayleden *attacked*
ayther *either, each*
baldelike *securely*
baret *fighting*
barfot *unshod*
barnage *king's vassals of high rank*
barre *bar used to fasten a door*
bat *club*
bathe *both*
bedden *lodge in bed*
bede *a prayer, announce*
bedel *messenger of justice*
beite *bait (worry, as with dogs)*
beneysun *grace at a meal*
bermen *porters*
bern *child*
berwen, burwe *protect, save the life of*
bidden *enjoin, command*
bidene *completely*
bihote *promise*
bihove *for the benefit of*
bimene *signify*
birde, birthe, bire *had cause to*
birthene *load*
bise *north wind, whirlwind*
bi-southe *on the south of*
bi-stond, bi-stod *stood alongside*
bistride *sit astride*
biswike *treated tracherously*
bitaken *hand over to*
bite *bite, drink*
bitechen *hand over, entrust to, commit to commed to the care of*
blac *black, clad in black, grimy; fair-complexioned, pale*

blakne *turn pale*
blame *disrepute, reprobation, transgression*
bleike *pale*
blenkes *tricks*
blinne *desist, cease from effort*
blisse *happiness, general rejoicing*
blithe *happy*
blome *fairest flower*
bloute *soft*
bode *summons, command*
boute *unless, but, except; remedy, reward*

child *youth, squire; knight*
clepede/clepe *called*

datheit *cursed be*
dawe *dawn; day*
del *part*
dere *precious; harm*
dighte *prepare, make worthy; rule, govern, direct; save*
don *do, does, did, etc.*
doute *fear*

eft *soon, again*
ek(e) *also*
eyr *heir*

fale *many*
fel(e) *many*
ferde *went*
feren, (y-)fere *companions*
forthi *because, for that reason, therefore*
fre *generous, noble*

gan *intensifier (translate as did)*
geilers *jailors*
Goddot *God knows*

harde *fiercely*
he *he; they*
helde *age, adulthood*
hem *them*
hende *courteous; gentle*
heo *she, her*
here *their; army*
heved *head*
hevere *ever*
highte *was called*
hii/hi *they*
hire *their*
hit *it*

i-, y- *past participial prefix (e.g., i-caught)*
ich *I*
ilk *each*
icham *I am*
ichave *I have*
is *is; his*

kynmerk *a birthmark signifying royalty*

lemman *sweetheart, dear one*
levedi *lady*
lith *light; limb*
lith(e) *relief, pleasure, rest; gently, kindly, obedient; quickly, easily*
lough *laughed*
loverd *lord*

masager/messager *messenger*
mekel/mikel *great*
mouthe *mouth; might; must*
muthe *mouth*

nam *took; (I) am not*
nas *(I) was not (contraction of ne was)*
ne *not*
nolde *would not (contraction of ne wolde)*

nouthe *not*
nu *now*

ok *also*
onon *soon, quickly*

payn(e) *pagan*
pine *suffering, pain*

recke *reckons, cares*
reke/rake *reach, go; reached, gone*
ri[c]th *right, justice*
rit *rode*

sagh *saw*
samen *together*
schupes *ships*
sithen *since, because; next, afterwards*
sket *quickly*
stounde *hour*
stronde/stonde *beach, shore*
sumdel *somewhat*
swike *traitor, scoundrel*
swilke *such*
swithe *very; quickly*

tale *tale; tally, in number*
te *go; take [myself]; to*
tene *pain, suffering, anxiety; anger*
than *then; when*
the *the, you; they; though*
ther *there; where*
tho *then, when; though*
thusgate *in this regard*
til *to, until*
to gadre *together*
trome *rank of warriors, body of armed men*
tun *town, fortified area, village, hamlet, populated area*

ure *our*
ut(h) *out*

wende *go, turn, travel; think*
wiste *knew*
wit *intelligence; with*
wite/witen *know*
wost *know*
wreke(n) *avenge*

yaf *gave*
yeme(n) *take care of, protect*
y-nowe *enough*
yow *you*
ywis *truly, certainly, indeed*

Volumes in the Middle English Texts Series

The Floure and the Leafe, *The Assembly of Ladies*, and *The Isle of Ladies*, ed. Derek Pearsall (1990)

Three Middle English Charlemagne Romances, ed. Alan Lupack (1990)

Six Ecclesiastical Satires, ed. James M. Dean (1991)

Heroic Women from the Old Testament in Middle English Verse, ed. Russell A. Peck (1991)

The Canterbury Tales: Fifteenth-Century Continuations and Additions, ed. John M. Bowers (1992)

Gavin Douglas, *The Palis of Honoure*, ed. David Parkinson (1992)

Wynnere and Wastoure and The Parlement of the Thre Ages, ed. Warren Ginsberg (1992)

The Shewings of Julian of Norwich, ed. Georgia Ronan Crampton (1993)

King Arthur's Death: The Middle English Stanzaic Morte Arthur and Alliterative Morte Arthure, ed. Larry D. Benson and Edward E. Foster (1994)

Lancelot of the Laik and Sir Tristrem, ed. Alan Lupack (1994)

Sir Gawain: Eleven Romances and Tales, ed. Thomas Hahn (1995)

The Middle English Breton Lays, ed. Anne Laskaya and Eve Salisbury (1995)

Sir Perceval of Galles and Ywain and Gawain, ed. Mary Flowers Braswell (1995)

Four Middle English Romances: Sir Isumbras, Octavian, Sir Eglamour of Artois, Sir Tryamour, ed. Harriet Hudson (1996)

The Poems of Laurence Minot (1333–1352), ed. Richard H. Osberg (1996)

Medieval English Political Writings, ed. James M. Dean (1996)

The Book of Margery Kempe, ed. Lynn Staley (1996)

Amis and Amiloun, Robert of Cisyle, and Sir Amadace, ed. Edward E. Foster (1997)

The Cloud of Unknowing, ed. Patrick J. Gallacher (1997)

Robin Hood and Other Outlaw Tales, ed. Stephen Knight and Thomas Ohlgren (1997)

The Poems of Robert Henryson, ed. Robert L. Kindrick (1997)

Moral Love Songs and Laments, ed. Susanna Greer Fein (1998)

John Lydgate, *Troy Book: Selections*, ed. Robert R. Edwards (1998)

Thomas Usk, *The Testament of Love*, ed. R. Allen Shoaf (1998)

Prose Merlin, ed. John Conlee (1998)

Middle English Marian Lyrics, ed. Karen Saupe (1998)

John Metham, *Amoryus and Cleopes*, ed. Stephen F. Page (1999)

Four Romances of England: King Horn, Havelok the Dane, Bevis of Hampton, Athelston, ed. Ronald B. Herzman, Graham Drake, Eve Salisbury (1999)

Other TEAMS Publications

Documents of Practice Series:

Love and Marriage in Late Medieval London, by Shannon McSheffrey (1995)

A Slice of Life: Selected Documents of Medieval English Peasant Experience, edited, translated, and with an introduction by Edwin Brezette DeWindt (1996)

Sources for the History of Medicine in Late Medieval England, by Carole Rawcliffe (1996)

Regular Life: Monastic, Canonical, and Mendicant Rules, selected with an introduction by Douglas J. McMillan and Kathryn Smith Fladenmuller (1997)

Commentary Series:

Commentary and Notes on the Book of Jonah, Haimo of Auxerre, translated with an introduction by Deborah Everhart (1993)

Medieval Exegesis in Translation: Commentaries on the Book of Ruth, translated with an introduction by Lesley Smith (1996)

Nicholas of Lyra's Apocalypse Commentary, translated with an introduction and notes by Philip D. W. Krey (1997)

Rabbi Ezra Ben Solomon of Gerona: Commentary on the Song of Songs and Other Kabbalistic Commentaries, selected, translated, and annotated by Seth Brody (1998)

To order please contact:

MEDIEVAL INSTITUTE PUBLICATIONS
Western Michigan University
Kalamazoo, MI 49008–3801
Phone (616) 387–8755
FAX (616) 387–8750

http://www.wmich.edu/medieval/mip/index.html